BASICS OF

R/C MODEL AIRCRAFT DESIGN

PRACTICAL TECHNIQUES FOR BUILDING BETTER MODELS

BY ANDY LENNON

796.154
L548b

OIL CITY LIBRARY
2 CENTRAL AVE.
OIL CITY, PA 16301

About the Author

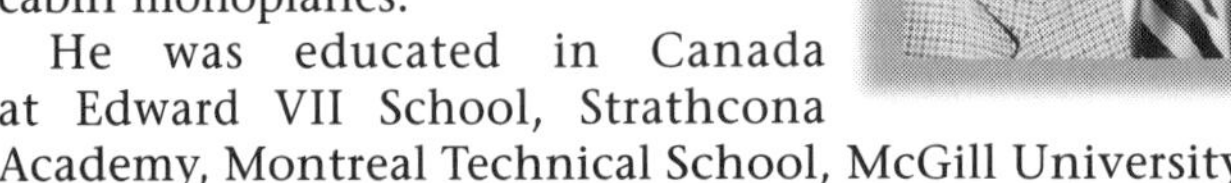

Longtime modeler Andy Lennon has been involved in aviation since the age of 15, when he went for a short ride in a Curtis Robin. He soon joined the Montreal Flying Club and began flying D. H. Gypsy Moths and early two-place Aeronca cabin monoplanes.

He was educated in Canada at Edward VII School, Strathcona Academy, Montreal Technical School, McGill University and the University of Western Ontario, London, Ontario.

Andy entered the Canadian aircraft manufacturing industry and later moved to general manufacturing as an industrial engineer. Throughout his career, he continued to study all things aeronautical, particularly aircraft design, aviation texts, NACA and NASA reports and aviation periodicals. He has tested many aeronautics theories by designing, building and flying nearly 25 experimental R/C models—miniatures of potential light aircraft. His favorite model, Seagull III, is a flying boat with wide aerobatic capabilities.

Andy is a valued contributing editor to *Model Airplane News*, and he has written for *Model Aviation*, *Model Builder*, *RC Modeler* and *RC Models and Electronics*. His two other books are "R/C Model Airplane Design" and "Canard: A Revolution in Flight."

He continues to fly full-size airplanes and is licensed in both Canada and the U.S. And when he isn't at his drawing board or in his workshop, he's likely to be at the flying field testing yet another model aircraft design. ▲

Group Editor-in-Chief **Thomas J. Atwood;** Technical Editor **Bob Kress;** Publication Manager **Debra D. Sharp;** Copy Director **Lynne Sewell;** Senior Copyeditor **Katherine Tolliver;** Art Director **Leslie Costa;** Image Technician **Christopher Hoffmaster.**

Copyright© 1996 by Air Age Inc. ISBN: 0-911295-40-2; reprinted 1999; 2002.

All rights reserved, including the right of reproduction in whole or in part in any form. This book, or parts thereof, may not be reproduced without the publisher's permission.

Published by Air Age Inc., 100 East Ridge, Ridgefield, CT 06877-4606 USA.

Chairman of the Board **Aldo DeFrancesco**; President and CEO **Louis V. DeFrancesco Jr.**; Senior Vice President **Yvonne M. DeFrancesco**.

PRINTED IN THE USA

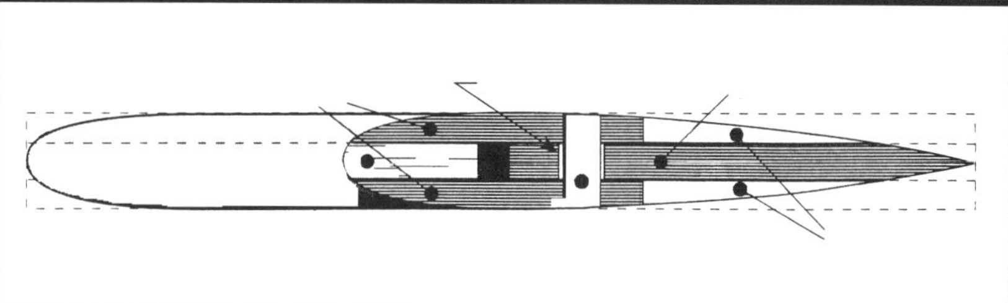

Contents

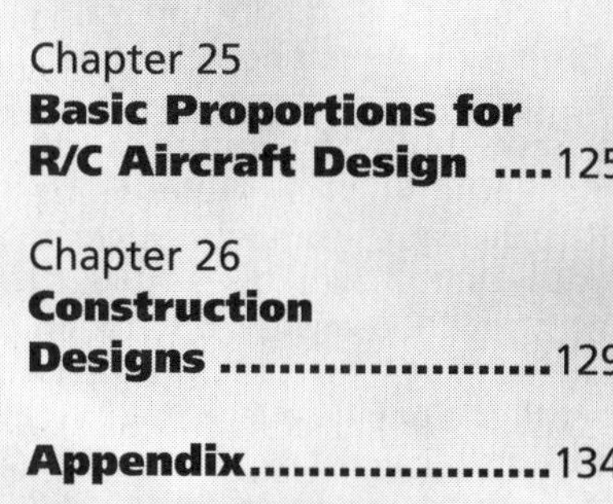

Introduction

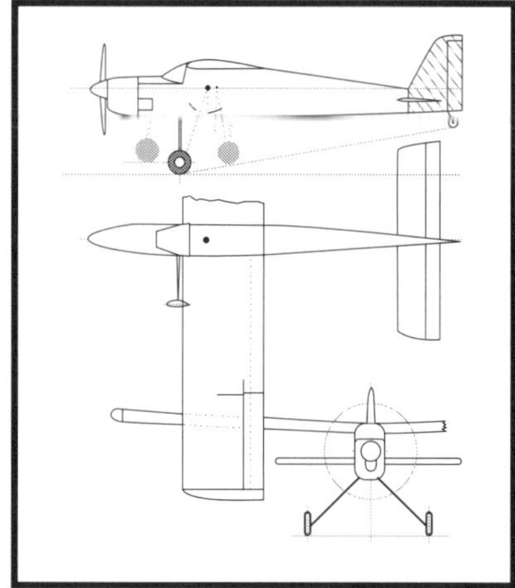

Andy Lennon has written an outstanding book that covers all required aspects of the preliminary design process for model aircraft. Further, much of the content is equally applicable to military RPV and homebuilt aircraft design. Reviewing the book was something of a nostalgia trip for me after 46 years of designing full-scale and model aircraft. Would that I had been able to carry this book with me to an unsuspecting aircraft industry when I graduated college in 1951!

My areas of disagreement here and there as I read were mostly on exotic topics and did not amount to much. When reviewing my notes jotted down while reading the draft, I found that many of my comments simply amplified what is said in the text and reflected events from my own career related to the book topic at hand. The chapters on pitch and lateral/directional stability and control reminded me of some Grumman history. We seemed to blow an aerodynamic fuse on every fifth aircraft prototype—to wit, the XF5F Skyrocket, most of which landed in Long Island Sound, and the XF10F, which, about all axes, was said to be "as stable as an upside-down pendulum." The only thing that worked flawlessly was the variable sweep, which we feared the most! Maybe Andy's book could have helped. Sadly, Grumman never got the chance to go beyond the F-14 and try an F-15F.

The design process begins with weight estimation and structural optimization in the name of reduced weight. The book covers these topics for models better than any sources I have encountered previously. Next in design comes drag analysis and reduction, which are covered professionally yet in an understandable way for the amateur designer. What a treat to see the consequences of flat-plate drag from seemingly small items like landing-gear-wire legs properly illuminated. I recently had this topic driven home dramatically when I went all out to clean up the drag of my electric fan A-6 Intruder prototype. The improved performance after the clean-up surprised me quite pleasantly. What I did could have been drawn directly from this book.

Stability and control, after performance, is what we see as an immediate result of our efforts. Results vary from joy to the blackness of the re-kitting process. Andy's book will keep you away from the latter end of the band through proper selection, arrangement and sizing of the aircraft components contributing to both longitudinal and lateral/directional stability and control.

The book is oriented mainly toward gas/glow-powered model aircraft design. With gas models, available power rarely is a problem. Coping with marginal thrust simply results in using a bigger engine and a tendency to ignore drag! Not so with electric models, which are rapidly becoming popular. They are clean, noiseless and thoroughly enjoyable alternatives to gas/glow. However, the design process challenges our ability to build strong but light models with low zero-lift and induced drag and an optimized thrust system, be it prop or jet. Short of information on the design of electric powerplant systems, this book gives you everything you otherwise need, even the impact of carrying heavy batteries. Perhaps Andy will tackle electric powerplants at a future date. ▲

— Bob Kress
Retired Vice President, Grumman

Chapter 1

Airfoil Selection

One of the most important choices in model or full-scale airplane design is the selection of an airfoil. The wing section chosen should have characteristics suited to the flight pattern of the type of model being designed.

There exist literally hundreds of airfoil sections from which to choose. They are described in "airfoil plots" similar to E197 (see Figure 1). Selection of an airfoil demands a reasonable understanding of this data so that one can read, understand and use it to advantage.

Providing this understanding is the subject of this chapter. Referring to E197, note that the data is given in terms of coefficients, except for the angle of attack. These coefficients are C_L for lift, C_{Do} for profile drag and C_M for the pitching moment around the ¼-chord point.

The actual lift, total drag and pitching moment of a wing depend on seven factors not directly related to its airfoil section. These are:

- **Speed.** Lift, drag and pitching moment are proportional to the square of the speed.
- **Wing area.** All three are proportional to wing area.
- **Wing chord(s).** Pitching moment and Reynolds number are proportional to chord.
- **Angle of attack (AoA).** In the useful range of lift, from zero lift to just before the stall, lift, profile drag and pitching moment increase as the AoA increases.
- **Aspect ratio (AR).** All three are affected by aspect ratio.
- **Planform**, i.e., straight, tapered or elliptical. All impact lift, drag and pitching moment.
- **Reynolds number (Rn).** This reflects both speed and chord and is a measure of "scale effect."

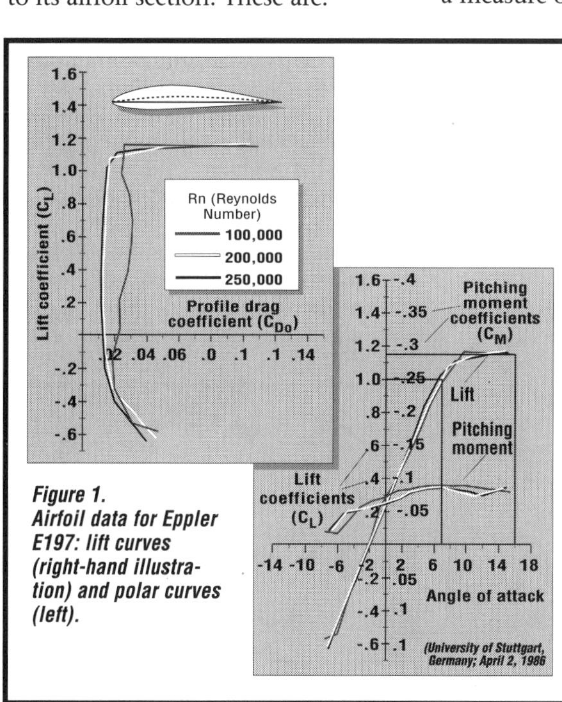

Figure 1. Airfoil data for Eppler E197: lift curves (right-hand illustration) and polar curves (left).

In developing these airfoil plots, aerodynamics scientists have screened out six of these factors, leaving only the characteristics of lift, profile drag and pitching moment unique to each individual airfoil. The seventh, Rn, is referenced separately on the airfoil plot. Formulas that incorporate all six variables and these coefficients permit accurate calculation of the lift, total drag and pitching moments for your wing and choice of airfoils.

In the airfoil selection process, however, it isn't necessary to perform laborious calculations for each potential airfoil. Direct comparison of the curves and coefficients of the candidate airfoils is more easily done, without deterioration of the results. This comparison calls for an understanding of the data. Start by examining the right-hand illustration of Figure 1—Eppler E197—in detail.

Eppler E197 is 13.42 percent of its chord in depth. This plot is the result of wind-tunnel tests performed at the University of Stuttgart in Germany under the direction of Dr. Dieter Althaus.

The horizontal line is the AoA (α, or alpha) line in degrees (measured from the airfoil's chord line)—positive to the right and negative to the left.

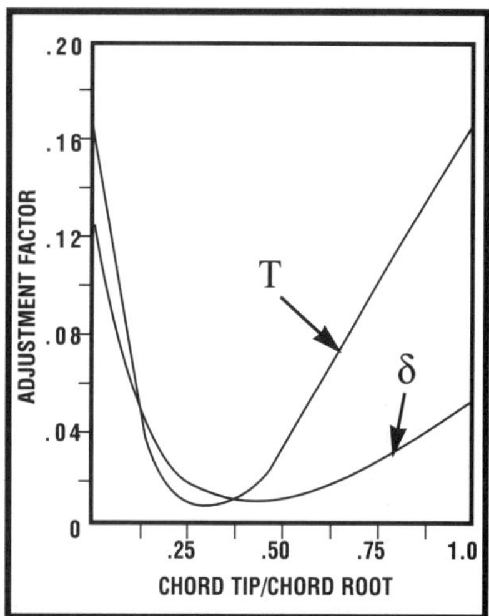

Figure 2. Taper-wing correction factor for non-elliptic lift distribution.

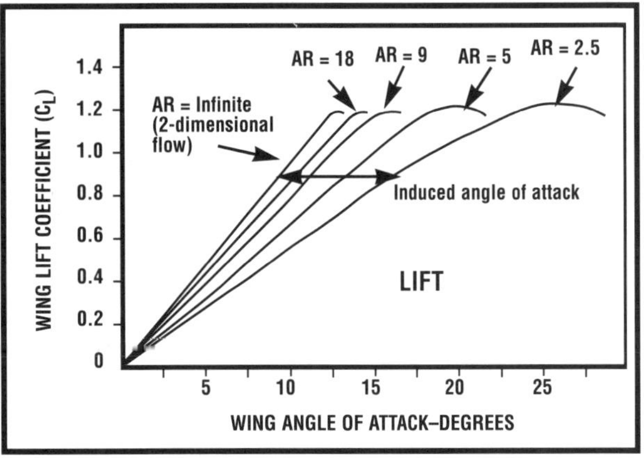

Figure 3.
How aspect ratio affects the stall angle of attack.

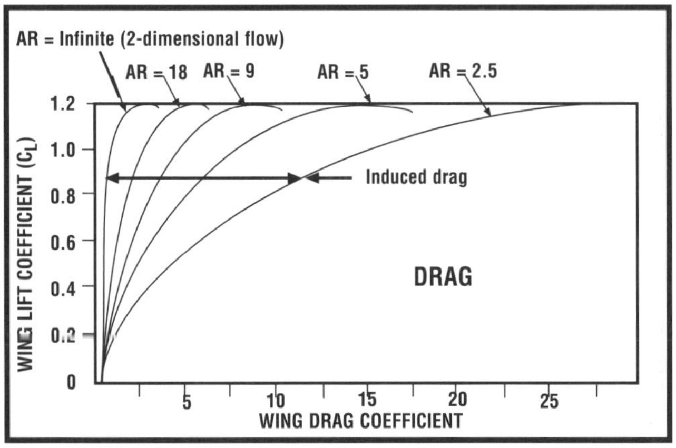

Figure 6.
How aspect ratio affects drag at a given lift.

The vertical line, on the left, provides the C_L, positive above and negative below the horizontal line.

On the right of the vertical are the pitching moment coefficients, negative (or nose down) above, and positive (or nose up) below the horizontal line.

In the center are the three Rns covered by this plot, coded to identify their respective curves.

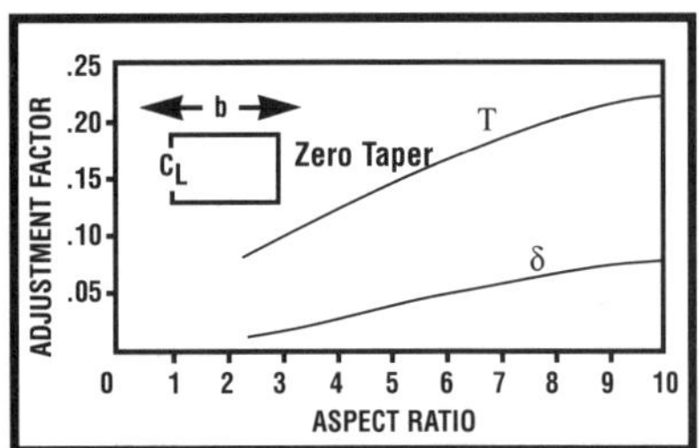

Figure 4.
Straight-wing correction factor for non-elliptic lift distribution.

In the left-hand illustration, E197's chord line is straight and joins leading and trailing edges. The dotted, curved line is the "mean" or "camber" line, equidistant from both upper and lower surfaces.

The vertical line is graduated identically with the C_L line on the right. C_L is positive above and negative below the horizontal line, which is itself graduated to provide the profile drag coefficient C_{Do}.

Now, back to the curves in the right-hand illustration. The lift lines provide the C_L data on the E197 airfoil. Note that this section starts to lift at the negative AoA of minus 2 degrees and continues to lift to 16 degrees, for a total lift spectrum of 18 degrees. C_L max is 1.17.

These lift curves are section values for "infinite aspect ratios" and two-dimensional airflow. For wings of finite AR and three-dimensional airflow, the slope of the lift curve decreases as shown in Figure 3. At these finite ARs, the AoA must be increased to obtain the same lift coefficient. These increases are called induced AoAs.

For example, Figure 3 shows that if, with a wing of AR 5, you can achieve a C_L of 1.2 with an AoA of 20 degrees, then with an AR of 9 you can achieve the same C_L with an AoA of 17 degrees. A higher AR wing will stall at a lower AoA.

In addition, the AoA must be increased to compensate for the fact that straight and tapered wings are not as efficient as the ideal elliptical wing planform. Figures 2 and 4 provide adjustment factors (T, or tau).

The pitching moment curves quantify the airfoil's nose-down tendency, increasing with increasing AoA, but not linearly like the lift curves.

The curves in the left-hand illustration of Figure 1, called "polar curves," compare C_L to C_{Do}. Note that E197 shows very little increase in profile drag despite increasing lift, except at the lowest Rn.

Again, these are section values. The profile drag values do not include induced drag, defined as "the drag resulting from the production of lift" and which varies with AR as shown in Figure 6.

Wing planform also affects induced drag. As shown in Figures 2 and 4, the curves identified by δ, or delta, provide the adjustment factor to adjust induced drag to compensate for the wing's planform. The total wing C_D is the sum of profile and induced drag coefficients.

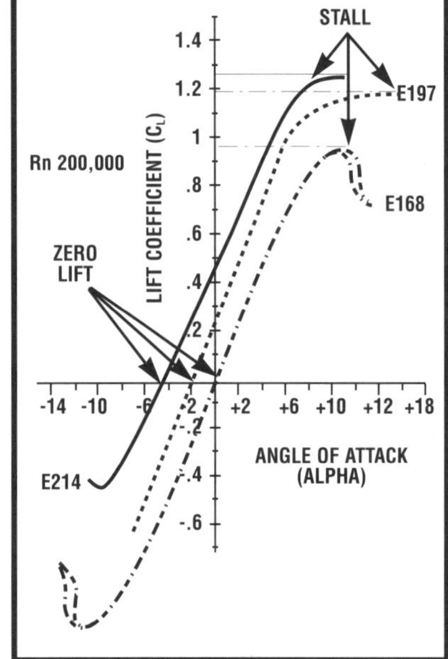

Figure 5.
Lift curves of three airfoil types. Note that E168 lifts equally well inverted.

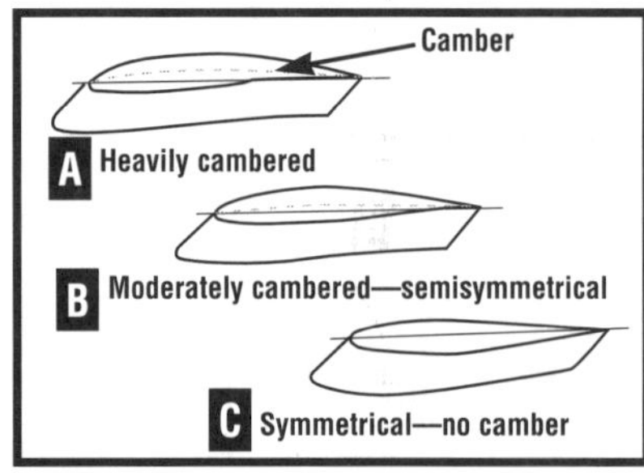

Figure 7.
Broad types of airfoil sections.

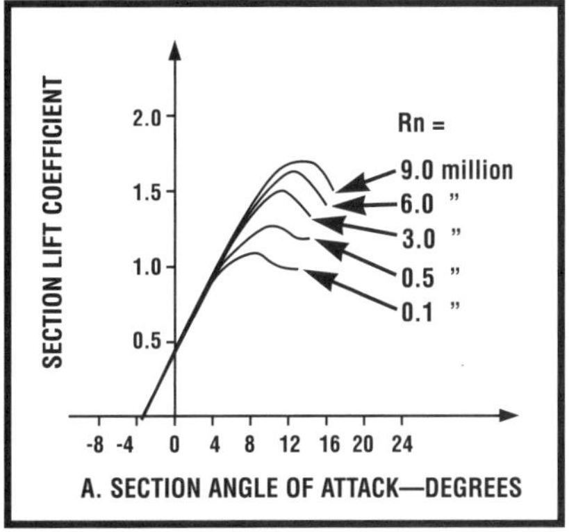

Figure 8.
Effects of Reynolds number on section characteristics.

In clarification, AoA is the angle at which the wing strikes the air (in flight) measured from the chord line.

Angle of incidence is a drawing reference and is the angle of the wing's (or horizontal tail's) chord line relative to the aircraft's centerline or reference line.

AIRFOIL PLOT COMPARISONS

There are three broad types of airfoil (as in Figure 7): heavily cambered (such as E214), moderately cambered (such as E197) and no camber, or symmetrical (such as E168). Each type has its own characteristics (see Figure 5). Greater camber increases C_L max, i.e., moves the lift curve to the left so that the angle of zero lift becomes increasingly negative, and the positive AoA of the stall is reduced. Note that symmetrical airfoils lift equally well upright or inverted.

STALL PATTERNS

There are three major types of airfoil stall pattern, as in Figure 9: sharp, as for E168; sudden lift reduction; and the soft, gentle stall as for E197.

E168 has another airfoil quirk (see Appendix). At the stall, lift drops off but doesn't return to full value until the AoA is reduced by a few degrees. This phenomenon is more pronounced at low Rn. This "hysteresis" is caused by separation of the airflow on the wing's upper surface at the stall that does not re-attach until the AoA is reduced. Some airfoils have a more emphatic version of this phenomenon.

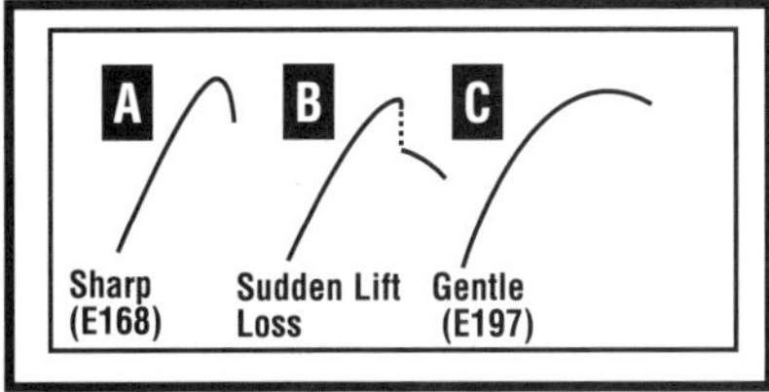

Figure 9.
Types of airfoil stall.

PITCHING MOMENT

Compare pitching moments of airfoils E197, E168, E214 and E184 in the appendix. The more heavily cambered the section is, the greater the negative pitching moment.

The symmetrical section in E168 has virtually no pitching moment except at the stall, where it becomes violently negative. This is a stable reaction. The airfoil strives to lower its AoA. E168 would be an excellent pattern-ship airfoil selection; C_L max is good, and it's thick enough for sturdy wing structures.

Airfoil E184 has a reflexed mean line toward its trailing edge. This acts like "up-elevator," reducing the pitching-moment coefficient, but also reducing C_L max. In airfoils, you don't get anything for nothing. E184 is designed for tailless models—and note the zero lift AoA shift to the right at low Rn.

DRAG AND REYNOLDS NUMBER

The polar curves of airfoils E197, E168, E214 and E184 show the adverse reaction, in both C_L and C_D, to lower Rn and to increasing AoA. Each airfoil has a different reaction—and this should be a serious consideration for narrow wingtips and small tail-surface chords, particularly where, at low Rns, there's a reduction in the stall AoA and higher profile drag.

The highest Rn in these plots is Rn 250,000. For a wing chord of 10 inches flying at sea level, this is equivalent to a speed of 32mph—ideal for sailplanes, but low for powered models, except at landing speeds. A 10-inch chord flying 90mph is at Rn 700,000 at sea level.

Figure 8 indicates that both lift and drag improve at higher Rns, improving E197's good performance.

MISSION PROFILE

The final selection of an airfoil for your design depends on the design and on how you want the airfoil to perform, i.e., its "mission profile."

For a sailplane, high lift, low drag and pitching moment at low Rns is the choice. For an aerobatic model, a symmetrical section with low C_M and the capacity to operate both upright or inverted is desirable, along with a sharp stall for spins and snap rolls and as high a C_L max as can be found. For a sport model, an airfoil like E197 is ideal. It has high C_L max, low drag and a moderate pitching moment. The stall is gentle. Note that the so-called "flat bottom" airfoils like the Clark Y (popular for sport models) are, in fact, moderately cambered airfoils.

FORMULAS

Now for those "dreaded" formulas. Don't be alarmed; they're simple arithmetic with just a touch of algebra. Their solutions are easily computed on a hand calculator that has "square" and "square root" buttons.

These formulas have been modified for simplicity, and to reflect model airplane values of speed in mph, areas in square inches, chords in inches, pitching moments in inch/ounces and weight, lift and drag in ounces.

Formula 1: Reynolds number (Rn)

$$Rn = speed\ (mph) \times chord\ (in.) \times K$$

(K at sea level is 780; at 5,000 feet is 690; and at 10,000 feet is 610)

Formula 2: Aspect ratio (AR)

$$AR = \frac{span\ (in.)^2}{wing\ area\ (sq.\ in.)}$$

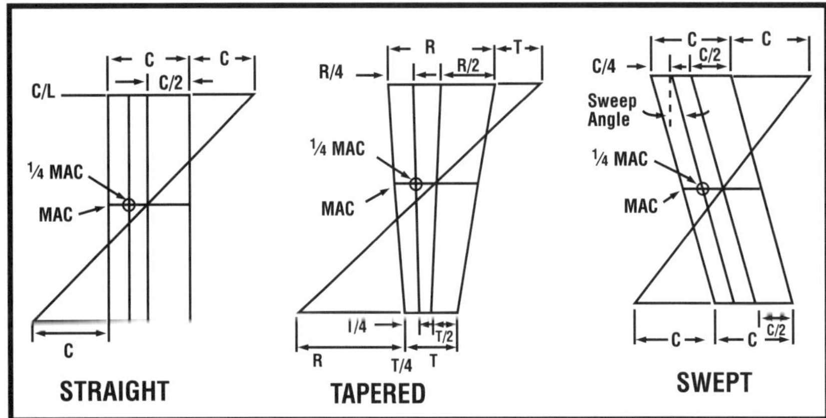

Figure 10.
Method for locating the mean aerodynamic chord (MAC).

Formula 3: Taper ratio (λ—lambda)

$$\textit{Taper ratio} = \frac{\textit{tip chord (in.)}}{\textit{root chord (in.)}}$$

(A straight wing has a taper ratio of 1.)

Mean aerodynamic chord (MAC)
Figure 10 provides a graphic method for locating the MAC and its ¼-chord point. The MAC is defined as "that chord representative of the wing as a whole and about which the lift, drag and pitching moment forces can be considered to act."

Formula 4: Total of section and induced angle of attack (AoA)

$$\alpha\ (alpha) = \alpha_o + \frac{(18.24 \times C_L) \times (1 + T)}{AR}$$

where α = total of section AoA and induced AoA;
α_o = section AoA from airfoil plot;
C_L = lift coefficient at section AoA from airfoil plot;
AR = aspect ratio;
T (tau) = planform adjustment factors (Figures 2 and 4).

Formula 5: Total of profile (section) and induced drag coefficients

$$C_D = C_{Do} + \frac{(0.318 \times C_L^2) \times (1 + \delta)}{AR}$$

where C_D = total of profile and induced drag coefficients;
C_{Do} = section profile drag coefficient at C_L chosen from airfoil plot;
C_L^2 = lift coefficient chosen "squared";
AR = aspect ratio;
δ (delta) = planform adjustment factor (Figures 2 and 4);

COEFFICIENT CONVERSIONS

Up to this point, coefficients have had only abstract values. To convert these to meaningful figures, we'll use the six variables mentioned previously in these formulas.

Formula 6: Lift (or weight)

$$\textit{Lift (or weight)} = \frac{C_L \times \sigma \times V^2 \times S}{3519}$$

If you want to determine the lift coefficient needed for a given air speed and weight:

Formula 7: Lift coefficient required

$$C_L = \frac{lift \times 3519}{\sigma \times V^2 \times S}$$

If you want to know the model's speed at a given C_L and weight:

Formula 8: Model speed

$$V = \sqrt{\frac{lift \times 3519}{\sigma \times C_L \times S}}$$

Formula 9: Total profile and induced wing drag

$$\textit{Total drag} = \frac{C_D \times \sigma \times V^2 \times S}{3519}$$

Formula 10: Pitching moment

$$\textit{Pitching moment} = \frac{C_M \times \sigma \times V^2 \times S \times C}{3519}$$

where in formulas 6, 7, 8, 9 and 10:
C_L = lift coefficient (formula 7);
C_D = total drag coefficient (formula 5);
V^2 = speed in mph squared;
S = wing area in square inches;
C = mean aerodynamic chord in inches (see Figure 10);
C_M = pitching moment about the ¼ MAC at the calculated C_L in inch/ounces;
σ (sigma) = density of air (sea level, 1.00; 5,000 feet, 0.8616; 10,000 feet, 0.7384).

SPECIAL PROCEDURES

A: Lift coefficient per degree of angle of attack adjusted for aspect ratio and planform.
Refer to Figure 1, Part 1 E197. At C_L 1.00 and AoA of 7 degrees, plus the 2 degrees negative, a_o is 9 degrees. Apply Formula 4 to obtain a. Divide C_L 1.00 by a to obtain C_L per degree.

B: Angle of attack (or incidence) for level flight. C_L required divided by C_L per degree of angle of attack.
Knowing wing area, weight and cruising speed, calculate the C_L needed as in Formula 7. Divide this C_L by C_L per degree as above to obtain lift spectrum. Deduct any negative AoA to zero lift.

C: Stall angle of attack adjusted for aspect ratio and plan.
Adjust the stall AoA for AR and planform as in Formula 4. Deduct any negative AoA to zero lift to obtain positive value of stall AoA. ▲

REFERENCES

Airfoil Design and Data, by Dr. Richard Eppler, and Profilaren fur den Modellflug, by Dr. Dieter Althaus, available from Springer-Verlag, New York Inc., P.O. Box 19386, Newark, NJ 07195-9386.

Airfoils at Low Speeds (Soartech #8), by Michael Selig, John Donovan and David Frasier, available from H.A. Stokely, 1504 North Horseshoe Cir., Virginia Beach, VA 23451.

Model Aircraft Dynamics, by Martin Simon, Zenith Books, P.O. Box 1/MN121, Osceola, WI 54020.

Chapter 2

Understanding Airfoils

The selection of an airfoil section for most powered models is considered not to be critical by many modelers and kit designers. Models fly reasonably well with any old airfoil, and their high drag is beneficial in steepening the glide for easier landings. Some years ago, there was a rumor that a well-known and respected Eastern model designer developed his airfoils with the aid of the soles of his size 12 Florsheim shoes.

In contrast, the R/C soaring fraternity is very conscious of the need for efficient airfoils. Their models have only one power source: gravity. The better the airfoil, the flatter the glide and the longer the glider may stay aloft.

This chapter is intended to provide readers with a practical, easy understanding of airfoil characteristics so that their selection will suit the type of performance they hope to achieve from their designs. It does *not* go into detail on such subjects as laminar or turbulent flows, turbulators, separation and separation bubbles, etc. (These are fully described in Martin Simon's "Model Aircraft Aerodynamics" and Selig-Donovan and Frasier's "Airfoils at Low Speeds"—see the source list at the end of this chapter.)

REYNOLDS NUMBERS

A most important consideration in airfoil selection is "scale effect." The measure of scale effect is the Rn. Its formula is:

Rn = Chord (in inches) x speed (in mph) x 780 (at sea level).

A full-scale airplane flying at 200mph with a wing chord of 5 feet (60 inches) is operating at Rn 9,360,000. A scale model flying at 60mph with a wing chord of 10 inches flies at Rn 468,000. When landing at 25mph, the model's Rn is reduced to 195,000.

In 1937, NACA issued Report No. 586, which shows the shocking adverse impact of scale on airfoil characteristics (based on tests in a variable-density wind tunnel over a wide range of Rns, as shown in

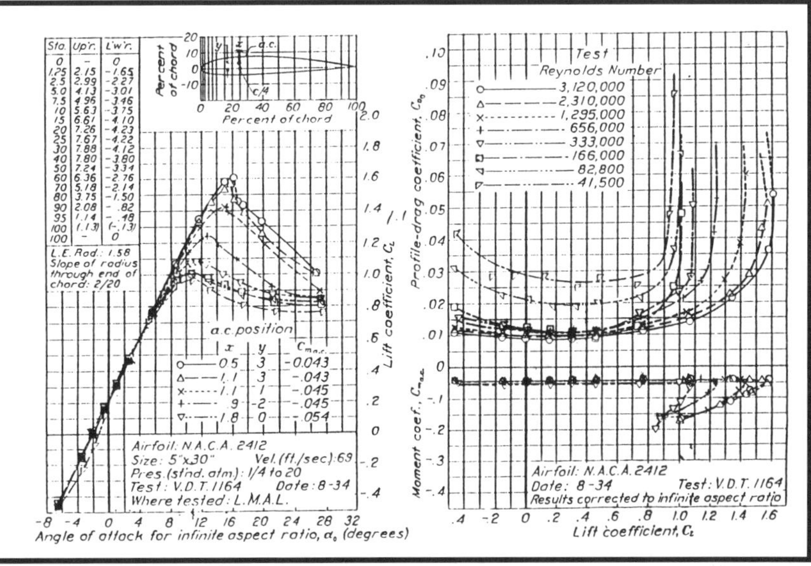

Figure 1.
Characteristics of NACA 2412 at various Reynolds numbers.

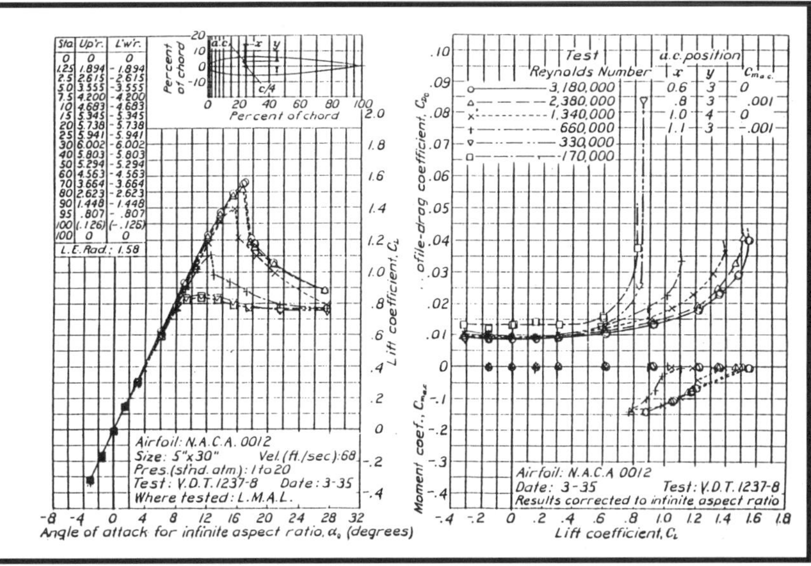

Figure 2.
Characteristics of NACA 0012 at various Reynolds numbers.

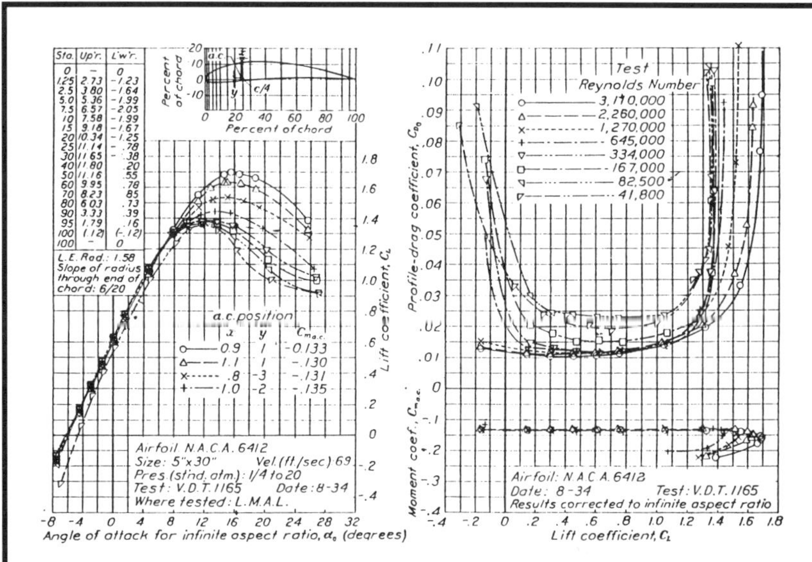

Figure 3.
Characteristics of NACA 6412 at various Reynolds numbers.

Figures 1, 2 and 3). Note that the Rns shown are "test" results and require correction for a "turbulence factor" that wasn't recognized during the tests. This factor is 2.64. Each Rn in Figures 1, 2 and 3 should be increased by this factor.

The airfoils involved in these figures are "related sections." NACA 0012 is symmetrical; NACA 2412 was developed by "wrapping" the symmetrical section around a cambered mean line so that the upper and lower surfaces were equidistant from the camber line. For NACA 2412, this mean line has a camber height of 2 percent of the chord length, with its highest point at 40 percent.

NACA 0012 in Figure 2 shows a shocking reduction in maximum lift coefficient from 1.55 for the highest Rn to 0.83 for the lowest—a difference of 54 percent of the higher value.

Similarly, the stall AoA is sharply reduced from 17 degrees for the highest Rn to 10 degrees for the lowest. One very interesting phenomenon is this airfoil's behavior beyond the stall at the lower Rns. It continues to lift up to 28 degrees at almost full value.

Profile drag at low Rns is almost double that at high Rns and increases very significantly at the stall and beyond—not surprising, considering the post-stall lift behavior.

NACA 0012 has a zero pitching moment, except beyond the stall where it's negative (nose down) and stabilizing.

NACA 2412 in Figure 1 is a popular sport-model airfoil. Compared with NACA 0012, the maximum lift coefficient is slightly higher at 1.6 at the highest Rn. At the lowest Rn, with the turbulence factor accounted for (41,500 x 2.64, which equals 109,560), the C_L max drops to 0.95, or 59 percent of that of the highest Rn. The stall angle is reduced from 16 degrees to 11 degrees. Both lift and stall angles are higher than for NACA 0012.

Profile drag increases almost threefold at the lowest Rn. Owing to this airfoil's cambered mean line, the pitching moment is minus 0.06.

For NACA 6412 in Figure 3, the C_L max goes from 1.7 to 1.35 (79 percent). The stall angle is reduced from 16 degrees to 12 degrees. Profile drag doubles at the lowest Rn.

It should be noted, however, that camber increase obviously improves C_L max and stall angle for this relatively thin (12 percent) section at low Rns.

The pitching moment, due to its higher camber, is 0.135 negative. A horizontal tail would need to produce a heavy download to offset this pitching moment, resulting in an increased "trim drag."

In 1945, NACA issued Report No. 824, "Summary of Airfoil Data"; it includes data on their "six-number" laminar-flow airfoils. NACA 64_1-412 is typical (see Figure 4). The lowest Rn is 3,000,000.

These airfoils were developed similarly to those in NACA Report No. 460: a symmetrical section wrapped around a cambered mean line. However, careful study of pressure distribution allowed this type of airfoil to obtain a very low

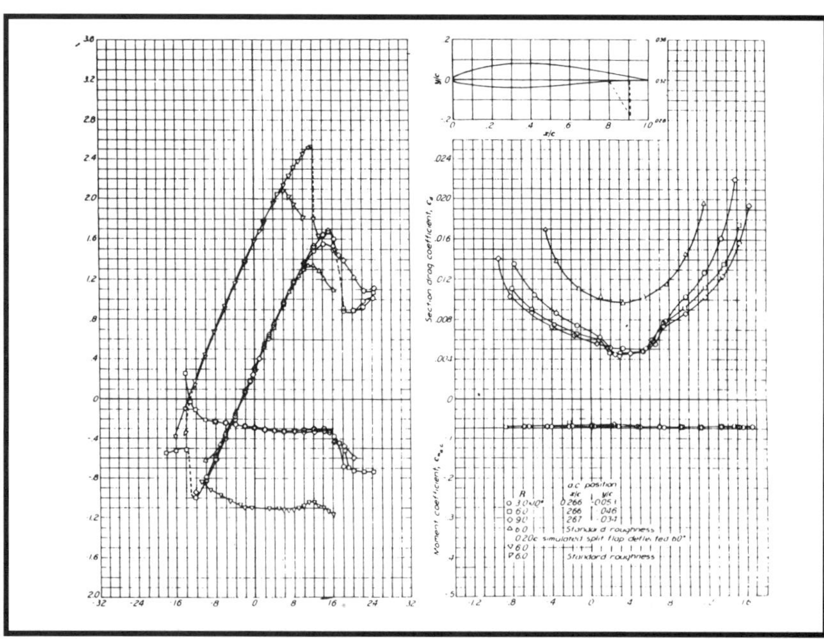

Figure 4.
Aerodynamic characteristics of the NACA 64_1-412 airfoil section, 24-inch chord.

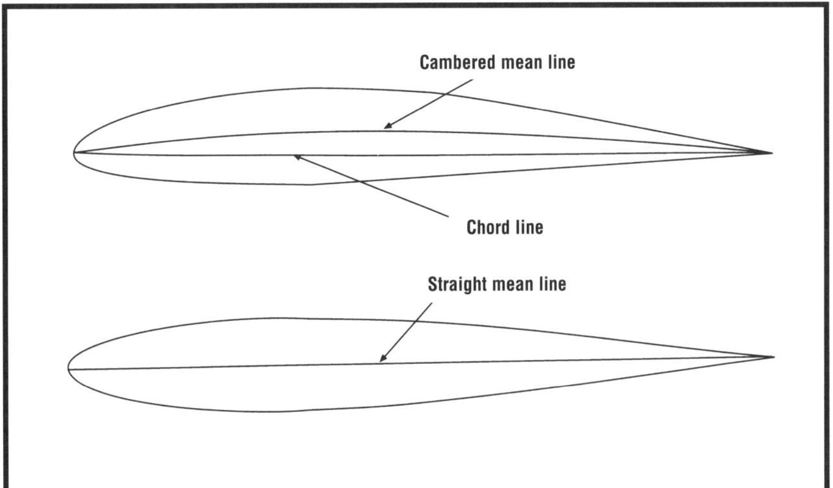

Figure 5.
The cambered mean line of E197 (top) was straightened out and the envelope redrawn, resulting in a symmetrical airfoil (bottom).

profile drag (over a limited range of lower lift coefficients). The P-51 Mustang WW II fighter employed airfoils of this type. The "low drag bucket" at C_L 0.4 shown in Figure 4 shows this drag reduction.

In 1949, NACA issued Technical Note 1945. This compared 15 NACA airfoil sections at Rns from 9,000,000 (9 x 10^6) to 700,000 (0.7 x 10^6).

The C_L max of NACA 64_1-412 at Rn 9 x 10^6 is 1.67, but it drops to 1.18 (70 percent of the highest Rn) at Rn 0.7 x 10^6. Profile drag increases from 0.0045 to 0.0072 for the same Rn range, and the stall angle is 16 degrees, but it drops to 12 degrees at the low Rn. Pitching-moment coefficient is 0.063.

This report concluded that at *low Rns*, the laminar-flow section did not offer substantial advantages over those in Report No. 460 and Report No. 610. NASA (NACA's successor) continued to do research into laminar-flow airfoils with much success; but at the high Rns of full-scale airfoils and aided by computer analysis.

The worldwide R/C soaring fraternity, however, has done much wind-tunnel testing and computer design of airfoils for model gliders (references 10 to 15 inclusive). Though the Rn range of these tests seldom exceeds Rn 300,000, any airfoil that offers good performance at this low Rn can only improve at the higher Rns of powered flight. A 10-inch-chord at 100mph is operating at Rn 780,000.

The selection of an airfoil for a design should start with a review of airfoil plots of the type in this chapter. In this author's experience, the plots of the University of Stuttgart published by Dieter Althaus are the clearest and most comprehensive. The airfoils developed by Dr. Richard Eppler are favored.

MEAN LINE CAMBER

A symmetrical airfoil has the lowest C_L max and stall angle. An airfoil with increased camber produces a higher maximum C_L, but it starts to lift at higher *negative* angles of attack with a broader range of lift before stalling. Increased camber, however, produces increased pitching moments.

Out of curiosity, the camber mean line for the E197 airfoil was straightened out and the envelope was redrawn as in Figure 5. The result was a symmetrical airfoil resembling the E168.

Some cambered airfoils have a lower surface trailing-edge "cusp" created by a localized and increased curvature in the camber mean line, as in the E214, Figure 6. The cusp increases both C_L max and pitching moment; it's called "aft loading." E197 in Figure 6 has a slight cusp; airfoils E207 and E209 are similar to E197, but they lack the trailing-edge cusp (reference 12). Airfoil E230 in Figure 6 has an upwardly reflexed camber mean line near its trailing edge. This produces a positive (nose-up) pitching moment. This airfoil would be suitable for a tailless or delta-wing model. Inevitably, C_L max is adversely affected.

THICKNESS

Thicker wings permit strong but light construction. They may also exact a small penalty in drag increase. Tapered wings with thick root airfoils that taper to thinner, but related, tip airfoils, are strong, light and efficient. Laying out the intervening airfoils between root and tip calls for much calculation—or computer assistance.

For high speed, an airfoil such as E226 shown in Figure 6 is suggested. Drag and pitching moments are low, as is the C_L max, and the airfoil performs almost as well inverted as it does upright. E374 would also be a good high-speed airfoil section.

The author has had success with the E197 for sport models. It has low profile drag, good lift and a gentle stall, but a fairly high pitching moment.

The E168 is suitable for strong horizontal or vertical tail surfaces, or for wings of aerobatic models. It performs as well upright as it does inverted.

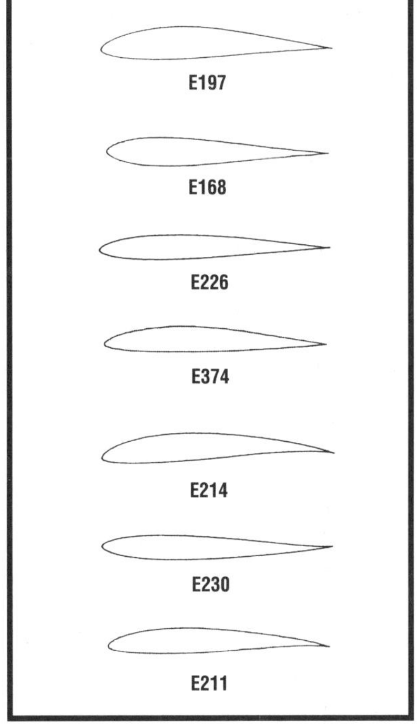

Figure 6.
Eppler airfoils.

PITCHING MOMENT

The airfoil's pitching moment is important both structurally and aerodynamically. In flight—particularly in maneuvers—the pitching moment tries to twist the wing in a leading-edge-down direction. This adds to the torsional stress placed on the wing structure by the ailerons and extended flaps. High-pitching-moment airfoils require wings that are stiff in torsion, and that favors thicker sections and full wing skins, particularly for high-AR wings.

Aerodynamically, the nose-down pitching moment requires a horizontal tail download for equilibrium. This adds to the lift the wing must produce and increases total drag—called "trim drag." The pitching moment is little affected by variations in the Rn.

STALL BEHAVIOR

One reason for preferring wind-tunnel test data over computer-developed performance curves is that the former provides an accurate "picture" of the airfoil's behavior at the stall and beyond.

In general, there are three broad types of stall (as shown in Figure 9 of Chapter 1, "Airfoil Selection"): sharp; sudden lift drop; and gentle.

For sport models, a gentle stall is desirable. Sharp stalls and those with a sudden lift drop are appropriate for maneuvers in which the ability to stall a wing easily is required, such as spins.

ZERO LIFT ANGLE

The angle of zero lift for a symmetrical-section airfoil is zero degrees AoA. Cambered airfoil sections such as E214 shown in Figure 6 start to lift at almost 6 degrees negative AoA, but for this airfoil, that angle is unaffected by variations in the Rn.

Contrast this with airfoil E211. This airfoil's angle of zero lift moves closer to zero degrees at the lower Rns.

The forward wing of a canard must stall before the aft wing; but, for longitudinal stability, the aft wing must reach its airfoil's zero-lift angle before the front wing's airfoil. If the foreplane's airfoil reaches zero lift first, a violent dive results and, because the aft wing is still lifting, a crash is almost inevitable.

The low-Rn behavior of the E211 means that, at low speeds—or narrow chords—this airfoil may reach zero lift more readily. Its use as a forward-wing airfoil on a canard is to be avoided. Airfoil E214 is more suitable.

MAXIMUM LIFT COEFFICIENT

From zero lift, higher camber results in a higher C_L max and higher stalling angles. This impacts the model's takeoff, stall and landing speeds. A high C_L max permits slower flight in all three points; a lower C_L max reverses these conditions.

SUMMARY

In aerodynamics, nothing is free. In general, high lift means increased drag and pitching moments; for high speeds, C_L max is reduced and so on. The type of performance sought for a design dictates which airfoil characteristics are significant. Having selected these, any adverse characteristics must be accepted and compensated for. ▲

AIRFOIL CONSTRUCTION

Most powered model aircraft operate in an Rn range from 200,000 to well over 1,000,000. This is above the critical range of Rns at which turbulators are considered to be effective.

For the more recently developed airfoils, there is a considerable degree of laminar flow that significantly reduces their profile drag. This flow is easily upset by protuberances on the wing's surfaces.

For smooth surfaces, full wing sheeting is suggested, with a film overlay—either over a foam-core or built-up construction—that will promote the most laminar flow and also result in a wing-stiff in torsion (see Chapter 13, "Stressed Skin Design").

There are large models whose wings have multiple spars on both top and bottom surfaces and are covered only in plastic film.

Because it shrinks on application, the film tends to flatten between each rib and each spar. As a result, multiple ridges run both chordwise and spanwise, rendering laminar flow impossible.

Contrast this with the very smooth surfaces of high-performance R/C soaring gliders.

NACA AND NASA DATA

1. Report 460*: The characteristics of 78 Related Airfoil Sections from Tests in the Variable Density Wind Tunnel; 1933; Jacobs, Ward and Pinkerton.

2. Report 586*: Airfoil Section Characteristics as Affected by Variations of the Reynolds Number; 1937; Jacobs and Sherman.

3. Report 610*: Tests of Related Forward Camber Airfoils in the Variable-Density Wind Tunnel; 1937; Jacobs, Pinkerton and Greenberg.

4. Report 628*: Aerodynamic Characteristics of a Large Number of Airfoils Tested in the Variable-Density Wind Tunnel; 1938; Pinkerton and Greenberg.

5. Report 824*: Summary of Airfoil Data; 1945; Abbott, von Doenhoff and Stivers.

6. Technical Note 1945*: Aerodynamic Characteristics of 15 NACA Airfoil Sections at Seven Reynolds Numbers from 0.7 x 106 to 9.0 x 106; 1949; Loftin and Smith.

7. Technical Note NASA TN 7428*: Low-Speed Aerodynamic Characteristics of a 17 percent Thick Airfoil Designed for General Aviation Applications; 1973; McGhee, et. al.

8. NASA Technical Memorandum TMX 72697*: Low Speed Aerodynamic characteristics of a 13-percent Thick Airfoil Section; 1977; McGhee, et. al.

9. NASA Technical Paper 1865*: Design and Experimental Results for a Flapped Natural Laminar-Flow Airfoil for General Aviation Applications; 1981; Somers.

10. Profilpolaren für den 1900 Ellflug, Book 1; 1980; Dieter Althus, Neckar-Verlag, Klosterring #1, 7730 Villingen-Schwenningen, Germany.

11. Profilpolaren für den 1900 Ellflug, Book 2; 1986; Dieter Althus, Neckar-Verlag, Klosterring #1, 7730 Villingen-Schwenningen, Germany.

12. Eppler Profile MTB 12; 1986; Martin Hepperle, Verlag für Technik und Handwerk GMBH, Postfach 1128, 7570 Baden-Baden, Germany.

13. Model Aircraft Aerodynamics, Second Edition; 1987; Martin Simons.

14. Airfoils at Low Speeds—Soartech 8; 1989; Selig-Donovan and Fraser, Zenith Aviation Books, P.O. Box 1, Osceola, WI 54020.

15. Airfoil Design and Data; 1980; Dr. Richard Eppler, Springer Verlag, New York, NY.

**Available from U.S. Department of Commerce, National Technical Information Service, 5285 Port Royal Rd., Springfield, VA 22161.*

Chapter 3

Understanding Aerodynamic Formulas

This book reflects a deep and lifelong interest in aviation; a close study of the vast amount of timeless aerodynamic research data, both full-scale and model, that is readily available.

This, coupled with the practical application of this data to the design, construction and flying of a wide variety of model airplanes, reflects those many years of study and experience.

(These models perform well, and photos and 3-view drawings of them are incorporated into this book and are compiled in Chapter 26, "Construction Designs.")

Layman's language is used, but inevitably some aerodynamic jargon and symbols have to be introduced. The many charts, curves and formulas may be intimidating to those readers who are not familiar with the use of the mass of information they contain. Once actual numbers replace symbols in the formulas, only plain, old, public-school arithmetic is needed. A pocket calculator with "square" and "square-root" buttons simplifies the work.

The problem seems to be "how and from where to obtain the numbers." This chapter is designed to answer this. The various figures are marked to illustrate the sources of those numbers, and the specifications of an imaginary model airplane are used as samples.

The most important formulas deal with lift, drag and pitching moment.

LIFT

The airfoil plot of Eppler E197 (see Figure 1) shows this airfoil's behavior for "infinite AR," i.e., no wingtips.

Airplane wings, even very high-AR glider wings, have "finite" ARs and do have wingtips. Lift is lost at those tips; the wider the tip chord, the greater the loss.

The wing's AoA must be increased (induced AoA) to obtain the C_L needed as AR decreases. Induced drag increases at low ARs.

Airfoil plots must be adjusted to:

- reflect the AR of your wings; and
- reflect the wing's planform—straight (constant chord) or tapered.

An elliptical wing planform needs only the adjustment for AR.

The formula for both AR and planform adjustments is:

$$a = a_o + \frac{18.24 \times C_L \times (1. + T)}{AR}$$

where a = total AoA (AoA) needed;
a_o = "section" or airfoil plot AoA;
C_L = C_L at that AoA;
AR = aspect ratio;
T = Planform adjustment factor.

Refer to Figure 2. E197 produces lift of C_L 1.00 at 9 degrees AoA, from *zero lift*, for infinite AR.

A constant-chord wing of AR 6 has an adjustment factor T of 0.17 (see Figure 4 of Chapter 1).

Replace the symbols with these numbers:

$$a = 9° + \frac{18.24 \times 1.00 \times 1.17}{6} = 12.5°$$

Had the wing been tapered with a taper ratio of 0.6 (tip chord 7.5 inches divided by root chord 12.5 inches, or 0.6), the planform

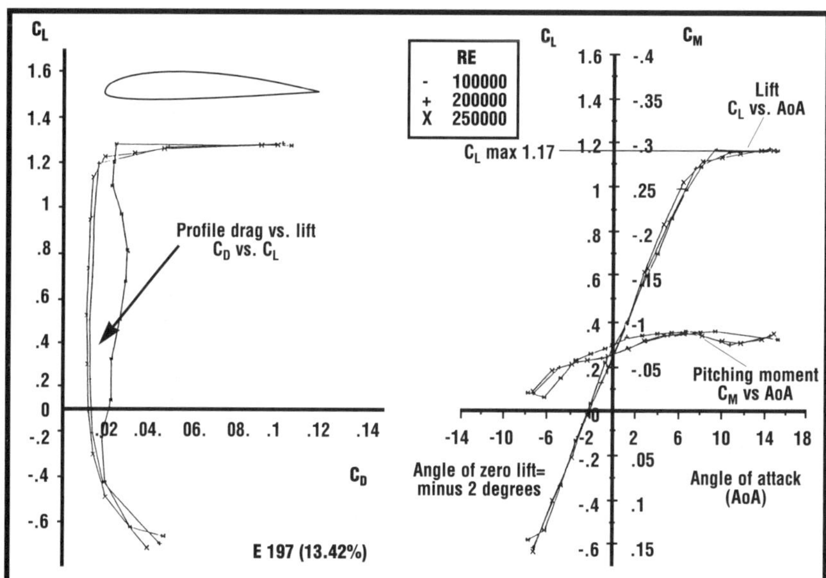

Figure 1.
Eppler E197 airfoil plot.

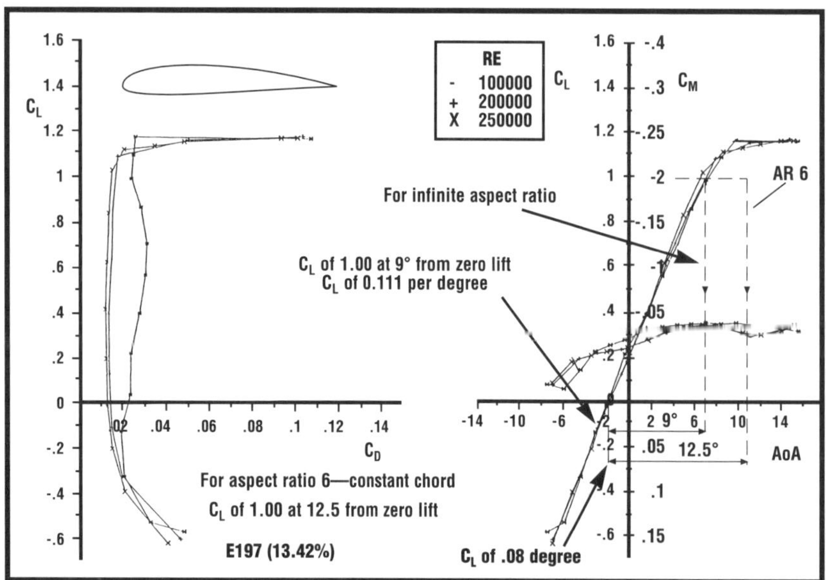

Figure 2.
Eppler airfoil E197 produces lift of C_L 1.00 at 9 degrees AoA, from zero lift, for infinite AR.

adjustment factor would be 0.0675, reflecting the lower tip lift losses from the narrower tip chord.

A C_L of 1.00 for 12.5 degrees is 1.00 divided by 12.5, or 0.08 per degree. This is the "slope" of the lift curve at AR 6 and constant chord.

Our example model design has the following specifications:

- Estimated gross weight of 90 ounces;
- Wing area of 600 square inches (4.17 square feet);
- Wing chord of 10 inches;
- Span of 60 inches;
- Estimated cruising speed of 50 mph; and
- Wing loading of 90 divided by 4.17, or 21.6 ounces per square foot.

The three-surface "Wild Goose" was designed to the aerodynamic and structural principles in this book; specifically those described in Chapter 22, "Canard, Tandem Wing and Three-Surface Design." It's an excellent flier.

There are two solutions to the determination of the wing's AoA to support the plane in level flight at the estimated cruising speed.

SOLUTION No. 1

Refer to Figure 3. At a wing loading of 21.6 ounces per square foot and at a speed of 50mph, the wing needs a C_L of close to 0.20.

Our wing develops a C_L of 0.08 per degree AoA. To produce C_L 0.20 would require an AoA of 0.20 divided by 0.08, or 2.5 degrees from zero lift, which for E197 is minus 2 degrees.

The wing would thus be set at (2.5 minus 2) or 0.5 degree AoA—and at 0.5 degree angle of incidence to the fuselage centerline on your drawings.

Note that a symmetrical airfoil's angle of zero lift is zero degrees AoA. If our wing used a symmetrical section, its AoA would be 25 degrees, as would its angle of incidence.

This is the "rigging" for a sport model, using a cambered airfoil such as E197, i.e., 0.5 degree AoA. Most pattern ships use symmetrical wing and horizontal tail airfoils; such airfoils have no pitching moment and perform as well inverted as they do upright, but with lower maximum lift coefficients (C_L max) compared with cambered airfoil sections. (See Chapter 2, "Understanding Airfoils.")

These agile models have chords of both wing and tail airfoils set at zero degrees relative to their fuselage centerlines. A symmetrical airfoil at zero degrees AoA will produce no lift.

What happens is that, to take off, the pilot commands up-elevator, thus adjusting the wing to a positive AoA, and it lifts. The lift produces downwash that strikes the horizontal tail at a negative (or downward) angle causing a download on the tail that maintains the wing at a positive, lifting AoA. In both upright and inverted flight, the fuselage is inclined nose up at a small angle, and with some added drag.

SOLUTION No. 2

This method is more accurate and involves one of the "dreaded" formulas, as follows:

$$Lift = \frac{C_L \times \sigma \times V^2 \times S}{3519}$$

Because we want to obtain the C_L needed, this formula is modified to:

$$C_L = \frac{Lift \times 3519}{\sigma \times V^2 \times S}$$

where C_L = C_L needed;

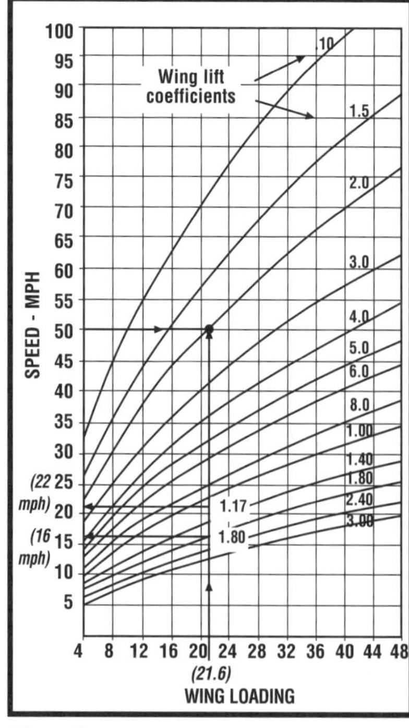

Figure 3.
Nomograph for quick determination of wing loading, lift and speed at sea level.

Lift = model's gross weight in ounces;

V^2 = estimated cruise speed in mph "squared";

S = wing area in square inches;

σ = density ratio of air (at sea level, it's 1.00; at 5,000 feet, it's 0.8616; and at 10,000 feet, it's 0.7384).

A modeler living in Denver, CO, at 5,000 feet above sea level would use a σ of 0.8616.

For our model, at sea level, this would be C_L = (90 x 3519) divided by (1.00 x 502 x 600), or 0.211.

Our sample wing has a C_L of 0.08 per degree. The wing's AoA would be 0.211 divided by 0.08, or 2.64 degrees, less the E197's 2-degree negative to zero lift, or 0.64 degree, rounded out to the nearest ¼ degree, or 0.75 degree.

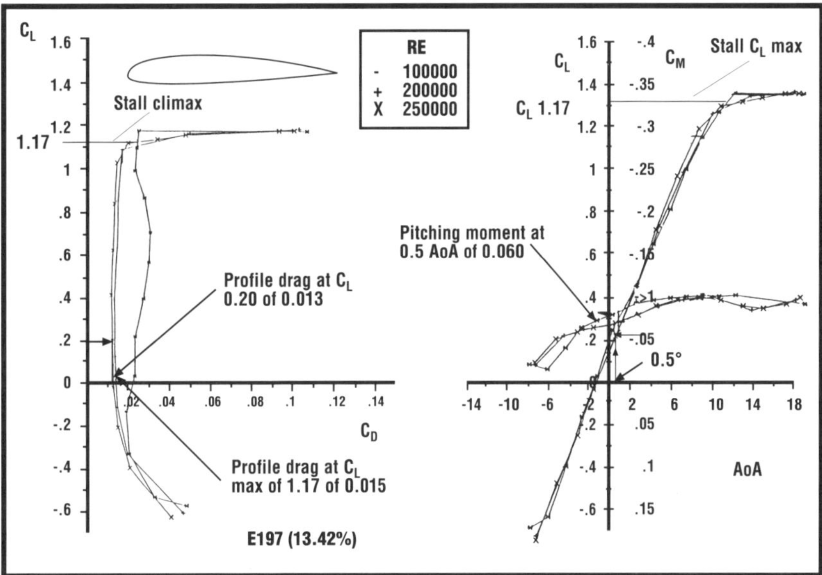

Figure 5.
Profile drag and pitching moments.

FIGURE 3

This nomograph is one of the most useful charts in this author's "bag of tricks." It compares three important factors: speed (mph), wing loading (oz./sq. ft) and wing C_L. It reflects the impact of changes in these factors.

For example, our paper design has a wing loading of 21.6 ounces per square foot of wing area; the wing has airfoil E197, which has a C_L max of 1.17. Using Figure 3, its stall speed is 22mph. Adding 20 percent, its landing speed, under good control, would be 26.4mph.

This nomograph is most useful in the early stages of a model's design. For example:

■ **At constant speed,** it shows the effect of changes in wing loading, i.e., wing area and/or weight, on the CL needed for level flight. As wing loading increases, so must the C_L.

■ **At constant wing loading,** it displays the effect of the C_L on speed (or vice versa). For illustration, if our sample model had slotted flaps that, when extended, increased the wing's C_L max to 1.80, the stall speed would decrease to 16mph from the unflapped 22mph, or become 27 percent slower.

■ **At constant C_L,** changes in wing loading are reflected in the speed needed for level flight, and vice versa.

STALLING ANGLES

In Figure 4, at infinite AR, the E197 stalls very gently at about plus 11.5 degrees, or 13.5 degrees from zero lift. For our wing of AR 6 and constant chord, this would be:

a = 13.5 + (18.24 x 1.17 x 1.17 divided by 6), or 17.5 degrees from zero lift, or 15.5 degrees AoA at altitude.

For landing, however, this stall angle is greatly modified by:

■ **Ground effect.** As shown in Figure 6, at 0.15 of the wingspan (60 x 0.15, or 9 inches) above ground, the stall angle is reduced to 0.91 of its value at altitude, or to 14 degrees.

■ **The level flight wing AoA.** Because the wing is at 0.5 degree, it will stall at 13.5 degrees higher AoA.

■ **High-lift devices.** As Figure 7 shows, slotted flaps extended 40 degrees would cause a further

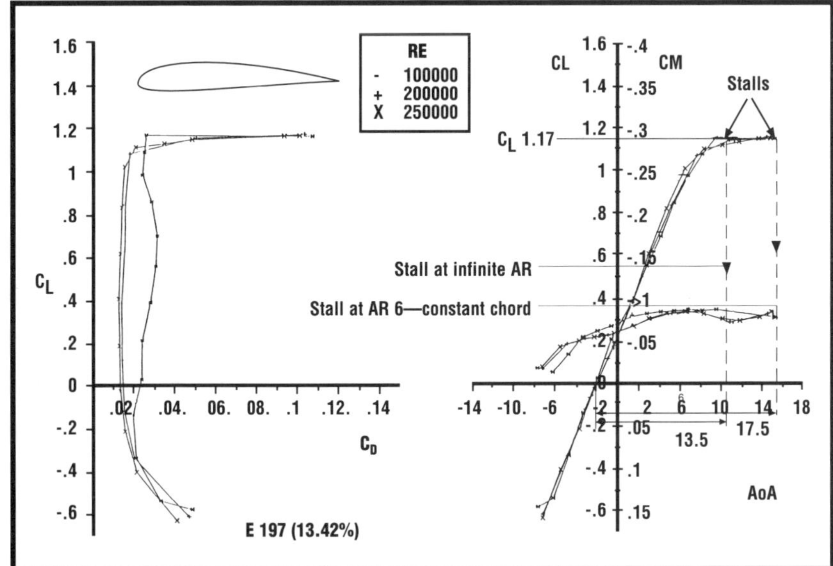

Figure 4.
The stalling angles of Eppler airfoil E197.

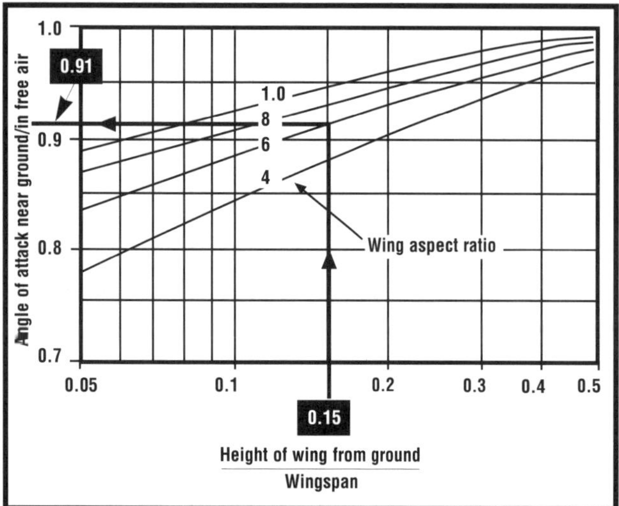

Figure 6.
Impact of ground effect on angle of attack.

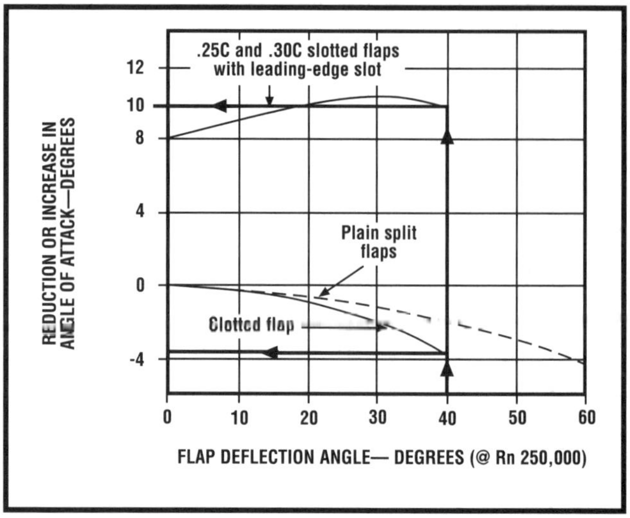

Figure 7.
The effect on flaps and LE slots on the angle of attack at maximum lift.

reduction of 4 degrees to 9.5 degrees stall angle. Had the slotted slaps been combined with fixed leading-edge (LE) slots, there would be a gain of 9 degrees, to 22.5 degrees stall angle.

The model's landing stall angle has a major impact on landing-gear design. (Chapter 16, "Landing Gear Design," goes into this in detail.)

Figure 8 shows the geometry of a fixed LE slot. Note how the slot tapers from the lower entry to the upper exit.

Figure 9 displays the benefits of an LE slot in added C_L and additional effective angles of attack before the stall. Drag is little affected.

Figure 10 shows the additional C_L to be obtained from various types of flap alone, or in combination with LE slots.

Slotted flaps and fixed LE slots combine to more than double the C_L of most airfoil sections, producing STOL performance.

For example, our E197 C_L max is 1.17. Equipped with deployed 30-percent-chord slotted flaps with extended lip and LE slots, both full-span, the wing's C_L max would be 1.17 plus 1.25, or 2.42.

Our sample model so equipped would stall (Figure 7) at 14mph.

Figure 11 shows the added profile C_D to be added to the section's profile C_D, when calculating the total of both profile and induced drags, discussed under "drag," as follows.

DRAG

The drag coefficients shown in Figures 5 and 11 are profile drag only. The C_L max profile drag of the unflapped E197 is 0.015 (Figure 5) and for full-span slotted flaps would be an additional 0.121 (Figure 11), for a total of 0.136 in profile drag. Induced drag is not included. Note the very small increase in E197's profile drag for C_L 0.20 to C_L max 1.17.

The formula for calculation of total wing drag is:

$$C_D = \frac{C_{Do} + 0.318 \times C_L^2 \times (1 + \sigma)}{AR}$$

where C_D = total of both profile and induced drags;

C_{Do} = section profile drag coefficient at the chosen wing C_L;

C_L^2 = wing lift coefficient "squared";

AR = aspect ratio;

σ = planform drag adjustment factors.

Our model's wing has a C_{Do} of 0.013 at C_L 0.20 (Figure 5) and a drag planform adjustment of 0.05 (see Figure 4 of Chapter 1).

Replacing symbols with numbers for the plain wing:

$$C_D = \frac{0.013 + 0.318 \times 0.2^2 \times 1.05}{6}$$

or 0.01523.

If our sample wing had full-span slotted flaps that extended 40 degrees and that were 30 percent of the wing chord, the total C_D, at a C_L max totaling (1.17 + 1.05), or

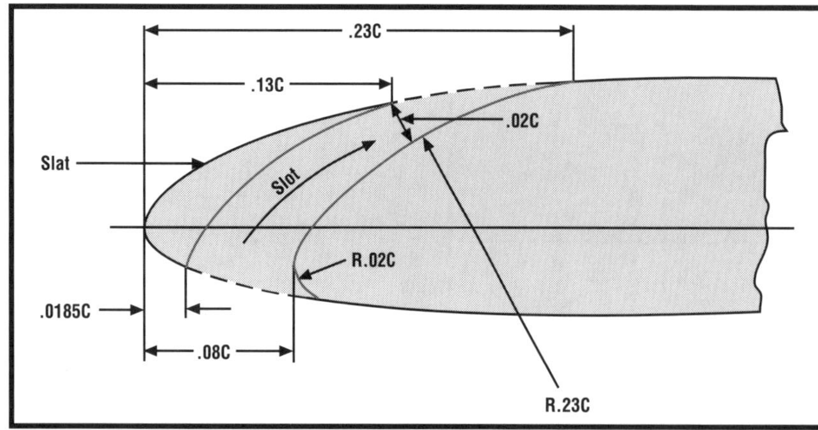

Figure 8.
Geometry of the fixed leading-edge slot.

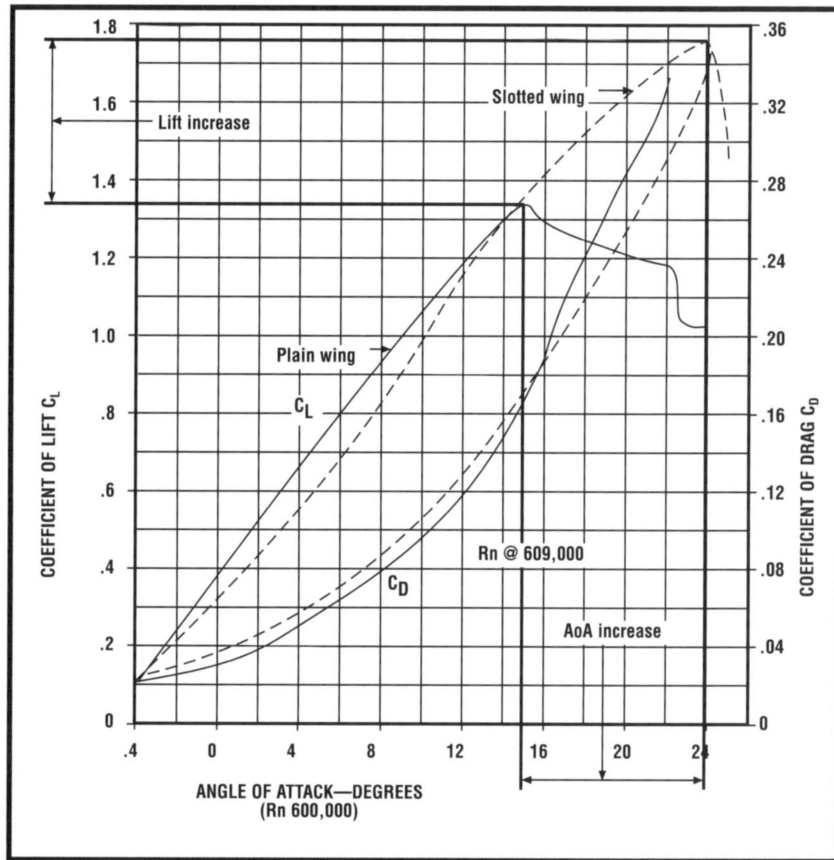

Figure 9.
The benefits of the fixed leading-edge slot.

2.22 (Figure 10), would be:

$$C_D = (0.15 + .121) + 0.318 \times 2.22^2 \times 1.05$$

or 0.410.

(Figures 5 and 11)

The formula for total wing drag is :

$$Drag\ (oz.) = \frac{C_D \times \sigma \times V^2 \times S}{3519}$$

Replacing the symbols with numbers for the plain wing at 50mph:

$$Drag\ (oz.) = \frac{0.01523 \times 1 \times 50^2 \times 600}{3519}$$

or 6.5 ounces.

And for the full-span, slotted-flap version at a stalling speed of 14mph, 30-percent-chord flaps at 40 degrees:

$$Drag\ (oz.) = \frac{0.410 \times 1 \times 14^2 \times 600}{3519}$$

or 13.7 ounces.

(Note: in Figure 2 of Chapter 1, the lower drag correction factor σ for the tapered wing, of taper ratio 0.6, is 0.02 compared to that for a constant-chord wing of 0.05.)

SCALE EFFECT

Scale effect is measured by Rn. In E197, lift and pitching moments are little affected by the reduction in Rn from 250,000 to 100,000, but profile drag increases substantially.

The formula for Rn is simple:

$$Rn = speed\ (mph) \times chord\ (in.) \times K$$

K at sea level is 780; at 5,000 feet, it's 690; and at 10,000 feet, it's 610.

Our sample model's wing chord is 10 inches, and at a landing speed of 26.4mph and at sea level, its Rn would be 26.4 x 10 x 780, or 205,920.

In Denver, the Rn would be 26.4 x 10 x 690, or 182,160.

A quicker solution at sea level is given in Figure 12. Laying a straightedge from "speed" left to "chord" right, Rn is read from the center column.

The Wild Goose shown with slotted flaps on both front and main wings extended for slow, stable landings.

Note that a tapered wing's root chord always flies at a higher Rn than its tip chord at any speed, owing to the narrower tips (which can be prone to tip-stalls as a result).

Full-scale airfoil research data may be used for model airplane wing design—with careful regard for the major effect of scale on particularly lift, drag and stall angles.

PITCHING MOMENTS

These have nothing to do with baseball! All cambered airfoils have nose-down, or negative, pitching moments. Symmetrical airfoils have no pitching moments, except at the stall. Reflexed airfoils may have low nose-down or low nose-up pitching moments.

Nose-down pitching moments must be offset by a horizontal tail download that is achieved by having that tail's AoA set at a negative angle to the downwash from the wing. (Chapter 8, "Horizontal Tail Incidence and Downwash Estimating," goes into detail.)

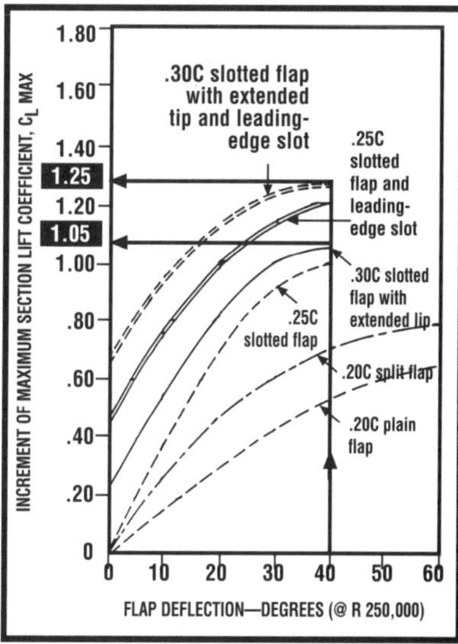

Figure 10.
Increments of maximum lift due to flaps and leading-edge slots.

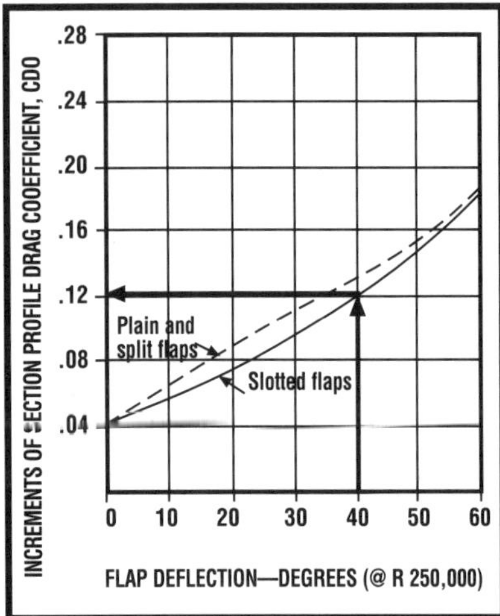

Figure 11.
Increments of profile drag coefficient at C_L max or increasing flap deflections.

As Figure 5 shows, the E197 airfoil has a negative C_M of 0.060 at an AoA of 0.5 degree. Note that C_M, like C_L, varies with the AoA.

Also, the C_M applies to the wing's ¼ MAC; on our straight wing of 10 inches chord, at a point 2.5 inches from its leading edge.

The pitching moment formula is:

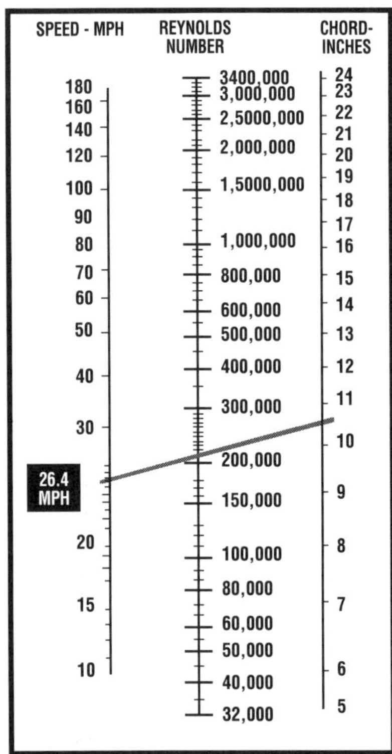

Figure 12.
Nomograph for quick determination of Reynolds numbers.

$$PM \text{ in in-oz.} = \frac{C_M \times \sigma \times V^2 \times S \times C}{3519}$$

where C_M = airfoil pitching-moment coefficient at the AoA of level flight;

V^2 = speed in level flight "squared";

S = wing area in square inches;

C = chord in inches;

σ = density ratio of air.

Our sample wing's nose-down PM is:

$$PM = \frac{0.060 \times 1 \times 50^2 \times 600 \times 10}{3519}$$

or 255.75 in-oz.

A moment is a force times a distance. In our sample, if a tail-moment arm distance were 30 inches, the tail download to offset the nose-down moment would be 255.75 divided by 30, or 8.52 ounces. (Chapter 8 goes into this in detail.)

RPM, SPEED AND PITCH NOMOGRAM

Figure 13 was developed to help model designers choose prop pitches and diameters suitable for both plane and engine to obtain optimum performance.

This is explained in Chapter 8. Figure 13 should be used with Figure 3, "Wing Loading Lift Speed Nomograph." Don't use Figure 13 alone to estimate the speed of any prop/plane/engine combination; if the prop pitch and diameter aren't suitable for a model's characteristics, the nomogram will not be accurate.

It would obviously be poor judgment to use a high-pitch, low-diameter propeller on a large, slow flying, draggy model with low wing loading. Similarly, a low-pitch, large-diameter prop on a low-drag, fast airplane with a high wing loading would be a poor choice.

I hope that this chapter will overcome any problems some readers may have with formulas in this book. To succeed, one must try! No effort, no success! ▲

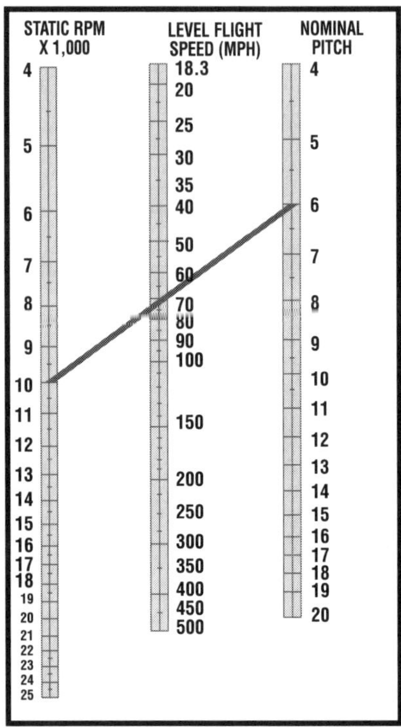

Figure 13.
Nomogram for choosing suitable prop pitches and diameters.

Chapter 4

Wing Loading Design

Wing loading is simply your model's weight in ounces (including fuel) divided by its wing area in square feet. It's expressed as "ounces per square foot of wing area."

In the initial stages of design of a new model aircraft, many major decisions have to be made that will determine its ultimate size and configuration:

- the size and make of engine (if any);
- the type of performance goals sought; (basically, is it a sport model of moderate speed and maneuverability or one that's fast and aerobatic? As a glider, is it a thermal seeker or a fast, sleek, aerobatic sailplane?);
- the wing planform (straight, tapered or elliptical);
- the airfoil; and
- the estimated weight.

Your model's wing loading is one of these major decisions—and should be "performance-objective oriented."

Wing loadings vary widely; gliders and sailplanes have wing loadings that range from less than 10 ounces per square foot to 15 ounces per square foot. Sport models are usually in the 15 to 20 ounces per square foot range. Pattern models have wing loadings from 23 to 26 ounces per square foot. Scale models are miniatures of existing aircraft. None of my scale modeling friends knows or cares what his model's wing loading is. They relate gross weight, in pounds, to engine displacement to ensure adequate power.

Scale models don't often involve the same design latitude as other types of model, but some are fantastic examples of excellent workmanship.

HIGHER WING LOADINGS

I personally favor higher wing loadings because they result in smaller, stronger, faster and—if you're careful in the design and construction phases—less "draggy" aircraft.

Higher wing loadings, however, result in higher stall and landing speeds. Level flight requires a higher angle of attack or greater speed. The most serious impact of a higher wing loading is on centrifugal loads when engaging in maneuvers that involve heavy elevator action. Such maneuvers include tight turns, sharp pull-ups or dive-recoveries.

An advantage of a higher wing loading is that, at any given speed, the wing must operate at a higher lift coefficient that's further up the slope of the lift curve and closer to the stall. Entry into maneuvers that involve wing stalling, such as spins, snap rolls and avalanches, is more readily achieved.

Once you've estimated your design's gross weight (with fuel) and decided your wing loading, the wing area (in square inches) is simply:

$$\frac{\text{model gross weight (oz.)}}{\text{wing loading (oz./sq. ft.)}} \times 144$$

LANDING SPEEDS

Wing loadings and landing speeds are closely related. Refer to Figure 2, and read up from the 16 ounces per square foot point at the bottom of the chart to the C_L of 1.00 (most airfoils' C_L max is close to 1.00). On the left side of the chart, you'll see that the stall speed is 20mph. Do the same thing on the 36 ounces per square foot line, and you'll see that the stall is 30mph. Adding a "safety margin" of 20 percent to each stall-speed estimate results in landing speeds of 24 and 36mph. The latter is too fast for comfort.

CENTRIFUGAL FORCE

Centrifugal force is expressed in multiples of "G", where 1G is normal gravity. Its formula, including the model's 1G weight, is:

Gap seal
Hinge
60°
25% C
60°

Figure 1.
The author proposes the use of plain flaps, depicted above, on pattern ships (see text).

$$N = 1 + \frac{(1.466 \times mph)^2}{R \times G}$$

where N = load factor in G's;
mph = speed in mph;
R = maneuver radius in feet;
G = acceleration of gravity (32.2 feet/second per second).

Aerodynamically clean model aircraft that have powerful engines and are correctly "propped" can achieve very high speeds. The norm for pattern ships is 100mph. My "Swift" has a top speed of 125mph; its gross weight is 92 ounces, and its wing loading is 22 ounces per square foot. At 90mph, it flies at a C_L of 0.072.

In a steep turn of a 50-foot radius, the load factor would be

$$N = 1 + \frac{(1.466 \times 90)^2}{50 \times 32.2} = 11.8\ G\text{'s}$$

In this maneuver, the Swift's wing has to lift 11.8 x 92, or 1,086, ounces—a shocking 68 pounds.

Just think what this means both aerodynamically and structurally. This is why I favor stiff, strong, fully sheeted and stress-skinned structures.

The lift coefficient in this turn would increase 11.8 times to C_L 0.85, well within its E197 airfoil's capacity of C_L max 1.17. There's a healthy margin before the stall.

If the Swift's airfoil were E168 with a C_L max of 0.98, however, then this margin would be greatly diminished. (See appendix for Eppler airfoil data.)

It's impossible to gauge accurately the model's turning radii from several hundred feet away, hence this safety factor is needed to avoid "high-speed stalls" (which would probably result in uncommanded snap rolls).

SLOTTED FLAPS

The Swift—slotted flaps up—will land at 30mph. With flaps down 40 degrees, at a C_L max of 1.9, its landing speed is 22mph. Flaps thus eliminate the adverse effect that higher wing loadings have on landing speeds.

In high-speed, short-radius turning maneuvers, 20 degrees of flap deflection would increase the Swift's C_L max to 1.6 (from flaps-up 1.17). Tighter turns are possible without danger of a high-speed stall. The Swift's sturdy flaps are strong enough to accept this treatment.

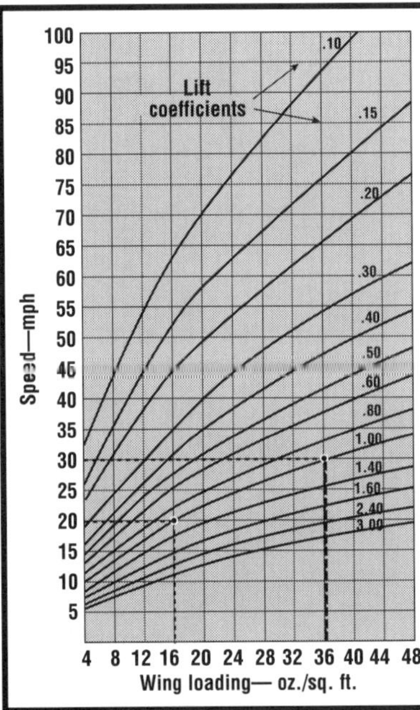

Figure 2.
From wing loading at the bottom, read vertically to the appliicable lift coefficient and then move left (horizontally) to find the speed in miles per hour. The stall speed is based on an airfoil's maximim lift coefficient.

The Swift wasn't designed to be a stunt model; it's a "sport-for-fun" model with a wide speed range and low landing and takeoff speeds, i.e., with flaps deployed. Its slotted flaps aren't suitable for the wide range of aerobatics that pattern ships perform, both upright and inverted.

PLAIN FLAPS

Plain flaps (Figure 1), however, in wings with symmetrical airfoil sections, such as E168 (standard on pattern models) would function equally well angled down (for upright flight) or up (for inverted flight). They achieve their C_L max at 60 degrees of deflection and would add an additional C_L of 0.62 at that angle, plus additional drag to slow the model. At 20 degrees of deflection, the additional C_L would be 0.25.

If we assume:

- outboard ailerons of 25-percent chord that are 35 to 40 percent of the semi span in length;
- plain flaps inboard of the ailerons to the fuselage; and
- E168 with a C_L max of 0.98, then the fully deployed flap at 60 degrees would provide a wing C_L max of 1.30 and, at 20 degrees of deflection, a wing C_L max of 1.13.

The pilot could extend these flaps up or down at any angle to suit the maneuver in progress. Landings, with a 60-degree flap deployment, with a high wing loading of 28 ounces per square foot, would be at 28mph—a comfortable speed.

In addition, for sharp-turning maneuvers, lowering these flaps partially to 20 degrees would prevent high-speed stalls.

At 100mph in level flight, a C_L of 0.068 is required. For a turn radius of 50 feet at 100mph, the load factor would be 14.34G's. This calls for a C_L of 0.97, which is dangerously close to the E168's C_L max of 0.98. The 20-degree flap deflection would provide a C_L of 1.13, which would be safer.

With flaps up, the higher loading would move the level-flight C_L higher up the lift slope, closer to C_L max. In turn, this provides easier entry into any maneuver requiring that the wing be stalled.

A .60-powered pattern model that weighs 8 pounds (128 ounces), and has a wing loading of 28 ounces per square foot would have a wing area of 4.57 square feet, or 658 square inches.

Pattern ships have evolved over time into beautiful configurations of startling similarity to one another. It's time to consider some fresh approaches to their design. Perhaps flaps and higher wing loadings are such approaches. ▲

Chapter 5

Wing Design

The Swift's design is the central theme in this chapter. It weighs 92 ounces fueled, has 600 square inches of wing area (4.17 square feet), an AR of 6.3 and is powered by an O.S. Max 0.46 SF engine rotating a 10x9 or 10x10 APC prop. Its top speed is 125mph, and flaps fully extended, it will stall at 18mph. Its wing loading is 22 ounces per square foot, and its power loading is 200 ounces per cubic inch of engine displacement.

A detailed analysis of the Swift's weight of 92 ounces reveals that 46.5 ounces (or 50.4 percent) of that weight can be classified as "fixed." This weight, over which the designer has no control, consists of:

- Power unit—spinner, prop, engine, muffler, cowl, tank and fuel;
- Control unit—receiver (6-channel), battery (700mAh), five servos, an on/off switch, and foam shock insulation;
- Landing gear—tricycle with 2-inch-diameter wheels.

WING DESIGN VARIABLES

These each require decisions:

- Airfoil selection
- Wing planform
- Aspect ratio
- Stall patterns, lift distribution and stall avoidance
- Wingtip design
- Flaps

To aid in decision making, each of these variables will be discussed in some detail, except airfoil selection, which is covered in Chapter 1.

The remaining weight of 45.5 ounces (or 49.6 percent of the gross) is composed of wing, fuselage and tail surfaces. This portion *is under the control* of the designer. The wing loading he selects will dictate the wing's area, and generally, the size of fuselage and tail surfaces. It will also influence the structure; lower wing loadings and lower speeds reduce flight loads, particularly those due to centrifugal force, permitting lighter, less rugged structural design.

It's possible to design a model of 800 square inches of wing area (5.56 square feet) with the same gross weight as the Swift by use of a more open structure. This model would have a lower wing loading of 16.5 ounces per square foot and would stall at 18mph.

Thus, flaps for landing wouldn't be needed. The weight of the fifth (flap) servo; the additional weight of the 700mAh battery (versus 500mAh); and the additional weight of the flaps, their hinging and their actuation would all be "saved." The performance of this model would not be as good as the Swift's, however, largely owing to the increased total drag resulting from its larger size.

The point of all this is that the type of performance desired by the designer dictates the wing loading and, to a large extent, the structure. For the Swift, high speed and maneuverability were the objectives, calling for a rugged, stress-skinned and low-drag design. Thus, within reasonable limits, wing loading governs performance and structural design.

WEIGHT ESTIMATING

Having selected the power and control units and type of landing gear, it isn't difficult to closely estimate their *fixed* weights.

Similarly, having decided on the wing loading, the *variable* weight of wings, tail surfaces and fuselage may be estimated with reasonable accuracy. My own estimates have only rarely been "right on"; the tendency was to underestimate. In compensation, the Swift's gross was overestimated at 100 ounces, whereas the actual is 92 ounces—8 ounces difference. While not perfect, this rational but practical approach shouldn't result in a difference between the estimate and actual of more than 10 percent.

With weight estimates of both fixed and variable components achieved and the wing loading selected, the wing area is easily calculated:

$$\text{Wing area in square inches} = \frac{\text{Weight in oz.} \times 144}{\text{Wing loading in oz. per sq. ft.}}$$

It's useful at the initial stages of a new design to have a preliminary estimate of the new model's total weight and wing area. In Chapter 13, "Stressed Skin Design," the weight versus wing area of 14 models is analyzed, disclosing a surprising consistency in the weight versus area relationship of 0.1565 ounce per square inch—or 22.5 ounces per square foot. For those adopting stressed-skin construction, these figures provide an easy weight-estimate basis.

For others who prefer lighter, more open structures, a study of construction articles and product reviews will help.

A word on tank size. It makes no

sense to provide a 16-ounce fuel tank on a model powered by a .40 to .50ci engine. Most sport flights seldom last more than 25 minutes so, on landing, the 16-ounce tank is still half-full. Your model is penalized to about ½ pound carrying this useless weight. A guide to tank size relative to engine displacement is 20 ounces per cubic inch of engine displacement. Thus, for a .40ci engine, an 8-ounce tank is right on.

Now, let's consider the many other design decisions to be made. It's fun!

WING PLANFORMS

■ **Elliptical wings.** This is the "ideal" wing planform. It has the lowest induced AoA and induced drag and stalls evenly across its span. These factors increase for tapered or rectangular wings. For example, a rectangular wing of AR 6 would require an induced AoA (T) 17 percent higher and with induced drag (δ) 5 percent higher than an elliptical planform. (See Figures 2 and 4 of Chapter 1.)

Structurally, the elliptical wing is difficult to produce. Each rib is different and wing skins all have a double curvature, chordwise and spanwise. The Spitfire's elliptical wing is a classic example.

■ **Rectangular wings**. This is the easiest type to design and build. All ribs are the same, and wing skins have a single chordwise curvature. While it suffers in comparison with the elliptical, for small models, it maintains a constant Rn across its span, whereas a tapered wing of the same area could have tip Rns in the high drag/lower lift and stalling-angle range of low Rns, leading to premature tip-stalls at low speeds.

Structurally, the wing roots need reinforcing, owing both to narrower root chords and higher bending moments. The center of lift of each wing half is farther from the centerline than an elliptical or tapered wing.

■ **Tapered wings.** A tapered wing with a tip chord of 40 percent of the root chord comes closest to the ideal elliptical planform in both induced AoA and induced drag (see Figure 2 of Chapter 1). For wings of smaller models, this taper ratio results in narrow tip chords and undesirably low Rns at low speeds. Increasing the taper ratio produces larger tip chords. The resulting loss in efficiency isn't great and is the "lesser of the two evils."

Structurally, the tapered wing has lower root bending moments, and the wider, deeper root chord provides the greatest strength where it's needed most—at the root. A tapered wing can be lighter yet stronger than a rectangular wing of the same area.

■ **Sweptback wings.** This causes similar behavior to decreased taper ratio (smaller tip chord) and leads to early tip-stalls with a nose-up pitch, since the tips, being behind the CG, lose lift. It has a dihedral effect; 2½ degrees of sweepback (measured at 25 percent of the chord) is roughly equivalent to 1 degree of dihedral. It also promotes directional stability; if yawed, the advancing wing's center of drag moves away from the CG, and the opposite, retreating wing's center moves inward. The resulting drag imbalance works to oppose the yaw. Large sweptback angles increase induced drag and lower the wing's maximum lift.

Wings of moderate taper ratios (0.5 to 0.6) with straight-across trailing edges and sweptback leading edges are popular for pattern ships. These wings tip-stall readily for easy entry into wing-stalling maneuvers such as snap rolls, spins, etc.

Structurally, a sweptback wing's lift tends to reduce the wingtip's AoA, particularly at high speeds and high centrifugal force loads. A stiff wing structure will prevent potentially damaging wing flutter.

■ **Swept-forward wings.** These tend to stall at the wing root first. The unstalled tips promote good aileron control at high angles of attack. The root stall reduces lift aft of the CG, causing a nose-up pitch.

Forward sweep is destabilizing in yaw. The centers of drag and lift of the advancing wing panel move inboard; on the opposite, retreating panel, these centers move outboard. The unequal drag moments increase the yaw, while the unequal lift moments cause a roll, but in a direction opposed to the yaw. Control of this instability calls for increased vertical tail surface area and effectiveness, along with generous dihedral.

Structurally, a wing very stiff in torsion is required to overcome the wingtips' tendency to increase their AoA. Any flexibility could be disastrous at high speeds.

In full-scale airplanes, modest sweep forward moves the wings' main spar aft, out of the way, and

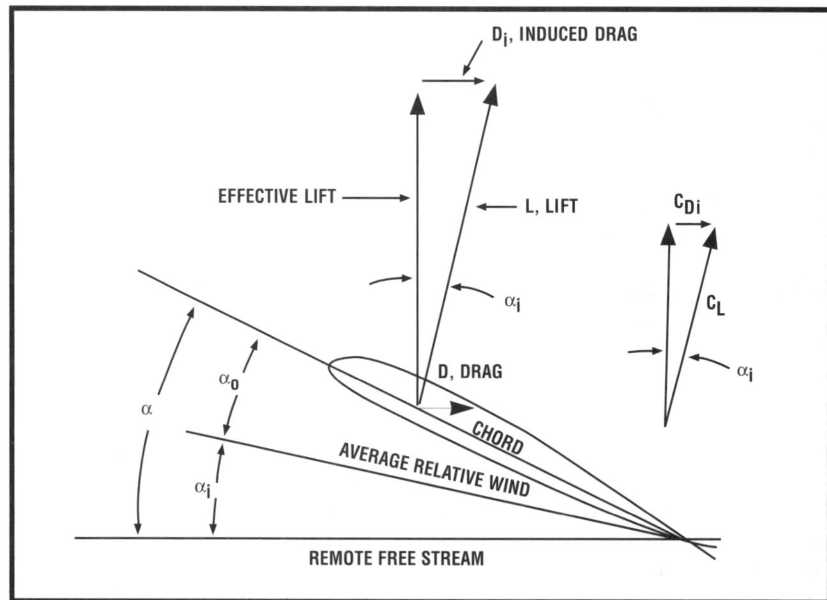

Figure 1.
The origin of induced drag.

improves the pilot's forward and downward vision.

■ **Delta wings.** The triangular shape of a delta wing is so called because of its resemblance to the capital letter delta (Δ) in the Greek alphabet. These have very low ARs. Low-AR wings stall at high angles of attack—but with high induced drag. Vortex flow is high, since a delta wing is virtually all "wingtip."

Deltas don't need flaps for landing owing to their high AoA capability, but should be landed with some power-on to overcome their high induced drag. Power-off, they have the glide characteristics of a brick!

A tailless delta-wing model, with the whole trailing edge composed of elevons, is highly maneuverable and will not spin, but requires symmetrical or reflexed airfoil sections for longitudinal stability.

Structurally, deltas are very strong. The deep, wide center chord promotes strength, and the low AR reduces the bending moments at the wing's center.

■ **Combined rectangular and tapered wings.** This planform is rectangular for roughly 50 percent of the semispan (inboard) and tapered for the remaining 50 percent to the wingtip. Piper Warriors and Cessna 172s typify this planform. It comes close to the elliptical in shape and efficiency, yet is more easily produced than a tapered or elliptical wing. The comments earlier regarding the hazards of low Rns of narrow wingtips apply. The rectangular inner portion is wider in chord, which provides a strong wing root, and bending moments are lower than for a rectangular wing.

ASPECT RATIO

This important ratio is that of wingspan to mean chord. Its formula is:

$$\frac{Span^2}{Area} = Aspect\ ratio$$

The Swift's wingspan is 61.625 inches and its area is 600 square inches. Its AR is:

$$\frac{61.625^2}{600} = 6.3$$

TABLE 1 Model type	Power loading oz./cid 2-stroke	Wing loading oz./sq. ft.	Aspect ratio
High-speed, highly maneuverable	200-250	22 to 26	4 to 6
Moderate-speed sport	250-300	16 to 22	6 to 8
Low-speed trainer	300 and up	12 to 16	8 to 10
Slope gliders	—	12 to 14	8 to 10
Soaring gliders	—	8 to 12	10 to 15

The AR of a wing has a major impact on its "induced drag"—defined as that drag caused by the development of lift—and is separate from the drag caused by the wing airfoil's form and friction, called "profile drag."

As Figure 1 indicates, increasing the AoA causes the lift to tilt rearward, resulting in a horizontal vector that produces induced drag.

The classical formula for the induced drag coefficient is:

$$\frac{Lift\ coefficient^2}{\pi\ x\ Aspect\ ratio}$$

or

$$\frac{0.318\ x\ C_L^2}{AR} = C_{Di}$$

Obviously, the higher the AR, the lower will be the induced drag coefficient—and the lower the induced drag. This is why soaring gliders have such long, narrow high-AR wings.

An airplane's total drag is composed of two types: parasite drag (including profile drag), which doesn't contribute to lift; and induced drag, which results from the wing's production of lift. Figure 2 illustrates this relationship.

Induced drag has a very significant difference from both lift and parasite drag. The latter two are proportional to the square of the speeds; induced drag, however, is inversely proportional to the square of the speed. It's lowest at high speeds and highest at low speeds. Lift and parasite drag are low at low speed and high at high speed.

At 100mph, the total of profile and induced drags for the Swift is 22.4 ounces, of which the induced drag is 0.215 ounce—or less than 1 percent. At 30mph, total wing drag is 4.3 ounces, of which 2.3 ounces, or 54 percent, is induced drag—useful in slowing this model for landing.

It's this relationship that explains the power-off, brick-like glide of a delta wing. The low AR and high lift coefficients result in very high induced drag for low-speed delta flight.

Figure 2 depicts typical airplane drag curves. Where the induced drag equals the parasite drag is the speed of the maximum lift-to-drag ratio and of the maximum range.

Range, for model airplanes, is not a factor of any consequence, except in rare instances, since most powered R/C flights seldom exceed half an hour in duration.

ASPECT-RATIO PROS

For a given wing area, increasing the wing's AR will reduce the induced drag. The narrower chord tips result in smaller wingtip vortices; the lift per degree of AoA increases so that the model flies at a lower AoA. These all favor high ARs.

ASPECT-RATIO CONS

Lower chords on smaller models result in lower Rns—particularly at low speeds. Scale effect causes an increase in wing profile drag, a reduction in maximum lift and lower stalling angles.

The centers of lift of each wing half are farther from the fuselage for high-AR wings, resulting in substantial increases in root bending loads. In addition, long, narrow wings must be stiff in torsion to prevent twisting under loads from two sources—pitching-moment changes as the model maneuvers and the opposed action of ailerons. Wings weak in torsion have been known to

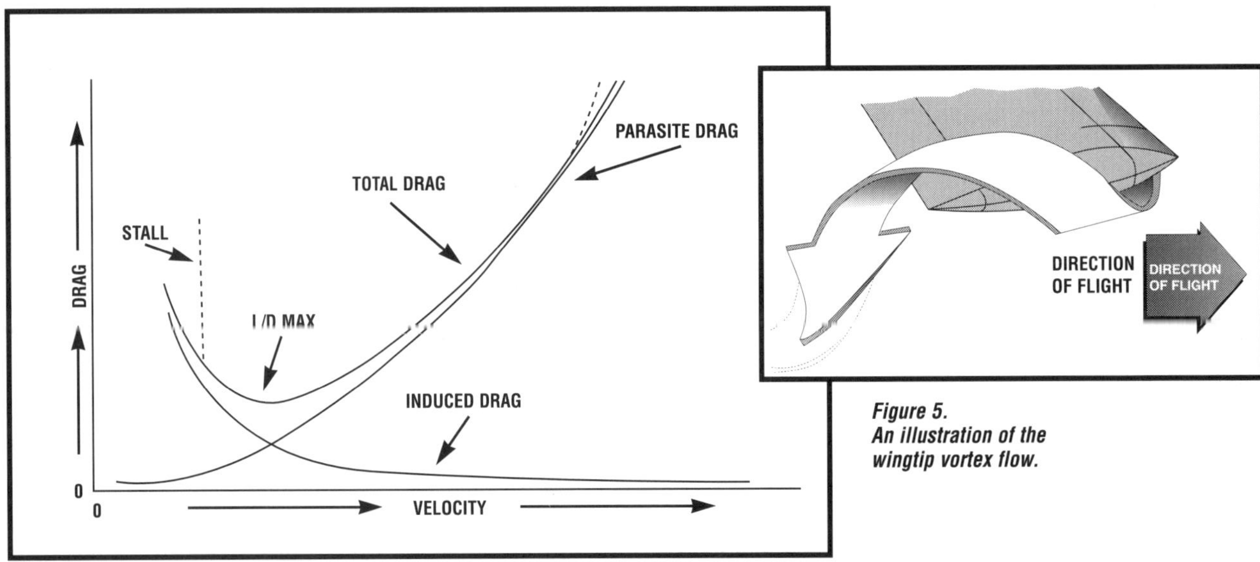

Figure 2.
Typical airplane drag curves. Parasite drag varies directly as the speed squared; induced drag varies inversely as the speed squared.

Figure 5.
An illustration of the wingtip vortex flow.

experience "aileron reversal." This occurs when heavy down-going aileron action twists the wing leading edge down. The up-going twists the leading edge up. The model banks in a direction opposite to that intended by its bewildered pilot.

High ARs result in weight increases, particularly for models designed for high speeds where high centrifugal loads are encountered. Increased weight results in higher wing loadings and higher parasite drag. Obviously, there must be some compromises.

With his neck "stuck way out," this author suggests the following classifications for radio-controlled model aircraft (see Table 1):

From this designer's point of view, to obtain the maximum efficiency, careful drag reduction is needed along with sound propeller selection. Higher flight speeds result with lower lift and profile drag coefficients and lower induced drag until the total drag equals the thrust. To provide the optimum strength-to-weight ratio to overcome high centrifugal force loads, stressed-skin structural design is suggested. To reduce landing and takeoff speeds, slotted flaps are recommended.

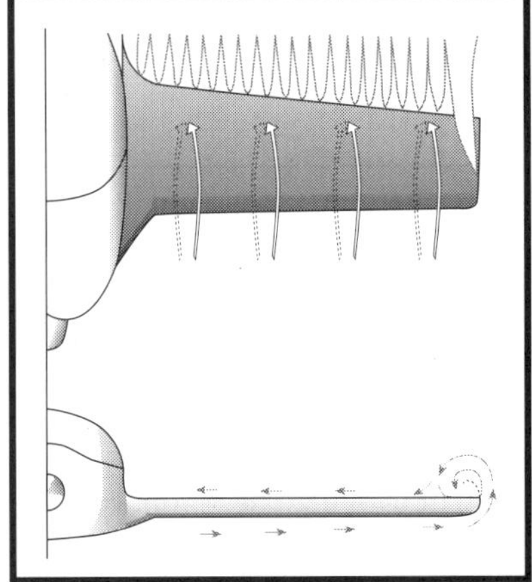

Figure 4.
As air flows past a wing from leading edge to trailing edge, positive pressure is created below the wing, while negative pressure exists above. At the wingtip, the positive-pressure bottom wing air flows around the tip and is drawn into the negative pressure region above the wing. This action gives rise to the wingtip vortex, as well as to lesser vortices along the trailing edge.

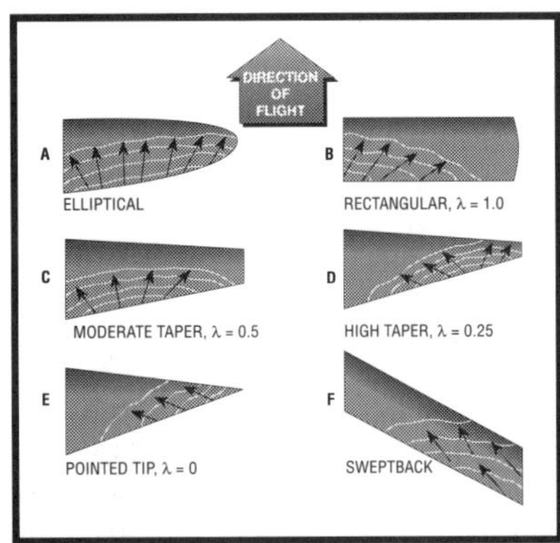

Figure 3.
Stall progression patterns for various planform wings.

STALL PATTERNS

Figure 3 illustrates how the various wing planforms stall at high angles of attack. Note that the rectangular wing stalls root first, permitting effective aileron control well into the stall.

There are a variety of ways in which tip-stalling may be delayed to higher angles of attack. The best and simplest form is the NASA-developed and tested partial-span wing-leading-edge droop. This feature has been used very successfully on six of my model designs.

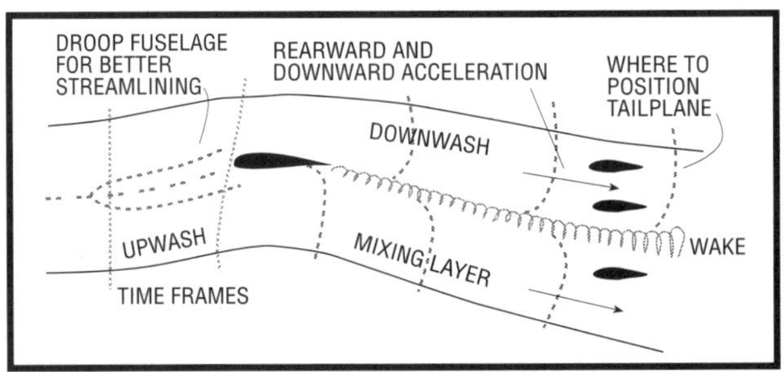

Figure 6.
The downwash and wake for a conventional, rear-tailed, aircraft. Note the suggested droop fuselage that would decrease drag. Time frames above the wing are spaced farther apart to illustrate higher-velocity air.

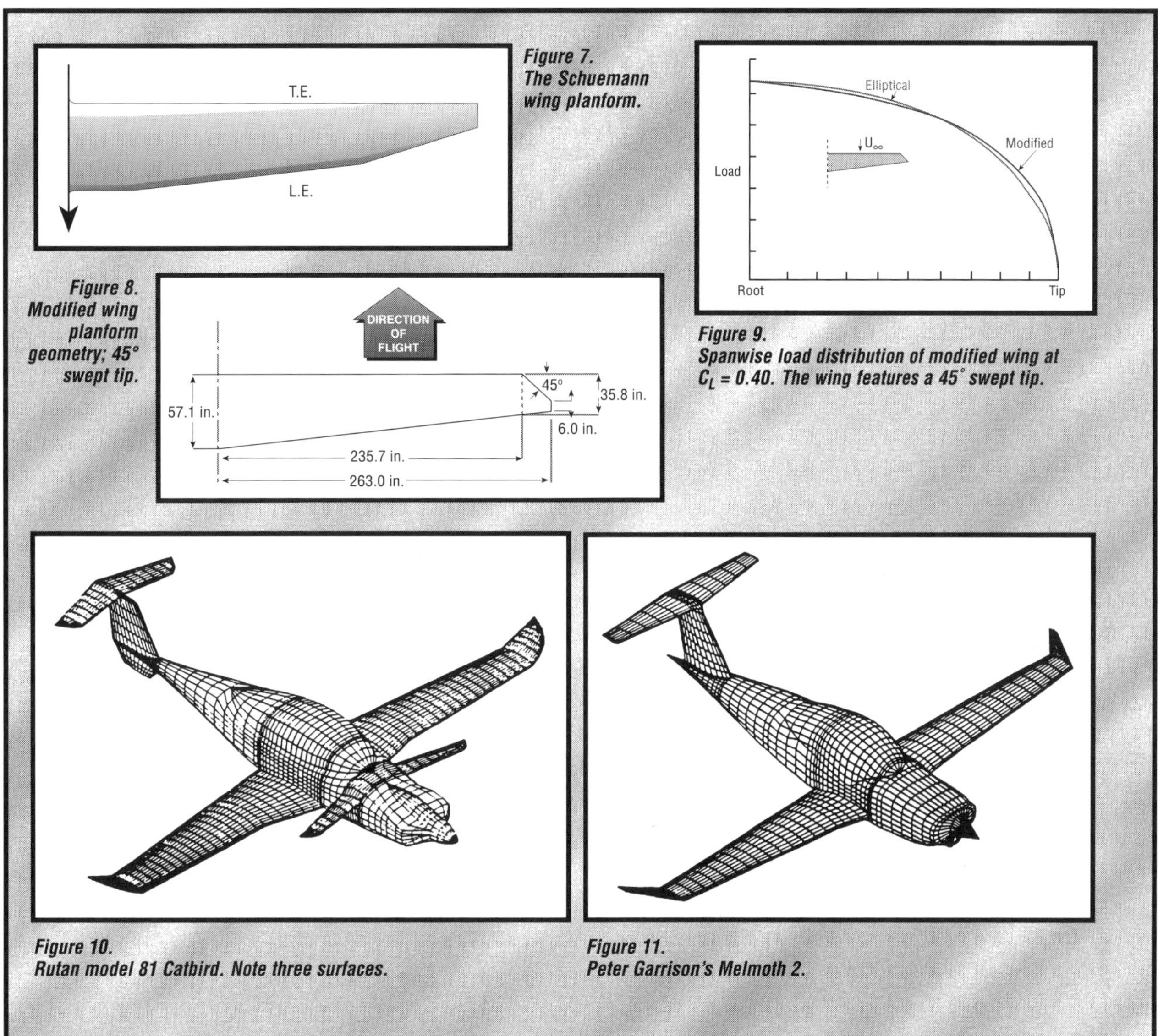

Figure 7. The Schuemann wing planform.

Figure 8. Modified wing planform geometry; 45° swept tip.

Figure 9. Spanwise load distribution of modified wing at $C_L = 0.40$. The wing features a 45° swept tip.

Figure 10. Rutan model 81 Catbird. Note three surfaces.

Figure 11. Peter Garrison's Melmoth 2.

WINGTIP DESIGN

The major difference in efficiency between the elliptical planform, considered the best, and other planforms is largely due to wingtip losses. The elliptical has no pronounced tip—one could say it is "all tip"—whereas the rectangular planform has the widest tip. Tapered wingtip widths vary with taper ratio.

Figures 4 and 5 portray the airflow over and under a wing and particularly the tip vortex flow. Figure 6 shows the wake and downwash resulting from the wing's production of lift.

Obviously, the narrower the tip, the lower the tip losses with due regard to stall patterns and scale effect, particularly at low speeds. A tip-stall close to the ground may be damaging to both model and its designer's ego!

Over the years, aerodynamicists have explored many wingtip configurations in their search for improved wing performance. Two forms, somewhat resembling each other, have emerged.

First is the Schuemann planform (Figure 7).

The second is the "sheared" wingtip, largely developed by C.P. Van Dam of the University of California. Figures 8 and 9 provide an outline of a sheared tip along with its spanwise load distribution. Note how close "modified" is to "elliptical" in Figure 9. This form of tip has been, or is being, applied to full-scale aircraft designed by such noted aerodynamicists as Burt Rutan and Peter Garrison. Figures 10 and 11 illustrate these designs.

This author uses a modified sheared wingtip that is both simple and rugged. Figure 13, a top view of the Snowy Owl's wing, illustrates this tip form.

FLAP CHORDS

Earlier model designs, such as the Snowy Owl, had slotted flaps whose chord was 26 percent of the wing's chord and were close to 60 percent of the wing's semi-span in length (see Figure 13).

After being throttled back and having their flaps fully extended, these models porpoised upward suddenly. Elevator down-trim applied simultaneously with flap extension would prevent this behavior, which was annoying.

Analysis disclosed that the

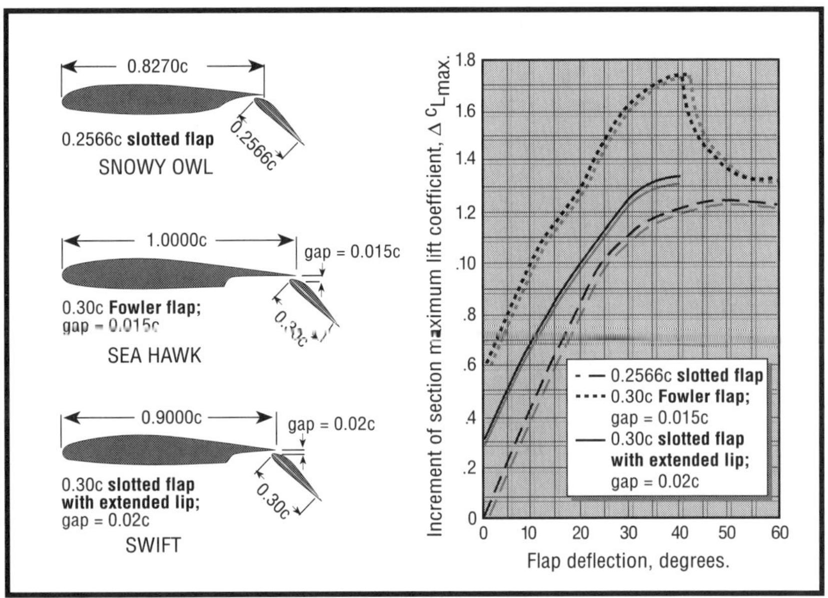

Figure 12.
Comparison of increments of section maximum lift coefficient for three flaps on a NACA 23012 airfoil.

increase in angle of downwash from the extended flaps was forcing the tailplane down and creating a greater force than the increase in nose-down pitch. The wing's AoA and lift increased, and the model zoomed upward until the excess speed bled off. The model then nosed over into the flap-down, slow glide.

Experience with three of my models (Sea Gull III, Sea Hawk and Swift) has proven that widening the flap chord to 30 percent of the wing chord produces a balance between these "nose-up" and "nose-down" forces, flaps fully extended. All three models exhibit no change in pitch on lowering flaps—but fly much more slowly.

On landing approach, ground effect reduces the downwash angle and increases the nose-down pitch. The glide close to the ground steepens, but appropriate up-elevator action raises the nose so that a gentle, slow landing results. ▲

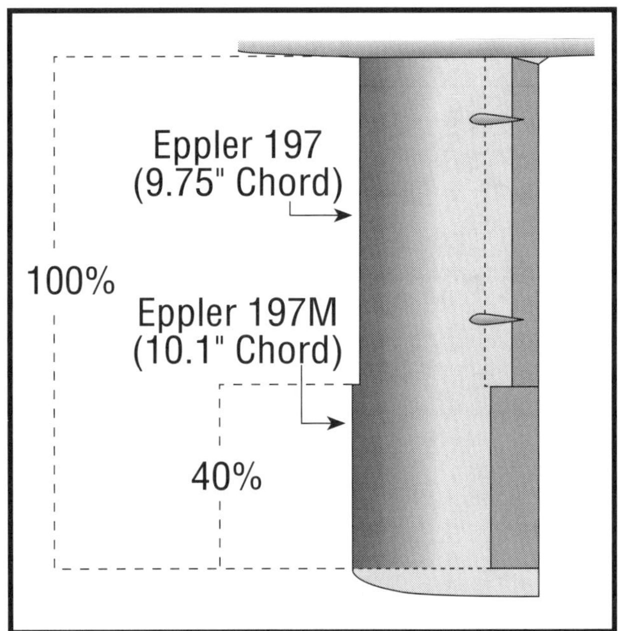

Figure 13.
Snowy Owl's flaps were 60% of the wing semi-span.

Chapter 6

CG Location

The location of the center of gravity has a major impact on longitudinal stability, the selection of the horizontal tail's angle of incidence and on the model aircraft's maneuverability. For sport models, it's customary to locate the CG at the wing's aerodynamic center (25 percent of MAC).

There is, however, a range of CGs both ahead of and behind the wing's aerodynamic center. These positions result in varying degrees of longitudinal stability. The steel ball in a saucer is a very graphic manner of describing pitch stability at various CGs (see Figure 1). Note that at position 4, the neutral point, the ball is on a flat surface and may be moved in any direction without returning to its original location in contrast to positions 1, 2 and 3, where the ball does return. At point 5, the ball will roll off the inverted saucer, indicating serious instability.

The following will outline the various CG advantages and limitations.

FORWARD CG

The most forward CG possible depends on the downward lifting capability of the horizontal tail. When I designed the Swift, the tail download needed to offset its wing airfoil's pitching moment was calculated at 15.4 ounces at 60mph level flight. A CG at 5 percent of the MAC, almost 2 inches ahead of the aerodynamic center, would further increase the required tail download. This results in three things:

- It increases the weight the airplane's wing must support.

- It reduces the horizontal tail's pitch maneuverability. This is because a major part of the tail's lift capacity is taken up with overcoming the nose-down combination of pitching moment and CG.

- This limited capacity makes achieving a full stall attitude difficult, if not impossible, in ground effect (this pressure of the ground reduces downwash). Moreover, with slotted flaps fully extended, the wing's nose-down pitching moment is further increased even with full up-elevator.

However, at this forward CG, the model's longitudinal stability would be high, and it would recover by itself from any pitch disturbance, returning to level flight. It would be easy to fly, but not highly maneuverable. Moving the CG rearward improves maneuverability but reduces pitch stability.

REAR CG AND THE NEUTRAL POINT

Modern aerodynamic analysis for assessing the stability of an airplane is based on the fact that a wing and tailplane represent a pair of airfoils in tandem. Each has its own aerodynamic center, but the combination will also have a corresponding MAC equivalent to the point where the total lift (and drag) forces of the two airfoils effectively act. This MAC is called the "neutral point" (NP). It follows that the NP will lie between the aerodynamic centers of the two airfoils and closest to the larger or more effective lift producer, i.e., the wing of conventional combinations, or the aft wing of a canard. Any disturbance in pitch that momentarily upsets the normal flight path of the aircraft will cause a change in AoA of both air-

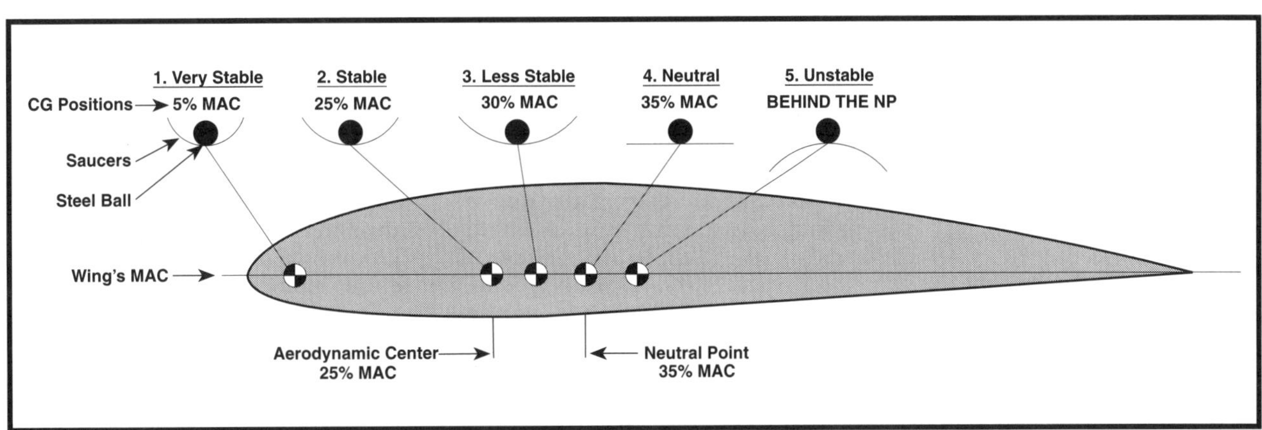

Figure 1.
In this illustration, a ball bearing in a saucer simulates the relative pitch stability of various CG locations.

WEIGHT ANALYSIS FOR THE SWIFT

FIXED WEIGHTS	OUNCES	PERCENT
POWER: Spinner, prop, engine, muffler, engine mount, fuel tank, fuel cowl (3 oz.), fuel tubing, nuts and bolts.	26.35	28.7%
CONTROL: Receiver (6-channel), 700mAh battery, five 5148 servos, switch, two extension cables, foam-rubber protection for receiver and battery.	15.0	16.3%
TRICYCLE LANDING GEAR: 2-inch-diameter wheels, 5/32-inch-diameter music-wire legs, fairings, nose-wheel bracket and steering arm, nuts and bolts.	7.0	7.6%
FIXED SUBTOTALS	*48.5 oz.*	*.52%*
VARIABLE WEIGHTS	**OUNCES**	**PERCENT**
WING: 600 square inches at 0.039 oz./sq. in., 1/16-inch-thick balsa skins, two spars, ailerons, slotted flaps (control cables included).	23.4	25.4%
HORIZONTAL TAIL: 120 square inches at 0.028 oz./sq. in., 1/16-inch-thick balsa skins and elevators; 40% (mass balanced.)	3.4	3.7%
VERTICAL TAIL: 40 square inches at 0.030 oz./sq. in., 1/16-inch-thick balsa skin, one spar and rudder. (Mass balanced.)	1.2	1.3%
FUSELAGE: Length from the engine bulkhead to the rudder tail post is 34.5 inches, 6 inches deep and 4.5 inches wide. This comes to 931.5 cubic inches at 0.017 oz./ci assuming 3/32-inch-thick balsa skins and 3/16-inch-thick balsa corners (control cables included).	15.8	17.0%
** Experience with several models indicates an average fuselage weight of 0.017 ounces per cubic inch, given the construction noted.*		
VARIABLE SUBTOTALS	*43.8 oz.*	*47.%*
TOTAL WEIGHTS	*92.3 oz.*	*100%*
WEIGHT (gross per square inch of wing area):	92.3/600 = 0.1538 oz./sq. in.	

foils. This will be translated as an increase (or decrease) in the total lift at the NP. The system is longitudinally stable if this change in lift produces a correcting effect, which it will if the NP is behind the CG. A nose-up disturbance increasing lift would apply this lift increase at the NP, behind the CG, causing the nose to drop and vice versa.

The degree of inherent stability is governed by the distance between the CG and the NP aft of it. It's called the "static margin." For the same setup, moving the CG aft would reduce this static margin (and, thus, the inherent longitudinal stability) until a condition of neutral stability is reached when the CG and NP coincide. Further movement of the CG aftward to behind NP would result in serious longitudinal instability.

The NP's position governs the margin of stability available (static margin, or distance between CG and NP). It's also the farthest aft position possible for the CG while still avoiding instability.

Calculation of the NP's precise location is very complex. There are many factors involved:

- tailplane efficiency;
- areas of wing and tailplane;
- distance between wing's and tail's aerodynamic centers;
- slopes of the respective airfoil's lift curves;
- fuselage area distribution in plan view;
- downwash variations; and
- the many effects of the propeller's rotation.

Full-scale practice is to calculate the NP's approximate position and then to finalize its precise location by wind-tunnel tests and/or by actual flight tests at increasingly rearward CGs.

For practical model design purposes, the "power-on" NP is located at 35 percent of MAC from its leading edge. The "power-off" NP moves a few percentage points farther aft, so that a model is more stable in an "engine-idling" glide.

With CG at 25 percent MAC and NP at 35 percent, there's a healthy stability margin of 10 percent. The minimum suggested stability margin is 5 percent, or a CG of 30 percent MAC.

Locating the CG farther aft, say at 33 percent MAC, would be dangerous. As fuel is consumed, the CG moves back and could easily reach a point behind the NP, leading to pitch instability under power.

Pattern-ship designers recognize this risk and position their fuel tanks on the model's CG. As fuel is consumed, the CG does not shift. Engine-driven pumps force the fuel to the carburetor.

These designers use symmetrical wing airfoils (with lower C_L max) because of their little or no pitching moments and aft CGs close to the NP. A small tailplane upload balances the aft CG. The result is a highly maneuverable model—but

Using the techniques described in this chapter, the Swift's CG was right on the money. No ballast was needed.

one that must be constantly "flown," demanding intense concentration from its pilot.

Since the stability is close to neutral, any disturbance will divert the model from its flight path, but the aircraft will not seek to return to its original course voluntarily, as a positively stable model would.

IN THE WORKSHOP

You have designed and built your very own model airplane. Wisely, before you go out to the flying field, you decide to check the physical location of your model's CG. To your dismay, you find it's well away from its design location. You are not alone; it has happened to others, including this author.

To correct this situation, you'll find that you don't have as much flexibility in rearranging things as you might think. Your engine, fuel tank and servos are in fixed locations. The only items that are readily moveable are the receiver and battery.

SERVO INSTALLATION AND CG

Questions of CG inevitably lead to a consideration of the arrangement of internal components and linkages. Bitter experience indicates that wiring from servos to receiver should be kept well away from both receiver and antenna to avoid radio interference. This author dislikes dowel pushrods from servos to rudder and elevator, and wire pushrods plus bellcranks for ailerons and flaps. Such installations require that rudder and elevator servos be located near the wing trailing edge and that the fuselage be "open" internally back to the tail surfaces. In addition, they vibrate heavily when the engine is running, doing both servos and control surfaces no good. Bellcranks lead to "slop" at the control surfaces.

Stranded steel cables running in plastic tubing permit the fuselage servos to be moved forward for easy access; the cables are run down the inside walls of the fuselage, or through the wing ribs, out of the way, and permit direct "no-slop" linkage between servos and control surfaces. No bellcranks are needed; cables do not vibrate as do linkages fashioned from pushrods and bellcranks. With this setup, radio/interference hasn't been an issue for at least 10 models.

As the photo of the Swift's wing clearly illustrates, the wing center section is open ahead of the main spar and behind the aft spar. This helps in providing access.

This author makes the following suggestions for the installation of the control components:

- Position the receiver aft so that it and the antenna are away from the wiring to the servos—and keep the antenna as far away from the control cables as possible.
- Position engine, rudder and elevator servos close behind the tank.
- Position servos for ailerons and flaps in the open wing center section, between the main and aft spar.
- The receiver's battery should be located so that "major surgery" isn't required for its removal and replacement.
- Finally, all in-fuselage and in-wing equipment should be readily accessible.

These objectives have been realized in the Swift. The front top of the fuselage is removed by unscrewing one bolt. Similarly, the lower engine cowl is even easier to remove. All components are readily accessible for adjustment, replacement or any other reason. The tank is fueled with the fuselage top "off." Straightening the nose gear after a hard landing is easy (you simply unscrew the steering arm setscrew and remove the gear).

Getting back to your new design; if you are unable to relocate your actual CG to where you want it, your only recourse is to add ballast, either up front for tail-heaviness—or aft for nose-heaviness. Lead shot, lightly coated with epoxy or dissolved cellulose

Side view of the Swift plan with power, control and landing-gear components. The balance-line fulcrum is in position at the lower center. (I used a triangular draftsman's scale as a fulcrum, but a spare piece of 3/4-inch balsa triangle stock would also work well.)

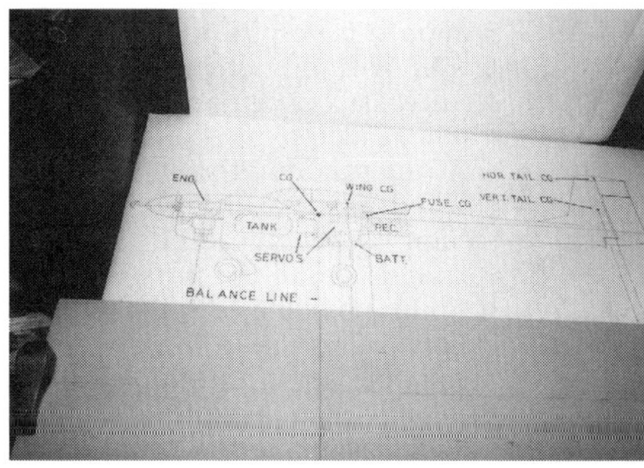

The balance beam is on the fulcrum and the weight—at the short end—is positioned so that beam and weight (a draftsman's "duck") balance on the fulcrum.

cements (like Sigment or Ambroid), may be stuffed into convenient corners and is self-adhering. Having to add much ballast isn't good design practice, however. Added weight doesn't improve the model's performance.

WEIGHT ANALYSIS

In Chapter 5, "Wing Design," an analysis revealed that over 50 percent of the Swift's gross weight was composed of three groups of items of fixed weight:

■ power components and fuel;

■ control components; and

■ landing-gear components.

Once selected, these are items over which the designer has no weight control; the engine is an example. If you don't already have these components on hand, their individual weights are easily obtained.

Don't be fooled by the tank size. The fuel in an 8-ounce tank, topped off, weighs only 5 ounces. Tank sizes are nominal, in fluid ounces, which is a measure of volume, not weight. Use your scale to weigh the tank, both empty and full. The difference is fuel weight!

A scale is essential for good design. The author uses an old beam scale, but the type used for weighing ingredients in cooking is available at low cost. It is recommended that you use one with a 10-pound capacity—graduated in pounds, ounces and ounce fractions.

THE BALANCING ACT

Concern with correctly locating the actual, physical CG during the design process lead to development of the technique that I refer to as the "balancing act." This procedure has been used successfully on many models—and the resulting CG's physical and design locations coincided or were very close.

It may be used on any configuration, conventional, canard, flying boat, etc. Used for the Seagull III flying boat during the design stage, the balancing act resulted in moving the engine nacelle forward 2 inches; its weight of 31 ounces compensated for a substantial tail heaviness. On completion, this model required no ballast. Time spent on the balancing act avoided major and difficult modifications to the finished model—or addition of a substantial weight of ballast up front.

Here are the steps needed:

■ Gather all the fixed-weight components that you possess. For those you don't have, make "dummies" of the same weight. Your scale is used here. Expired AA, C and D batteries, lead shot, fishing sinkers, etc., are useful for "dummy" purposes.

■ Similarly, make dummies for each of the variable weight items and wing, fuselage and tail surfaces, both horizontal and vertical.

The Swift's wing is bolted in position. Note that all components remain accessible.

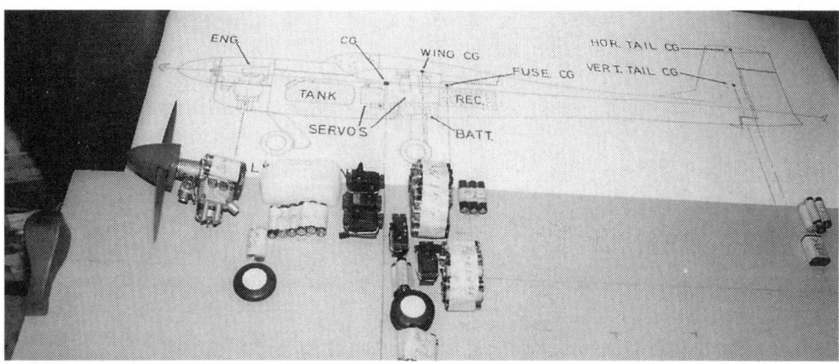

All the actual and dummy, fixed and variable weights in position—and again the balance beam is level. The actual and design CGs now coincide.

■ Position the CGs of the variable-weight items as follows:
—wing with flaps: 50 percent MAC
—wing without flaps: 40 percent MAC
—horizontal tail: 40 percent MAC
—vertical tail: "eyeball" the CG
—fuselage: normally 40 percent of the distance from engine bulkhead to rudder post. (Because of the concave aft contours of the Swift's fuselage, this was advanced to 35 percent.)

The Swift's fuselage is designed for easy access.

Seagull III. The original design had the engine nacelle farther back. The "balancing act" indicated that it was tail heavy. The nacelle was moved forward 2 inches; no ballast was needed when the model was completed.

■ Draw a side view, full-scale, of your design showing the positions of your fixed-weight items. Show your design's CG clearly—but don't detail any internal structure.

■ Locate and identify the CGs of your variable-weight items—wing, fuselage and horizontal and vertical tails. Draw vertical lines from their CGs to the board that will be used as a balance beam.

■ Place a fulcrum, e.g., a spare piece of ¾-inch balsa angle stock, on your worktable. The fulcrum should be vertically in line with the model's CG.

■ Place the "balancing beam" on the fulcrum and weight the short end so that the beam is balanced on the fulcrum.

■ Carefully position the fixed and variable weights, actual components and/or dummies in their respective positions, vertically below their design positions.

If balance is achieved—good. If the beam tilts down at the tail end, your design is tail heavy. Slight forward movement of power components, nosewheel unit and possibly fuselage servos should achieve balance. Measure the distance of this forward move, and elongate the design's fuselage accordingly.

If the beam tilts down at the front, your design is nose heavy. The best solution is to move the design's wing forward.

Carefully move the beam and its weights backward—then move wing, wing servo and landing gear (or dummies) forward to the original positions relative to your side view. Some trial-and-error movement will achieve balance. The distance the beam is moved backward will indicate the distance the wing must be moved forward to get the actual and design CGs to coincide.

Now that the positions of all the components have been established for the correct CG, mark your drawing accordingly. The fuselage internal structure then may be detailed. (See Chapter 13, "Stressed Skin Design.")

The balancing act is not too time-consuming, is certainly dependent on reasonably accurate weight estimates for the variable weight items and has proven itself to be a valuable design tool. Having to add gobs of weight, fore or aft, to your model to pin down that elusive CG to its design location is not good engineering. The balancing act will surely reduce the amount of weight needed, if it doesn't eliminate it entirely. ▲

The Swan canard, flaps extended on its cradle. Twelve ounces of ballast were needed—and provided for—as a result of using the "balancing act."

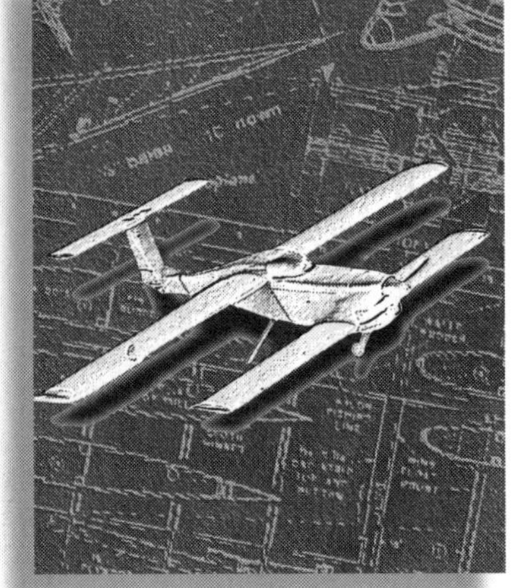

Chapter 7

Horizontal Tail Design

The design of an airplane's horizontal tail surface raises many questions. What area should it have? How far behind the wing should it be located? Where should the tail be located vertically, relative to the wing? What angle of incidence should it have? What airfoil? What proportion of its area should the elevators have? And what type of construction should be used? This chapter will answer these questions.

FORCES AT WORK

An airplane in steady level flight is a remarkable "balancing act." Lift must equal the model's weight; forces causing the model to nose down must exactly equal forces causing a nose-up reaction; thrust must equal drag.

What are these forces?

■ **CG placement.** A CG ahead of the wing's center of lift causes a nose-down reaction. Behind the wing's center of lift, a nose-up action takes place. A CG vertically in line with the wing's aerodynamic center, i.e., at approximately 25 percent of the MAC, exerts no nose-up or nose-down force.

■ **Pitching moment.** The pitching moment of semisymmetrical or flat-bottomed airfoils causes the aircraft to nose down. Symmetrical or reflexed airfoils have no pitching moment. Symmetrical sections are popular for aerobatics; they fly equally well upright or inverted. Reflexed sections are used on tailless models.

■ **Upwash and downwash.** Upwash originating ahead of the wing strikes both propeller disk and fuselage at an angle, ahead of the wing, and this causes a nose-up reaction. Downwash from the wing's trailing edge strikes both the aft fuselage and the horizontal tail downward, and this also causes a nose-up reaction.

■ **Thrust line.** A thrust line above the CG causes a nose-down reaction. If it is below the CG, a nose-up reaction results.

■ **Center of drag.** A high-wing model has its center of drag above the CG. A nose-up reaction occurs. A low-wing model reverses this reaction.

A mid- or shoulder-wing location permits the centers of lift, drag, thrust and gravity to be closer to each other. This, in turn, minimizes the imbalance of forces that frequently oppose one another.

The horizontal tail supplies the balancing force to offset the net result of all these forces, and its chord line must be at an angle to the downwash that provides either the upward load or (most often) the download required.

WAKE AND DOWNWASH

The tail surfaces of a conventional, rear-tailed airplane operate in a very disturbed atmosphere. The air sweeps downward off the wing's trailing edge as the result of the lift generated. This airstream is called the "wake." This wake is turbulent, and it influences the air—both above and below itself—in a downward direction called "downwash." (See Chapter 8, "Horizontal Tail Incidence and Downwash Estimating," for further discussion.)

Obviously, no self-respecting horizontal tail should find itself located in this very disturbed wake.

The angle of the downwash depends on the lift coefficient at which the wing is flying. An airplane has many level flight speeds, from just above the stall at low engine rpm to its maximum speed at full throttle.

At low speed, the wing's angle of attack must increase, as does its lift coefficient, and the downwash angle is high. At top speed, the reverse is true, and the downwash angle is low.

At low speed, the horizontal tail's downward lift must be increased to force the wing's airfoil to a higher AoA. Part of this download is supplied by the increase in the downwash angle. At high speed, the tail's download must be reduced to lower the wing's AoA—but again, since the downwash angle is reduced, the tail download is reduced.

The point of all this is that as the model's level flight speed varies with the throttle setting from low

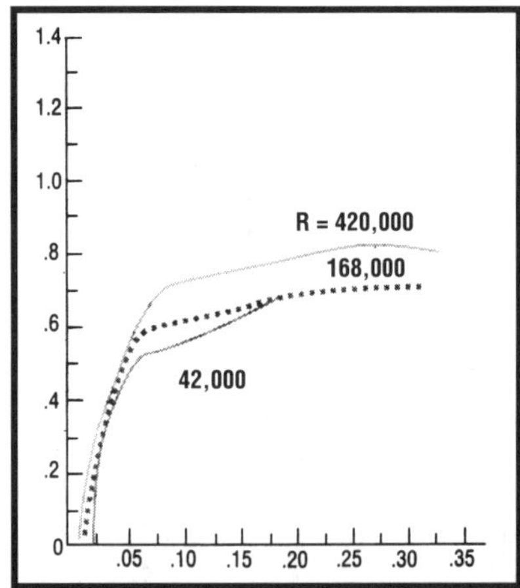

Figure 1.
Polar curves for a flat-plate airfoil at low Reynolds numbers.

to high—or vice versa—the horizontal tail's lift must vary accordingly. On model airplanes, this is accomplished by changing the angle of the elevators. This angle is controlled by the elevator trim lever on the transmitter—literally at one's fingertips (a little up-elevator at low speed and some down for high speed).

The angle of incidence of the fixed portion of the horizontal tail, i.e., the stabilizer, is important but not too critical. For semisymmetrical or flat-bottomed wing airfoils, an angle of incidence of minus 1 degree (as measured against the datum line) is appropriate. For symmetrical wing airfoils, an angle of incidence of zero degrees is suggested. There are some exceptions to these rules, as you will see.

VERTICAL LOCATION OF THE HORIZONTAL TAIL

In addition to the downward deflection of the air by the wing, resulting from its production of lift, both profile and induced drags "pull" the air along with the wing, so that by the time it reaches the tail, it has lost some of its velocity. (This is easier to visualize if one considers the airplane fixed with the air passing at level flight speed, as in a wind tunnel.) This reduction adversely affects the tail's effectiveness.

The greater the vertical distance between the wing's wake and the horizontal tail, the smaller (flatter) the downwash angle is and the less the reduction in velocity of the air is. A T-tail location, atop the vertical tail surface, raises it well above the wing's wake and puts it in less disturbed air.

Other T-tail advantages are:

- The elevator may be situated above the prop slipstream.
- It is out of the fuselage's boundary layer.
- It does not blanket the rudder, for better spin recovery.

For high-wing models, a low-set horizontal tail brings it well below the wake.

In addition to its vertical location, the effectiveness of the horizontal tail surface depends on three factors:

- area and tail moment arm;
- airfoil section; and
- aspect ratio.

AREA AND TAIL-MOMENT ARM

The tail-moment arm (TMA) is the distance between the mean aerodynamic chords of the wing and tail. It is, in effect, the lever on which the tail's area works.

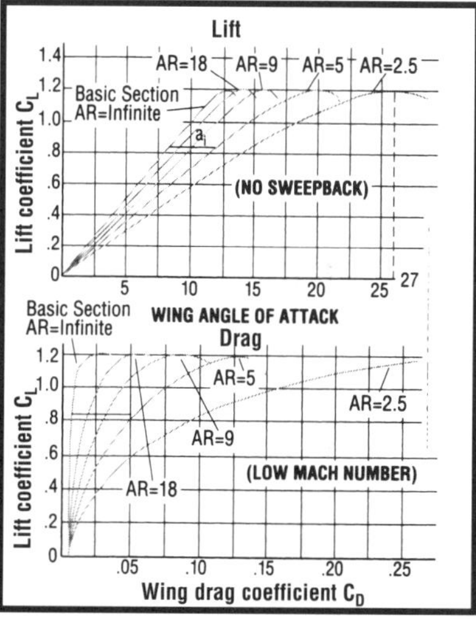

Figure 2.
Effect of aspect ratio on wing characteristics.

Based on experience, this author uses a simple method for establishing the horizontal-tail area (HTA). If you have a wing AR of 6 and a tail-moment arm that is 2.5 times the wing's MAC, then a tail area of 20 percent of the wing area is adequate.

Here is the formula:

$$HTA = \frac{2.5 \times MAC \times 20\% \times WA}{TMA}$$

where HTA = horizontal-tail area in square inches;
TMA = tail-moment arm in inches;
WA = wing area in square inches;
MAC = wing's mean aerodynamic chord in inches.

For short TMAs, this formula will increase the tail area; for long TMAs, area is reduced, but what aerodynamicists call "tail volume," i.e., area times TMA, will remain constant.

TAIL AIRFOIL SECTIONS

Since the horizontal tail surface has to provide lift—both up and down—symmetrical airfoils such as Eppler E168 are recommended. Many models incorporate flat balsa sheet or flat built-up tail surfaces. These are less effective, aerodynamically, than symmetrical airfoils.

Figure 1 shows polar curves (C_L versus C_D) for a flat plate airfoil at low Rns. Lift is greater, and drag is less for E168.

As explained in Chapter 13, "Stressed Skin Design," symmetrical tail surfaces may be made lighter and stronger than sheet balsa and much stronger than built-up surfaces (and only slightly heavier).

TAIL ASPECT RATIOS

The upper portion of Figure 2 illustrates the effect of AR on lift and AoA. For AR 5, the stall occurs at a 20-degree AoA, and at AR 2.5, the stall is at 27 degrees—both at a lift coefficient of 1.2. Thus, at AR 5, the tail surface responds more quickly to changes in AoA than at AR 2.5 since the lift per degree of AoA is greater.

For smaller models, however, the tail's chord should not be less than 5 inches to avoid unfavorable low Rn effects. An AR of 4 to 5 with constant chord is recommended.

SLOTTED FLAP EFFECT

When slotted flaps are fully extended, several things occur:

- Both lift and drag increase substantially, and the model's speed decreases.
- The wing's nose-down pitching moment increases sharply.
- The downwash angle also increases in proportion to the lift increase from the lowered flaps. This increases the horizontal tail download.

Experience with the Seagull III, the Seahawk and the Swift indicates that the flap chord (in percent of the wing's chord) influences the model's flaps-down behavior.

Flaps with wider chords—up to 30 percent of the wing's chord—generate very little pitch change when extended. The increase in tail down-

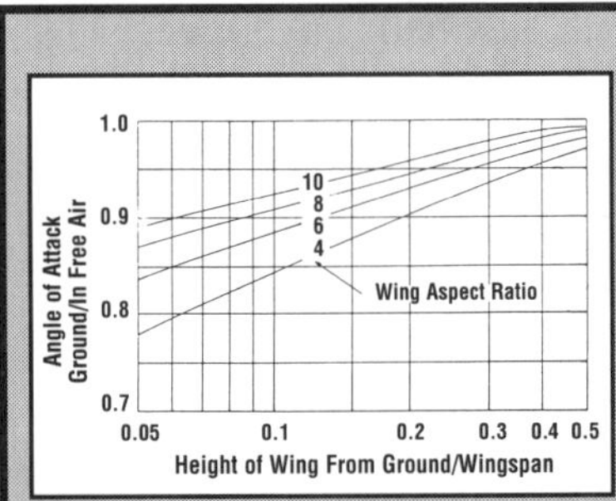

Figure 3.
Impact of ground effect on angle of attack.

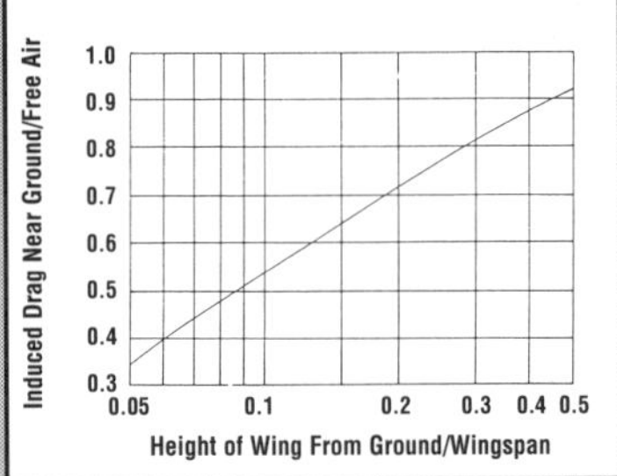

Figure 4.
Impact of ground effect on induced drag of a wing.

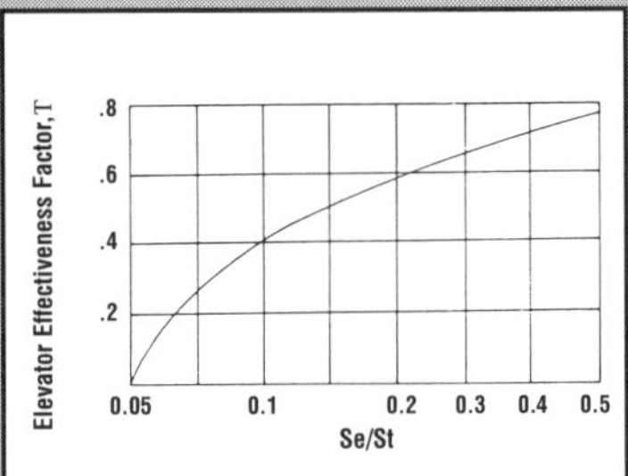

Figure 5.
The elevator effectiveness factor and how it varies with the elevator's percentage of the horizontal tailplane area.

load that tends to cause a nose-up reaction is equalized by the wing's higher nose-down pitching moment. It is very satisfying to lower full flap, after throttling back and have the model continue on its merry way, without nosing up or down, but flying noticeably slower.

For narrower chord (25 percent) flaps, the flap-induced tail download is greater than the nose-down wing pitching moment. When the flaps are extended, this causes the model to nose up sharply and rather alarmingly.

GROUND EFFECT

When an airplane is on final approach and descends to half its wingspan above ground (or water) level, "ground effect" occurs. When a plane is in ground effect:

- The wing behaves as though it had a higher AR; lift increases and the stall AoA decreases (see Figures 2 and 3).

- The induced drag of the wing decreases (see Figure 4).

- The most important change is a severe reduction in the downwash angle to about half its value at higher altitude.

Lowering flaps causes an increase in the downwash angle and in the nose-down pitch; but the severe downwash angle reduction, due to ground effect, reduces the tail's download, causing the model to nose-down in a shallow dive. This is particularly noticeable for models with wide-chord (up to 30 percent of the wing's chord) slotted flaps.

This behavior requires considerable up-elevator force to stop the dive and to raise the aircraft's nose to the near-stall touchdown posture.

ELEVATOR EFFECTIVENESS

The larger the elevator area, in proportion to the horizontal tail's total area, the more effective the elevator, as shown in Figure 5.

For slotted flapped models, an elevator area of 40 percent of the horizontal tail's area is suggested. This proportion provides adequate elevator authority to achieve near-full-stall landings, with flaps extended and in ground effect.

Without flaps, a proportion of 30 to 35 percent is adequate.

Full elevator deflection of 25 degrees, both up and down, is appropriate. This may, at first, prove sensitive but, with practice, has proven to be no problem. At high speeds, elevator low dual rate is suggested.

CG LOCATIONS

The optimum CG is vertically in line with the wing's aerodynamic center at 25 percent of its MAC.

There are, however, advantages and disadvantages inherent in positioning the CG ahead of or behind the wing's aerodynamic center.

FORWARD CG

See Figure 6. A CG ahead of the wing's aerodynamic center has only one advantage: it improves longitudinal stability, since it increases the "stability margin." (See Chapter 6, "CG Location.") A forward CG has these consequences:

- The model's maneuverability is reduced, particularly when centrifugal force comes into play. (More on this subject further on.)

- The tail download to balance the forward CG adds to the load the wing must support, in addition to the model's weight. Profile and induced drags (called "trim drag") of both wing and tail increase.

- In ground effect, and particularly for a flapped model, more powerful tail downlift is needed to raise the model's nose for a flaps-down landing. This is more pronounced for wings using cambered, i.e., semisymmetrical or flat-bottomed, airfoils owing to the wing's nose-down pitching moment. For symmetrical-wing airfoils, the tail download need only balance the nose-down moment of the forward CG and the nose-down pitch from the extended flaps.

- The forward CG should be no farther forward than a point 16 percent of the MAC, i.e., measured aft of the leading edge.

- With respect to any maneuver involving centrifugal force (and there are few that don't), that force acts at the CG and also substantially increases the load the wing must support. (See Chapter 4, "Wing Loading Design.").

In a tight turn at high speed, centrifugal force increases the wing lift and the weight at the CG ahead of the wing's aerodynamic center. A force couple results that resists the turn. This imposes a heavy additional load on the horizontal tail that, even with full up-elevator, it may be unable to support—and it stalls—limiting the model's maneuverability.

For a CG vertically in line with the wing's center of lift, these

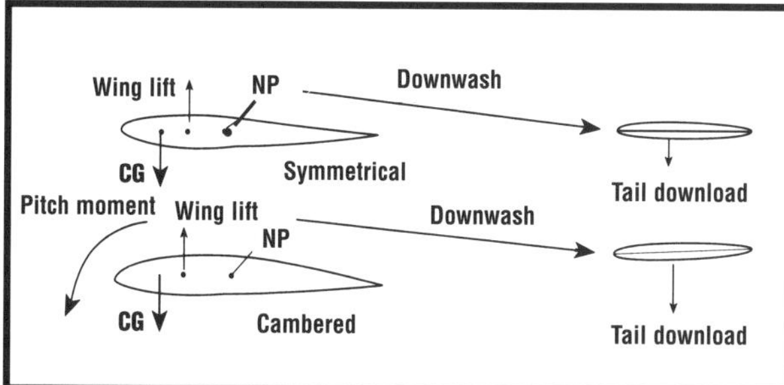

Figure 6.
Forward CG force diagrams.

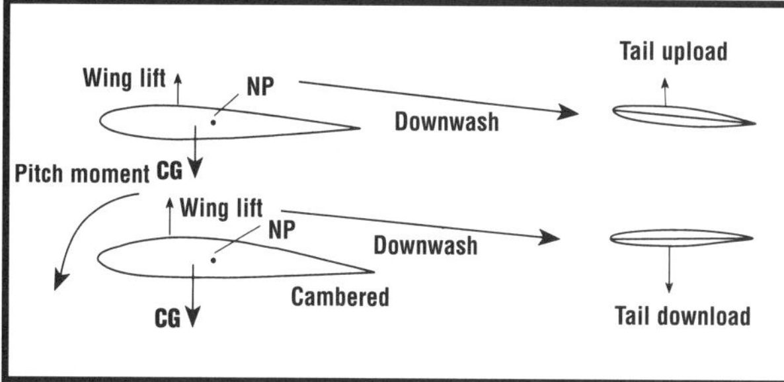

Figure 7.
Aft CG force diagrams.

forces are directly opposed and do not add to the tail's load.

AFT CG

See Figure 7. A CG behind the wing's aerodynamic center offers advantages, but has serious potential disadvantages:

■ Maneuverability is increased—centrifugal force acting on the aft CG actually reduces the tail loads needed for these maneuvers.

■ Owing to the nose-down pitching moment of a cambered airfoil, the horizontal tail normally has a download requirement. The aft CG's moment about the wing's aerodynamic center reduces this tail download.

For symmetrical airfoils, the horizontal tail's airfoil is set at a positive AoA, *relative to the downwash*, to produce an upload to offset the aft-CG's nose-up moment. The wing's total load and trim drag are both reduced.

The disadvantages of an aft CG are:

■ The stability margin is reduced, which could have serious implications for stability and flight control.

■ Attempting to reduce trim drag by moving the CG too far aft can cause problems. This requires an increase in the tail's positive AoA for equilibrium. In a shallow dive, the wing's AoA and C_L both decrease. Since the downward angle of the downwash is proportional to the wing's C_L, the dive reduces the downwash angle, which becomes more nearly parallel with the fuselage centerline. The tail's AoA and lift increase, resulting in a sometimes violent "tuck under." Soaring gliders with CGs so located have lost wings in the resulting steep dive. Moving the CG forward and reducing the tail's AoA is the remedy.

■ This author is nervous about the use of an aft CG coupled with slotted or Fowler flaps. The large increase in downwash angle created by the extended flaps could change the tail's AoA substantially, converting a positive upload (or mild negative download) to a heavy download. The combination of an aft CG and a heavy tail download might well result in a disastrous stall.

NEUTRAL-POINT MANIPULATION

There are ways to have both a modestly aft CG and a healthy stability margin between the CG and the NP. The major factors influencing the neutral point's location are:

■ The relative size of the areas of the horizontal tail and wing. Enlarging the tail will move the NP rearward for a larger static margin.

■ Similarly, a longer tail moment arm will move the NP aft.

■ The relative vertical positioning of the wing and horizontal tail has a significant bearing on the tail's effectiveness, or efficiency. A tail located close to the wing's wake, in heavy downwash, loses effectiveness. At this location, the tail is in reduced dynamic air pressure caused by the drag of both wing and fuselage. This reduces that tail's effectiveness to under 50 percent. In contrast, a T-tail is 90 percent effective.

This reduced efficiency affects the NP location. It acts like a reduction in tail area; it moves the NP forward and reduces the static margin. The larger the vertical separation between wing and tail, the better. For models whose wing is on or in the middle of the fuselage, a T-tail is best. For high wings above the fuselage, a low tail is indicated.

There is another aspect to all this. For the same NP, a high, more efficient tail may be reduced in area, yet would have the same effectiveness as the lower, larger tail. If made larger in area, the more efficient higher tail will move the NP aft, thereby enlarging

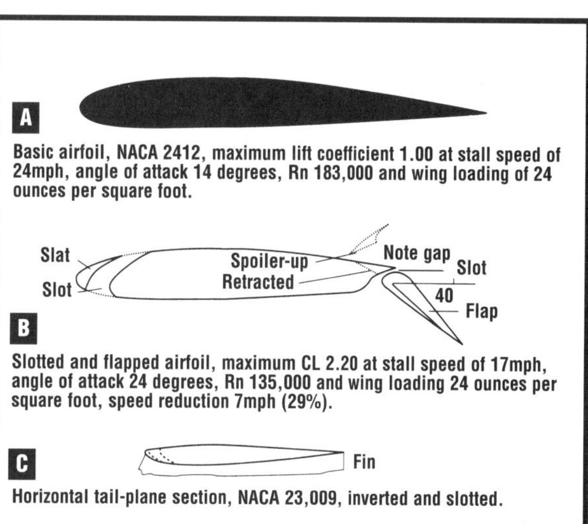

Figure 8.
Crane wing and tail sections.

the static margin.

Structurally, a tail in the fuselage presents few problems. A T-tail does impose heavy loads on the vertical fin. If thicker symmetrical airfoils, such as the Eppler 168 or NACA 0012, are employed for the vertical tail along with stressed-skin construction (see Chapter 13), the fin will have adequate strength.

A simple formula for estimating the most aft CG location, but still leaving an adequate static margin for safe, controllable flight is:

$$.17 + \left(.30 \times \frac{TMA}{MAC} \times \frac{SH}{SW} \times HTE\right) \times 100 =$$

CG location, in percent of the MAC, measured from the MAC's leading edge, where:

TMA = *tail-moment arm in inches*
MAC = *mean aerodynamic chord in inches*
SH = *horizontal tail area in square inches*
SW = *wing area in square inches*
HTE = *horizontal tail efficiency, estimated at between 40 and 90 percent and based on the tail's vertical location relative to the wing's wake*

This formula reflects the fuselage's contribution to the NP location. Depending on its size and shape, the neutral point can advance up to 15 percent of the wing's MAC under the fuselage's influence. Calculation of the fuselage's contribution is complex and beyond the scope of this article.

Using the Swift's actual and imaginary modified values will illustrate all this.

Actual

TMA—25.5 in.; MAC—9.75 in.; SH—120 sq. in.; SW—600 sq. in.; HTE—90 percent.

Modified

TMA—29.25 in.; MAC—9.75 in.; SH—150 sq. in.; SW—600 sq. in.; HTE—90 percent.

The actual most rearward CG is at 31 percent of the MAC. Since the design CG is at 25 percent MAC, there is a healthy static margin. In the modified version the most rearward CG would be at 37 percent of the MAC.

Thus, the modified version would also have a healthy stability margin with a CG at 31 percent of the model's MAC, well behind the wing's aerodynamic center of lift at 25 percent MAC.

CAMBERED AIRFOIL SECTIONS

Semisymmetrical or flat-bottomed airfoil sections may be used in the horizontal tail. They have a wider range of AoAs before the stall and a higher C_L at the stall than symmetrical airfoils. Where a powerful up or download is required, such sections are useful. For uplift, the tail airfoil is right side up; for downlift, the airfoil is inverted. It should be noted that a cambered airfoil starts to lift at a negative AoA, not zero degrees as for symmetrical sections. The Eppler 205 section and the Eppler 222 section are suggested as tail airfoils (see Appendix). Note the shift to lower negative angles of zero lift at low Rns.

An example of the need for a powerful download, in ground effect, is the "Crane," a short takeoff and landing (STOL) model. This model had full-span, fixed, leading-edge slots and, flaps down, it stalled at 20 degrees AoA. After some trials, this model was able to achieve full-stall landings. An all-moving tail with an inverted, cambered and leading-edge-slotted airfoil, called a "stabilator," as in Figure 8, was required ▲

REFERENCES

Report 648*: Design charts for predicting downwash angles and wake characteristics behind plain and flapped airfoils, by Silverstein and Katzoff, 1939.

Report 651*: Downwash and Wake Behind Plain and Flapped Airfoils, by Silverstein, Katzoff and Bullivant, 1939.

*Both reports are available from the National Technical Information Service, 5285 Port Royal Rd., Springfield, VA 22161.

Chapter 8

Horizontal Tail Incidence and Downwash Estimating

An airplane in level flight at its selected cruising speed is a classic balancing act. To achieve this balance, both nose-down and nose-up moments must be evaluated. The horizontal tail must balance the net result of these moments. (A moment is simply a weight or force multiplied by a distance—also called "arm".) The horizontal tail's AoA, relative to the wing's downwash, should be sufficient to provide the upward, or most often, the downward lift required to provide this equilibrium.

The penalty for having an incorrect tail incidence is heavy elevator deflection at cruise speed. This adds drag and could result in a lack of adequate elevator authority to bring the airplane to a near-stall landing posture while in ground effect, with full flap deflection and with a CG located ahead of the wing's aerodynamic lift center.

Establishing the appropriate tail incidence calls for:

■ An evaluation of the moments, in inch-ounces, both nose-up and nose-down to obtain the net result. Nose-up moments are offset by nose-down moments;

■ A determination of which type of tail lift—upward or downward—in ounces is required to provide the balancing moment at the model's selected cruising speed.

■ A calculation of the tail angle of attack required to provide this tail lift.

■ An estimate of the downwash angle at the horizontal tail's location.

■ Setting the tail's inciden(relative to the downwash at the c culated AoA to provide the balar ing moment.

MOMENT EVALUATION

The following details the fo major moment sources. There are others, which are beyond the scope of this article, but small elevator trim adjustments would compensate for their minor values.

■ **CG location.** A CG that's ahead of the wing's ¼ MAC causes a nose-down, or negative, moment. Its value is the horizontal distance between the CG and ¼ MAC, in inches, multiplied by the model's gross weight in ounces. Having the CG behind the wing's ¼ MAC causes a positive or nose-up moment. Its value is calculated in the same way as for a forward CG, but it has positive value. In level flight, a CG that's vertically in line with the wing's lift (at ¼ MAC) contributes neither up moment nor down moment.

■ **Airfoil pitching moment.** Symmetrical sections have no pitching moment; semisymmetrical and flat-bottom airfoils have such moments, which are always negative, or nose-down. Their value is calculated using Formula 10 (pitching moment) in Chapter 1, "Airfoil Selection."

■ **The wing's drag moment.** The wing's total of both profile and induced drags, in ounces, at the wing's AoA for the design cruising speed, is calculated using Formulas 5 ("Total of profile [section] and induced drag coefficients") and 9 ("Total profile and induced wing drag"), of Chapter 1.

The drag moment is the drag in ounces multiplied by the vertical

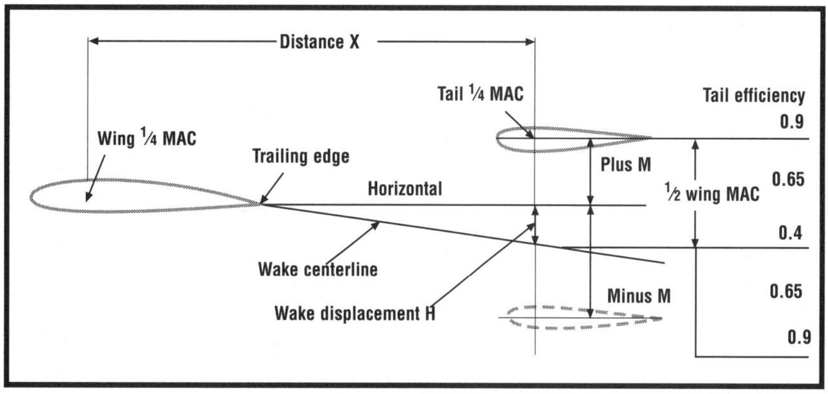

Figure 1.
Wake and downwash determination.

Vertical Location of the Horizontal Tail

In addition to the downward deflection of the air by the wing that results from its production of lift, both profile and induced drags "pull" the air along with the wing, so that by the time it reaches the tail, it has lost some of its velocity. (This is easier to visualize if one considers the airplane fixed with the air passing at level flight speed, as in a wind tunnel.) This reduction adversely affects the tail's effectiveness.

The greater the vertical distance between the wing's wake and the horizontal tail, the smaller (flatter) the downwash angle is and the less the reduction in air velocity is. A T-tail location, atop the vertical tail surface, raises it well above the wing's wake and puts it in less disturbed air.

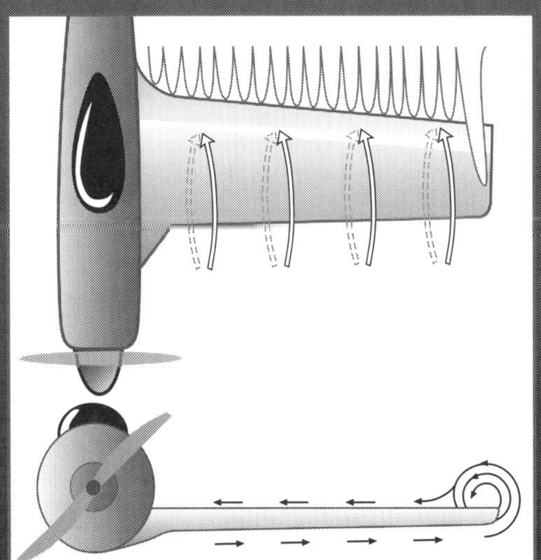

As air flows past a wing from leading edge to trailing edge, positive pressure is created below the wing, while negative pressure exists above. At the wingtip, the positive-pressure bottom-wing air flows around the tip and is drawn into the negative-pressure region above the wing. This action gives rise to the wingtip vortex, as well as to lesser vortices along the trailing edge.

distance, in inches, between the CG and the wing's ¼ MAC on the airfoil's chord line. If the wing is below the CG, the moment is nose-down, or negative. If it's above the CG, the moment is nose-up, or positive. If the wing is on the CG, it contributes *no* drag pitching moment.

■ **Thrust moment.** A thrust line above the CG promotes a nose-down (negative) moment. Below the CG, the moment is nose-up (positive). The thrust, in ounces, is difficult to pin down without a wind-tunnel test. An educated guess is a thrust of 40 percent of the model's weight for level flight at the design cruise speed. The moment, in inch-ounces, is the estimated thrust multiplied by the vertical distance in inches from thrust line to CG. If the thrust line passes through the CG, there is no thrust pitching moment.

■ **Net result.** The net sum of these four moment sources will provide the balancing moment that the horizontal tail plane must provide. Usually, the net result is a nose-down, or negative figure.

TAIL LIFT NEEDED

Dividing the net moment figure given in the previous section by the tail's lever (or tail moment arm—the distance from CG to the tail's ¼ MAC in inches) will tell how much lift, in ounces, the tail must develop to provide the balance moment. If the net moment is negative, or nose-down, the tail must lift downward. If positive, the tail lift must be upward.

TAIL ANGLE OF INCIDENCE

The tail lift required, in ounces, should be adjusted to compensate for the tail's efficiency (or lack thereof). See Figure 1. That adjustment would be: lift required divided by tail efficiency. For a T-tail where the lift required is 100 ounces, this would increase to 100 divided by 0.9, or 111 ounces.

To calculate the tail AoA needed to provide that lift, use Formula 7 ("Lift coefficient required"; special procedure A: "Lift coefficient per degree angle of attack adjusted for aspect ratio and planform" and special procedure B: "Angle of attack (or incidence) for level flight" in Chapter 1. Identify whether the angle is positive (upward lift) or negative (downward lift).

DOWNWASH ANGLE ESTIMATING

The first step is to determine the location of the wake centerline at the tail (Figure 1) so as to obtain the wake displacement H. With H and two other dimensions from your drawings, plus (or minus) M and distance "X," you can easily locate the wake centerline relative to the tail.

■ **Wake centerline.** Factors controlling the wake displacement are

—wing aspect ratio;
—wing planform; and
—wing's C_L at the design cruising speed.

If a thorough design job has been done, the C_L will have been determined in calculating the wing's angle of incidence for level flight For more detail, see Chapter 18, "Propeller Selection and Speed Estimating."

Refer to Figure 2, A to F. This was extracted from NACA Report No. 648 and is not difficult to use. First, note that all the dimensions are given as a percentage of the wing's semi-span.

■ The column on the left covers the wing planforms, both straight and tapered, for aspect ratios of 6, 9 and 12. Dihedral and sweepback may be ignored. Select the planform closest to your design.

■ The center column provides the wake displacement for each of the planforms for a C_L of 1.00. Note the decrease with increasing aspect ratio. If your wingspan is 60 inches, the semi-span is 30 inches. If distance X in Figure 1 equals 24 inches, then wake displacement is 24 divided by 30, or 80 percent of the semi-span. In the center column, Figure 2A, the wake displacement at 80 percent of semi-span is 8 percent of the semi-span, for a C_L of 1.00. If your wing's C_L is, say 0.3, this displacement would be reduced to 0.3 multiplied by 8, or 2.4 percent of the semi-span (distance H in Figure 1).

Now convert distance M into a percentage of the wing's semi-span. If, for your design, M equals 4 inches, wake displacement is 4 divided by 30, or 13.3 percent of semi-span. Note that M is negative for tails below the wake centerline.

Adding distances H and M gives the vertical location of the horizontal tail relative to the wake C_L. In our example, H plus M, 2.4 percent plus 13.3 percent is a total of 15.7 percent, and distance X is 80 percent of the wing semi-span.

DOWNWASH ANGLE

Refer to the third vertical column in Figure 2A. At 80 percent "Distance behind" and 15.7 percent "Vertically above," the downwash angle, for a C_L of 1.00, is between 5.4 degrees and 4.8 degrees, or 5 degrees. For our C_L of 0.3, this would be 0.3 x 5, or 1.5, degrees and is the downwash angle at the horizontal tail's location.

In Figure 1, there is a dotted outline of a tail below the wake centerline—the tail location for many high-wing aircraft. The downwash-angle-estimating procedure applies, but the difference is that distance M would be a minus figure and H a positive figure, which would reduce the vertical displacement. Note how the downwash angles are reduced as the vertical displacement is increased.

TAIL INCIDENCE

In the example above, the downwash angle is 1.5 degrees. If the tail AoA needed for balance were minus 2 degrees, that 2 degrees would be relative to the downwash angle. Figure 3 diagrams this relationship and shows that the tail's angle of incidence (relative to the model's centerline, for this example) should be minus 0.5 degree. CAUTION: for cambered airfoils, the angle of zero lift is not the chord line as it is for symmetrical sections, but it can be several degrees negative as shown in the airfoil plots for the section concerned. This must be considered when establishing the AoA relative to the downwash. Note also that there's a major difference between angular settings for upright cambered sections and inverted cambered sections.

PATTERN-SHIP DESIGN

Pattern ships have evolved into configurations in which the four major moment sources have been reduced to a minimum:

- The CG is on or close to the wing's lift center (¼ MAC).
- The symmetrical airfoils have no pitching moment.
- With the wing on the CG, the wing's drag moment is nonexistent.
- The thrust line passes through the CG. Tail surfaces are generous in area. "More is better" is the prevailing belief. These large areas move the NP aft, improving the static margin and permitting the CG to be behind the wing's ¼ MAC. In maneuvers, centrifugal force, acting at the aft CG assists; the model is more agile.

The wing and tail airfoils are both set at zero incidence—a "no-lift"

Wake and Downwash

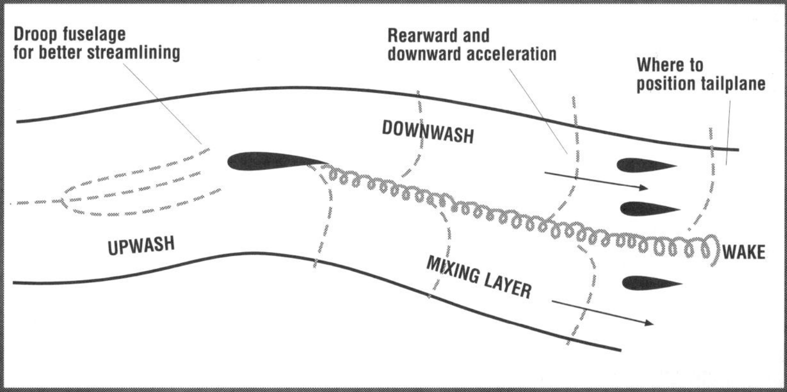

The downwash and wake of a conventional, rear-tailed aircraft.

The tail surfaces of a conventional, rear-tailed airplane operate in a very disturbed atmosphere. As the figure illustrates, the air sweeps downward off the wing's trailing edge as the result of the lift generated. This airstream is called the "wake." This wake is turbulent, and it influences the air—both above and below itself—in a downward direction called "downwash."

Obviously, no self-respecting horizontal tail should find itself in this very disturbed wake.

The downwash angle depends on the lift coefficient at which the wing is flying. An airplane has many level flight speeds, from just above the stall at low engine rpm to its maximum speed at full throttle. At low speeds, the wing's angle of attack increases, as does its lift coefficient, and the downwash angle is high. At top speed, the reverse is true, and the downwash angle is low.

At low speeds, the horizontal tail's downward lift must be increased to force the wing's airfoil to a higher angle of attack. Part of this download is supplied by the increase in the downwash angle. At high speeds, the tail's download must be reduced to lower the wing's angle of attack; but again, because the downwash angle is reduced, the tail download is reduced.

The point of all this is that as the model's level flight speed varies with the throttle setting from low to high—or vice versa—the horizontal tail's lift must vary accordingly. On model airplanes, this is accomplished by changing the angle of the elevators. This angle is controlled by the elevator trim lever on the transmitter—literally at one's fingertips (a little up-elevator at low speeds and some down for high speeds).

The angle of incidence of the fixed part of the horizontal tail, i.e., the stabilizer, is important, but not too critical. For semisymmetrical or flat-bottom-wing airfoils, an angle of incidence of minus 1 degree (as measured against the datum line) is appropriate. For symmetrical-wing airfoils, an angle of incidence of 0 degrees is suggested. (There are some exceptions to these rules.)

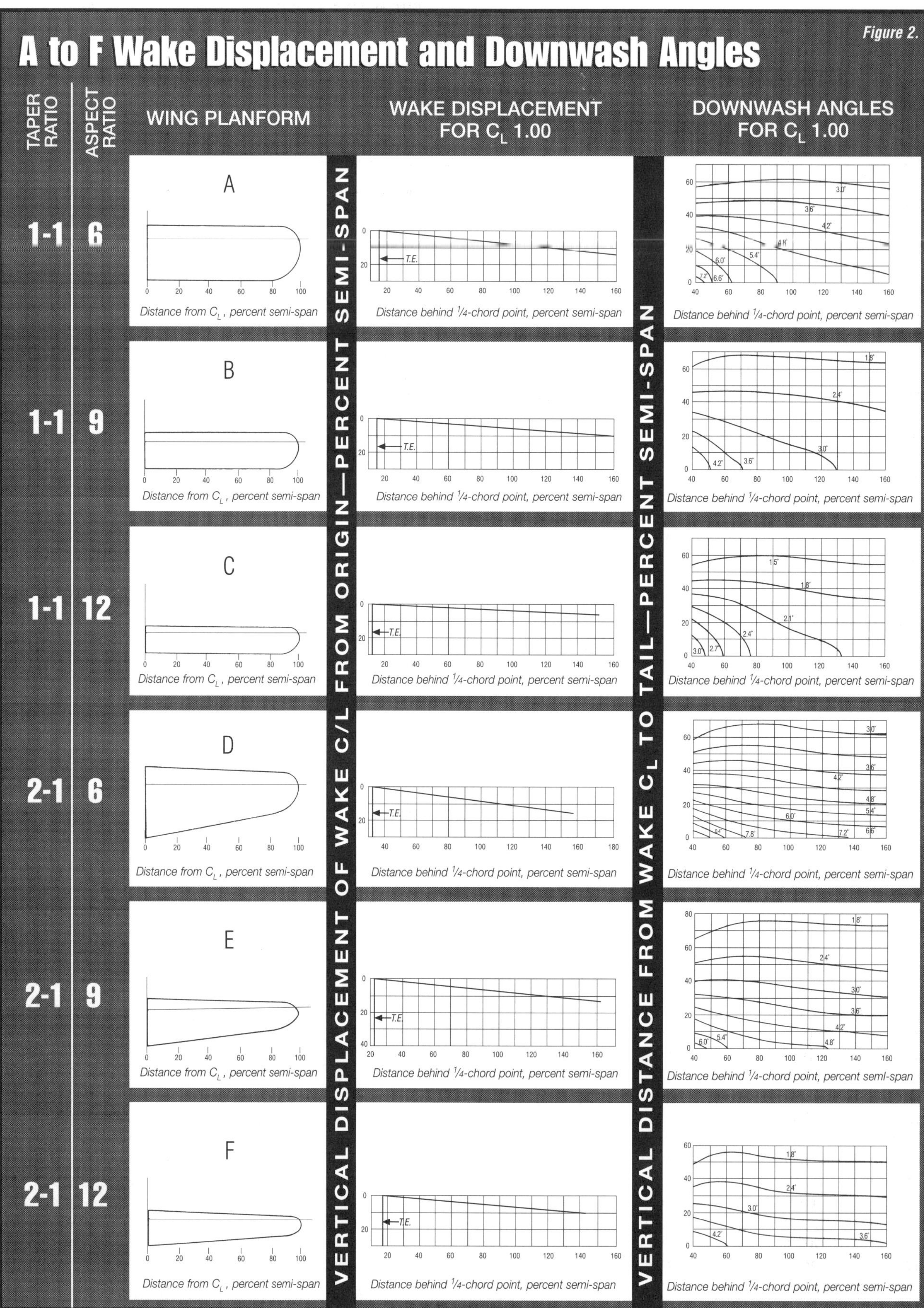
Figure 2.
A to F Wake Displacement and Downwash Angles
TAPER RATIO
ASPECT RATIO
WING PLANFORM
WAKE DISPLACEMENT FOR C_L 1.00
DOWNWASH ANGLES FOR C_L 1.00
VERTICAL DISPLACEMENT OF WAKE C/L FROM ORIGIN—PERCENT SEMI-SPAN
VERTICAL DISTANCE FROM WAKE C_L TO TAIL—PERCENT SEMI-SPAN
1-1 6 A
1-1 9 B
1-1 12 C
2-1 6 D
2-1 9 E
2-1 12 F
T.E.
Distance from C_L, percent semi-span
Distance behind 1/4-chord point, percent semi-span

condition. However, as soon as up-elevator is applied, the wing's AoA becomes positive; both lift and downwash are produced. That downwash strikes the horizontal tail at a negative angle, producing tail downlift that maintains the wing at a positive lifting angle. Inverted, the same conditions apply. In both positions, the fuselage is inclined at a slight nose-up angle to provide the wing's lift.

TAIL DEEP STALL

Some authorities state that, at high angles of attack, the wake from the wing may blanket the horizontal T-tail, and the airplane will have difficulty recovering from a stall. This condition is called "deep stall."

Cases of full-scale deep stall have resulted in fatal crashes. All have involved test-flights of twin or tri-jet aircraft with aft, fuselage-mounted engines and rearward CGs for the tests. In a stalled condition, the wing and engine-pod wakes may blanket the horizontal tail.

There are many prop- and jet-driven aircraft with T-tails that have no deep-stall problems.

RECENT DESIGN ANALYSIS

The following models are further discussed in Chapter 26, "Construction Designs."

■ **The Swift.** The Swift's thrust line, wing drag and CG are in line, and the CG is vertically in line with the ¼ MAC of the wing. The only significant moment is the result of the wing's airfoil pitching moment. At 60mph cruise speed, a tail setting of minus 1 degree proved to be correct.

■ **Seagull III flying boat.** This model had two major nose-down moments: the high thrust line and the wing's airfoil pitching moment. Centers of lift and drag coincided with the CG. The pusher engine arrangement was chosen so that the horizontal tail would be partly submerged in the powerful prop slipstream in the hope that pitch changes caused by power (rpm) variations would be minimized. Luckily, this was successful; the model exhibits no change in pitch as rpm are varied.

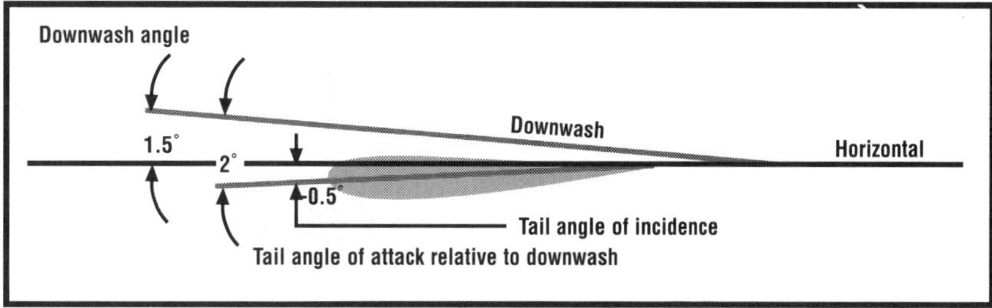

Figure 3.
Tailplane angle of incidence.

■ **Swan canard.** The nose-down pitch of the high thrust line is offset by the aft wing's drag moment. Pitching moments of both fore and aft wings add to the foreplane's load. The foreplane downwash reduces the wing's AoA and lift in the area shadowed by the foreplane. The wing's AoA in this area was increased to compensate.

■ **Seahawk float and tricycle gear.** Here, the major nose-down moments are caused by the wing's drag, below the CG, and the wing's airfoil pitching moment. A thrust line above the CG adds to the nose-down moment. The ¼ MAC is vertically in line with the CG and produces no moments in level flight.

■ **Osprey tail-dragger and twin float plane.** The major moments caused by wing drag and the wing's airfoil pitching moment oppose each other. Thrust line and CG coincide, and the latter is vertically in line with the ¼ MAC in level flight. ▲

Chapter 9

Vertical Tail Design and Spiral Stability

Vertical tail design is more complex than one might imagine. It involves consideration of wing dihedral, fuselage and landing-gear side areas, CG location and the important vertical tail area.

A brief summary of model airplane history is timely. In the 1930s, models were light, tissue-covered and rubber-band powered. To fly properly, they depended solely on their inherent stability.

The small, single-cylinder gasoline engine, such as the Brown Jr., with its fuel tank, ignition coil, condenser and battery, revolutionized model aviation. Gas models were bigger, heavier and flew faster and longer. They still depended on inherent stability to avoid damaging crashes. Radio control was still ahead.

Early R/C "rudder-only" models still relied on the model's inherent stability. Rudder control really only "steered" the model. It became apparent that there was a serious spiral instability problem. Models were spiral-diving into the ground.

CENTER OF LATERAL AREA CONCEPT

In 1941, Charles Hampton Grant, then editor of *Model Airplane News*, published his center of lateral area (CLA) theories, in his book "Model Airplane Design." "Lateral area" refers to aircraft surface areas that face sideways. This theory, in a nutshell, states that if:

- the model's CLA was at about 25 percent of the tail moment arm aft of the CG;
- a line through CLA and CG was horizontal; and
- the wing joining the front CLA and the rear CLA sloped upward to the front,

then the model would be spirally stable. Figure 1 illustrates the layout required by this theory.

Put into practice by many modelers, this theory was proven time and time again and was applied in the early days of rudder-only R/C by such well-known and respected modelers as Hal deBolt and Bill Winter. The latter's beautiful "Cloud-Niner" (outlined in Figure 1) still reflects Charlie Grant's ideas.

Today, with the very precise, powerful and reliable control provided by modern R/C equipment, which permits unlimited aerobatics, this theory is less important, but nonetheless valid.

INERTIAL ROLL COUPLING

This author surmises that inertial coupling in rolling plays as big a part as side areas in understanding Grant's CLA ideas.

The mass of a model airplane is concentrated in two elements, one representing the mass ahead of the CG and the other, the mass behind the CG. There are thus two principal axis systems to consider:

- the aerodynamic, or wind, axis, through the CG, in the relative wind direction; and
- the inertia axis through the CG, joining the two element masses (see Figure 2).

If, in level flight, the aerodynamic and inertial axes are aligned, no inertial coupling will result from rolling motion.

If, however, the inertial axis is inclined to the aerodynamic axis, as in Grant's theory, rotation about the aerodynamic axis will create centrifugal forces that, through the

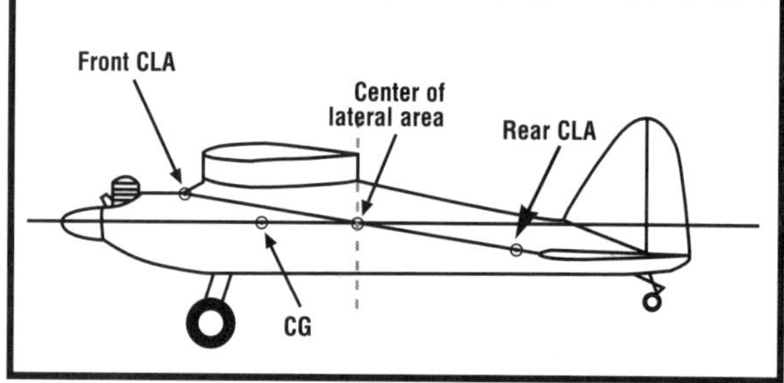

Figure 1.
Side view of "Cloud-Niner" with estimated CG and CLA locations.

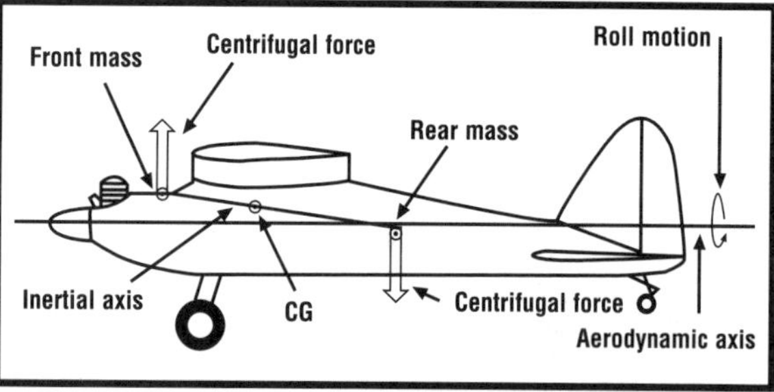

Figure 2.
Side view of "Cloud-Niner" showing estimated aerodynamic and inertial axis.

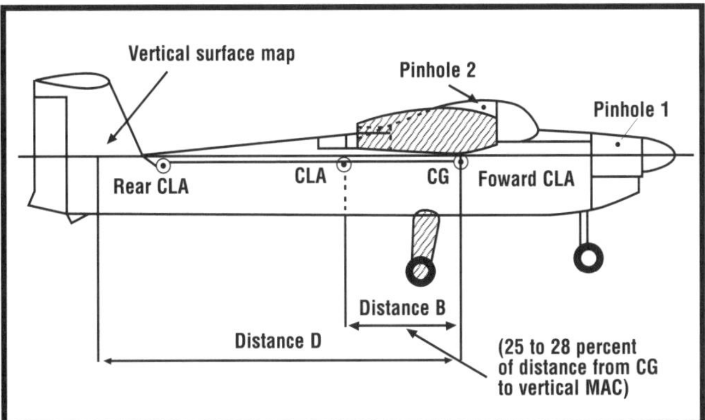

Figure 3.
The center of lateral area (CLA) relative to the CG.

action of inertial forces, cause a pitching moment. This is "inertial roll coupling" (see Figure 2).

Since the inertial axis slopes upward to the front, a nose-up pitch will occur when the model rolls. This prevents the fatal spiral dive. This type of spiral stability is great for sport models, but the inertial coupling must inhibit any maneuver where rolling is involved.

Look at the side view of the author's Swift (see Chapter 26, "Construction Designs"). The CLA is at 25 percent of the tail-moment arm, as per Grant, but the positions of the two element masses make the aerodynamic and inertial axes almost coincide. In rolling, noinertia coupling (that could interfere with aerobatics) will occur. Pattern models have similar configurations.

The Wasp was another .15-powered model—a tandem-wing biplane with 4 degrees of dihedral on each wing. The CLA was originally at 25 percent of the VTMA, but owing to doubts about the forward fuselage's impact on directional stability, the vertical tail area was increased to bring the CLA to 30 percent. The Wasp was spirally unstable and unpleasant to fly. Cutting off the fin tops to the rudder top levels (finotomy!) and adding small streamlined caps improved the spiral stability and the model's behavior. The CLA was then back to 25 percent of VTMA as originally planned.

DIHEDRAL

With today's modern radio control and ailerons, the high dihedral angles that were built into free-flight and rudder-only models are no longer needed. For powered R/C models with ailerons, the following dihedral angles are suggested:

- high wing—2 degrees
- mid wing—3 degrees
- low wing—4 degrees

Sweepback also has a dihedral effect. Two to 3 degrees of sweepback is equivalent to 1 degree of dihedral.

LOCATING THE CLA

The following procedure has been used by this author for many years and on many models—all successful fliers—to determine vertical tail area. It is applicable to all configurations, flying boats, canards, floatplanes, etc.

In his "full-scale" book, "The Design of the Aeroplane," British aerodynamicist and author Darrol Stinton recommends a very similar procedure.

Cut out a cardboard profile of your design, full size, that represents the lateral surfaces of the aircraft. For two lateral surfaces, e.g., for the right and left sides of the fuselage, a single cardboard profile cutout will suffice. If there are more than two stacked lateral surfaces (viewing the plane from the side), e.g., the wing's dihedral, landing-gear or vertical-tail surfaces, an additional piece of cardboard will have to be layered on the profile to reflect the additional pair of surfaces. Add the necessary layers of cardboard as shown crosshatched in Figure 3. Note that for this configuration, at the wing, three layers would be needed, two for the wings' side areas (because of dihedral, each wing has a left and right "lateral surface" comprised of the vertical rise in the wing, as seen from the side) and one for the canopy outline.

Size your vertical tail surface to an area that looks right. You'll soon find out how accurate your estimate was.

To locate the CLA of this profile, simply establish its CG. It is easily done by inserting a pin through the profile at pinhole no. 1, in Figure 3; push the pin into some vertical surface, door jamb, or edge, and allow the profile to hang free under gravity. Make a loop at one end of a 3-foot length of string, and slip it over the pinhead; to the other end of the string, tie a small weight, e.g., a nut, key, or paperclip. Allow it, too, to hang free under gravity.

The profile's CG will be somewhere along the thread line; mark this line on the profile. Repeat this procedure from another point, somewhat distant from pinhole 1. In Figure 3, this is shown as pinhole 2.

Where the two thread lines intersect is the cardboard profile's CG and your model's first CLA. The CG (and CLA) will not, in all probability, be at 25 percent of TMA; reduce or add to your vertical surface area until it does. You may have to repeat this process several times to get the right tail area/CLA relationship—unless you are smarter than this author (which could well be!).

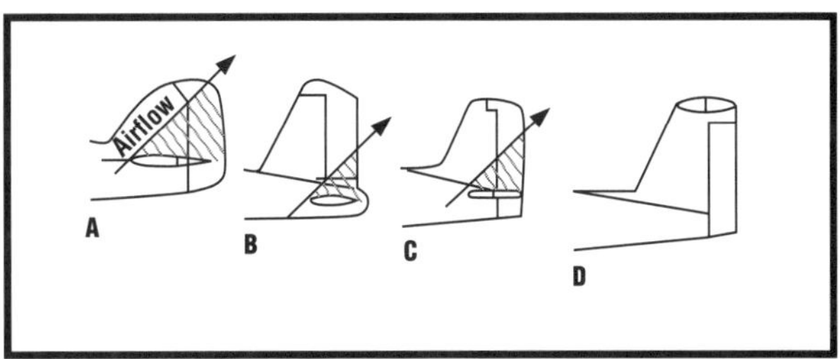

Figure 4.
Blanketing of the vertical tail in a spin, as affected by the position of the horizontal tail. Notice the absence of blanketing in a T-tail configuration (D).

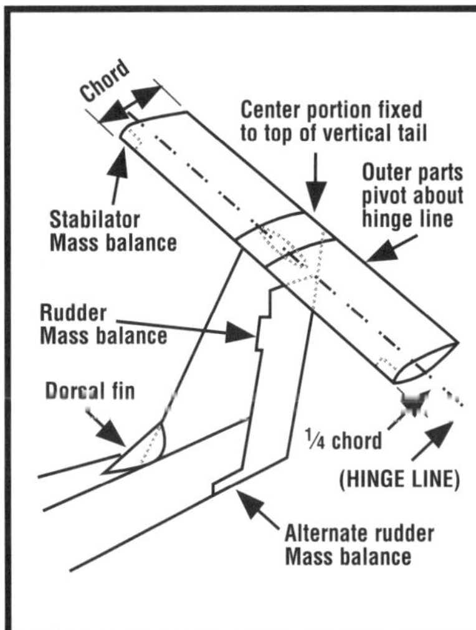

Figure 5.
Perspective drawing of an all-moving horizontal T-tail or stabilator.

VERTICAL-TAIL ASPECT RATIO

The AR of horizontal and vertical tails (and wings) bears on their effectiveness. Vertical-tail ARs of 2.5 to 3 are suggested. To determine your vertical tail's AR, use this formula:

$$ARv = \frac{1.55 \times Bv^2}{Sv}$$

where ARv = vertical tail aspect ratio;

Bv^2 = height of vertical tail from fuselage bottom, in inches, "squared"; and

Sv = vertical tail area in square inches, including fuselage below the fin.

A T-tail capping the vertical tail surface, as in the "Swift," effectively increases the vertical tail's AR effect.

Figure 4 shows how the horizontal tail could dangerously blanket the vertical surface in a spin. The T-tail in Figure 4D is not blanketed in this way.

DORSAL FINS

The Swift has a small dorsal fin. It has three useful functions:

- increases fuselage stability at high side slip angles;
- reduces vertical tail stalling; and
- just plain looks good!; it gives the impression that its designer knows what it is all about!

A dorsal fin area of 10 percent of vertical tail area is suggested.

ALL-MOVING HORIZONTAL T-TAILS

Figure 5 sketches an all-moving T-tail or "stabilator" that's suitable both for powered models and for sailplanes; for the latter, mass balancing may not be required if the glider is intended to fly at a relatively low speed. A "T" stabilator's area may be reduced 10 percent from that of a conventional stab-elevator horizontal tailplane.

RUDDER POWER

For powered sport models, a rudder area of 30 percent of the vertical tail area, with angular travel of 30 degrees either side of neutral, is suggested. For sailplanes with high-AR wings and for pattern ships, a rudder area up to 50 percent of the vertical tail area is recommended.

RUDDER AILERON EFFECT

A rudder that has its "area-center" above a horizontal tail line through the CG will act like an aileron when used. It induces a roll that is opposed to the rudder-forced yaw.

To avoid this, the rudder's area center should come close to or fall on the horizontal line through the CG. The portion below the CG opposes and neutralizes the rolling action of the portion above the CG (Figure 1), and the rudder action causes yaw only.

Upwardly dihedral V-tails have pronounced anti-yaw roll action when the ruddervators act as rudders. Downwardly dihedralled (anhedralled) V-tails have rolling action in the same direction as the yaw.

SPIRAL STABILITY

To assess an existing model airplane's spiral stability—or lack of it—is easy. In level flight, at the model's normal cruising speed and at a reasonable altitude, put it in a 15- to 20-degree bank, then neutralize the controls and watch its behavior closely.

- **Spirally stable.** If it returns to normal level flight, upright, in turning up to 270 degrees of its circular path, it is spirally stable. The rapidity with which it rights itself is a measure of its degree of spiral stability.

- **Neutrally spirally stable.** If it continues to turn without the angle of bank increasing, it is neutrally spirally stable.

- **Spirally unstable.** If the angle of its bank slowly increases as it turns and its speed gradually increases in a descending spiral, it is spirally unstable. The rapidity with which it increases its bank angle is an index of its degree of instability.

LEVELS OF SPIRAL STABILITY

High spiral stability is needed for free-flight models (for obvious reasons) and for trainers. When a novice pilot gets into trouble, if his model has good spiral stability, he need only neutralize his controls and the model will, on its own, recover, provided it has enough altitude.

For sport models, a moderate degree of spiral stability is desirable. This applies also to flying boats, floatplanes, canards and particularly to rudder- and elevator-only models, both powered and gliders.

For pattern and aerobatic models, neutral stability or mild spiral instability is needed for good maneuverability. The spiral dive is slow to develop, so the expert pilot has no problem controlling the model.

A high degree of spiral instability

Snowy Owl was a .40-powered model with 5 degrees of dihedral, slotted flaps, a T-tail and a CLA at 25 percent of its VTMA. It flew well, but in slow, nose-high, flaps-down, level flight at low rpm, it developed a mild Dutch roll. Theorizing that turbulence, from both the nose-up posture and the lowered flaps, was blanketing the vertical tail, I doubled the dorsal-fin area; this corrected the problem. The 5-degree dihedral was found to be too high for good inverted flight.

is not desirable, nor is too much spiral stability, which inhibits maneuverability.

Testing the spiral stability of an existing model as noted above is hindsight. The old saw that, "Foresight, as good as hindsight, is a damn sight better" applies. We need a way to incorporate the desired degree of spiral stability in a design while it is still on the drawing board.

LATERAL AND DIRECTIONAL COUPLING

Spiral stability requires a balance between lateral (roll axis) and directional (yaw axis) forces. The extremes are:

■ Large dihedral angles on the wing along with a small vertical tail area leads to "Dutch roll" (characterized by tail wagging coupled with a slight side-to-side roll) or even a stall-spin crash. The lateral forces are too high.

■ A large vertical tail area along with little or no dihedral leads to sideslip; the large tail resists the slip, and a killer spiral ensues. The directional forces are too great.

Somewhere between these extremes lies the correct balance of lateral and directional forces that will produce the degree of spiral stability that suits the designer's performance objectives.

BALANCE OF FORCES

Since spiral stability requires a balance between lateral and directional forces, i.e., a balance between the effects of dihedral angle and vertical tail surface area, the design procedure is to establish the lateral parameters (dihedral) first, and then to balance the directional parameters (vertical tail area) to match, at the chosen CLA position.

■ Lateral stability

—*Dihedral.* The wing's dihedral angle is a major contributor to lateral stability. See the chart "Suggested Dihedral Angles."

The relative positions of wing aerodynamic center (AC)—25 percent of the MAC—and CG bear on the dihedral angle. A high wing enjoys some pendulum stability that's absent from mid- and shoulder-wing positions. With CG above the wing AC (as in a low-wing setting) there is pendulum instability, hence, the different dihedral degree figures.

Suggested dihedral angles (degrees)

	With ailerons	Without ailerons or with forward sweep
High wing	2	5
Mid- or shoulder-wing	3	6
Low wing	4	7

—*Sweepback* acts like dihedral. In level flight, 2 to 3 degrees of sweepback are equivalent to 1 degree of dihedral. The dihedral effect increases both with angle of sweepback and C_L and so, unlike normal dihedral, it increases with higher AoAs.

Many pattern ships use tapered wings with straight-across trailing edges and sweptback leading edges. The angle of sweepback on the quarter-chord line is about 7 degrees on a wing of AR 6 and taper ratio (root to tip) of 1:0.6 and needs no dihedral. Without dihedral, there are no side areas projected by the wing ahead of the CLA, and that reduces the vertical tail area needed.

High sweepback angles on full-scale aircraft increase lateral stability to such an extent that negative dihedral (anhedral) is introduced to reduce lateral stability for better lateral control. The Lockheed Galaxy is an example.

—*Forward sweep.* Heavy forward sweep (20 degrees or more) is very destabilizing both laterally (in the roll axis) and directionally (in the yaw axis). When yawed, one wing advances and the other retreats; the centers of lift and drag of the advancing wing panel have reduced moment arms to the CG. The moment arms on the retreating panel are increased. The differential in drag moments increases the yaw; but the lift-moment differential causes a roll in a direction that's opposed by the yaw. The model will "corkscrew" and probably crash unless there is sufficient vertical tail area and/or vertical-tail moment arm to prevent the yaw.

This requires: 1) an area that's sufficient to bring the CLA to the 30 to 35 percent of vertical-tail moment arm (VTMA) position; 2) higher dihedral (as discussed above); and 3) a limit in the forward sweep to not more than 30 degrees measured on the quarter-chord line.

In addition, the model will be spirally unstable. The major advantage of forward sweep is that the wing stalls at the root first. Roll damping and effective aileron control continue to high AoAs before the wingtips stall. This permits slow, high-AoA flight.

■ Directional stability. The major factors are the amount of vertical tail area and its moment arm to the CG (i.e., vertical tail volume). The vertical-tail AR, like that of a wing, is a contributing factor. Higher-AR vertical tails have steeper lift-curve slopes; they are therefore more sensitive, but stall at lower AoAs. At high side-slip angles, a high-AR vertical tail can stall, resulting in reduced control. A dorsal fin is recommended to overcome a lack of vertical-tail effectiveness at high AoAs, such as when flaps are extended and at high sideslip angles.

Sweepback aids directional stability. When yawed, the advancing wing's centers of lift and drag have greater moment arms than those of the retreating wing. The drag-moment differential reduces the yaw, and the lift differential promotes a roll in the direction of the yaw.

—*Ailerons.* Good aileron design, with differential, reduces or eliminates aileron-induced adverse yaw. (See Chapter 10, "Roll Control Design.")

—*CG location.* If the CG location of

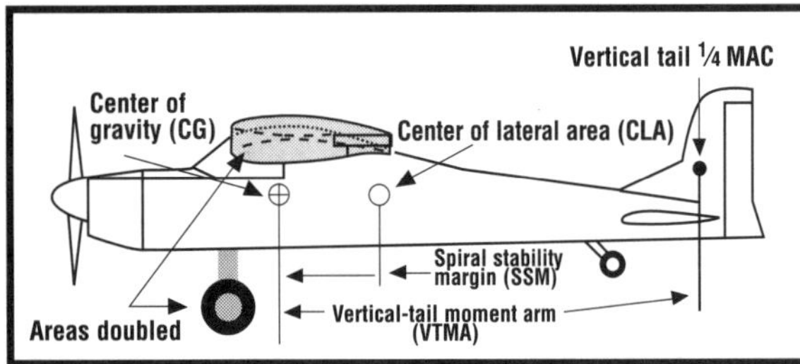

Figure 6.
Conventional profile model.

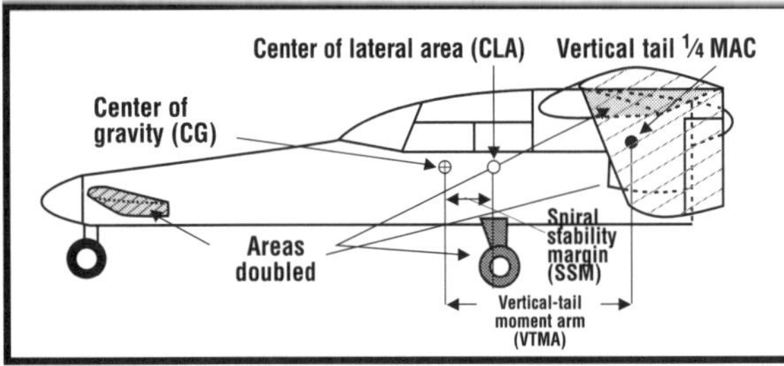

Figure 7.
Canard profile model.

an existing model is moved forward from a position that's vertically in line with the wing's AC, it lengthens both the VTMA and the distance from CG to CLA (spiral stability margin or SSM). For example, the Swift has a VTMA of 24 inches, and with the CG under the wing's AC, the SSM is 25 percent of the VTMA, or 6 inches. Moving the CG forward 1 inch increases the VTMA to 25 inches, and the SSM becomes 7 inches, or 28 percent of the VTMA. This is enough to change the spiral stability from mildly positive to neutral.

If the CG is moved aft of the wing AC by 1 inch, both VTMA and SSM are reduced. For the Swift, the VTMA would be 23 inches and the SSM 5 inches, or a CLA location 21.7 percent aft of the CG. This is a very spirally stable location.

SPIRAL STABILITY MARGIN

Refer to Figures 6 and 7. These static stability margins are suggested:

SSM as % of VTMA	
Super spiral stability	22
Good spiral stability	25
Neutral spiral stability	28
Mild spiral instability	30
Very spirally unstable	33 and up

The increase in vertical tail area required to move the CLA aft is surprisingly large. For one model, the Skylark, an increase in vertical tail area of 60 percent would have been needed to move the CLA aft from 22 percent to 30 percent of its vertical-tail moment arm—a distance of 1.65 inches.

CONCLUSION

The profile method for balancing lateral and directional factors, at the selected center of lateral area, is certainly not high-tech, but it's simple, effective and applicable to the great majority of conventional planform configurations.

The CG/CLA relationship and the SSM bear a remarkable resemblance to the CG-neutral point and static-margin concept in the longitudinal stability considerations outlined in Chapter 6, "CG location" and the material discussed here will well reward the model airplane designer. These techniques have worked well on a variety of designs built and flown by the author, and they're a good stepping-off point for further exploration of stability considerations in model design.

POSTSCRIPT

While reading an old (1947) NACA Report No. 868—"Summary of Lateral Control Research"—I found some very significant data (the data in NACA reports are timeless). Though expressed in general terms, without specifics, they reinforce the ideas expressed in this article and Grant's CLA theories.

■ **Lateral stability.** High, positive, effective dihedral combined with weak directional stability, i.e., small vertical tail area, results in a large opposing action to any rolling motion (experienced with the Skylark) and can lead to a predominance of lateral oscillation, i.e., Dutch roll. Since the banking motion is opposed by the effect of the dihedral, that dihedral should be no larger than is necessary to meet other criteria.

■ **Directional (weathercock) stability.** Modifications that increase directional stability, such as an increase in vertical tail area, permit greater roll rates to be obtained and make the performance of a given banking maneuver possible with decreased aileron deflection.

The effect on lateral maneuverability of changing the tail length while maintaining the same directional stability, i.e., the same tail volume, and thereby increasing the damping in yaw, is negligible.

■ **Adverse yaw.** The effects of adverse yawing moments on rolling velocity may be decreased by increasing directional stability, or by decreasing dihedral.

In Frank Zaic's 1935/36 yearbook, under the heading, "Determination of Rudder Area," a similar profile method is described. In it, the CLA is called the "directional center." It was intended for use on rubber-powered, free-flight models. Grant's procedure was a refinement of this early method. Thanks to Martin Simons for bringing this to my attention.

Those who are interested should read NACA Technical Note No. 1094 of 1946: "Experimental Determination of the Effects of Dihedral, Vertical Tail Area and Lift Coefficient on Lateral Stability and Control Characteristics." ▲

Powered by a .45 converted to diesel operation, Osprey was designed as a trainer with 3 degrees of dihedral, slotted flaps and a generous dorsal fin. CLA was at 25 percent of the VTMA, and tail-dragger landing gear was used. It was a stable, yet maneuverable model to fly. Banked 15 to 20 degrees and controls neutralized, it would return to upright level flight in about 90 degrees of a circle. Flaps down, it was stable, and on floats, it was pure fun.

Chapter 10

Roll Control Design

Desirable roll or lateral control characteristics are important for good and easy maneuverability.

There are several types of roll control in use on today's model aircraft:

- none or minimal (via roll coupling)—on rudder and elevator-only models;
- conventional ailerons;
- external airfoil ailerons;
- flaperons;
- spoilers and slot lip ailerons;
- all-moving wings (pitcherons); and
- all-moving horizontal tails (stabilators).

NONE (OR MINIMAL)

This form of rudder-only lateral control is popular for sailplanes and some powered sport models. Wings for this type need additional dihedral. For powered models, this would be 5 degrees for high wings, 6 degrees for mid wings and 7 degrees for low wings.

Thermal gliders have polyhedral—typically 5 degrees from root to 3/5 of the semi-span, with an increase of 3 degrees from the polyhedral joint to the wingtip. On this type, when rudder is applied, the model yaws. Air strikes the wing at a slight diagonal. For the wing on the outside of a turn, the wind that strikes the wing at any given point on the LE exits from the TE at a point slightly closer to the fuselage. Because of the dihedral, there is an effective increase in AoA. This situation is reversed on the opposite wing. Both cause the model to roll. It is important that such models have good spiral stability.

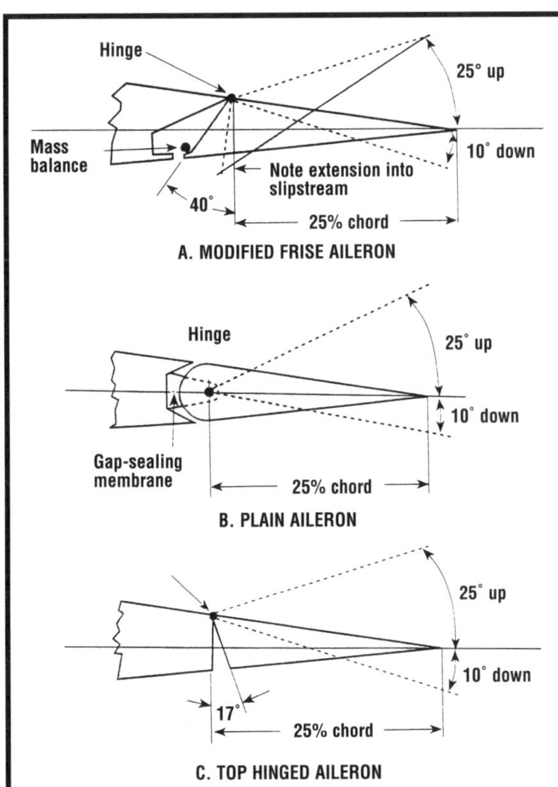

Figure 1.
Outboard ailerons.

CONVENTIONAL AILERONS

In general, this type falls into two categories: outboard, or "barn door," and strip ailerons. Outboard ailerons (see Figure 1), usually are 25 percent of the wing chord in width and 35 to 40 percent of the semi-span in length. Being farther from the model's CG, they have more leverage. One serious disadvantage is that, with equal up and down movement, they produce greater adverse yaw than do strip ailerons. The downgoing aileron has more drag than the upgoing, and this unequal drag tends to yaw the model in a direction opposite to the turn commanded.

A remedy for this condition is aileron differential, where the upgoing aileron's angular travel is two to three times that of the downgoing. This author uses a modified Frise, top-hinged aileron with a differential of 2.5:1. The extended lower, forward lip projects into the airstream below the wing when the aileron is raised, producing drag that favors the turn (see Figure 1A). Turns are made without use of rudder. Figures 1B and 1C show two other forms of barn-door ailerons.

The outboard location permits use of flaps spanning 60 to 65 percent of the wing's semi-span. This wide, short type of aileron should be mass balanced for flutter elimination.

Two other forms of ailerons developed to overcome adverse yaw are slotted and Frise ailerons. Use of differential aileron is more effective in producing desirable yaw moments than is the use of either of these two aileron types. Both slotted and Frise ailerons require

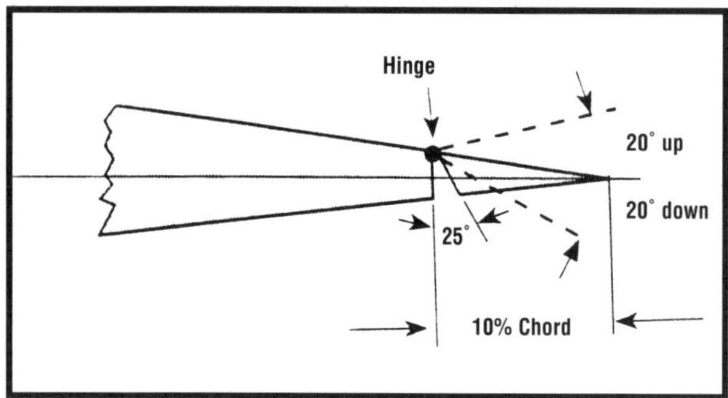

Figure 2.
Strip aileron.

more deflection than plain ailerons for the same roll rate.

Strip ailerons (see Figure 2) are long, narrow and almost full span. They simplify wing construction, and they produce less adverse yaw than outboard ailerons, since their center of area is closer to the CG.

Most are actuated by servos moving horns on their inboard ends so that differential is easily introduced. Made of solid balsa TE stock, they are prone to flutter and should be mass balanced at the outboard end to avoid this problem.

EXTERNAL AIRFOIL AILERONS

External ailerons were a Junker's development and may be seen on some full-scale ultralight aircraft flying today. As Figure 3 shows, these consist of small, separate wings that are tucked under the main wing's TE, which provides a slot effect over the small wing. These are full span; the outboard portions form ailerons, and the inboard form a type of slotted flap. Hinged externally, they should be mass balanced for flutter elimination.

FLAPERONS

Flaperons are a form of plain aileron that can be operated as ailerons and drooped simultaneously as flaps. They extend for most of the wing's semi-span, like strip ailerons. When in the fully lowered position as flaps, and then used as ailerons, there is a high degree of adverse yaw that cannot be overcome by aileron differential action. Rudder control, either manual or electronic, must be introduced to counter the adverse yaw of this type of roll control. Mass balancing is recommended.

SPOILERS AND SLOT-LIP AILERONS

Figure 4 shows a typical spoiler. Provided its leading edge is beyond 70 percent of the wing chord, there is no lag in the control's aerodynamic action. Only one spoiler operates at one time—the one on the inside of the turn. The opposite spoiler stays retracted. They provide positive into-the-turn yaw, work inverted, and require no mass balancing. A version of the spoiler, sometimes called the "slot-lip aileron" is shown in Figure 5.

This form of roll control proved very effective on both my Crane I and II. The roll rate was fast and worked inverted. With flaps lowered, roll control was very crisp at low speeds, since raising the spoiler destroyed the slot effect over the flap, reducing its additional lift. Yaw was favorable. This model's performance, at low speeds particularly, was spectacular.

PITCHERONS

These are a recent development for R/C sailplanes. Each wing panel rotates around spanwise pivots located at the wings ¼ MAC. Both are controlled by one servo, but considerable differential is needed to offset adverse yaw.

Very few degrees of rotation are needed since each wing panel

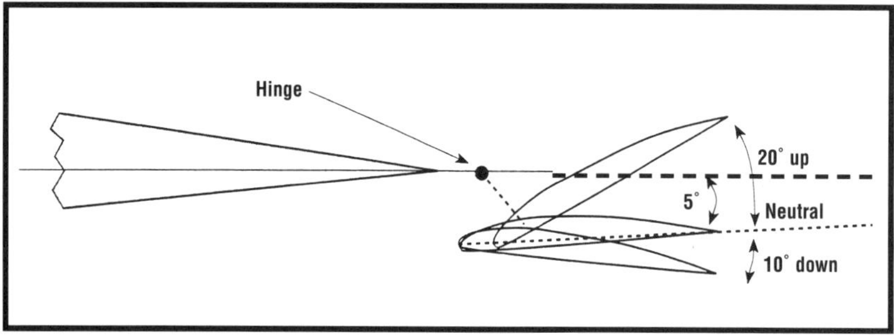

Figure 3.
External airfoil aileron.

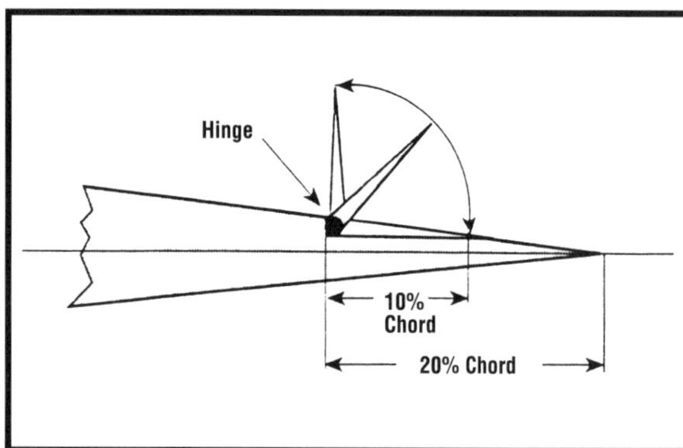

Figure 4.
Spoiler.

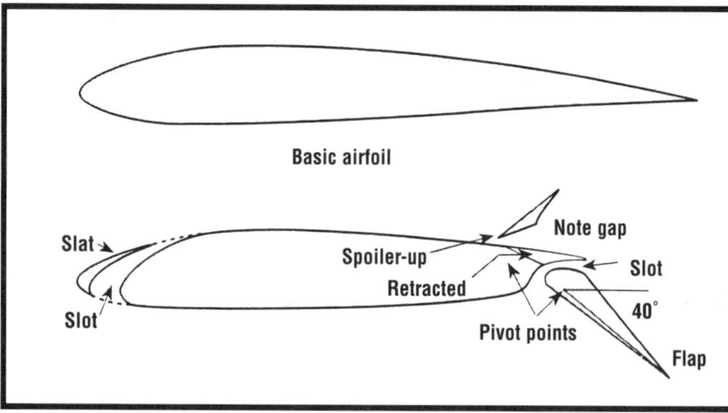

Figure 5.
Slotted and flapped airfoil.

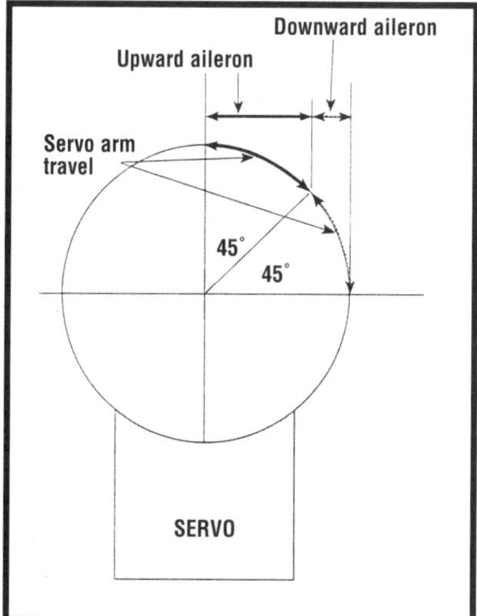

Figure 6.
Aileron differential (schematic for one aileron linkage).

rotates in its entirety. The wing-fuselage joint would need special attention to avoid local separation and increased drag.

STABILATORS

Some recent jet fighters use such tails. They move in opposite directions for roll control, and up or down for elevator action—or any combination of the two. They seem very effective and, for a model, higher ARs would provide longer moment arms. Adverse yaw would be small.

Pivoting on the spanwise pivots at ¼ MAC would result in low operating loads, as for all moving wings. This form of roll control might have application on pattern ships, leaving the wing free for full-span flaps.

AILERON DIFFERENTIAL

Figure 6 shows how to use a servo's rotation to produce aileron differential.

GAP SEALING

Wind-tunnel tests have proven that a 1⁄32-inch gap on a 10-inch-chord wing will cause a loss of rolling moment of approximately 30 percent. A gap seal for all control surfaces is suggested. The sidebar "Flap and Aileron Actuation Hinges" of Chapter 14, "Design for Flaps," provides a hinging method that has proven durable and inherently gap sealing. For other types of hinging, some form of gap seal is advised.

Figure 7 provides suggested proportions for ailerons, strip ailerons and spoilers that were developed by NACA. They are good starting points when you are creating your own designs. ▲

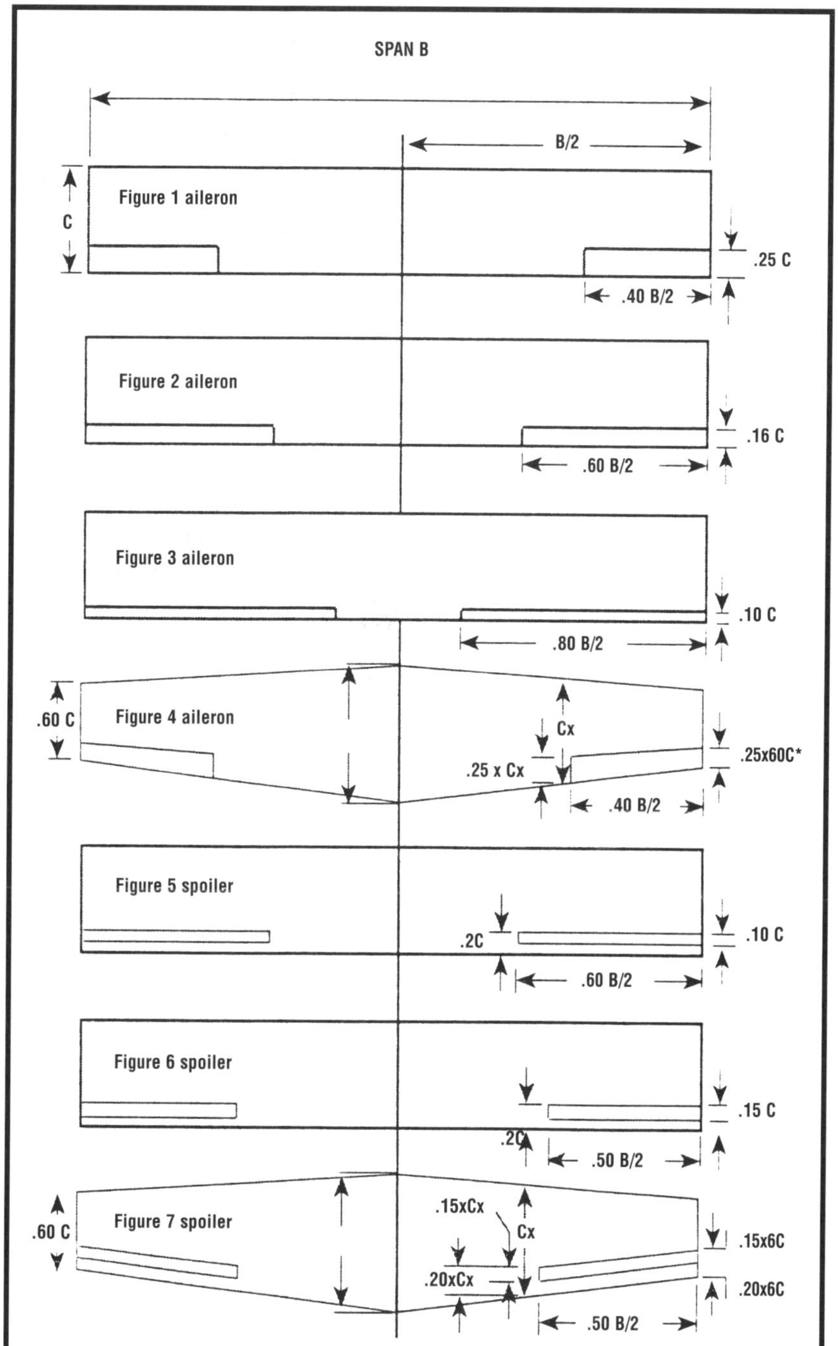

Suggested aileron and spoiler geometries for model aircraft, from NACA Report No. 605, Resume and Analysis of NACA Lateral Control research, Weick & Jones, 1937.

* 25% of 60% of the full chord.

Figure 7.
Typical control-surface geometries.

Chapter 11

Weight Distribution in Design

An analysis of the weight of the average .40 to .50 glow-powered, radio-controlled model aircraft with ailerons discloses that the power and control units, combined, weigh very close to 50 percent of the aircraft's gross weight.

The power unit (PU) is composed of spinner, prop, engine, muffler, engine mount, fuel tank, fuel, cowl, fuel tubing and nuts and bolts. The control unit (CU) is made up of receiver, battery, servos, switch, extension cables, foam protection for receiver and battery and servo screws. In the design of a model, the distributions of these heavy units along the length of the fuselage has a major effect on that model's maneuverability.

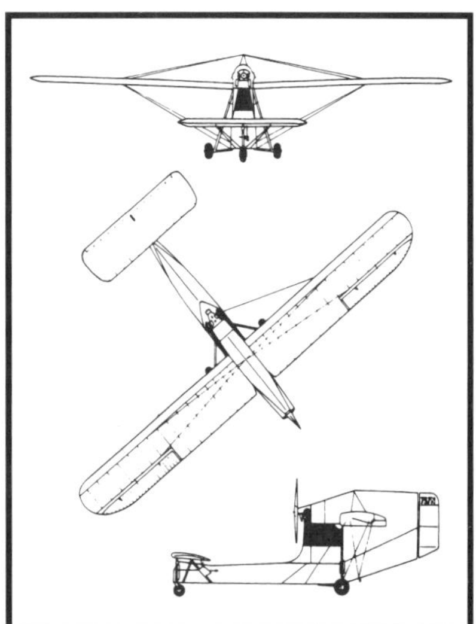

Figure 1.
Three-view drawing of Granville canard.

Massing both units as close together and as close to the CG as possible while keeping that CG in its design location will result in a highly maneuverable model.

Moving the power unit forward by elongating the fuselage ahead of the wing requires that the control unit move aft to keep the CG at its design location. Maneuverability will be reduced as a result. A few simple definitions will help in understanding this reduction:

■ **Moment.** A force times a distance.

■ **Inertia.** The resistance of an object to any change in its motion or to being moved from a state of rest.

■ **Moment of inertia.** The inertia resistance times its distance from some related point. In our case, that "related point" is the model's CG.

■ **Momentum.** An object in motion has momentum equal to its mass times its velocity. In maneuvers, both the PU and CU acquire momentum in a direction different from the original line of flight.

The PU's weight multiplied by its distance from the model's CG is its "moment of inertia." The same applies to the CU.

Obviously, the greater the distance of both the PU and CU from the model's design CG, the greater those moments of inertia will be and the greater the resistance to the maneuver.

Also, longer moment arms (in this case, distance of the PU and CU from the CG) require both PU and CU to move through greater distances, for a given angular displacement, as the aircraft maneuvers.

Longitudinally, the moment to overcome the moments of inertia of both units for maneuvers is the model's TMA multiplied by the force generated by deflecting the elevators. The model's TMA is measured from CG to ¼ MAC of the horizontal tail. For a given TMA and elevator force, the greater the moments of inertia of the PU and CU, the slower the model's reaction. Loops will have greater diameter, and the model will be less agile.

With the maneuver underway, both the PU and CU acquire momentum. To stop the maneuver, this momentum must be overcome. Larger moments of inertia produce larger momentum and slow the recovery from that maneuver.

Directionally, the same applies. The rudder will have less effect in yawing the model. Also, as explained in Chapter 9, "Vertical Tail Design and Spiral Stability," elongating the fuselage ahead of the CG increases its directionally destabilizing side area, requiring increased vertical tail area for stability and control, further aggravating the situation. Greater moments of inertia have one advantage: they offer more resistance to any disturbance. In level flight, the model will "groove."

SPINNING

In a tailspin, one wing panel is fully stalled, but the opposite panel continues to lift. The model rotates rapidly, nose-down, around a vertical axis through its CG. Up-elevator and rudder into the spin maintain the rotation.

Centrifugal force acting on the model's components comes into play. The longer moment arms of both the PU and CU result in these units rotating at higher speeds, generating greater centrifugal forces, which act horizontally, away from

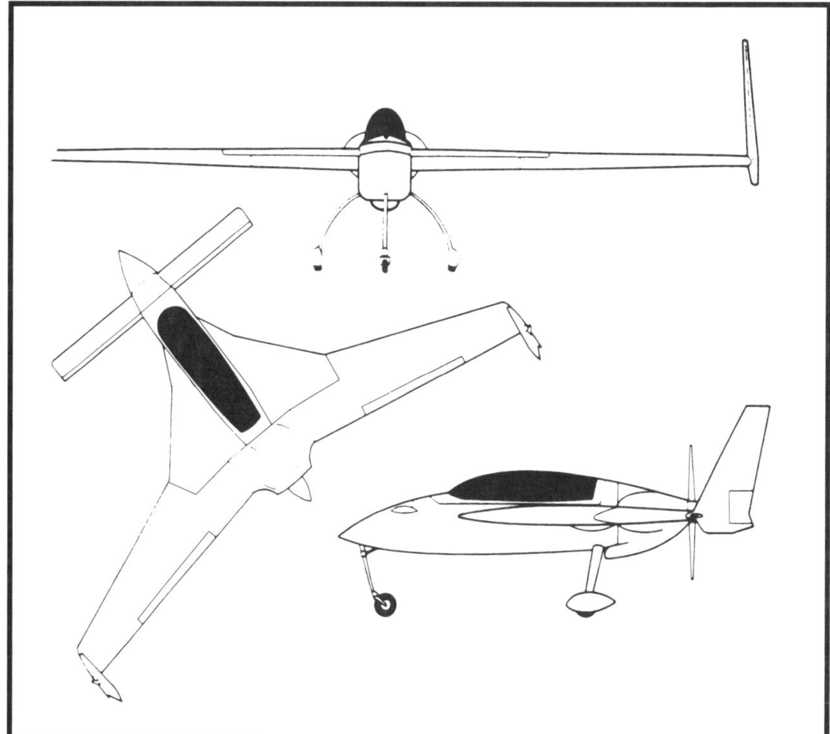

Figure 2.
Three-view drawing of Long-EZ.

the spin axis. This action flattens the spin.

The longer moment arms increase the momentum, reduce the rudders' effectiveness in stopping the spin and delay the spin recovery, which could lead to a damaging crash.

LATERAL CONTROL

Inertia roll coupling is a consideration in lateral control. For those designs in which the aerodynamic and inertia axes coincide, axial rolls are little affected by larger moments of inertia. In snap rolls and barrel rolls, centrifugal force comes into play, as it does for spins, resulting in slower initiation of and recovery from these maneuvers.

The model's wing is a factor, as it weighs close to 25 percent of the model's gross weight. For good lateral maneuverability, keeping the wing panel's CG as close to the fuselage center line helps. This results from:

- Tapered wing of moderate AR.
- Ailerons, mass balanced to avoid flutter, permit aileron and flap servos to be positioned in the wing center section.

While aileron mass-balance weights work against lateral maneuverability, keeping the ailerons light reduces the mass-balance weight correspondingly. Freedom from dangerous aileron flutter greatly outweighs the small reduction in maneuverability that's occasioned by the mass-balance weights. The same comments apply to mass balancing of elevators and rudder.

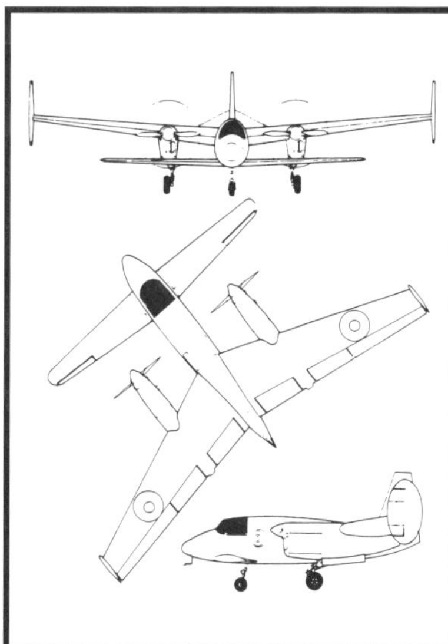

Figure 3.
Three-view drawing of the Miles M.39B Libellula.

REAR-ENGINE CANARDS

For conventional designs, it is not difficult to position both power and control units so as to minimize their moments of inertia.

Rear-engine canards, without aft wing sweep, are a different matter. Such aircraft have their CGs between fore and aft wings, closer to the latter. The PU at or behind the aft wing is balanced by locating the CU as far forward as possible. In most cases, additional ballast is required up front to locate the CG correctly. The moments of inertia of both units (and ballast) could not be greater.

My Swan canard was not intended to be aerobatic, but in level flight, it grooved beautifully. There are canard configurations that have lower moments of inertia.

- **Granville canard (Figure 1).** Both PU and CU (the pilot) are located close to the CG for good maneuverability. A modernized version of this clever design would be interesting.

- **Rutan's Long-EZ (Figure 2).** The sweptback aft wing permits the PU to move forward, shortens the fuselage and permits the CU (pilot) to move aft, close to the CG. The big wing-root strakes house the fuel on the CG. The wingtip vertical surfaces have reasonable moment arms for good directional control, but their location increases the wing's moment of inertia, reducing lateral maneuverability.

- **Miles Libellula (Figure 3).** This was a British wartime design. The twin engines ahead of the moderately swept aft wing bring the power units closer to the CG longitudinally. Both fore and aft wings have flaps. Note the high-AR foreplanes on both the Long-EZ and the Libellula. ▲

Chapter 12

Reducing Drag

It will come as a surprise to most modelers (and some model designers, too) to find how much air resistance, or drag, their miniature aircraft generate in flight. The sources of much of it are such things as exposed or partially cowled engines; wire landing-gear legs; fat tires; dowels and rubber bands that are used to hold down the wings; large, exposed control horns and linkages; and thick TEs on wings and tail surfaces.

This doesn't imply that the models don't fly well; they do! In fact, the high drag is beneficial: it causes fairly steep glides—engine throttled—that make the landings of these relatively low-wing-loading models easy to judge. Their performance suffers in all other flight aspects, however.

Many years ago, *Model Airplane News* published a very significant article by Hewitt Phillips and Bill Tyler, titled "Cutting Down the Drag." It was based on wind-tunnel tests conducted at the Massachusetts Institute of Technology Aeronautical Laboratory at model airplane speeds of from 15 to 40mph. The test models were 48 inches long and of typical model airplane construction.

Figure 1 summarizes the results, which are given in terms of their C_Ds. The actual drag in ounces of a model fuselage depends on three factors:

- airspeed;
- cross-section area; and
- shape of the fuselage.

The C_D for each reflects the drag value of that shape. When used in a formula that includes cross-section area and speed, it will accurately provide the actual drag in ounces. For our purposes, the C_D provides the relative drag value of each shape. Analysis of the C_Ds in Figure 1 will provide some surprising results.

Deducting the .198 C_D of fuselage 1 from that of fuselage 8 (.458) gives a C_D of .260 for the landing gear only—or more than the drag of fuselage 1. This gear was 1⁄8-inch-diameter music wire, and the wheels were the thin, symmetrical, cross-sectioned type that was popular at the time. Current tricycle landing gear with their large, fat tires would, conservatively, double the C_D to .520—or more than 2½ times that of fuselage 1.

Deducting the .198 C_D of fuselage 1 from that of fuselage 9 (.775) provides a C_D of .577 for the stationary propeller. From fuselage 11's C_D of 1.261, deducting the prop C_D of .577, the landing gear C_D of .260 and the .340 C_D of fuselage 2, results in the exposed engine-cylinder drag of C_D .084. A fully exposed engine, muffler and firewall would, conservatively, have a C_D four times as great: .336.

Fuselage 11, which is 48 inches long and 33 square inches in cross-section, looks representative of many of today's fuselage shapes. From its C_D of 1.261, deducting the prop C_D of .577 and adding the extra drag of .260 for tricycle gear/tires and of .336 for the fully exposed engine, results in a worst-case C_D of 1.28. At 40mph, this would generate a 19-ounce drag; at 50mph, a 30-ounce drag. Surprised? This doesn't include wing and tail-surface drag. A good drag-reducing design could lower this to a C_D of .38 (5.7 ounces) at 40mph but, again, this wouldn't include wing and tail-surface drag. Figures 3 and 4 from

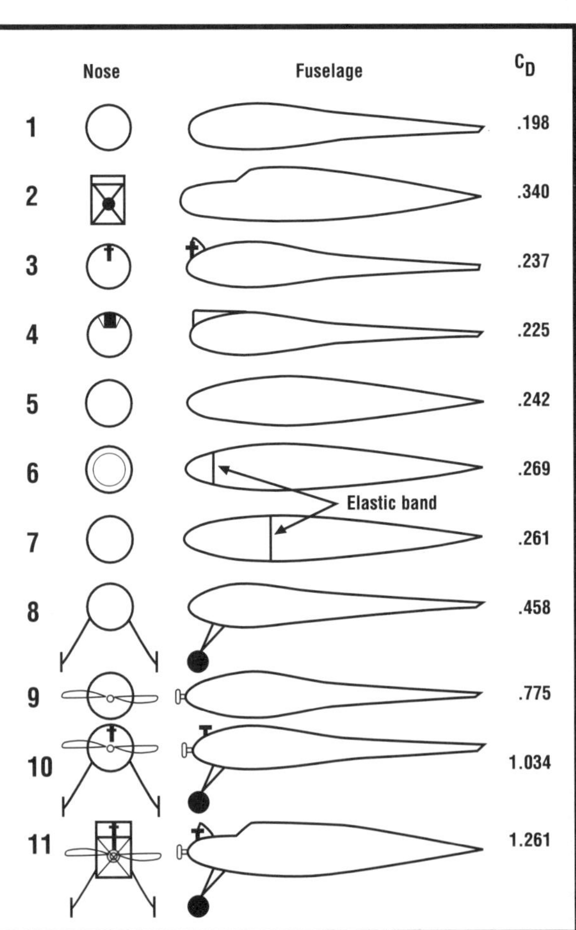

Figure 1.
Drag coefficients of various fuselages.

Figure 3.
High-drag airflow around wire landing-gear leg.

This chart permits accurate scale construction of the fuselages depicted in Figure 1.

Station	Fuselage no. 5	Fuselage no. 1
0%	0.0000%	0.0000%
5%	0.0475%	0.0750%
10%	0.0660%	0.0980%
20%	0.0920%	0.1130%
30%	0.1080%	0.1030%
40%	0.1130%	0.0750%
50%	0.1030%	0.0520%
60%	0.0900%	0.0390%
70%	0.0710%	0.0325%
80%	0.0490%	0.0250%
90%	0.0250%	0.0180%
100%	0.0000%	0.0000%

Figure 2.
Fuselage diameter as a percentage of fuselage length for least-drag circular fuselages.

Phillips and Tyler's article illustrate the high drag caused by unfaired landing-gear legs. Figure 2 provides data for reproducing fuselages 1 and 5 in Figure 1.

TYPES OF DRAG

Here's a list of the various types of drag and their causes:

■ **Skin friction** is proportional to the amount of exposed surface area and its roughness as well the Rn at which the model flies. The smooth, reflexed, pressure-recovery shape of fuselage 1 in Figure 1 has the least surface area, and this contributes to its low drag.

■ **Interference drag** is caused by the breakdown of smooth airflow owing to such things as landing-gear legs, bracing struts, dowels, open cockpits, etc., that disturb the air flow over the aircraft aft of the cause (Figure 5 gives examples).

■ **Separation drag.** An example of this is a thick, low wing on a round fuselage. The air has to expand from the high point of the wing to the TE and also fill the re-entrant corner formed at the TE and the lower fuselage. The resultant turbulent flow causes high drag and reduces tail-surface effectiveness. The cure is wing-root fairings, e.g., those on the Spitfire, but they're difficult to make.

■ **Wing and tail-surface profile drag.** These are similar to skin-friction drag and depend on the shapes of the airfoils and on the Rns at which they fly.

■ **Induced drag** results from the production of lift, and it depends on several factors: the wing area, the wing AR, the wing planform, the flight speed and the C_L at which the wing (and the tail surfaces) operate. It's normally less than the wing-profile drag.

■ **Powerplant drag.** This is caused by exposed engines, cylinder heads, mufflers and tuned pipes.

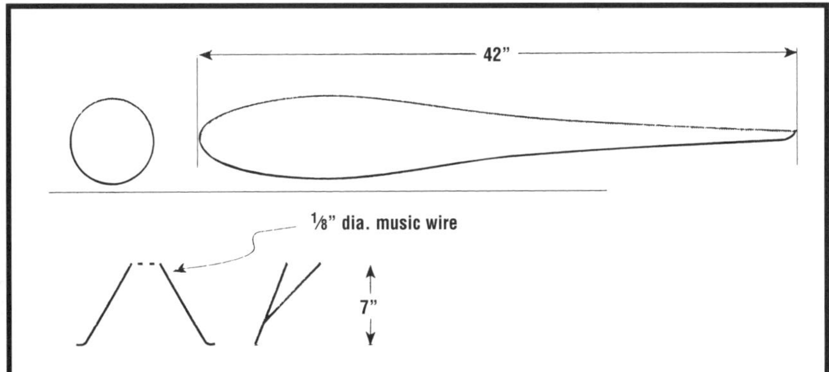

Figure 4.
These two objects give the same drag.

■ **Trim drag.** Consider a 100-ounce model, which has its CG 1 inch ahead of its wing's center of lift. A nose-down moment of 100 oz.-in. results. To maintain level flight, the horizontal tail must lift downward. Using a TMA of 25 inches, that download would be 100 ÷ 25 = 4 ounces.

To achieve this negative lift, the horizontal tail surface must be at a negative angle to the wing's downwash; this would result in increased induced drag. Since that extra 4 ounces must be supported by the wing, its induced drag also increases.

There are other forces that cause nose-up or nose-down actions and, to achieve level flight, the horizontal tail must overcome the net resultant force:

■ **Wing-pitching moment.** This is a nose-down moment, except for symmetrical or reflexed trailing-edge sections, which have little or no pitching moment.

■ **Upwash/downwash.** In level flight, air doesn't flow horizontally onto the wing's LE, or from its TE. Ahead of the wing, the air flows upward to the LE (called upwash) and downward off the TE (downwash).

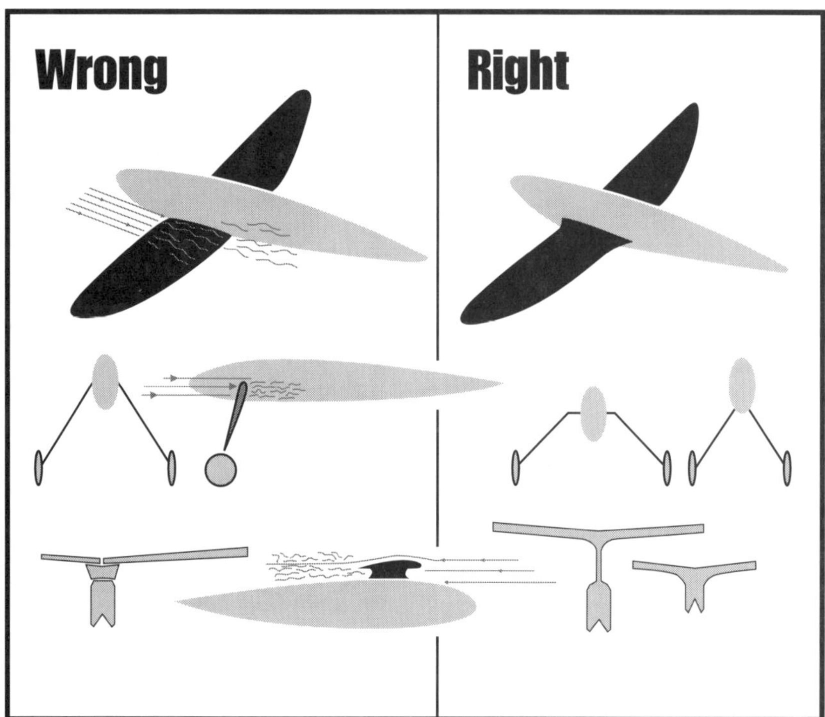

Figure 5.
Causes of interference drag.

Upwash causes a nose-up force on the fuselage ahead of the wing and on the propeller, because air flows into the propeller disk at a slight, upward angle. Downwash impacts on the aft fuselage and on the horizontal tail surface, and it causes a nose-up action.

■ **Thrust-line location.** If it's above the CG, it produces a nose-down couple; below the CG, a nose-up couple.

■ **Center-of-drag location.** If it's above the CG, it causes a nose-up force; below the CG, a nose-down force.

Some readers may question the value of the drag-reduction techniques outlined in this chapter, particularly since they involve extra time, effort and cost to achieve. Reduced drag has the following benefits:

■ Improved acceleration and, with proper propeller pitch and diameter selection, higher flight speeds and better vertical performance. A drag of 30 ounces at 50mph increases the model's weight by that amount when climbing.

■ At slower speeds and lower rpm, fuel consumption is reduced.

■ The fully balsa-cowled engine and muffler are distinctly quieter.

■ The use of slotted flaps as outlined in Chapter 14, "Design For Flaps," will provide very quick takeoffs when half extended, and slow, steep landing approaches and gentle touchdowns when fully extended. By selecting the angle at which the flaps are deployed (from 0 to 40 degrees) and adjust-ing engine rpm, it's possible to fly at any chosen speed from just above the stall at 20mph to the maximum speed; for the Swift, that's at 138mph.

■ The quickly and easily removed engine cowl and upper fuselage make servicing of the engine, fuel tank, servos, etc., very convenient.

■ The model will look sleek and fast even standing still; one can be proud of both its appearance and performance.

■ Flying a low-drag, slotted-flap-equipped model provides a new and thrilling experience.

The following deals with drag reduction for wings and tail surfaces and the engine and muffler.

WINGS AND TAIL SURFACES

There are three major considerations in wing design: wing cross-section or airfoil; aspect ratio; and planform.

■ **Airfoils.** Of the three, airfoil selection is the most critical. Select from those airfoil sections for which there are wind-tunnel test curves at model airplane Rns.

In the Eppler E197 section (see appendix), the lift curves show a maximum C_L of 1.17 with a gentle stall. The pitching moment is fairly constant for all AoAs. The polar curves show the profile C_D versus the C_L. Note that the profile C_D is low despite the increasing C_L, except at the low Rn of 100,000. A wing of 6 inches in chord flying at 20mph would be operating near Rn 100,000. Table 1 provides the data for reproducing E197 for any chord length. This airfoil is 13.42 percent of its chord in depth, permitting strong, but light, wing structures.

For tail surfaces, see the curves for the symmetrical Eppler E168 section. Note the higher profile drag at Rn 60,000. A 4-inch chord flying at 20mph would be operating at Rn 60,000. Avoid chords of less than 5 inches on tail surfaces. Table 2 provides data for duplicating this section.

■ **Aspect ratio.** This has an impact on induced drag; the higher the AR,

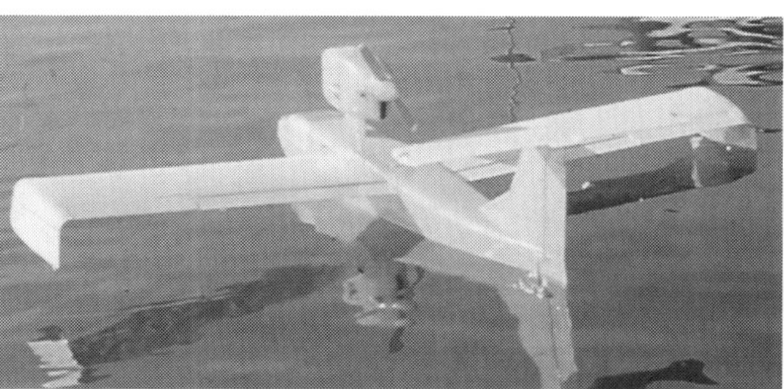

The Seagull III is an example of a low-drag airplane design.

The Canada Goose is a canard that uses the low-drag techniques described in this chapter.

the lower that drag. This is why soaring gliders have long, slender, high-AR wings. For models, high AR results in narrow chords that have higher profile drag at low Rns. This defeats the lower induced drag benefits of the high ARs.

Long, slender wings impose greater stresses at the wing roots and require stronger structures. In aerobatics, they slow any maneuvers involving rolls.

For R/C sport models, ARs of 5 to 7 are suggested—a nimble airplane results and, on smaller models, prevents narrow chords and low Rns.

■ **Planform.** This is the wing's shape as viewed from above. It may be straight, tapered, a combination of straight and tapered, or elliptical. It may also be swept back or swept forward.

The elliptical is the most efficient planform, but it's difficult to make. In addition, the tips fly at low Rn and are prone to tip-stalling.

Tapered wings with taper ratios (ratio of tip chord to root chord) of .5 to .6 are close to elliptical wings in efficiency. Each rib is different, and laying them out is time-consuming. The wing is strongest at the root, but, on small wings, the lower tip chord results in lower Rns, higher drag, and risk of tip-stalling at low speed.

This also applies to combined straight and tapered wings, in which the wing is straight for 50 to 60 percent of the semi-span and the outboard 40 to 50 percent is tapered.

A modest sweepback of 5 to 10 degrees is popular in pattern models because it improves aerobatic performance. Sweptback wings tend to tip-stall more readily. Forward sweep reduces tip-stalling, but it imposes heavy torsion loads on the wing structure.

Straight, untapered wings of AR of 6; use of the NASA "safe-wing" LE droop ahead of the ailerons (see Chapter 15) and hollowed balsa block wingtips are recommended.

Horizontal tail surfaces should have lower ARs (4 to 4.5) to keep chords above 5 inches and to avoid low Rn profile drag. Streamlined

Table 1: Eppler 197 Aerodynamic Zero -2.7 Degrees

Chord Station XU	Upper Surface YU	Chord Station XL	Lower Surface YL
.000	.000	.000	-.200
.318	.789	.279	-.640
1.104	1.683	1.164	-1.278
2.335	2.633	2.555	-1.893
3.996	3.600	4.438	-2.454
6.075	4.556	6.797	-2.945
8.551	5.478	9.610	-3.365
11.402	6.345	12.852	-3.706
14.599	7.139	16.493	3.955
18.112	7.844	20.495	-4.125
21.902	8.442	24.818	-4.195
25.933	8.918	29.414	-4.185
30.159	9.250	34.231	-4.085
34.551	9.413	39.236	-3.855
39.085	9.394	44.415	-3.535
43.735	9.191	49.723	-3.165
48.474	8.806	55.091	-2.765
53.282	8.246	60.447	-2.365
58.146	7.542	65.718	-1.965
63.028	6.752	70.834	-1.595
67.860	5.920	75.725	-1.266
72.575	5.079	80.323	-.965
77.105	4.254	84.564	-.715
81.384	3.466	88.388	-.505
85.349	2.733	91.738	-.325
88.939	2.068	94.572	-.185
92.096	1.478	96.864	-.075
94.778	.960	98.572	-.009
96.960	.530	99.637	-.005
98.604	.219	100.000	.000
99.642	.050		
100.000	.000		

Table 2: Eppler 168

NR	Chord Station X/T	Upper Surface YO/T	Lower Surface YU/T
1	1.00000	0.00000	0.00000
2	0.99893	0.00006	-0.00006
3	0.99572	0.00027	-0.00027
4	0.99039	0.00071	-0.00071
5	0.98296	0.00142	-0.00142
6	0.97347	0.00238	-0.00238
7	0.96194	0.00352	-0.00352
8	0.94844	0.00477	-0.00477
9	0.93301	0.00609	-0.00609
10	0.91573	0.00754	-0.00754
11	0.89660	0.00914	-0.00914
12	0.87592	0.01094	-0.01094
13	0.85355	0.01293	-0.01293
14	0.82767	0.01513	-0.01513
15	0.80430	0.01754	-0.01754
16	0.77779	0.02014	-0.02014
17	0.75000	0.02293	-0.02273
18	0.72114	0.07588	-0.02588
19	0.69134	0.02898	-0.02898
20	0.66072	0.03219	-0.03219
21	0.62941	0.03547	-0.03547
22	0.59755	0.03879	-0.03079
23	0.56526	0.04210	-0.04210
24	0.53270	0.04535	-0.04535
25	0.50000	0.04848	-0.04818
26	0.46730	0.05143	-0.05143
27	0.43474	0.05415	-0.05415
28	0.40245	0.05650	-0.05658
29	0.37059	0.05865	-0.05865
30	0.33928	0.06027	-0.06029
31	0.30866	0.06146	-0.06146
32	0.27006	0.06211	-0.06211
33	0.25000	0.06220	-0.06220
34	0.22221	0.06169	-0.06169
35	0.19562	0.06057	-0.06057
36	0.17033	0.05881	-0.05881
37	0.14645	0.05640	-0.05640
38	0.12408	0.05335	-0.05335
39	0.10332	0.04971	-0.04971
40	0.08427	0.04555	-0.04555
41	0.06699	0.04094	-0.04094
42	0.05156	0.03595	-0.03083
44	0.02653	0.02535	-0.02535
45	0.01704	0.01980	-0.01980
46	0.00961	0.01444	-0.01444
47	0.00428	0.00910	-0.00910
48	0.00107	0.00460	-0.00460
49	-0.00000	0.00000	0.00000

Dicke/T... = 0.124 Ruecklage/T = 0.250
Woelbung/T = 0.000
Ruecklage/T = 0.001
Profiletiefe... = T

forms such as E168 have lower drag than ¼-inch-thick sheet-balsa surfaces. By use of stress-skinned techniques, they can be lighter and stronger.

For both wings and tail surfaces, avoid thick TEs; sand them to 1/16 inch thickness with rounded edges. Thick TEs have the same drag as wire landing-gear legs and are longer.

ENGINE AND MUFFLER

Exposed engine cylinders and mufflers are major sources of drag. Fully exposed engines, firewalls and mufflers are even worse.

Some mufflers permit cowling of both engine and muffler completely. This type of cowl has been used on several models powered by .40 to .45 and .46ci engines with absolutely no cooling problems.

The two cooling air outlets are at points of reduced air pressure on the sides of the fuselage. Remember, only the air that actually hits the engine cylinder does the cooling. This thick balsa cowl also acts as a sound damper. Engine noise is noticeably reduced. (See Chapter 17, Ducted Cowl Design.)

FUSELAGE

The fuselage with the lowest C_D, fuselage no. 1 in Figure 1, isn't entirely practical for an R/C model that seeks to simulate the appearance of its full-scale big brothers.

The Seahawk at rest, flaps extended.

The basic low-drag features may, however, be incorporated. Such a model is shown in the photo of the Seahawk. Another photo displays this airplane on its single float. The model's large Youngman flaps, fully extended, are very effective.

At a gross weight, on wheels, of 110 ounces, powered by a .46 engine turning an 11x8 prop, this model's performance is thrilling and justifies the drag-reducing techniques in this chapter.

In plan view, the fuselage sides should be straight and parallel at the wing-fuselage intersection to avoid separation drag. Reflexing starts just after the wing TE.

The angle of incidence at which the wing is set relative to the fuselage centerline is important. It's safe to assume that the fuselage's lowest drag occurs when it's flying, in level flight, with its centerline horizontal.

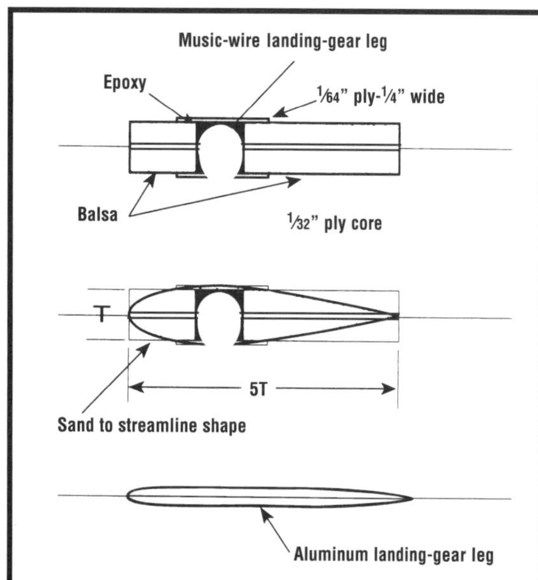

Figure 6. Streamlining landing-gear legs.

The wing's being fixed to the fuselage will cause variations in the fuselage's centerline attitude. At low speed, the wing must operate at a higher AoA to provide adequate lift for level flight. At high speeds, lower AoAs furnish the needed lift. Hence, the fuselage's centerline departs from the horizontal, nose up at low speeds, and nose down at higher speeds, both with increased drag.

The solution is to select a level-flight cruising speed and to adjust the wing's angle of incidence to provide the lift needed for level flight at that speed. At other speeds, the increase in fuselage drag must be accepted. Figure 2 of Chapter 4—the lift, wing loading and speed chart—is very useful in this connection. Using that chart, proceed as follows:

From the wing loading of your model at the bottom of the chart, read upward to the cruise speed you've selected. Where the vertical and horizontal lines intersect, you'll find the C_L needed. For example, a wing loading of 24 ounces per square foot at 60mph needs a C_L roughly halfway between C_L 0.15 and C_L 0.20—say C_L 0.17.

Refer to the lift-drag curves for the wing airfoil of your choice, and determine the AoA for C_L 0.17. Using Eppler E197 as an example, an angle of minus 0.5 degree will produce C_L 0.17. To adjust for the wing's AR of 6, another 0.5 degree should be added to this and the rectangular planform, bringing the AoA to zero degrees.

In your design, the angle of incidence of the wing to the fuselage centerline would be zero degrees to obtain the lowest fuselage drag at the 60mph cruise speed.

LANDING GEAR

This necessary, but drag-producing, appendage provides a significant opportunity for reducing drag. Aluminum landing-gear legs should have rounded LEs and TEs tapered to an almost knife-edge as in Figure 6.

OVERALL DESIGN

Good overall design will do much to reduce trim drag. A shoulder or mid-fuselage wing location, along with a high thrust line (inverted engine), will bring the centers of lift, thrust,

Below the Seahawk on its single float. Note the sub fin below the horizontal tailplane.

gravity and drag very close to one another, thus minimizing the horizontal tail's load, reducing its, and the wing's, induced trim drag. The model will also be more nimble.

THE SWIFT

This model aircraft's design was based on the concepts in this chapter and Chapter 14. See the 3-view of the Swift in Chapter 26.

This is a small, fast, highly maneuverable model, but with flaps down 40 degrees, the plane will stall at 17mph. A "safe" landing speed would be 25 percent greater, or about 21mph. Top speed is 138mph. Total drag at 50mph is estimated at 12.5 ounces, including wing and tail surfaces. At 90mph, this would increase to 42 ounces. The T-tail location was chosen to remove it from the fuselage boundary layer and the propeller slipstream into undisturbed air. Since this location results in only two corners, instead of the four of an in-fuselage location, drag is reduced.

The receiver and transmitter should have one extra channel of "proportional" nature so that flap extension may be tailored to the flying speed desired.

Figure 7 provides wing and tail-surface airfoil profiles and control-surface throws.

Ailerons, elevators and rudder are mass-balanced for flutter prevention. In a dive, this model's speed would be high.

A feature of this model is the removable fuselage top, from firewall to just aft of the wing. It's held by dowels at the front and one nylon bolt at the rear. Its easy removal provides access to all servos, receiver, fuel tank and nosewheel linkage, etc. This is a real convenience.

Note that the flap width is 30 percent of the wing's chord, rather than 25 percent. This provides greater drag when it's extended for a landing. The Swift is very clean aerodynamically, and the additional drag of the wider flap will prove beneficial.

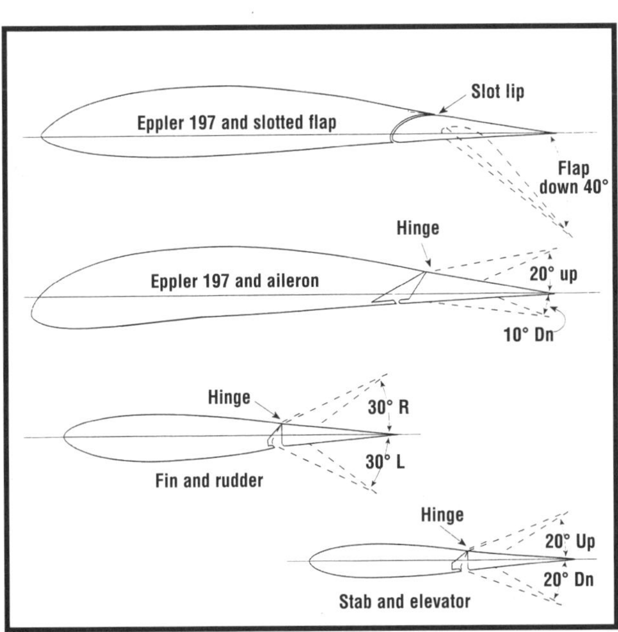

Figure 7.
Swift airfoil selections.

ENGINE/IDLE FOR LANDING

An aerodynamically clean model such as the Swift is capable of landing, flaps down, at air speeds in the 20 to 25mph range. It doesn't need much prop thrust to fly at very shallow angles, making landings difficult.

It's important that your engine be adjusted to its lowest, continual idle—around 2,500rpm. At anything higher, say 3,000 to 3,500rpm, it may be necessary to stop the engine in flight once the final approach has been established.

The model's structure is of stressed-skin construction. You'd enjoy flying a model such as this! ▲

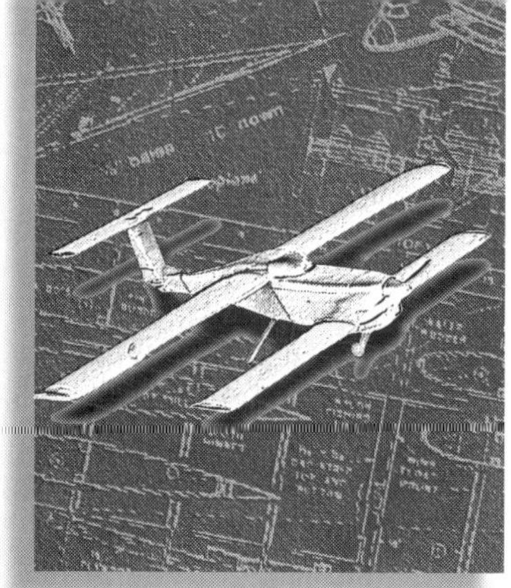

Chapter 13

Stressed-Skin Design

It's a sound engineering principle that, to maximize strength and to minimize weight, the structural material should be located as far from the "neutral axis" as possible.

This chapter will explain, in simple terms, what this neutral axis business is all about and how to arrange the structure of your model for maximum strength without adverse weight penalty.

To start with, a nodding acquaintance with basic forces is needed. There are only four:

■ **Tension.** Pulling on an elastic band puts it under tension.

■ **Compression.** Opposite of tension. A column supporting a roof is under compression.

■ **Shear.** Forces opposed to one another. Cutting paper with scissors is "shearing." Each blade opposes the other.

■ **Leverage.** A 90-pound person sitting 2 feet away from the balance point of a seesaw will be exactly balanced by a 60-pound person sitting 3 feet from the same point, but on the opposite side. The greater leverage on the lighter person's side offsets the other's greater weight. Both sides have 180 foot/pounds of leverage.

BENDING

These forces exert themselves in a variety of ways. Figure 1 shows a 1-inch-square balsa strip being bent; all four forces come into play here. The fibers on the outside of the bend are being stretched—under tension. On the inside of the bend, they're being pushed together under compression. These opposing forces develop shear. In our balsa strip, that shear acts on a line midway through called the "neutral axis."

Now look at Figure 2, illustration A. This shows the end view of the 1-inch-square balsa stick. The neutral axis and the leverage from the centers of the balsa areas above and below the neutral axis are shown.

Consider Figure 2, illustration B. The beam is composed of balsa 1x7⁄16-inch upper and lower flanges joined by a 1⁄16-inch-thick balsa web *with its grain vertical.* Both A and B have the same cross-section areas.

Obviously, the "leverage" from the neutral axis to the flange centers is greater in B than in A. B will be substantially stronger than A in bending *because the material is farther from the neutral axis.*

The balsa web in B is under shear in the bending of the beam. Balsa is much stronger in shear *across* the wood grain than *along* the grain; and stronger *along* the grain in both tension and compression.

Consider Figure 3. It displays the same beam as B in Figure 2, but without the balsa shear web—and as part of a wing structure under flight loads. The upper flange is under compression, and the lower is under tension.

Failure will occur by the upper flange *buckling* as shown in Figure 3, illustration B; and *in the absence of the web,* the opposing forces will distort the structure.

With the vertical-grain shear web in place, the buckling is resisted, as are the shear loads. These webs add much strength for little additional weight.

Obviously, the farther apart the flanges are, the stronger the beam; or, by reducing flange size and weight, obtain the same strength.

A thicker wing can be made strong but light; its spar flanges are farther apart and smaller.

TORSION

Torsion is composed of shear and tension. In Figure 4, a tube is being twisted in opposite directions at its ends. The arrows in the center show opposing shear forces; the twisting tends to elongate the fibers in tension.

The Canada Goose canard features stressed-skin construction. Power is a .35ci engine.

Figure 1.
Bending.

In Figure 5, A is a solid cylindrical rod; B is a hollow cylinder with the same cross-sectional area of material as A. Again, obviously, B is much stronger in torsion *and bending* than A because of the material's greater leverage from the neutral axis.

There is a limit to this leverage length, i.e., the point at which you can still retain the same cross-sectional area of material; beyond this limit, the outer skin would become so thin that it would fail by local buckling under load. Full-scale airplanes have thin-skinned fuselages reinforced by lateral frames and longitudinal stringers to resist buckling.

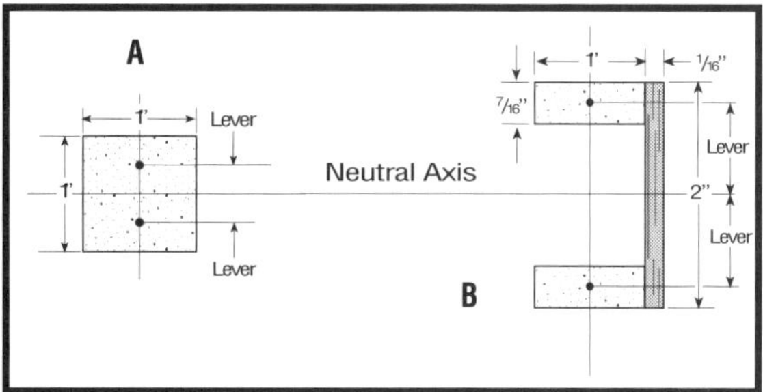

Figure 2.
Beam construction.

A beam such as that in Figure 2, illustration B, is weak in torsion. Figure 6 illustrates this beam in a wing. An airplane wing, in addition to bending loads from lift, must resist drag and torsion loads. Drag loads are due to air resistance or drag. Torsion loads result from the airfoils' pitching moment and from the twisting action of ailerons in opposite directions and the nose-down loads of flaps when extended. These loads are all substantially increased in high-speed maneuvers such as steep turns, sharp pull-ups, etc. where centrifugal forces come into effect.

The D-spar structure of Figure 6 is designed to resist all these loads. It combines a cylinder and a beam. Note that the material is as far from the neutral axis as possible and that the beam is close to the wing's thickest point.

Ailerons and flaps, as mentioned, impose loads that, on larger models, require a second spar in front of these surfaces, with some torsion-resisting structure. Full balsa sheeting in 1/16-inch balsa skins, top and bottom of the wing, maintains the airfoil section and adds little weight, but considerable strength. Ribs may be "capstripped" between spars with the covering sagging between the ribs, reducing the airfoil's integrity. Both fully and partially sheeted wings are covered with your choice of materials. The grain of the 1/16-inch skin runs parallel to the span to resist torsion and drag loads across the wood grain; and the skin aids the spars in tension and compression loads parallel to the grain.

Figure 3.
Flanges buckling under load.

The Snowy Owl has an external glow-plug power plug in the jack. Plug removal is safely away from the dangerous rotating prop. It's .40ci powered.

Horizontal and vertical tail surfaces have to contend with, principally, bending loads as elevators and rudder operate. The same structural principles apply.

Fuselages encounter a wide variety of loads in flight and particularly on landing. A tubular structure is best able to resist the heavy bending, twisting and tension loads. In balsa, a tubular or oval well-streamlined fuselage is difficult to produce. In fiberglass, it can be done, but the molds required are expensive for "one-off" models. The compromise, in balsa, is flat sheet sides, top and bottom with generous corner radius. This comes closest to the local round or oval cross-section.

It always surprises me to find how strong stressed-skin structures become after assembly of pieces of flimsy balsa. Built straight, they do not warp. Models built 10 years ago are in flyable condition today.

WINGS, AILERONS AND SLOTTED FLAPS

Figure 7 details the wing structure of the "Swift"—a model with slotted flaps that's designed for low drag. Its aerodynamic design was

The Sea Loon—a .15ci-powered twin-boom flying boat. Flaps are fully extended.

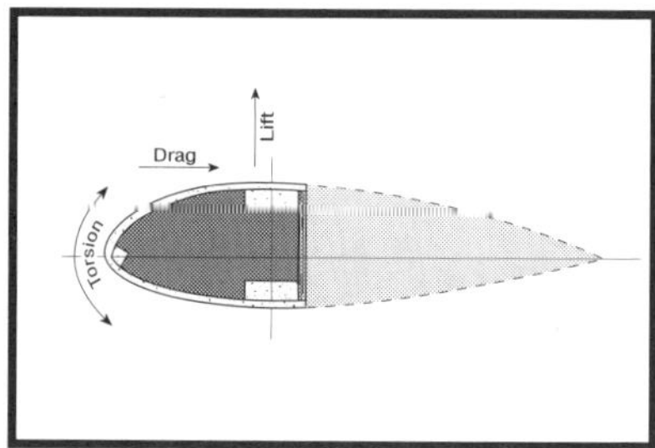

Figure 6.
D-spar wing structure.

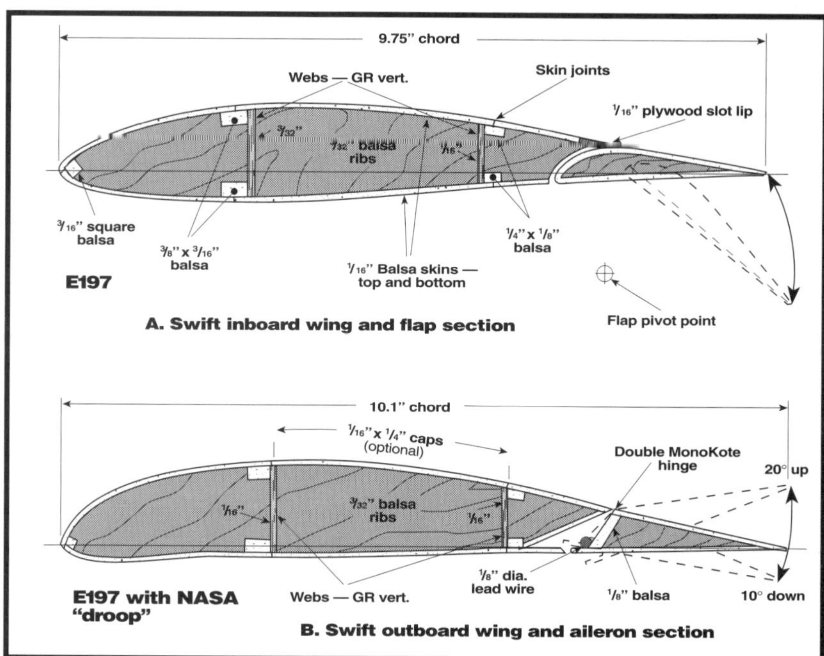

Figure 7.
The wing structure of the Swift.

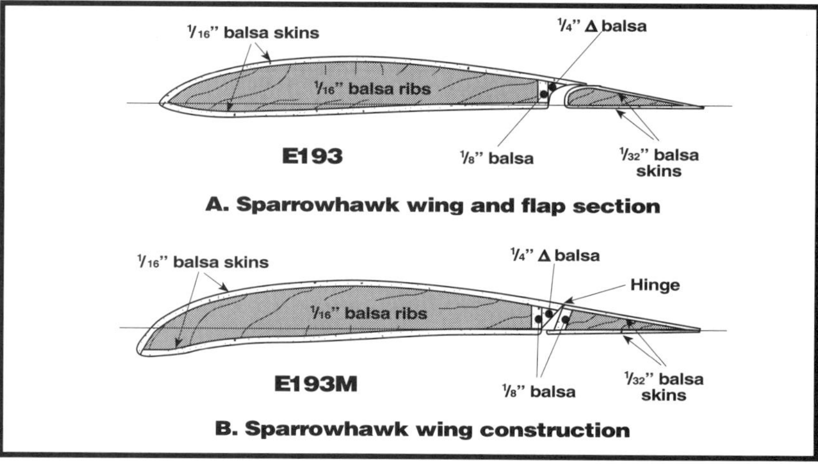

Figure 8.
The wing structure of the Sparrowhawk.

described in Chapter 12, "Improve Performance by Reducing Drag." The Swift's structure is based on the principles outlined previously in this chapter. "A" is a section cut through the flapped portion, and "B" is cut through the aileron and NASA "drooped" LE.

Figure 7A shows the Swift's two-spar wing with vertical-grained webs running from top to bottom flanges and between the wing ribs. The 3/16-inch-square LE spar adds little strength but provides gluing surfaces for joining top and bottom 1/16-inch balsa LE skins. The aft spar absorbs the flap drag and lift loads when flaps are extended.

Figure 7B shows the structure at the ailerons designed to resist aileron twisting loads. The diagonal 1/16-inch balsa sheet running from the lower flange of the aft spar to the upper skin stiffens the aileron attachment point. The ailerons and flaps are simple box structures.

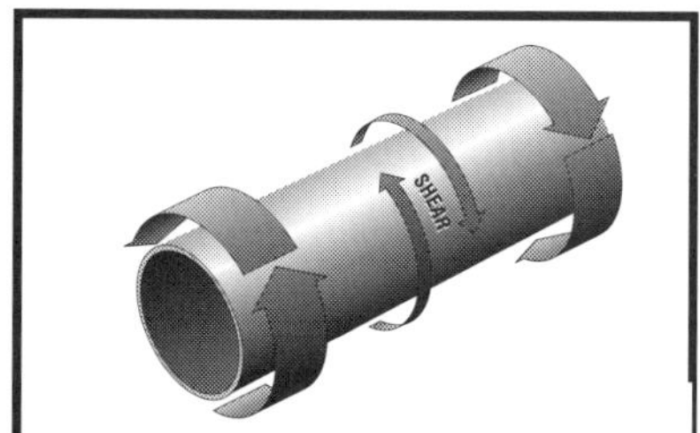

Figure 4.
Tube under torsion.

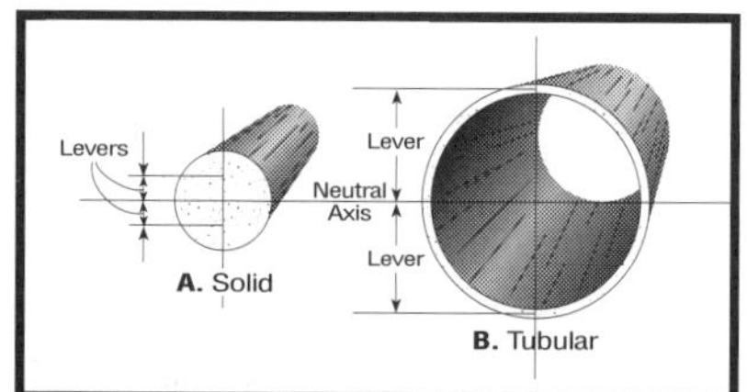

Figure 5.
Round structures.

The Swift's ailerons are of modified Frise design. With equal up and down travel of "barn-door" ailerons, the downward extension produces more drag than the upward one. This uneven drag pulls the wrong way—out of the turn—and requires coordinated rudder to correct the resulting adverse yaw.

The Swift's ailerons have differential travel—the upgoing moves twice the angle of the downgoing. Also, the lower forward lip of the upgoing aileron projects into the airstream below the wing, producing favorable drag as in Figure 7B.

These two factors combine to produce "into-the-turn" yaw. Rudder action isn't needed; the model turns on aileron action.

Both ailerons and flaps of this construction are strong, stiff units. Note the lead-wire, aileron mass balance.

The wing center section is open, with the center section main and aft spars running across the fuselage. This leaves the center section free for installation of aileron and flap servos where they're accessible by removal of the canopy as in Figure 10. It also provides access to the elevator, rudder and engine servos in the fuselage.

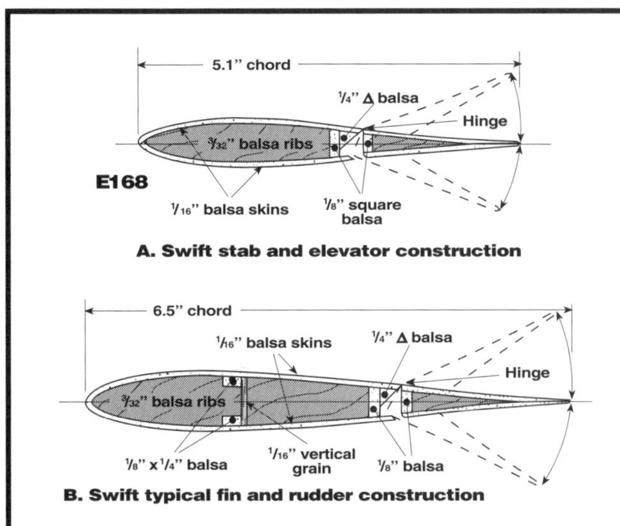

Figure 9.
Typical cross-sections of the Swift's tail.

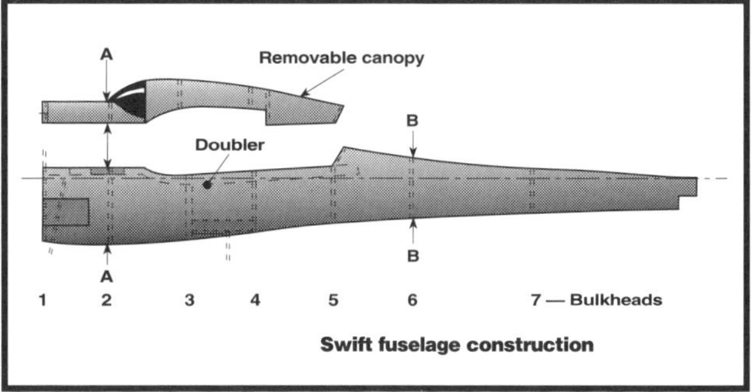

Figure 10.
Swift fuselage construction.

This open center section leaves it relatively weak in torsion. However, the wing is firmly bolted to the fuselage structure at four points. The torsion loads are absorbed by the fuselage structure, as are the main landing-gear loads.

HORIZONTAL AND VERTICAL TAIL SURFACES

Figure 9 details typical cross-sections of the Swift's tail. "A" displays the stab and elevator sections. The stab has one spar with tri-stock reinforcing the upper skin at the elevator's double MonoKote hinge.

Elevators are composed of 1/8-inch balsa L.E. spar and 1/16-inch balsa skins, top and bottom. Ribs are 3/32-inch balsa sheet.

Because the horizontal tail is mounted on top of the fin, the fin structure incorporates a spar and shear web, as in "B," to absorb the loads imposed by this T-tail location. The rudder construction is similar to that of the elevator's.

Figure 9, illustration A's construction has been used successfully on small model wings of up to 7-inch chord, as shown in Figure 8A and B. Flaps, ailerons, stabs, elevators, fins and rudders of the small models are all skinned in 1/32-inch balsa sheet with 1/16-inch balsa ribs.

FUSELAGE

Figure 10 provides an outline of the Swift's fuselage construction and Figure 11 shows typical fuselage sections for models with .40 to .60ci engines. The sides, top and bottom are all 3/32-inch firm balsa sheet with the grain running lengthwise of the fuselage. The generously radiused corners are of 3/16-inch balsa sheet and are as far from the neutral axis as possible.

The typical bulkhead is composed of four pieces of 1/8-inch balsa that are cemented together at the overlapping corners. Note the wood-grain orientation.

The firewall is 3/16-inch plywood and does triple duty. In front are motor mount and cowl, and landing-gear nosewheel brackets are on the rear. The wing and landing-gear attachment bulkheads are balsa with plywood reinforcement. The easily removable canopy and top in Figure 10 weaken the fuselage structure. Beneath the wing, the fuselage is reinforced by the four-bolt, wing-to-fuselage assembly.

Doublers along the fuselage top edges (Figure 10) reinforce these edges, along with triangular gussets at the upper-fuselage to bulkhead corners, as shown.

LANDING GEAR

Both main and nose-gear struts are 5/32-inch-diameter music wire. Fairings have to be added and shaped to streamline cross-sections.

The nose strut has a shock-absorbing coil that's entirely inside the fuselage for low drag. The main struts have a square "U" in that

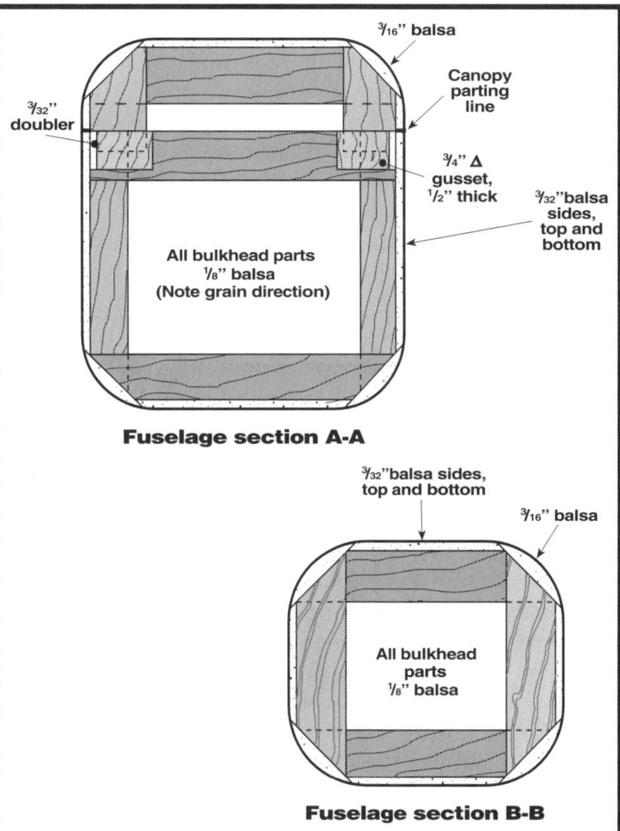

Figure 11.
Typical fuselage sections for models with .40 to .60ci engines.

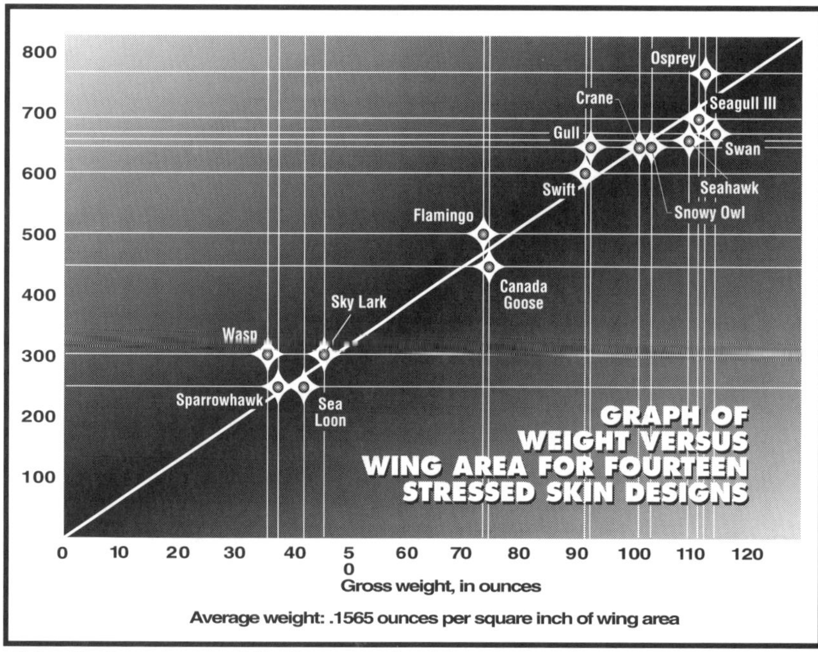

Notes: the Osprey was not fully sheet covered and, hence, was lighter. The Swan had 12 ounces of lead ballast in the nose to position the CG in the design location. The Wasp had only four servos, not five.

portion in the fuselage; the horizontal legs are shock-absorbing torsion bars that distribute landing loads over the same two bulkheads that absorb wing loads.

WEIGHT ESTIMATING

Estimating the weight of a model airplane while it's still in the conceptual stage is an important and difficult decision.

Over the years, this author has designed, built and flown 14 model aircraft, all R/C, and all of the type of stressed-skin structure described in this series. These are detailed in the Table, "14 Stressed Skin Designs" and plotted on the accompanying graph.

The total weight of the 14 was 1,151.75 ounces, and their combined wing areas totalled 7,359 square inches; the weight per square inch of wing area was 0.1565 ounce. Power loadings (ounces per cubic inch of engine displacement) varied from 200 to just over 300 ounces per cubic inch displacement. A model that has 625 square inches of wing area would weigh an estimated (625 x 0.1565) or 97.8 ounces.

Obviously, the lower the power loading, the greater the power-to-weight ratio, and the better the climb performance and top speed.

Anyone interested in designing a model to these structural principles, in the 0.15 to .46ci range, will find this tabulation a useful guide. Stressed-skin design results in the optimum weight-to-strength ratio.

There are logical justifications for all the Swift's design features—except one—the styling of the lower rudder TE. The author just likes it that way! ▲

14 Stressed-Skin Designs

Model	Eng. disp.	Model type	Gross weight (oz.)	Wing area sq. in./ sq. ft.	Wing loading oz./sq. ft.	Power loading oz./ci
1. Seahawk	**0.46**	**Sport trike**	**110.0**	**655/4.54**	**24.22**	**239.0**
2. Seagull III	0.46	Flying boat	112.0	694/4.81	23.28	243.0
3. Swift	**0.46**	**Sport trike**	**92.0**	**600/4.16**	**22.11**	**200.0**
4. Osprey	0.45	Tail-dragger	113.0	768/5.33	21.2	251.0
5. Swan	**0.45**	**Canard**	**115.0**	**669/4.64**	**24.78**	**256.0**
6. Crane	0.45	STOL trike	101.5	643/4.46	22.75	226.0
7. Gull	**0.40**	**Sport trike**	**93.0**	**643/4.46**	**20.85**	**232.5**
8. Snowy Owl	0.40	Sport trike	104.0	643/4.46	23.31	260.0
9. Canada Goose	**0.35**	**Canard**	**75.0**	**444/3.08**	**24.35**	**214.0**
10. Flamingo	0.35	Flying boat	74.0	500/3.47	21.32	211.0
11. Sparrowhawk	**0.15**	**Sport trike**	**38.0**	**250/1.73**	**21.96**	**253.0**
12. Wasp	0.15	Tandem wing	36.3	300/2.08	17.42	242.0
13. Sea Loon	**0.15**	**Flying boat**	**42.0**	**250/1.73**	**24.27**	**280.0**
14. Skylark	0.15	Spor trike	46.0	300/2.08	22.11	307.0

Chapter 14

Design for Flaps

An R/C model designed specifically for flaps opens up a new and exciting dimension in sport flying. This airplane will be fast, structurally rugged and well-streamlined, and it will have a higher-than-usual wing loading; but with flaps lowered, it will land at trainer speeds of around 20mph. It will also have a very wide speed range!

This chapter will first deal with the design of a model that will use flaps; then it will detail the design and actuation of the flaps themselves and give tips on flying with them.

To illustrate the features of a model designed for flaps, consider the Snowy Owl (see sidebar). This plane was built 15 years ago and is still flying. Powered by an old .40 engine, it weighs 104 ounces, has a wing area of just under 4½ square feet, a wing loading of slightly less than 24 ounces per square foot, and a power loading of 260 ounces per cubic inch of engine displacement. It features the NASA "safe wing" droop modification.

This model's performance has proven to be better than any other .40-powered model encountered so far. Takeoffs—flaps half extended—from grass require no more than 10 feet with a fast steep climb. Landing approaches—flaps fully extended and engine idling—may be very steep (almost vertical) without significant acceleration. This results from the high flap drag when the flaps are fully extended.

Stalls—flaps down—are at 17mph. On a low-wind day, full-stall slow landings are pure fun—like a bird landing on a branch—and ground roll seldom exceeds 4 feet.

With a 10x7.5 prop, the Snowy Owl's top speed is estimated at 75mph. It's fully aerobatic, but it refuses to do more than one or two turns of a spin, which is then converted into a fast spiral dive (courtesy of the NASA droop) and from which recovery is prompt upon neutralizing the controls.

On a windy day, it will hover, almost motionless, flaps fully extended, engine throttled back and with full up-elevator. Aileron control is still effective in this nose-high altitude, and no tip-stalls occur.

Figure 1. FLAP TYPES

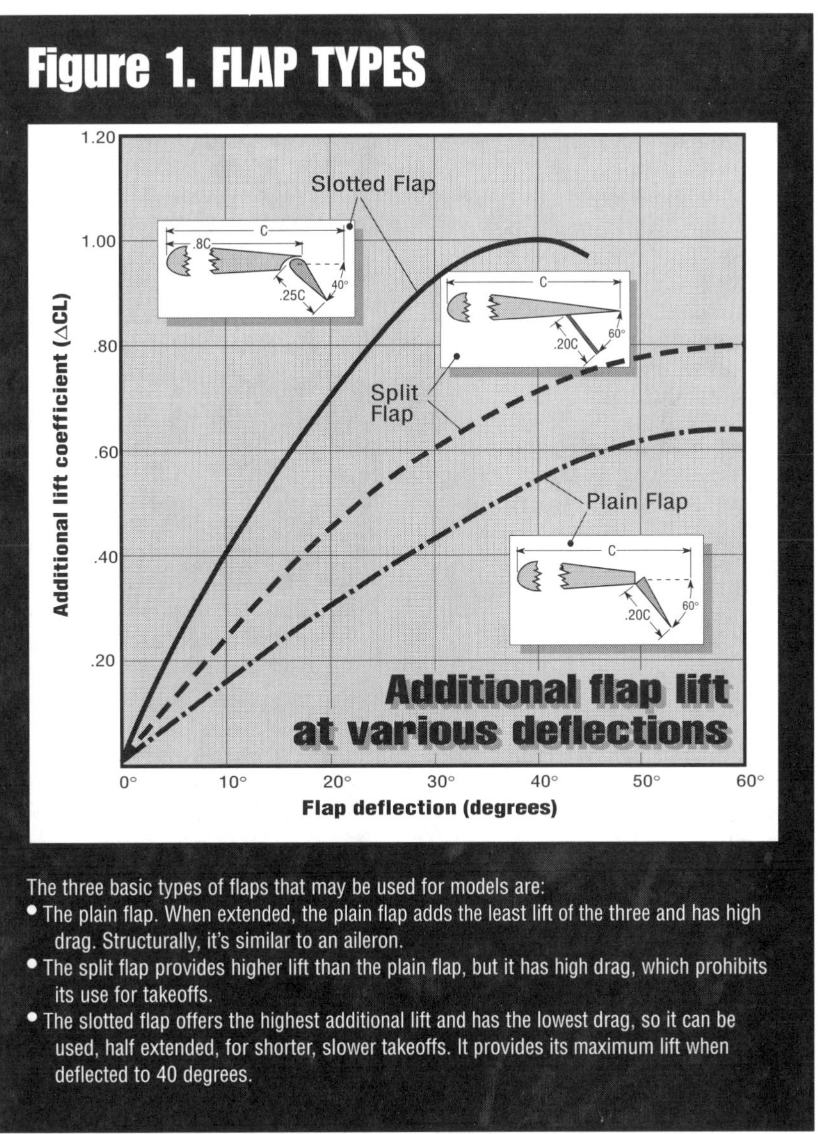

The three basic types of flaps that may be used for models are:

- The plain flap. When extended, the plain flap adds the least lift of the three and has high drag. Structurally, it's similar to an aileron.
- The split flap provides higher lift than the plain flap, but it has high drag, which prohibits its use for takeoffs.
- The slotted flap offers the highest additional lift and has the lowest drag, so it can be used, half extended, for shorter, slower takeoffs. It provides its maximum lift when deflected to 40 degrees.

The Seagull III—an amphibious flying boat. Powered by an O.S. Max 46SF engine, it weighs 113 ounces and is an excellent performer. Its large slotted flaps are fully extended for landing.

It's great fun to make a low pass—flaps fully extended; engine throttled; nose-high attitude—at about 25mph, followed by another pass with flaps up and engine wide open.

The Snowy Owl's speed range is remarkable. Maneuvers—flaps down—are very tight indeed. On a day with little or no wind, don't attempt to land the Snowy Owl flaps-up, because the glide is fast and very flat, and you could easily overshoot the flying field.

On the other hand, landings on a very windy day should be made flaps-up. The high wing loading provides good penetration, and the high airspeed gives good control. Thanks to the NASA droop, there are no wing-tip-stalls when making nose-high landings.

SNOWY OWL'S KEY DESIGN FEATURES

Which factors contribute most to Snowy Owl's good performance?

The Snowy Owl. Note its low-drag design and NASA safe-wing droop.

- **Most important is the careful attention to drag reduction. A 2½-inch spinner is faired into a ducted cowl that fully encloses (and quiets) the engine and muffler. The wing airfoil—Eppler 195—was developed specifically for the low Rns of model flight, and it has very low-profile drag. The tricycle landing-gear legs are stream-lined with rugged balsa-and-ply fairings. The wheels are 2½-inch-diameter, smooth-contour type. (Bare wire landing-gear legs and big, fat tires have an astonishing amount of drag.) The horizontal and vertical tail surfaces have low-drag, symmetrical airfoil sections. Though "slab-sided," the fuselage has generously rounded corners—no exposed dowels and rubber bands to hold the wing.**

  The rugged, fully balsa-sheet-covered flying surfaces have no lift-reducing, between-the-ribs, sags in the covering. The antenna is enclosed in the fuselage and fin, and the MonoKote covering provides a smooth, slippery surface. All control horns are internal, or only slightly exposed.

- **Second in importance are the rugged slotted flaps whose area is 13.6 percent of the total wing area, and which occupy 60 percent of the wing's TE. They may be extended at any airspeed.**

- **Third in importance is propeller selection. The make, diameter and pitch that provide the best performance can only be chosen after repeated trials.**

- **The NASA safe-wing modifications.**

- **Despite its higher gross weight (at least 15 ounces more than most .40-powered sport models), the greater wing loading results in a smaller model overall with a wing area of 4.5 square feet. (Most sport models run 5 to 6 square feet.)**

- **The high gross weight permits a rugged structure; flaps and their servos and linkage add 3 to 4 ounces; but the balance of the additional weight provides strong, stiff, fully balsa-sheeted surfaces (based on stressed-skin principles) that are absolutely warp-free.**

SLOTTED-FLAP DESIGN

Let's make a bold stab at designing a wing for a slotted-flap-equipped model called the "Swift." To a greater extent than the Snowy Owl, it will take advantage of the lift-increasing capacity of the extended flaps.

For this project, the chosen wing loading is 25 ounces per square foot of wing area. This is higher than Snowy Owl's and should result in a smaller, lighter model with even lower drag. By comparison, a gross weight (with fuel) of 100 ounces seems reasonable. The wing area would thus be 100 divided by 25 to equal 4 square feet, or 576 square inches. The Swift is powered by a .46 engine, and its power loading is 217.3 ounces/cubic inch displacement.

For this project, test-fly with 10x9 and 10x10 props to select the one that performs best for this model. At 11,000rpm, a 10x9 prop would produce an estimated top speed of 90mph.

Figure 2 shows the actual dimensions of the Swift's wing and the proportions of its features. With a wing loading of 25 ounces per square foot and a C_L max of 1.933, this model will stall at just under 18mph at sea level. If you have the C_L for a particular airfoil and wing loading, stall speed can be estimated quickly by using the curves

Sparrowhawk is a 15-powered airplane with a wing area of 250 square inches and a wing loading of 22 ounces per square foot. It's nimble and fun to fly.

shown in Figure 3 of Chapter 3. Add 20 percent to this stall speed for a safety margin, and this model would be capable of touching down, nose-high at 22mph under "no-wind" conditions. This is a comfortable landing speed.

Well-developed flaps on a model designed specifically for flaps will produce an aircraft that has high top speeds and is very strong and rugged. It will also have a very wide speed range, and this will permit slow landings (flaps-down) and flight at any speed desired within that speed range. The plane will be more versatile than the average sport .40 and much more fun to fly.

GUIDELINES

■ With flap extended, the slot formed between the upper forward surface of the flap and the underside of the slot lip should converge or narrow steadily from the slot entry in the wing underside to the exit over the flap top surface. This accelerates the airflow over the flap, delaying its stall and improving its lift. It's the reason the slotted flap is superior to either the split or the plane variety.

■ Air flowing from the slot should merge smoothly into the air flowing around the wing and the flap.

■ Having an appreciable length of slot lip on the upper wing surface is advantageous.

The Osprey is a tail-dragger. Powered by an O.S. Max 45 FSR, it weighs 113 ounces and has a wing loading of 26.5 ounces per square foot. Under "no-wind" conditions, it takes off from water in less than 40 feet on floats.

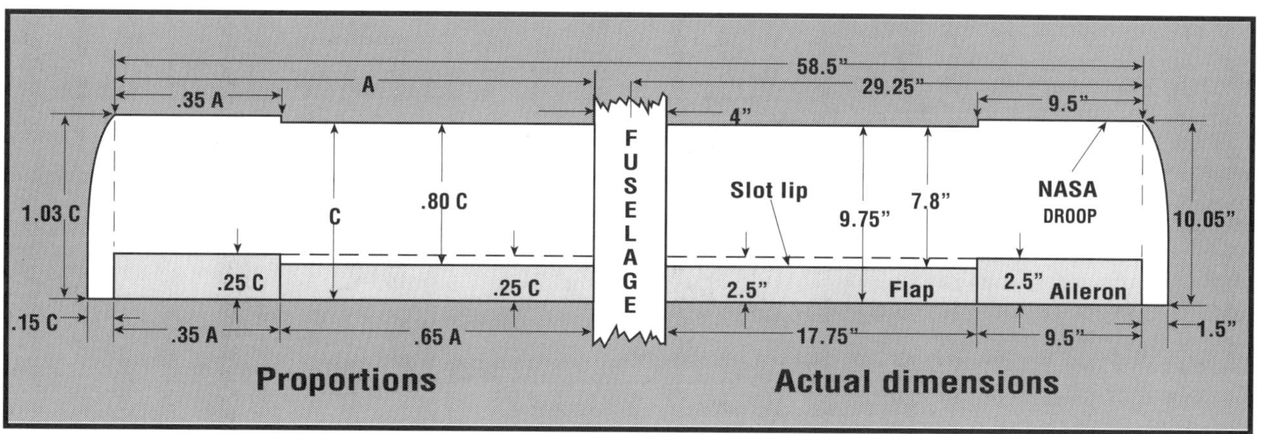

Figure 2.
Outline of the Swift's wing (576 square inches: aspect ratio of 5.94).

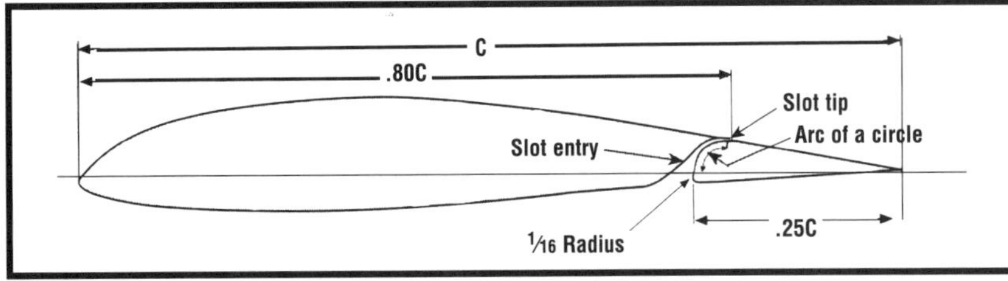

Figure 3.
Slotted flap proportions.

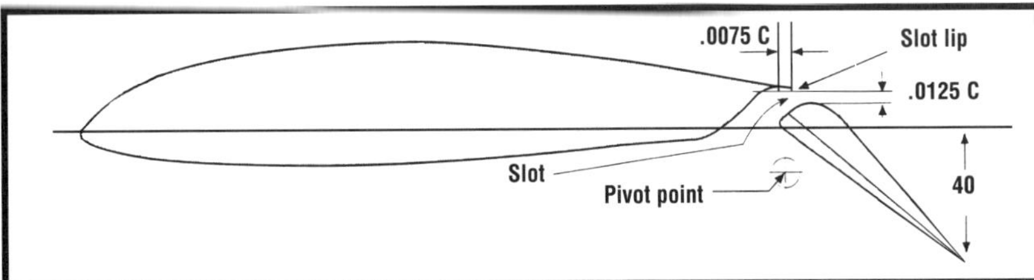

Figure 4.
Flap in the 40-degree-down position.

Figure 3 provides the proportions of a slotted flap for the Eppler 197 airfoil that conform to these guidelines. This is based on proportions developed in the wind-tunnel tests outlined in NACA Report 664, Flap Type 1b.

This flap extends by rotating around a fixed pivot, to 40 degrees. Note that only the top front and LE curves are added to form the flap's profile; the rest are provided free by the wing profile itself.

Figure 4 shows the flap in the 40-degree-down position and provides the proportions of the slot gap and the slot lip overhang. These proportions are important for good flap performance.

Positioning the pivot point so that the flap-up and 40-degree-down positions coincide with those shown on the drawing is done by a simple trial-and-error method.

Trace the flap profile and chord line on translucent material such as onion-skin paper, tracing paper or drafting film. Lay this tracing over the flap drawing in the *up* position. Using a pin as a pivot, rotate the tracing so that the flap extends. Trial and error will guide you to a pivot point where the tracing coincides exactly with the drawing of the flap, in both the up and the 40-degree-down positions. Mark this position carefully on your drawing.

FLAP CONSTRUCTION AND OPERATION

Figure 5 details the structure of both the wing and the flap. The 1/16-inch-thick plywood flap supports and the 3/32-inch-thick plywood pivot and horn ribs are shown in Figure 6. The enlarged section of the "Flap support—pivot rib" shows the sanding required to streamline this assembly.

The flap has 1/16-inch-thick balsa-sheet skins on the top and the bottom. Each flap has two pivot ribs and one horn rib—all made of plywood; the rest of the ribs are made of 3/32-inch-thick sheet balsa.

The form of slot entry shown in Figure 3 was used on Snowy Owl. Although this smoothes the airflow into the slot, it leaves a drag-producing gap when the flap is retracted. Later designs simply have the lower wing skin extended to the flap's LE (see Figure 5) without any apparent adverse affects.

HORIZONTAL TAIL SURFACES

When slotted flaps are extended in flight, a number of things happen:

- Wing lift increases substantially.
- Wing drag also increases, and this slows the model.
- The nose-down pitching moment increases.
- The angle of the downwash from the wing and the lower flap increases sharply; this impacts on the horizontal tail at a negative angle and leads to a tail download that induces a nose-up pitch.

The outcome of these force changes is some degree of nose-up pitch. This is overcome by applying nose-

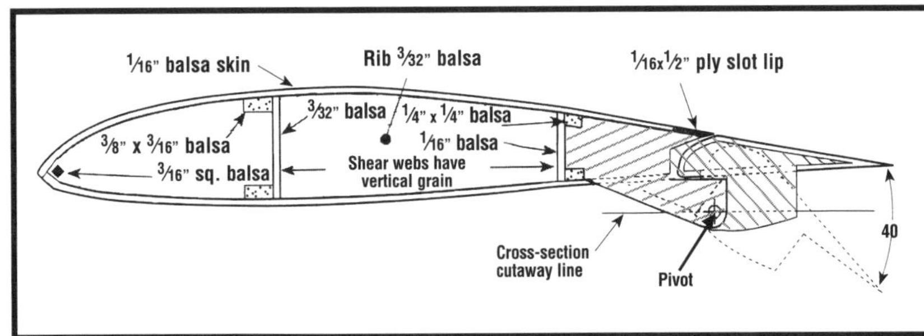

Figure 5.
Wing and slotted-flap construction and hinging.

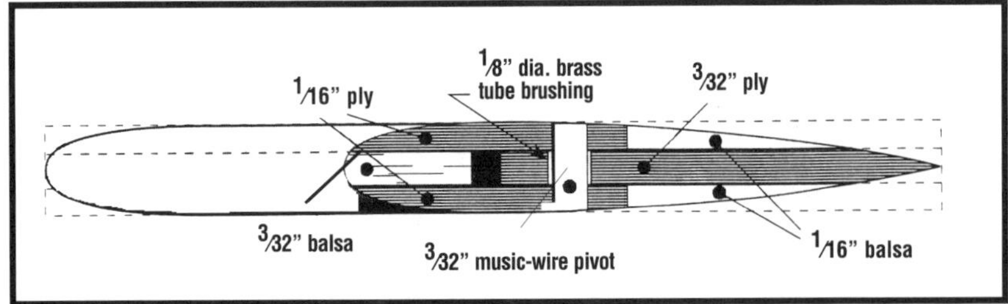

Enlarged cross-section of flap support-pivot rib.

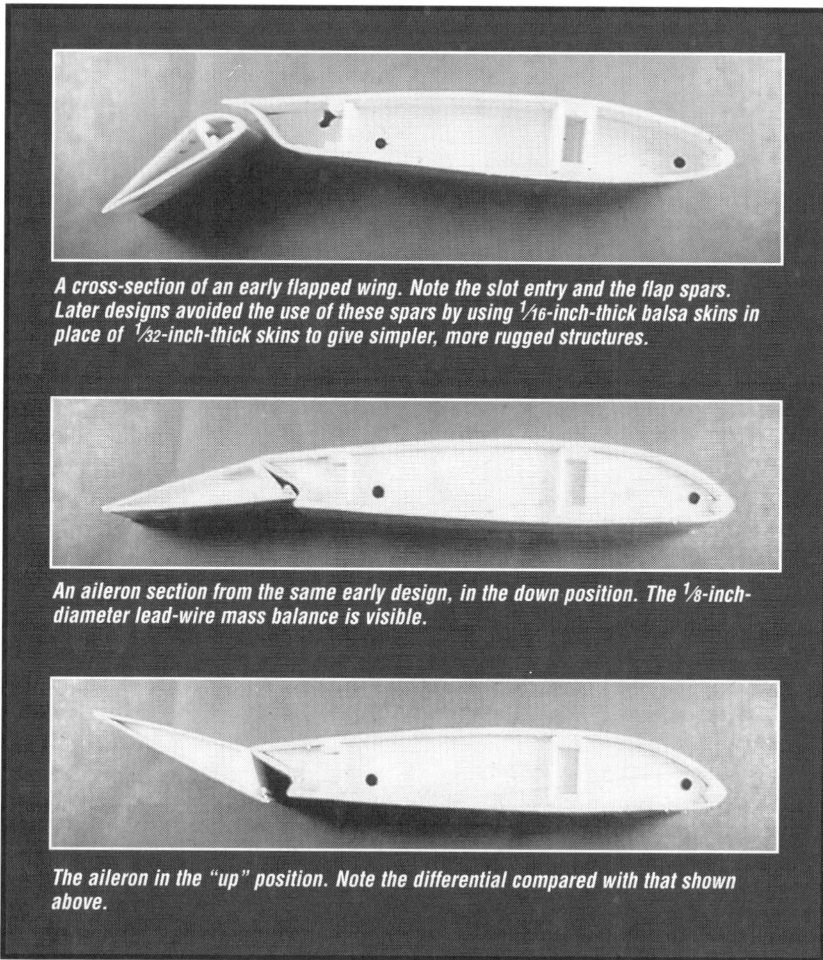

A cross-section of an early flapped wing. Note the slot entry and the flap spars. Later designs avoided the use of these spars by using 1/16-inch-thick balsa skins in place of 1/32-inch-thick skins to give simpler, more rugged structures.

An aileron section from the same early design, in the down position. The 1/8-inch-diameter lead-wire mass balance is visible.

The aileron in the "up" position. Note the differential compared with that shown above.

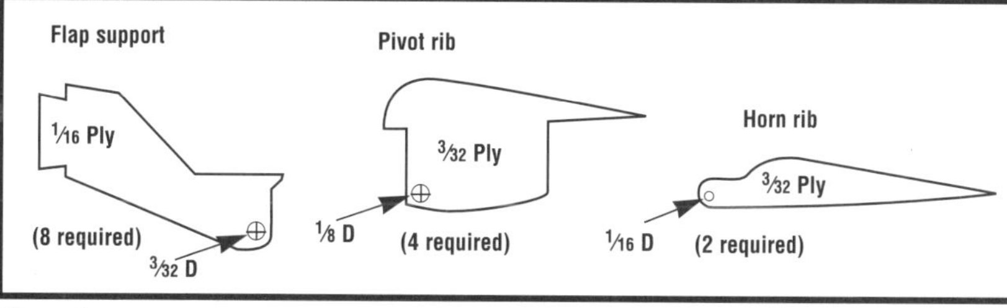

Figure 6.
Flap plywood components.

down trim by means of the elevator trim lever while simultaneously lowering the flaps. With a little practice, this becomes almost automatic.

The nose-up pitch varies with the speed at which the model is flying when you lower the flaps and the extent to which they're lowered.

Experience has proven that T-tail models, e.g., the Snowy Owl, pitch-up to a greater degree than those in which the horizontal tail is in the fuselage, e.g., the Osprey.

A T-tail operates in air that's only lightly disturbed by the downwash. It's thus more effective than a lower tail, which is in air that's disturbed by the fuselage, in heavier downwash and in the prop's slipstream. The T-tail is more affected by the increase in downwash angle on lowering the flaps.

GROUND EFFECT AND ELEVATOR DESIGN

In ground effect, at an altitude of less than half the wingspan, the wing and flap downwash angle decreases to roughly half of the angle at higher altitude. This reduces the tail download proportionately. This occurs at a bad point; the tail download should be increasing to raise the nose to a high angle for a slow landing. Powerful elevators are needed to produce the tail download required.

An elevator area of 40 percent of the total horizontal tail area with a travel of 30 degrees up and down is recommended for a model that's equipped with slotted flaps.

In normal flight—flaps up—these large elevators may be sensitive at first, but with experience, you'll adjust to them.

TAIL SURFACE AIRFOIL AND STRUCTURE

Figure 9 shows details of the tail-surface airfoil and the structural design used on several successful models. The depth of this section provides a very strong, light, simple structure with low drag. The same principles of airfoil and structure apply to the fin and the rudder.

FLUTTER PREVENTION

Well-streamlined model aircraft with fairly high wing loadings and powerful engines can achieve very high speeds, particularly when diving. This invites the very real danger of control-surface flutter, which could destroy that surface very quickly and would probably result in a disastrous crash.

This is particularly true of the wide-chord control surfaces inherent in "designing for flaps." The only certain way to prevent flutter is to offset the weight of the control surface behind its hinge with weight in front of the hinge, with both weights balancing at the hinge line.

The modified Frise aileron shown in Figure 7 lends itself to mass-balancing very easily. Shielded horn balsa tips on rudder and elevator permit this mass-balancing (see Figures 9 and 10). Flutter prevention for flaps has proven to be unnecessary. Thanks to their stressed-skin construction, wings and tail surfaces are torsionally very stiff and free of flutter.

See also Chapter 20, High-Lift Devices and Drag Reduction," for

FLAP- AND AILERON-ACTUATION LINKAGES

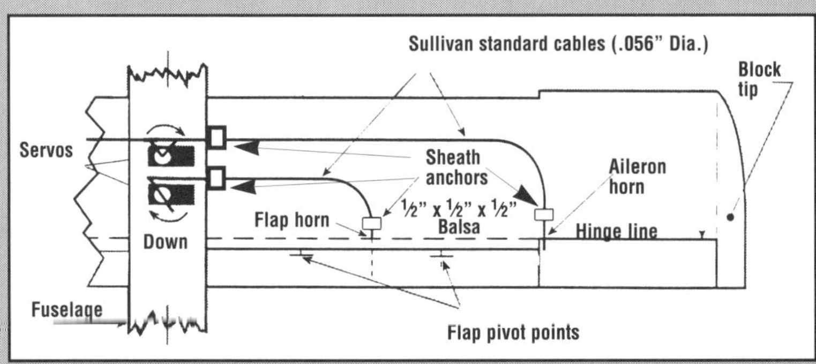

Figure 7.
Flap and aileron actuation.

To operate flaps, a standard servo is adequate. The servo-to-flap (and ailerons) linkage is flexible stranded 0.056-inch-thick cable running in ⅛-inch-o.d. plastic sheaths (see Figure 7). This system gives positive "no-slop" control movement, and I've used it for all control surfaces on several of my recent models.

Using CA, the cable is glued directly into clevises at the control-surface end and into threaded brass couplers at the servo end. The servo clevises are then threaded onto the couplers to allow the control-surface neutrals to be easily adjusted.

Anchor both ends of the plastic sheaths by using CA to glue them into small balsa blocks that are cemented firmly into the model's structure. Put a drop of CA to anchor the sheath to each rib or bulkhead through which it passes. These steel cables, which run down the fuselage and into the wings, haven't produced any radio interference, but keep the antenna as far away from them as possible.

Depending on the vertical distance from the flap pivot to the flap horn, the stroke needed to lower the flap fully may be more than a normal servo horn can provide. For a longer stroke, use Futaba's "E" horn or equivalent that has longer arms.

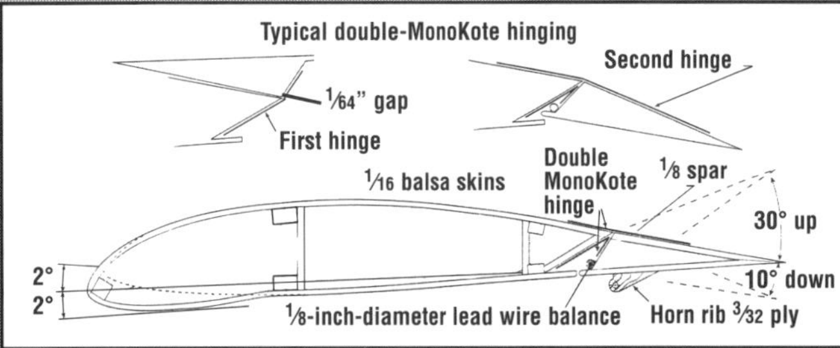

Figure 8.
NASA droop, aileron construction and hinging.

You'll need a fifth or sixth channel for flap control. Use either a sliding-switch type, which permits the flap to be extended to any position (from full-up to full-down), or a three-position snap switch, which provides full-up, 20-degree down for takeoffs and 40-degree down for landing.

Figure 8 shows a cross-section of the the aileron and wing structures showing the NASA "droop." The aileron's action is differential—down 10 degrees; up 30 degrees—and it provides "positive," into-the-turn, aileron yaw aided by the forward lower lip of the "up-going" aileron that extends into the airflow below the wing. This provides a small amount of favorable drag. Turns are made without any rudder action.

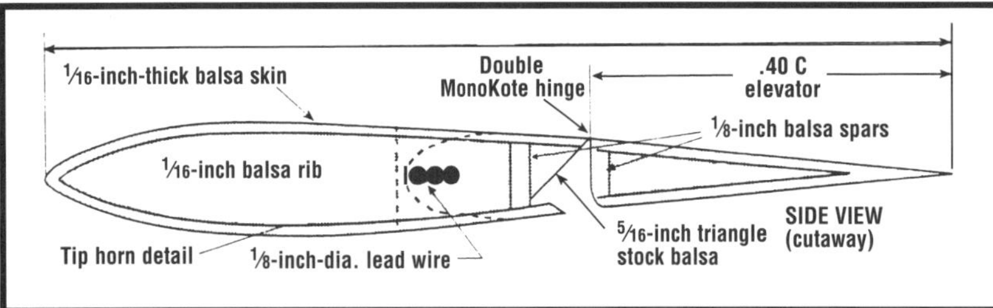

Figure 9.
Typical tail surface construction— E168 airfoil.

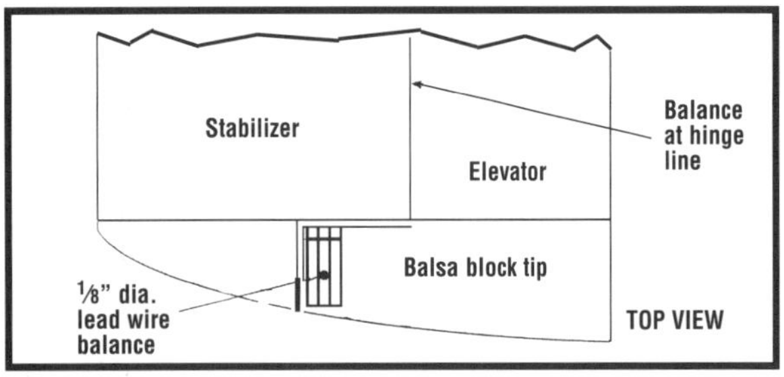

Figure 10.
Typical shielded horn and mass balance for elevator and rudder.

the benefits of 0.30c chord slotted flaps.

Flying R/C model aircraft is challenging, exciting and fun. I hope that "flapped flying" will add to your enjoyment of this sport. It has for me! ▲

Chapter 15

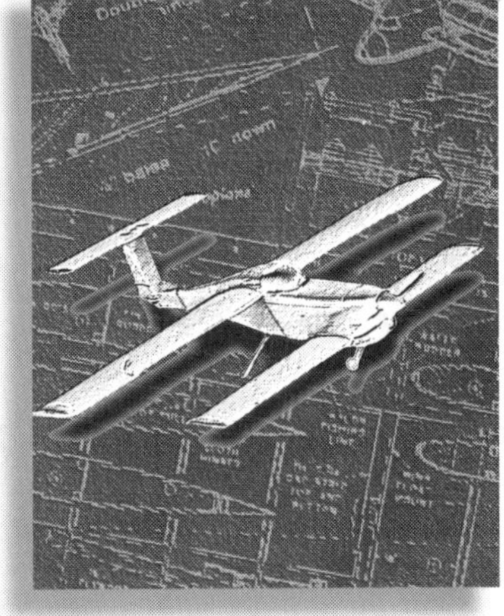

NASA "Safe Wing"

The Snowy Owl in slow-speed flight with flaps extended. The increasing leading-edge droop ahead of the ailerons is clearly visible.

Here's a grim statistic: roughly 30 percent of all fatal accidents involving light, full-scale airplanes are caused by stalling and spinning at low altitudes, and ground impact occurs before the spin fully develops. Several members of my club have discovered that R/C model aircraft are also prone to this insidious failure. What's happening?

As a private pilot, I've been interested in wing modifications that will improve the stall/spin characteristics of both full-scale and R/C model airplanes. Most modelers know that a model's wing lift is proportional to the square of its airspeed. At the same AoA, doubling the speed increases lift fourfold. Also, lift varies directly with the AoA, from the airfoil's zero lift angle to its stalling angle. In high-speed flight, the wing operates at a low AoA; at low speed, that angle must be increased to maintain level flight. The stalling angle of the wing's airfoil determines the lowest speed limit.

Centrifugal force plays a significant part in stalls and spins because it increases the weight that the wing must support. It's encoun-tered when banking steeply, sharply pulling up into climbs, and when you panic and use full-up-elevator when pulling out of dives at low altitude.

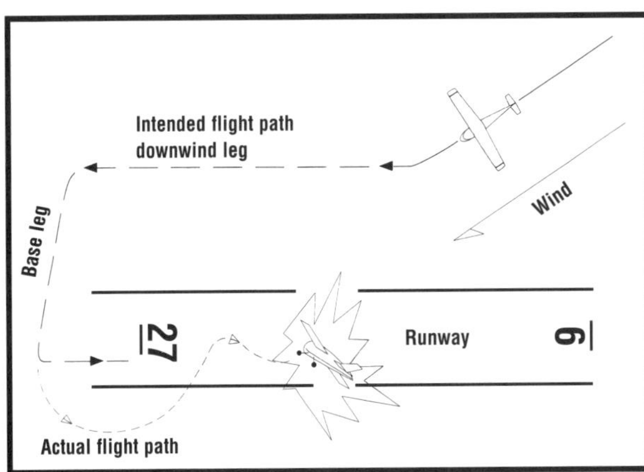

Figure 1.
Classic stall/spin flight path, frequently fatal. Wrong way to "hit" the runway.

For example, a full-scale Cessna 172 at gross weight stalls at 57mph. In a 60-degree banked turn, its stall speed increases by 42 percent to 81mph, and this is due entirely to the extra load imposed by centrifugal force. As a normal wing approaches the stalling angle, aileron-control effectiveness deteriorates markedly. Lowering an aileron to introduce a roll input at this angle increases the wing's AoA at that aileron, and may cause it to stall—just the opposite of the action commanded by the pilot.

A TRAGIC SCENE

Suppose an inexperienced pilot is flying a high-wing aircraft. He's in a left-hand pattern for landing at a busy airport, and a light crosswind is blowing from left to right. After turning onto the base leg of his approach, he slows the airplane by throttling back and increasing its AoA by applying up-elevator. While scanning the area for other traffic, he lowers the flaps, trims the aircraft and announces his intention to land.

At an altitude of 300 feet, he turns left again onto final approach, and our inexperienced aviator finds that the crosswind has made the plane drift well to the right of the centerline. To correct, he cranks in more left aileron to steepen his bank, and he adds up-elevator to accelerate his turn; both increase the centrifugal load. As the aircraft is realigned with the runway, the pilot applies heavy, right aileron to straighten up. The down-aileron (left) wing stalls, and over he goes to the left as the plane starts to spin. Unable to recover at this altitude, he becomes another statistic.

In an attempt to remedy the spin/stall syndrome, a variety of wing modifications were tested by

The Osprey, powered by a .45 diesel, about to start its takeoff run. The leading-edge droop shows clearly.

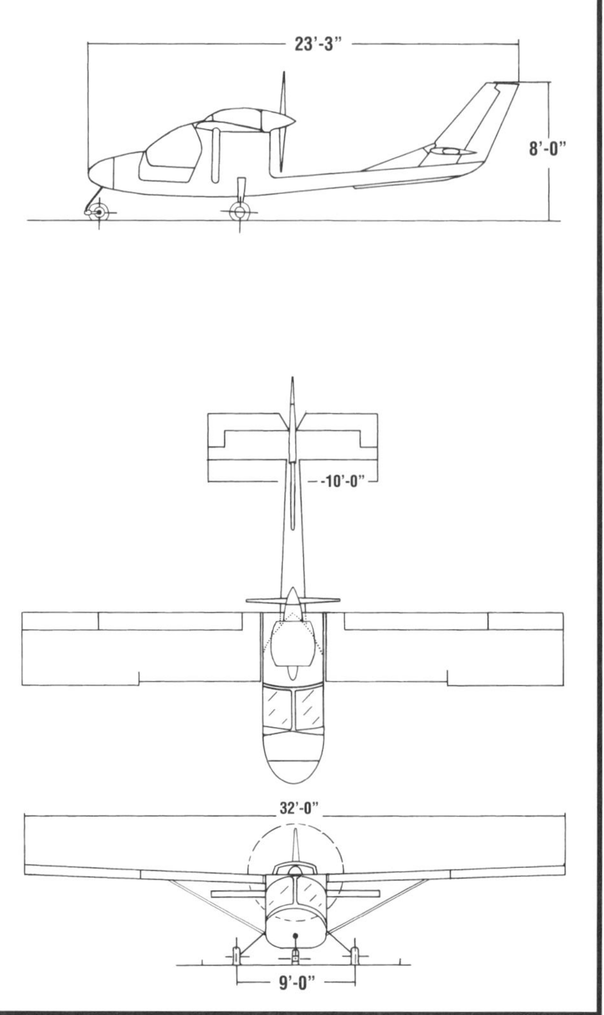

Figure 2. Verilite Aircraft Co. Inc. Sunbird.

aeronautical engineers: fixed or retractable LE slots; wing washout to reduce tip angles; greater camber at the wingtips and slot-lip ailerons. While modifications did improve stall behavior, they also aggravated spin characteristics. Many of these changes worsened aircraft performance and increased the complexity and cost of construction and maintenance.

NASA'S SOLUTION

In the late '70s, NASA's Ames Research Center initiated a program to develop an improved LE that would be inexpensive to manufacture and would require no maintenance. After determining the best wing modification through extensive wind-tunnel tests, NASA incorporated these design changes into an R/C scale model. Stall/spin characteristics were significantly improved, and, to confirm these R/C model results, four, full-scale light aircraft—a Grumman American Yankee, Beech Sierra, Piper Arrow and Cessna 172—were modified and flown extensively.

Because manufacturers pay such high insurance premiums, they're building fewer, full-scale light airplanes. Verilite Aircraft Co. Inc. has developed a new design that incorporates NASA's LE modifications. The Sunbird (Figure 2) is the first aircraft designed to provide spin resistance and thereby reduce stall/spin accidents. NASA has run extensive wind-tunnel tests on this aircraft, and it has built and tested a small scale model, a ¼-scale R/C model and a full-scale version. A 28-degree AoA was recorded before the stall was encountered.

On the previous page, a photo of my Snowy Owl (one of my earlier models) is in slow-speed flight with its flaps extended. The increasing LE droop ahead of the ailerons is clearly visible, and it reached its maximum at the wingtips. This modification succeeded in delaying the stall, but the ailerons proved ineffective in the attitude shown.

The Sea Loon in its natural element—water. The leading-edge droop starts at the inner-wing stripe.

NASA's LE droop has been successfully incorporated into seven R/C model aircraft: the .15-powered Sparrowhawk; the .40-powered Snowy Owl II; the .15-powered Sea Loon (a flying boat); the Swift; the Seagull III; the Seahawk; and the Osprey, which is a .45-powered craft designed to be used with both wheels and floats.

While the smaller models can be *forced* to spin, only one or two turns are achieved before the spin becomes a spiral dive, and recovery is instantaneous when the controls are neutralized. Aileron control is greatly improved in the stall, with the flaps up or down. Despite many attempts, I haven't been able to spin the larger models.

As the illustration of the airflow over the NASA wing shows, the outboard, drooped panels become very

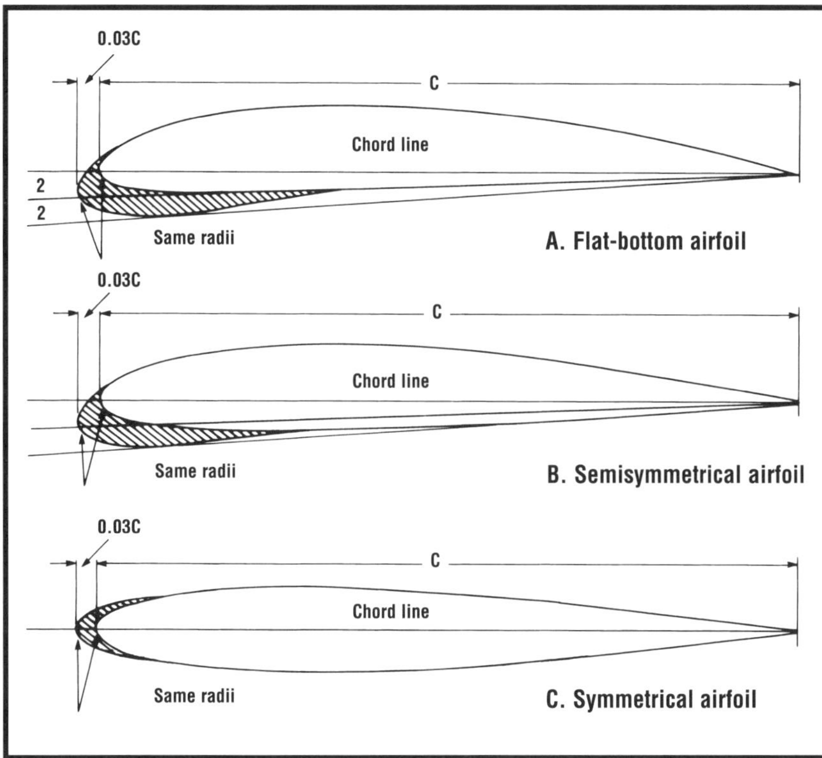

Figure 6.
NASA droop (cross-hatched areas) on various airfoils.

low-AR wings, with a stall that's considerably delayed. The droop itself, which delays the stall to approximately twice the stall angle of the basic wing, permits effective aileron control at the higher AoAs.

If you fly models with flat-bottom or semisymmetrical airfoils, you could modify the wings by adding droop. (See the cross-hatched areas in Figure 6 A and B). For evaluation purposes, I've done this by using Styrofoam, which is held in place with transparent tape.

As an alternative, you could add balsa ribs like the ones shown in the cross-hatched section, and a light LE spar. Cover them with bond paper or thin balsa, and glue this unit to the outboard wing LE. I haven't tried this droop on symmetrical airfoiled wings, but it might delay the stall in both upright and inverted flight (see Figure 6C).

Congratulations, NASA, for your major contribution to aviation safety. I hope this "safe" wing will be incorporated in future aircraft designs. ▲

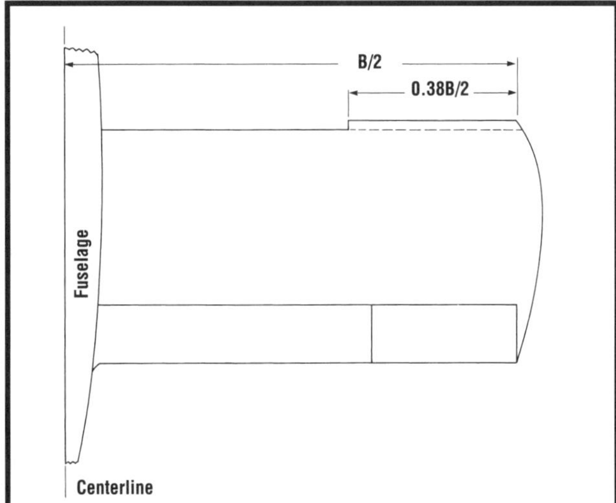

Figure 7.
The wing planform showing the proportions of the added leading-edge droop. Note that the corners formed by the inboard end of the droop must be sharp where the droop addition meets the normal airfoil.

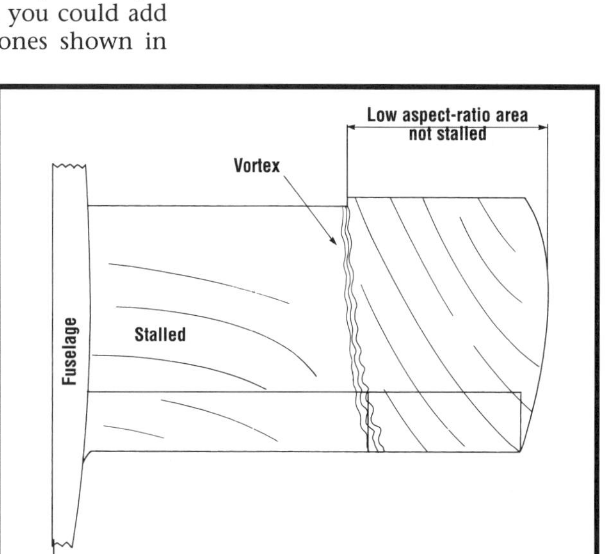

Figure 8.
The airflow over the NASA wing at high angles of attack. While the inboard, undrooped section is stalled, the sharp-cornered notch in the leading edge produces a chord-wise vortex that effectively separates the two areas.

Chapter 16

Landing-Gear Design

The landing gear of a propeller-driven aircraft has two major functions. The first is to provide adequate clearance between prop tips and the ground. The second, and no less important, is to permit the plane to rotate on both takeoff and landing so that the wing's AoA comes close to the stalling angle of its airfoil. At that AoA, the wing is near the airfoil's C_L max. This permits the lowest landing and takeoff speeds of which the model is capable.

On the ground, however, it should not be possible to rotate to or beyond the wing's stalling angle. Such a stall on takeoff or landing could be damaging, both to the model and to its designer's ego!

For windy-day flying, good judgment dictates flaps-up landings, and at a lower AoA for good control. The wind's speed reduces the model's ground speed accordingly.

This chapter deals with the landing-gear function. Intelligent determination of the AoA for landing and takeoff requires consideration of the following:

The Wasp tandem wing. The prop's position, just behind the main landing gear, has no clearance problem.

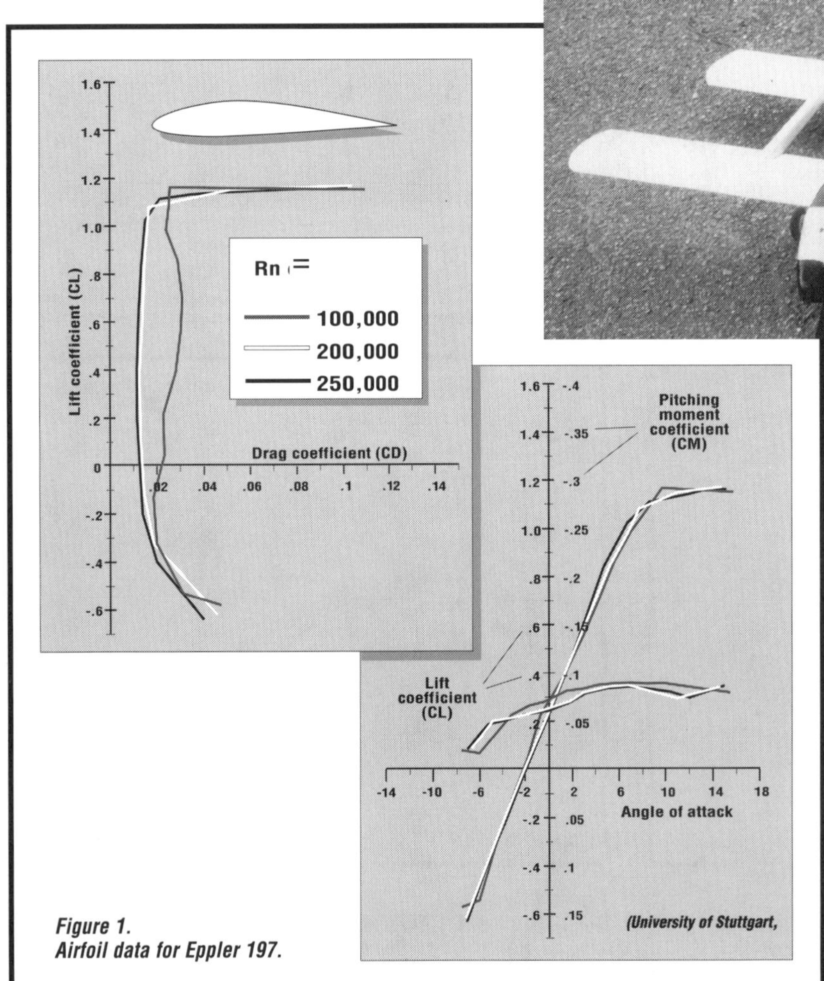

Figure 1. Airfoil data for Eppler 197.

- The airfoil's characteristics and the Rn at landing and takeoff speeds.
- Adjustment of "section values" to those for your wing's AR and planform.
- The effect on the stalling angle of flaps when extended.
- The impact of ground effect.
- The wing's AoA in level flight. If that angle is 3 degrees and the land-

ing/takeoff angle is 12 degrees, then the plane has to rotate through only 9 degrees to reach the 12-degree angle.

■ Wings incorporating the NASA "droop" will have an increase in landing/takeoff angles.

LANDING GEAR

For conventional models, the wing characteristics control the landing/takeoff AoA. For canard or tandem-wing models, lift is generated by both wings. Well-behaved canards or tandem wings have front wings that must stall first, so that for landing-gear design, only the fore-plane's characteristics are to be considered, not the aft wings.

Now, about those six factors: Figure 1 provides the lift, drag and pitching-moment characteristics of the Eppler 197. On the left, C_L 1.1 has been selected as the takeoff/landing C_L at an 8-degree AoA. This is well below this section's stalling angle of 16 degrees, and the stall is gentle with no hysteresis. Figure 1 of Chapter 14, "Design for Flaps," gives the additional lift coefficient that slotted flaps develop.

If you know (or can reasonably estimate) your model's wing loading in ounces per square foot, and if you calculate your wing's "close" to C_L max., as above, with slotted flaps deployed 20 degrees for takeoff and 40 degrees for landing, Figure 3 of Chapter 3, "Under standing Aerodynamic Formu-las," will provide the means to estimate both landing and takeoff speeds in mph. With the Rn under your belt, select the appropriate Rn curves of your airfoil. Note that Figure 1 offers different curves for different Rn numbers. For E197, lift is little affected, but profile drag increases at low Rn.

SECTION VALUE ADJUSTMENTS

The values in Figure 1 are called "section values" and are for "infinite AR." A model's wing has a "finite" AR and wingtips. In addition, the wing's planform (straight or tapered) has an impact. The formula previously discussed in Chapter 3 will help you to adjust the wing's AoA to provide the lift coefficient selected and compensate for both AR and planform.

Using the data in Figure 1 and noting that the E197 airfoil starts to lift at minus 2 degrees and achieves C_L 1.1 at plus 8 degrees, the section AoA would be 10 degrees. Using an AR of 6 (this depends on your design, of course), the total AoA equals 13.91 degrees. Let's say 14 degrees—less the minus 2 degrees (since it starts lifting at minus 2 degrees), or 12 degrees for the horizontal.

Summary: our AR 6 straight-wing with airfoil E197 would require a 12-degree AoA to achieve C_L 1.1.

The Canada Goose Canard's tricycle landing gear. Propeller clearance on takeoffs and landings is critical for rear-engine canards.

HIGH-LIFT DEVICES

Slotted flaps reduce takeoff and landing AoAs (as shown in Figure 7 of Chapter 3). A 20-degree flap deflection causes a reduction of 1 degree, but for the full 40-degree deflection, it is 4 degrees. Since landings are more critical than takeoffs, use 4 degrees. As one former jet fighter pilot puts it, "Takeoffs are optional; landings are unavoidable."

GROUND EFFECT

This phenomenon starts at half the model's wingspan above the ground (or water) and becomes more intense closer to the ground. Both landings and takeoffs, hence, are made in "ground effect." It acts like a substantial increase in AR. A reduction in the stall AoA and in

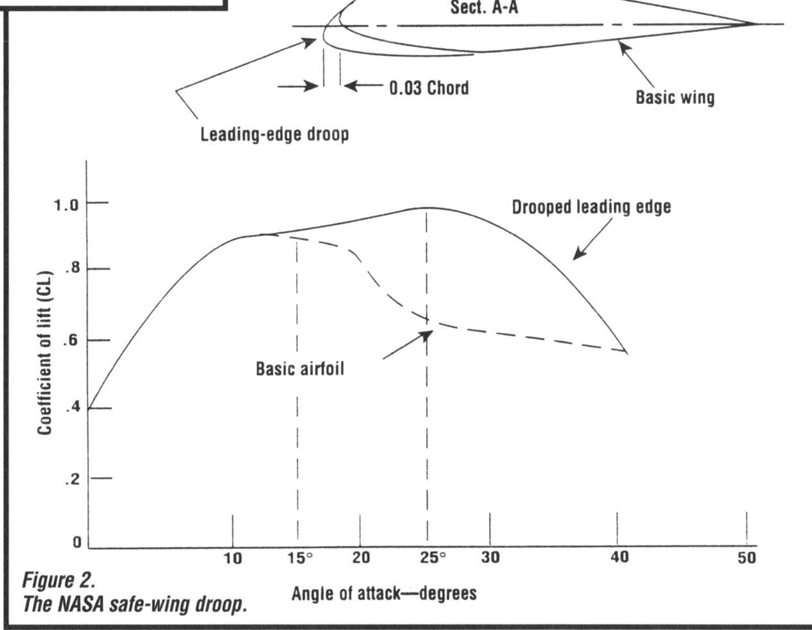

Figure 2. The NASA safe-wing droop.

induced drag results. For a model with a span of 60 inches, *and* with its wing 8 inches above the ground on touchdown *and* AR 6, this reduction would be 10 percent of our 12-degree AoA, or 1.2 degrees.

Using the Swift as an example, the wing's AoA for level flight is zero degrees, so no adjustment for a positive AoA is called for.

NASA SAFE-WING DROOP

This is recommended for sport models (see Figure 2). It delays tip-stalling and provides effective aileron control in the stall. Since the droop occupies 38 percent of the semi-span, it is estimated that it provides a full 4 degrees more in the takeoff/landing AoA.

Summary: the adjusted AoA for C_L 1.1 of airfoil E197 is 12 degrees; slotted flaps reduce this by 4 degrees; ground effect makes a further reduction of 1.2 degrees; and the NASA droop adds 4 degrees for a net AoA of 10.8 degrees.

For the Swift, this was increased slightly to 11 degrees to provide a 2-inch prop-tip ground clearance with a 10-inch-diameter prop. The Swift illustrates the benefit of a high thrust line provided by an inverted engine (see 3-view in Chapter 26). If the engine was upright and still fully cowled, the thrust line would be lowered by roughly 2 inches. A landing gear 2 inches longer, to preserve the 2-inch ground clearance, would be necessary. This could entail a substantial increase in the "tail angle," bringing the wing's AoA to above the stall for takeoffs/landings.

The remedy would be to lower the aft fuselage to reduce the tail angle so as to avoid the stall. This would affect spiral stability as discussed in Chapter 9, "Vertical Tail Design and Spiral Stability." The longer gear would increase both weight and drag.

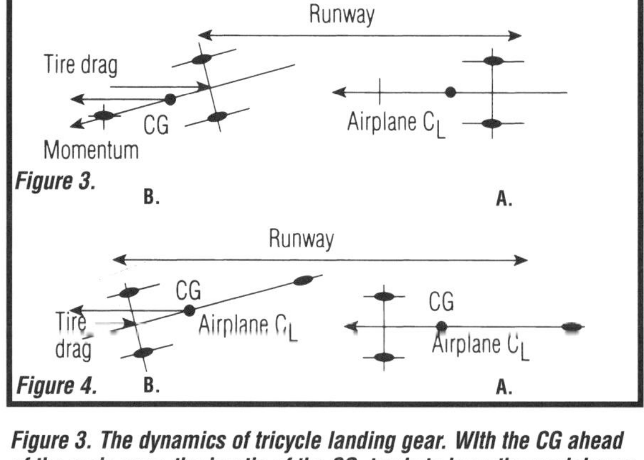

Figure 3. The dynamics of tricycle landing gear. With the CG ahead of the main gear, the inertia of the CG tends to keep the model moving straight forward. Figure 4. The dynamics of tail-dragger landing gear. With the CG behind the main gear, the inertia of the CG tends to exaggerate any divergence from a direct path straight forward.

THE "CRANE" II

The Crane II, a STOL model, had a very nose-high landing posture. It had an 11-inch-diameter variable-pitch prop; full-span LE slots and slotted flaps. Spoilers on the wing's upper surface provided roll control. The horizontal tail had an inverted and LE-slotted lifting airfoil to provide the high tail download that is needed to achieve the very high AoA (20 degrees) provided by the wing's slots and flaps.

The Crane II had a fueled weight of 101.5 ounces and a wing loading of 22.75 ounces/square foot; power was a .45 engine; power loading was 225 ounces per cubic inch or engine displacement (cid).

POWER LOADING

Power loading in ounces per cubic inch of engine displacement is a useful "rule of thumb" for evaluating the weight-to-power relationships of 2-stroke or 4-stroke models, but not 2-stroke versus 4-stroke.

The formula is simple:

$$\frac{1 \times \text{gross weight (oz.)}}{\text{engine cid}} = \text{power loading}$$

A trainer that weighs 80 ounces and is powered by a .40ci 2-stroke engine would have a power loading of 1 divided by .40 x 80 = 200 ounces/cid. The crane's power loading of 225 ounces/cid with a 2-stroke engine shows that it has greater weight for its power than the trainer.

CG AND LANDING GEAR

The CG location, in both the horizontal and vertical senses, is the focus around which the landing-gear geometry is established. For model aircraft, the only cause of a CG shift during flight is the reduction in the weight of the fuel as the flight progresses. For a conventional model, this causes a rearward shift of about 3 percent of the MAC. For a rear-engine canard, the fuel tank is typically behind the CG so that a similar, but forward, CG shift occurs. The vertical CG location is usually "eyeball" estimated. It is better to get it a bit higher than lower.

There are two major types of landing gear:

- **Tricycle.** The CG is ahead of the main wheels, and the nose wheel is steerable.

- **Tail-dragger.** The CG is behind

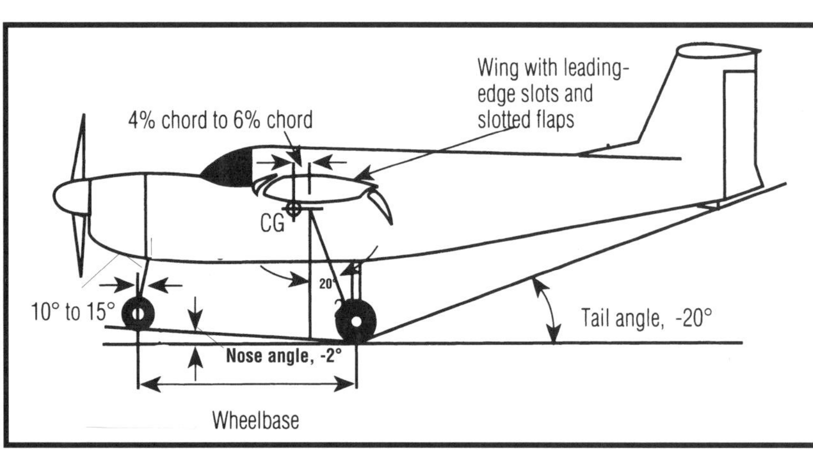

Figure 5.
Fuselage upsweep required to obtain a high tail angle and a short landing gear. This drawing shows the Crane, which was designed by the author.

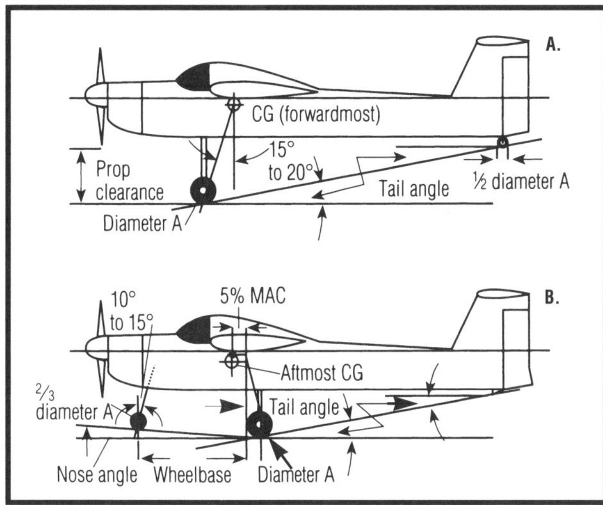

Figure 6.
The geometry of tail-dragger landing-gear design (above) and tricycle landing-gear design.

the main wheels, and the tail wheel is steerable.

Bicycle landing gear is a variant of tricycle gear; a single rear wheel replaces the normal tricycle main wheels; the front wheel is steerable, and tricycle geometry applies.

The single-wheel CG of some sailplanes is a variation on tail-dragger style and geometry. The high tail angle is not needed because there is no prop, and these gliders land in a nearly horizontal attitude.

LANDING-GEAR DYNAMICS

■ **Tricycle gear.** On the landing or takeoff run, tricycle landing gear—with the CG ahead of the main wheels—is self-correcting directionally (see Figure 3). The nosewheel steers, prevents the plane from "nosing over" and protects the propeller.

When a "trike"-geared model tips backward so that the tail skid rests on the ground, the CG rotates with it. If this rotation brings the CG behind the wheel axles, the model will stay tail-down—a most undignified posture! Shifting the landing gear rearward from the CG by 5 percent of the MAC, as shown in Figure 6, prevents this from occurring.

Most trikes sit with their longitudinal center line parallel to the ground. A nose-down angle of 2 to 3 degrees, as shown in Figure 6, is suggested. On landing, after the nose-wheel has made contact with the ground, this nose-down angle will bring the wing close to its angle of zero lift. The model will tend to cling to the ground. The potential for nose-gear damage is reduced, and experience has proved that this nose-down attitude has no adverse effect on takeoffs.

Figure 9 illustrates the trike geometry for a rear-engine canard such as the Canada Goose. Obviously, a very high thrust line is needed to avoid the need for an unduly long landing gear for prop-tip protection. The Swan canard illustrates this point. For such craft, add 5 degrees to the tail angle.

Figure 5 shows how fuselage upsweep may be used to reduce the length of the landing-gear legs for models that require large tail angles, such as the Crane.

This high tail angle moves the wheel axles farther behind the CG and requires heavy up-elevator deflection to rotate the model for takeoff; but as the tail goes down, the wing's lift ahead of the CG aids the model's rotation for quick takeoffs.

■ **Tail-draggers.** As soon as a tail-dragger's speed, on takeoff, permits the tailwheel to lift off, it becomes directionally unstable (Figure 4). The CG wants to get ahead of the main wheels (see "B" of Figure 4). Coarse rudder application is needed for directional control on takeoffs and on landings.

As the tail comes up, propeller torque and gyroscopic precession cause the model to veer. Compensating rudder is applied until the aircraft is just airborne.

If liftoff is forced by heavy up-elevator action, the model has ample dihedral and coarse rudder is still applied, a sudden snap roll may occur. Unless your reflexes are very quick, a damaging and embarrassing crash will occur. It has happened to this author!

Another disadvantage of a tail-dragger is its tendency to nose over, which is hard on props! Moving the wheels farther forward to reduce this tendency aggravates the model's directional instability on the ground. To avoid nosing over, taxiing, particularly on grass, should be done holding full up-elevator.

DETAIL DESIGN

Figure 6 illustrates the procedure for positioning the main landing-gear wheels for both trikes and tail-draggers. Take the tail angle described previously and, on a side view of your design, draw a line *that defines the tail-angle to the horizontal*, originating either at the tailskid or at the tail wheel.

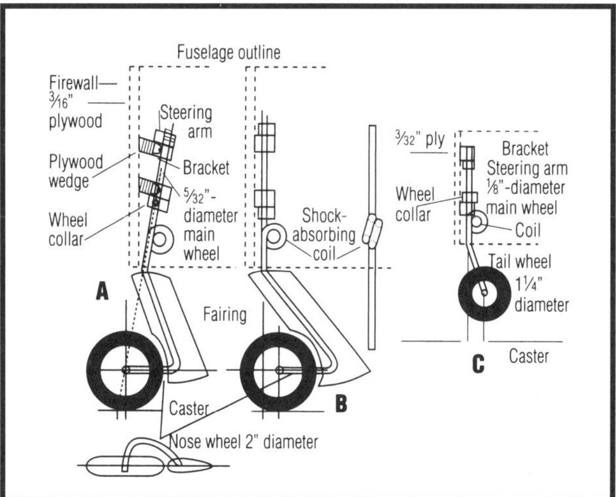

Figure 7.
Nose- and tail-gear detail (two arrangements for a nose wheel and one for a tail wheel).

■ **Tricycle gear.** To prevent the model from sitting back on its tail, follow this procedure. Draw a vertical line through the point that is 5 percent of the MAC behind the CG. Draw a second line through this point that defines the tail angle to the vertical line just drawn (see Figure 1). Notice that this tail angle is the same one as that defined by the line drawn from the wheel to the skid. Where these two tail-angle lines intersect, draw a horizontal line forward to the nose-wheel position, and then draw a short vertical line upward from the same intersection. The main wheel axles should be on the short vertical line, with the wheels' outside diameter resting on the horizontal line. Decide whether a nose-down angle is to be used, and if it is, draw the nose angle at 2 to 3 degrees to the horizontal line. Nose and tail gear will be discussed later.

■ **Tail-dragger.** Draw a line at 15 to 20 degrees from the CG, in front of the vertical, as in Figure 6A. Where the two lines intersect, draw both horizontal and vertical lines. The main wheels' outside diameters should rest on the horizontal line, with their axles on the vertical.

TREAD WIDTH

Both trike and tail-dragger landing gear should have a lateral spacing ("tread width," or the distance between the centerlines of each tire) of 25 percent of the wingspan of an AR 6 wing (see Figure 8).

If the wing has a higher AR, calculate what the span would be for AR 6 with the same area. The formula for AR equals span squared divided by the area. Knowing that the AR is 6, the imaginary span can be easily calculated; the wheel-tread dimension will be 25 percent of that span.

STATIC LOAD SQUAT

Models with music-wire or aluminum landing-gear legs originating in the fuselage and sitting on the ground bearing the model's gross weight (iG) will "squat." For .40 to .50ci-powered models, this squat is about ½ inch and reduces the tail angle for takeoff. To compensate, reduce your landing gear legs' "included angle" (see Figure 8) to lower the wheels and compensate for the squat.

WHEEL DIAMETER

Smaller wheels have less air drag. For paved runways, a 2-inch diameter is the recommended minimum; for grass, a 2¼- to 3-inch diameter is suggested.

NOSE- AND TAIL-WHEEL DESIGN

Steerable nose- or tail-wheel gear should incorporate a modest amount of caster. A modest amount of offset, as in the case of a grocery-cart caster wheel, facilitates steering. Similarly, in the case of landing gear, such gear tracks well and permits easy steering. Too much offset invites "shimmy." An offset of 20 percent of the wheel's diameter is sufficient. Figure 7 illustrates two

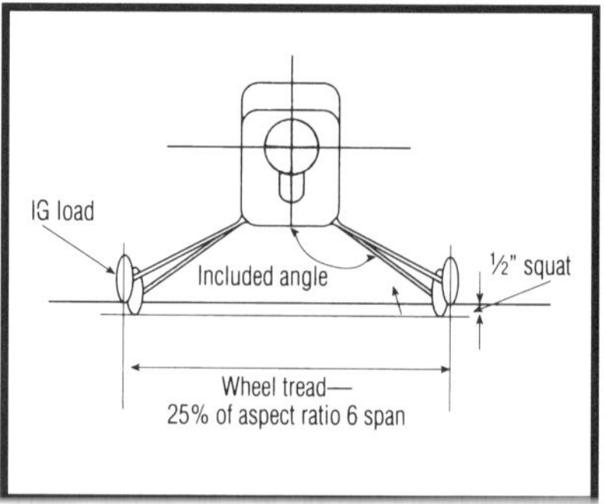

Figure 8.
Wheel tread and squat detail.

nose-wheel arrangements (A and B) and one for a tail wheel (C).

The nose-wheel gear is mounted on the rear surface of the ply engine-mount bulkhead. For a conventional design, this determines the position of the nose gear. For a canard with a rear engine, the nose wheel should be well forward, as in Figure 9. Note that, in Figure 7, A and B, the shock-absorbing coil is totally enclosed in the fuselage to reduce drag.

For tail-draggers, this author prefers a somewhat forward tail-wheel location, with the tail-wheel leg supported internally by nose-wheel brackets bolted to plywood, as in Figure 7C.

MAIN LANDING-GEAR LEGS

Main landing-gear legs should be a continuous piece of metal from wheel to wheel so that bending loads do not have to be absorbed by the fuselage structure, but are contained in the landing-gear legs themselves. ▲

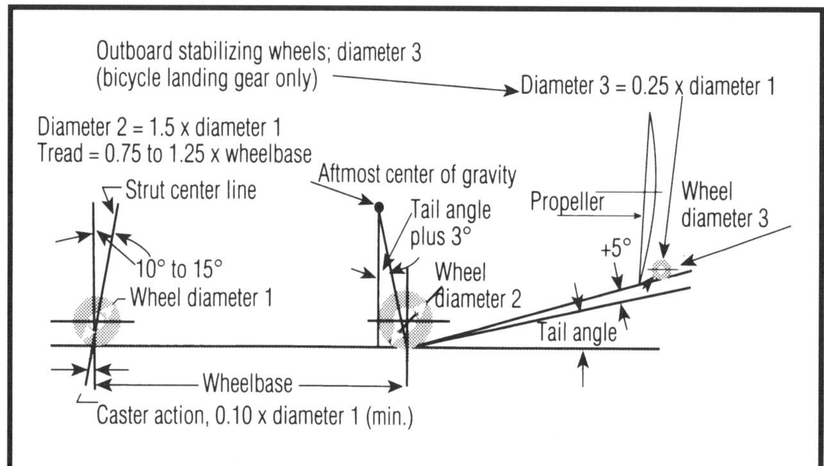

Figure 9.
Layout geometry for tricycle or bicycle landing gear for a pusher canard.

Chapter 17

Ducted-Cowl Design

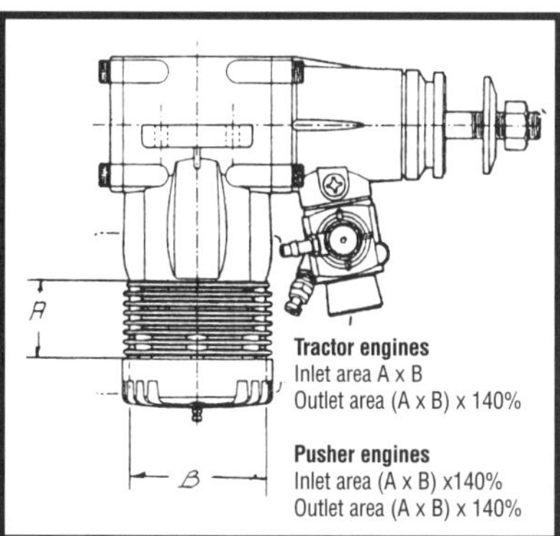

Figure 1. Sizing cooling-air inlets and outlets.

Our model airplane engines, by themselves, are beautiful, powerful examples of precision machining and engine technology.

Hung on the front of a model airplane and left uncowled, they are hideous from a drag point of view. Even when partially cowled but with the cylinder sticking out, they make a model look like a full-scale Cessna 172 with a garbage can above the engine just behind the prop–ugly!

A well-designed cowl greatly reduces drag, improves a model's appearance and actually improves engine cooling. Why are there so few cowled engines among the many models, both kit-built and original designs, at our flying fields? This author surmises that there are three major objections:

■ Removing a cowl to service the engine is a nuisance to be avoided. In most cases, it is necessary to remove the spinner, the prop, the needle-valve needle and up to a half-dozen small, easy-to-lose screws. Replacement reverses this boring sequence.

■ Cowls are difficult to make.

■ Fear that a cowled engine will not be adequately cooled.

The design, construction and fastening of the cowls described in this chapter responds to and overcomes all three objections:

■ The removable portion of each cowl described is almost ridiculously easy both to remove and to replace. Taking off the spinner, the prop and the needle-valve needle is unnecessary, and there are no screws to laboriously unscrew (and lose). The engine is easily accessible for servicing.

■ Such a cowl is easy to make, as this chapter will demonstrate.

■ Cooling is adequate, as proven by test runs on hot summer days at full rpm with the model stationary and consuming full tanks of fuel.

The Swift's cowl; note the jack location.

DUCTED-COWL DESIGN

For minimum drag, the cooling-air entry should be as small as possible, yet large enough for adequate cooling. Bear in mind that only the air that actually contacts the cylinder and muffler does the cooling. Air passing 1 inch away from the cooling fins does nothing.

A good, low-drag cowl design requires:

■ An inlet;

■ an expanding chamber, or "diffuser";

■ the item to be cooled: radiator, or cylinder and muffler;

■ a contracting part, or "nozzle(s)"; and

■ outlet(s) into the passing air stream at point(s) of low air pressure.

Prop-driven air enters the diffuser, slows down, cools the cylinder and muffler, expands because of the heat

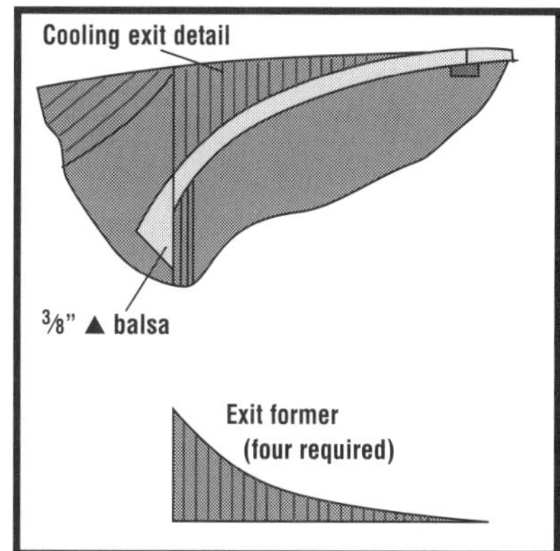

Figure 2. Cowl top view—internal muffler.

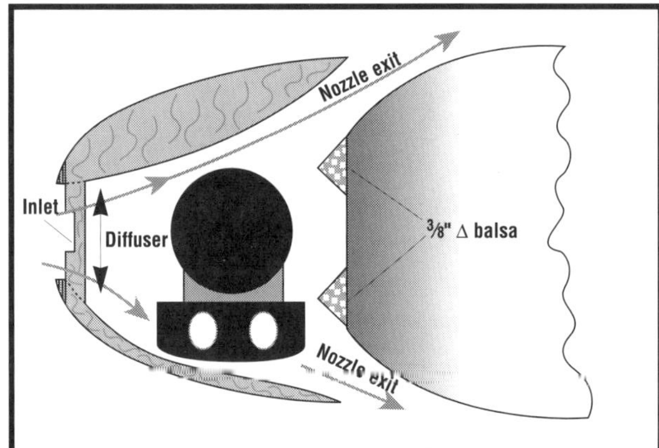

Figure 3.
Cowl section A-A (see also Figure 6—internal muffler).

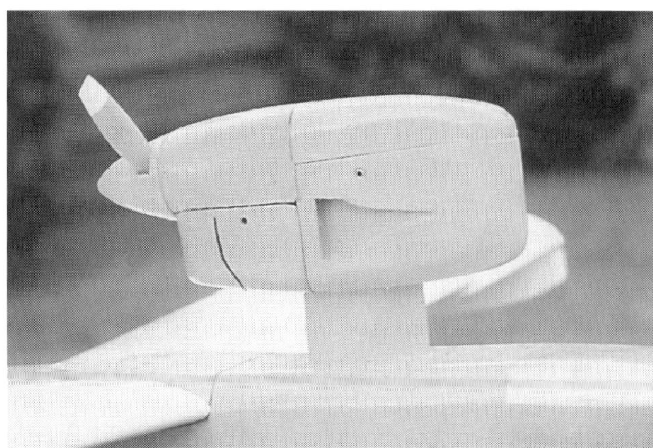

The pusher nacelle on the Seagull III flying boat. The NACA inlet and the outlet below the spinner show.

absorbed, speeds up in the nozzles and exits at considerable velocity. British WW II Hurricane fighters' ducted-engine coolant radiators were based on these principles; they contributed thrust, not drag. The hot, expanded air exiting the duct's nozzle provided some jet-like propulsion. This is not to suggest that these cowl designs will contribute thrust, but there will certainly be substantial drag reduction.

INLET AND OUTLET SIZING—TRACTOR ENGINES

Figure 1 shows the side view of a model engine. An empirical rule of thumb, based on experience, is to provide an air-entry area that's equal to the area of the finned portion of the cylinder, as shown. Whether the opening is round, square, or rectangular makes no difference provided the entry has the area described.

The cooling air exit(s)' rule of thumb is that the total exit area be 140 percent of the entry area. For example: an entry area of 1.25 square inches requires an exit of 1.75 square inches for one, or 0.875 square inch each for two exits.

ENGINE AND ENCLOSED MUFFLER

Figure 3 shows a horizontal cross-section through the Swift's cowl with a muffler. Both the engine and the muffler are wholly enclosed. It has an inlet, a diffuser, a cylinder, muffler and nozzles; and the exits are at points of reduced air pressure on the fuselage sides (they look like gills on a fish!). The fuselage must be widened to accommodate the engine and muffler as in Figure 3.

The "teardrop" fuselage was described in Chapter 12, "Improve Performance by Reducing Drag."

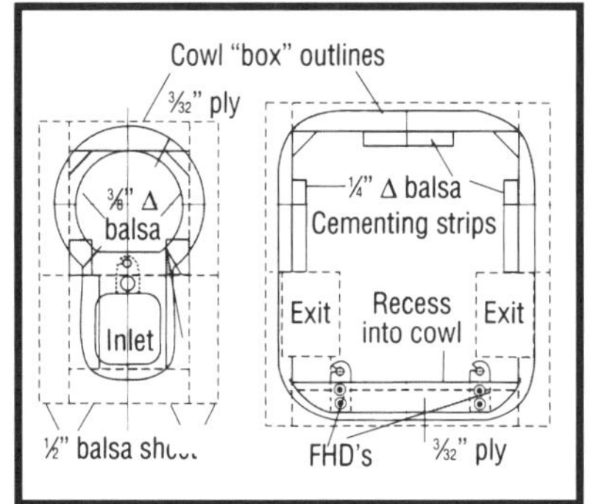

Figure 4.
Spinner ring/entry and rear hold-down detail.

This type of fuselage lends itself to a wider forward section without a drag penalty. Figures 3 and 6 detail the cowl installation.

Exhaust stacks may extend through the cowl, and the necessary holes must be elongated sideways 1/8 inch for cowl removal. They may also end just clear of the inside of the cowl with slightly larger, round holes.

ENGINE AND EXTERNAL MUFFLER

Figure 7 shows the cross-section of a cowl for an engine equipped with a stock muffler. While the muffler (and pressure tubing to the tank) is exposed, its drag is largely overcome by the jet-like exhaust gases squirting backward. With an external muffler, the fuselage may be narrower, as shown.

COWL FASTENING

The removable portion of the cowl is held in position by three "flat hold-downs" (FHDs). One is in the cooling air-entry former in front, and two are at the rear of the cowl (see Figures 4 and 6). All three engage no. 2 shoulder

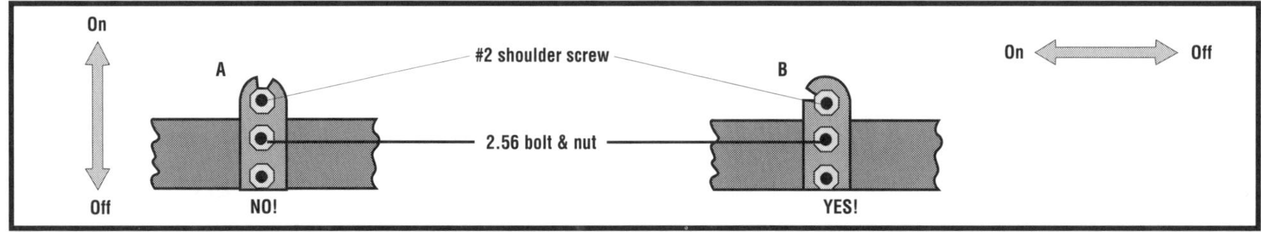

Figure 5 A and B.
Goldberg flat hold-down (FHD) installation.

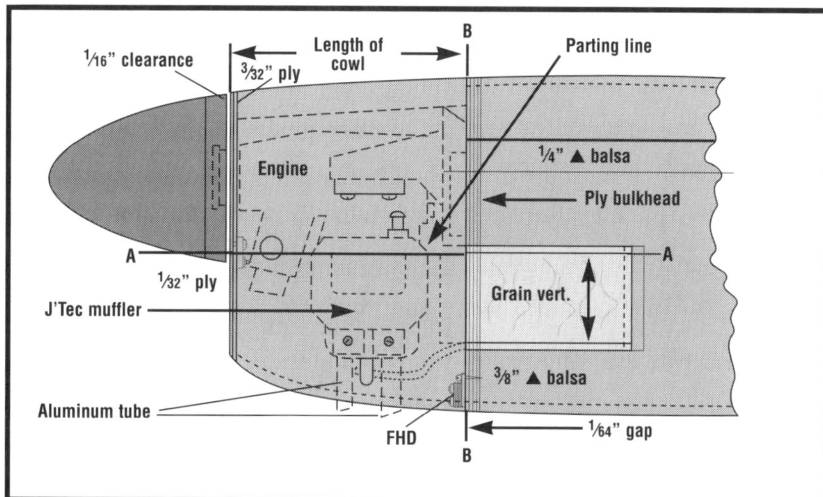

Figure 6.
Cowl side view—tractor engine; internal muffler.

screws; two are screwed into the plywood engine bulkhead, and one into the plywood spinner ring.

Initially, this author used these FHDs as shown in Figure 5A. A knife blade inserted at the parting line and then twisted, detached the cowl. On smaller models, this method was satisfactory. On larger models—and after losing several detachable portions in flight (none was ever found despite lengthy searches)—it was evident that this form of cowl attachment was unsatisfactory. It was belatedly realized that the wrong end of the FHDs was being used, and the arrangement shown in Figure 5B was employed very satisfactorily—no more lost cowls!

A useful byproduct of this change was that removal requires only a sharp knuckle rap on the removable portion's side opposite the muffler. Replacement requires the alignment of the "hooks" on the FHDs with the shoulder screws and a rap on the cowl's muffler side. It is amusing to have a startled onlooker exclaim, "How did you do that!"

CONSTRUCTION HINTS

Over the years, I have designed and built many types of cowl. They ranged from laboriously hollowed-out solid balsa to fiberglass-and-epoxy lay-ups on dissolvable foam mandrels. The ducted-cowl construction described previously has been used on at least seven model designs. The sound-deadening properties of thick balsa sheet are a definite advantage. In this chapter, I will give more details on ducted-cowl construction and also touch on design considerations for a cowl mounted in a pusher configuration.

That portion of the cowl behind the spinner and surrounding the engine crankcase is solidly CA'd to the engine bulkhead. The other, removable, portion surrounds the cylinder. The level of the parting line between these two parts is important. It must be horizontal, and it must separate through the center of the needle-valve needle—either just above or just below it. Obviously, a suitable slot or slots (half above and half below the parting line) is essential to clear the needle.

If an external muffler is used, then suitable cutout(s) must be made to clear the portion from the engine exhaust to the muffler. In Figure 9, note the 1/32-inch plywood parting-line separator that guides the shaping of the cowl both inside and outside. It is firmly cemented to the removable portion of the cowl.

ASSEMBLY AND SHAPING

Photo A shows balsa sheet, tri-stock and plywood components partially assembled into the cowl's two parts. Carefully trim the length of both parts of the cowl's balsa to suit the length of your installation, as shown in Figure 6.

At this stage, the fuselage should be finished (but not covered). Temporarily install the engine (less the needle-valve needle) and muffler on the engine mount so that the cowl can be shaped inside as shown in the photos and drawings. The ply parting-line separator guides this effort. A Dremel sanding drum and drill will do this quickly and easily.

The cowl structure around the crankcase requires only minor internal contouring to clear the muffler; the removable portion needs considerably more internal shaping to clear the cylinder and muffler.

The three flat hold-downs are both CA'd and bolted (2-56 bolts

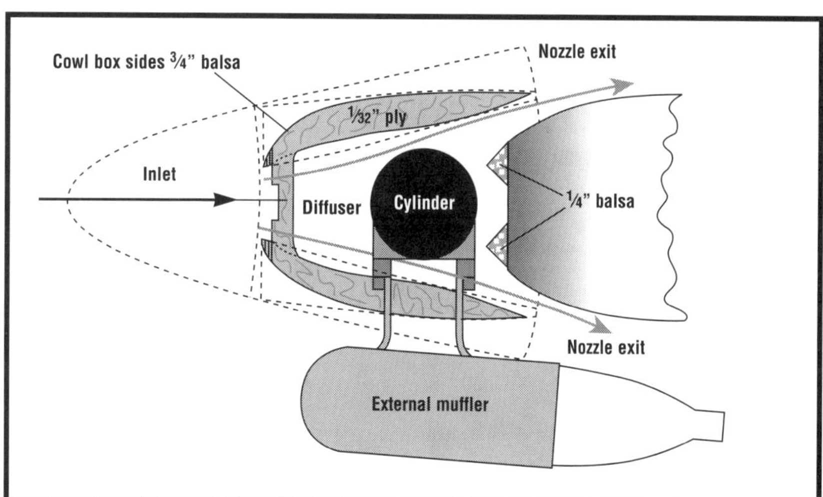

Figure 7.
Cowl section A-A; external muffler.

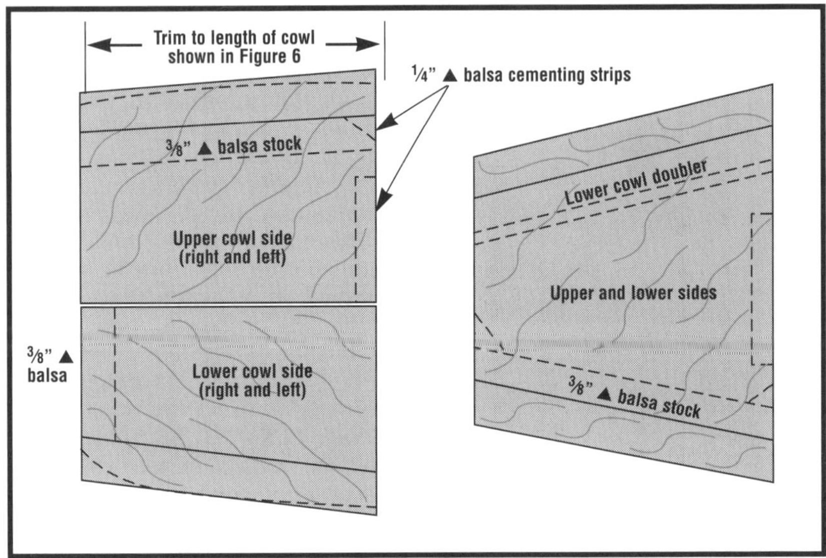

Figure 8.
Cowl box detail; 1/2-inch balsa sheet; internal muffler.

and nuts) to their plywood parts. (Note the bolt-orientation nuts inside.) File the round bolt heads level with the bottom of the screwdriver slot after they've been installed in the plywood.

Install and lightly tack-glue the cowl "box" to the engine bulkhead as shown in Photo B, with the spinner ring cooling-air entry assembly cemented to both portions of the cowl.

Using an old spinner backplate of the correct size, clamp the box into position by installing the prop nut and washer, putting a 3/32-inch balsa-sheet spacer between the spinner backplate and the ply spinner ring.

Shape and sand the outside surfaces to match the spinner; the cooling-air entry plywood parting line; the 1/32-inch ply separator and the fuselage contour, as shown in Photo C.

Next, remove the cowl and take the engine and muffler off the motor mount. Epoxy the rear FHD ply assembly in the removable portion of the cowl as shown in the photo. This requires some trimming of both the ply and the balsa. Note that the open side of all three FHD's "hooks" should face away from the muffler side.

Now clamp the cowl into position as you did before, carefully aligning it with the spinner and fuselage. Through the air-entry hole, using the rear flat hold-downs as guides, mark the positions of the no. 2 shoulder screws on the engine bulkhead. Remove the cowl, drill 1/16-inch holes in the bulkhead, put some CA in the holes, and install the two screws.

Photo B.
The cowl "box" has been clamped into position for external shaping.

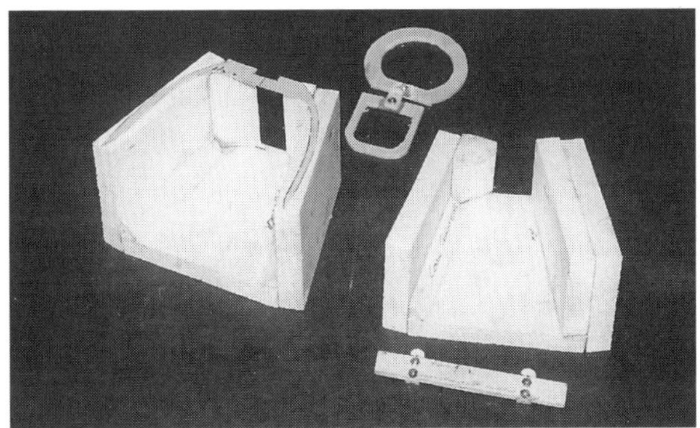

Photo A.
Cowl components are shown partly assembled.

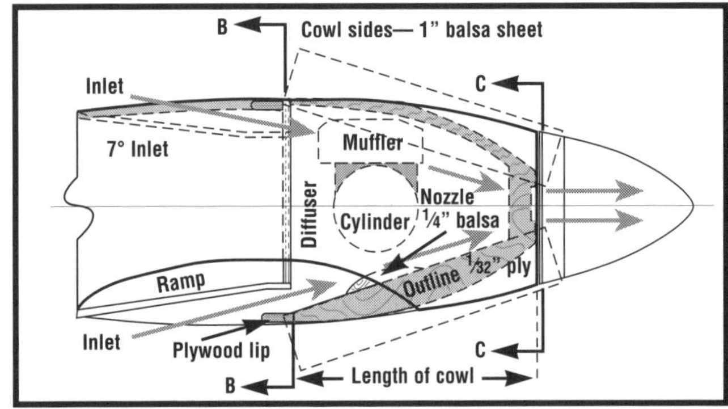

Figure 9.
Top view of pusher engine cowl.

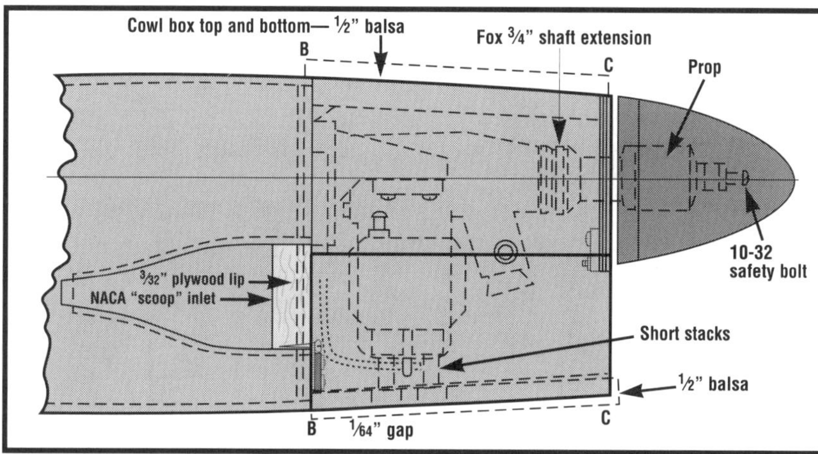

Figure 10.
Side view of pusher engine cowl.

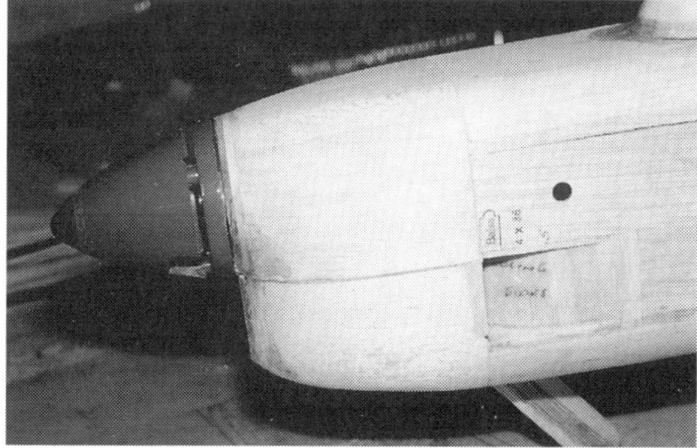

Photo C.
The shaped and sanded cowl. The upper portion has been CA'd to the engine-mount bulkhead.

Permanently install the engine and muffler, connect the carb-to engine-servo linkage, replace the needle-valve needle, install the fuel and muffler pressure tubing from the engine to the fuel tank, and connect the glow-plug clip to the glow plug.

Solidly CA the fixed portion to the engine bulkhead, and clamp the whole cowl into position as before, as shown in Photo C. In Photo D, both parts are ready for painting. The engine's accessibility is evident.

GLOW-PLUG ENERGIZING

With the engine enclosed, the glow plug is energized by means of a two-conductor, closed-circuit type, Radio Shack phone jack. To energize the plug, a mating, ⅛-inch, Radio Shack plug is wired to the external power source and inserted into the jack. This is a major safety feature because the jack may be located well away from that deadly, rotating prop for plug removal. Figure 6 details the bronze glow-plug clip that's easily disengaged from the glow plug when plug replacement is necessary.

The jack is mounted through a 7⁄32-inch-diameter hole in a small square of 1⁄16-inch plywood. Both are epoxied to the inside fuselage wall so that the jack's knurled nut projects through a 5⁄16-inch-diameter hole in that wall. Figures 12, 13 and 15 provide a wiring diagram and engine-servo detail for an "onboard" glow-plug energizing system that heats the plug in flight, but only at low rpm. The system ensures a reliable idle, particularly for 4-stroke engines.

ENGINE PRIMING

Priming a fully cowled engine is easy. Invert the model on your field box to bring the engine upright. With a squirt bottle, inject a few drops of fuel into the carburetor. If the carb is closed, the carb entry forms a small cup which, when filled, provides adequate priming. The cooling-air entry hole permits this method of priming without

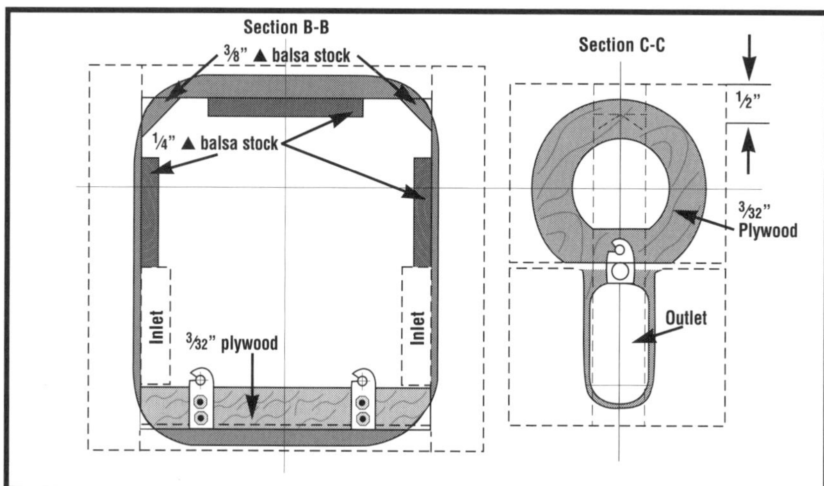

Figure 11.
Pusher engine cowl sections and hold-down detail (see Figure 10).

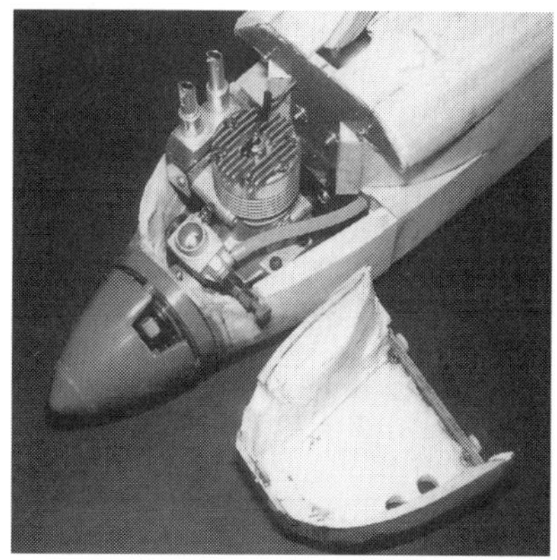

Photo D.
This cowl detail shows that servicing the engine is easy.

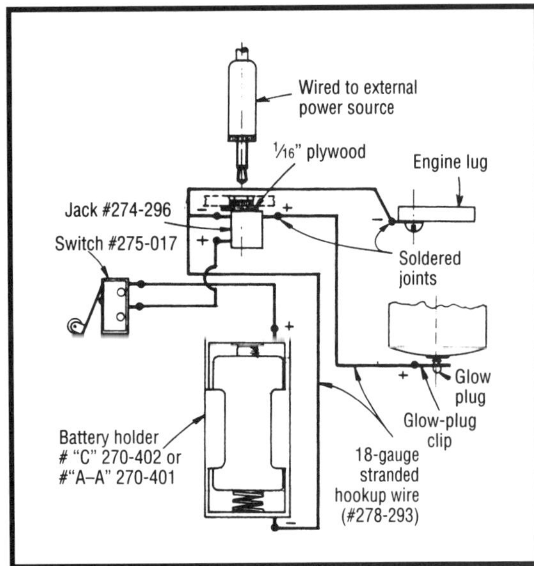

Figure 12.
Onboard glow-plug wiring diagram.

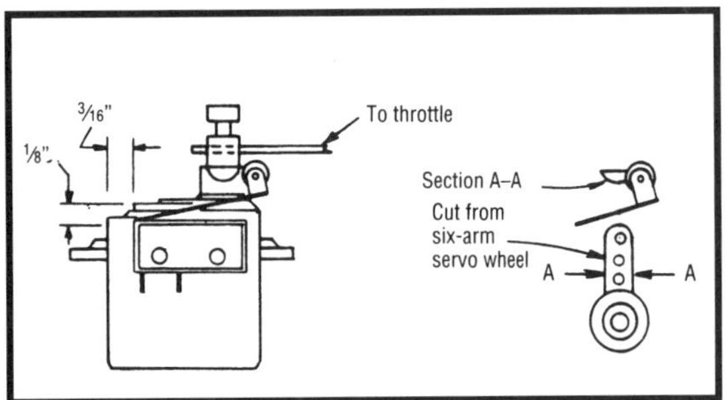

Figure 13.
Small engine servo (Futuba S33-S133).

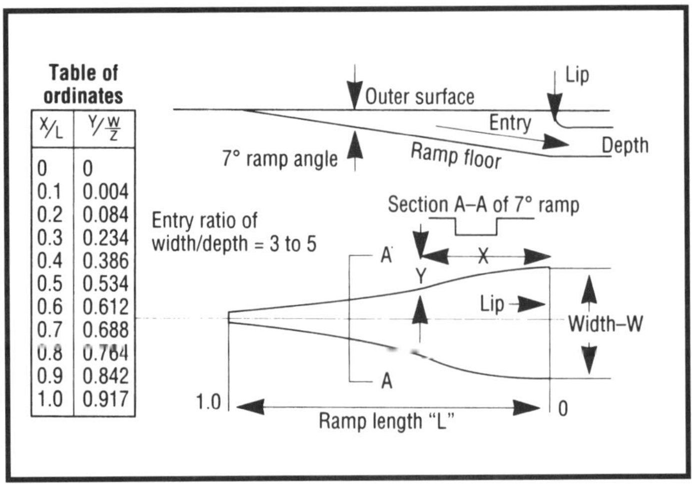

Table of ordinates

X/L	Y/(W/2)
0	0
0.1	0.004
0.2	0.084
0.3	0.234
0.4	0.386
0.5	0.534
0.6	0.612
0.7	0.688
0.8	0.764
0.9	0.842
1.0	0.917

Figure 14.
Details and ordinates of NACA submerged intake.

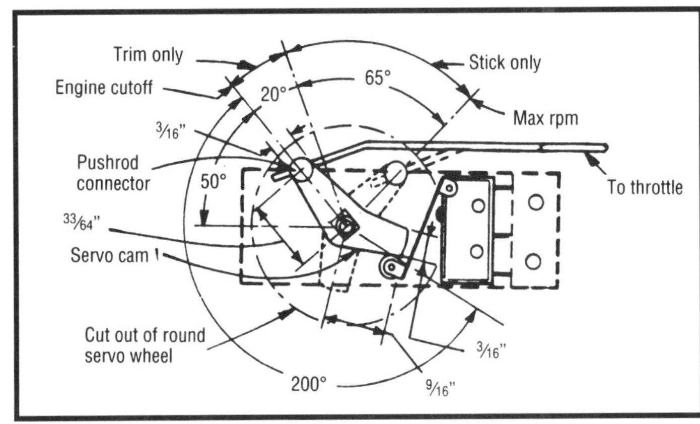

Figure 15.
Engine servo lengthwise in fuselage.

cowl removal. If, after a flight, the engine is stopped by closing the carb, subsequent engine starts don't require priming. To avoid "hydraulic lock"—having fuel trapped between the piston and the cylinder head—apply your electric starter with the model inverted (engine upright).

PUSHER ENGINE INSTALLATIONS

Figures 9, 10 and 11 show the pusher installation of the Seagull III—a flying boat. The engine sits in a nacelle above the hull.

For improved streamlining, a 3/4-inch crankshaft extension was used, as shown in Figure 12. An enclosed muffler is mandatory, because the external muffler would exhaust the wrong way, facing forward, and it could not be reversed, because that would foul the prop and prevent the propeller from rotating.

Cooling air enters the cowl through two, NACA-developed, low-drag, submerged air intakes recessed into the nacelle (or fuselage) sides ahead of the engine bulkhead. The combined areas of these intakes is the cylinder area described in Figure 1 plus 40 percent. The exit slot under the spinner has the same total area as the entries. The rotating prop "sucks" cooling air out of this cooling slot.

Construction, shaping and fastening the removable portion and glow-plug energizing are identical to the tractor installation.

NACA COOLING-INLET DESIGN

Figure 14 shows how to develop the shape of the NACA submerged intake. Note the intake width-to-depth ratio and the ramp floor at 7 degrees to the outside surface.

Over the years, I've used pusher engines cowled as described on five models. Cooling problems have not occurred.

Throughout this chapter, illustrations and photos show inverted engines (author's addiction). For upright installations, simply turn the photos and drawings upside-down! ▲

Chapter 18

Propeller Selection and Estimating Level Flight Speeds

The wide variety of propeller makes, shapes, materials, diameters and pitches available today can be somewhat confusing. The choice of a prop to suit your model, its engine and your style of flying requires some understanding of how a propeller functions. It also requires an appraisal of the weight, wing area and aerodynamic drag of your airplane and of the power loading of the model—plus some insight into its engine's power characteristics.

In addition, the propeller's high-speed rotation leads to effects that every modeler should be aware of. These are:

- Slipstream;
- asymmetrical blade effect;
- propeller pitching moment;
- torque; and
- gyroscopic precession.

This chapter will cover these points and help to narrow propeller choice for a given model to one or two diameters and pitches.

PROPELLER ACTION

A propeller generates thrust by forcing a column of air backward—called the "slipstream" as in Figure 1. In the slipstream, the air's velocity is increased above the aircraft's forward speed, and its pressure is reduced. In addition, a substantial part of this increase occurs ahead of the propeller. This slipstream swirls around the fuselage in the same direction as the propeller rotation.

A PAIR OF WINGS

A two-blade "prop" is actually a pair of small wings; each has an airfoil cross-section that is thick close to the hub for strength and rigidity, and that tapers to the tips. These small airfoils have all the characteristics of a wing's airfoil. They have:

- A chord line;
- an angle of zero lift;
- a stalling angle;
- increasing profile and induced drags as their AoA increases;
- a pitching moment; and
- upwash ahead, and wake and downwash behind the blades.

Propeller blades differ from the wing's airfoil in that they operate at much higher speeds than the wing. A 12-inch-diameter propeller that advances 5 inches per revolution and turns at 10,000rpm has a tip speed of 360mph, while the model it propels flies at only 47mph.

A wing normally flies at the same speed across its span. A propeller, however, operates at different speeds: high at the tip and progressively slower from tip to root. At half its diameter, its speed is half that at the tip. Stresses on the propeller are high, particularly at its center. These stresses result from a combination of centrifugal and thrust forces, plus the blade's airfoil pitching moment trying to twist them.

DIAMETER AND PITCH

Propellers are sized in both diameter and pitch in inches. Diameter is simply the length of the prop, tip to tip. It identifies the size of the imaginary cylinder in which the prop rotates and advances. Increasing the diameter increases the load

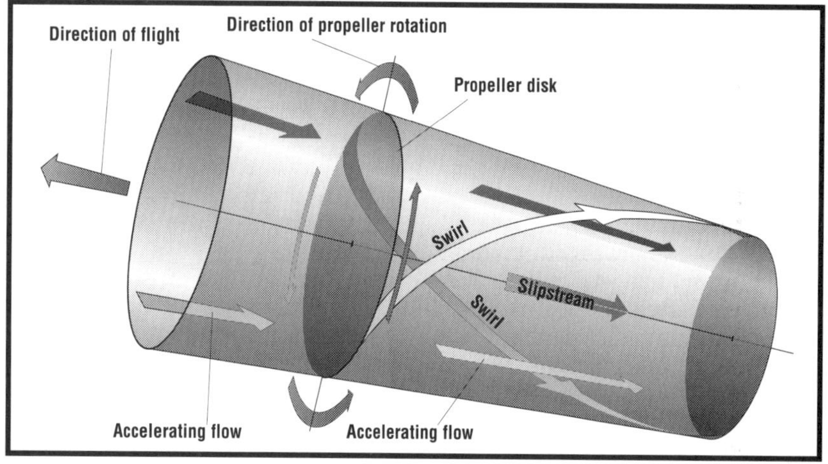

Figure 1.* *The propeller's action.

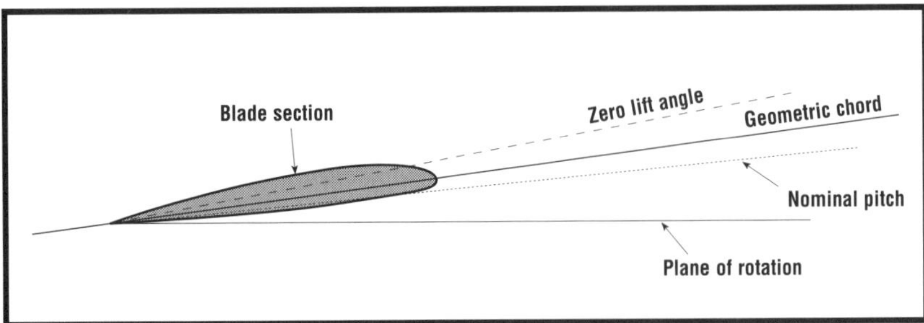

Figure 2.
Propeller pitches.

on the engine and reduces its rpm.

For each prop diameter, there are several different pitches available. For example, a 10-inch-diameter prop is typically offered in pitches from 6 inches to 10 inches. The higher the pitch, theoretically, the greater the advance per revolution, and the higher the engine load—again, reducing its rpm.

Thus, both diameter and pitch must be considered in propeller selection. For high-speed flight, reduced diameter and increased pitch apply; for slower flight, increased diameter and lower pitch prevails.

There are several variations for a given pitch dimension, as follows (see Figure 2).

■ The "nominal pitch" is measured across the flat back surface of the blade—usually measured at 75 percent of the diameter. This is what you buy!

■ The "geometric pitch" is measured across the airfoil's chord line.

■ The "true pitch" is the actual distance the prop advances per revolution. The difference between geometric and true pitch angles is the AoA at which the prop airfoil is truly operating and is called the propeller "slip."

PROPELLER AS AIRSCREW

A propeller has much in common with a screw. In fact, they are frequently called "airscrews." A screw being turned in a threaded hole will always advance its full pitch for each revolution. A propeller "screws" into air that is fluid. The advance per revolution is not fixed. A heavy model with high air drag and in a steep climbing attitude will offer high resistance. Under these conditions, the propeller must operate at higher AoAs or slip, with increased profile and induced drags. This reduces the engine's rpm. It should be noted that, while pitch is a major factor in speed, a plane obviously can't fly faster in level flight than a speed that is close to that permitted by its geometric pitch multiplied by the rpm.

In a dive, with the engine at full rpm, the actual advance per revolution may increase to a point where the prop's airfoil is operating at a very low or a negative AoA. The profile and induced drag reduce substantially, the prop "unloads" and the engine over-revs—which does it no good! Experienced fliers throttle back in dives for this reason.

CONSTANT-PITCH PROPELLERS

Each point on a propeller blade—rotating and simultaneously advancing—describes a helix inside an imaginary cylinder. Consider one blade advancing one revolution; imagine cutting the cylinder lengthwise down one side, from start to finish of that one revolution. Imagine opening and flattening it.

Figure 3 shows this flattened cylinder along with the geometric and actual pitches and blade cross-sections at 100 percent, 75 percent, 50 percent and 25 percent of the blade's length.

Note how the geometric angle of the blade varies from tip to root so that there is a constant AoA. Calling such a prop "constant pitch" is a bit of a misnomer; the blade is obviously twisted. "Constant angle of attack" is more accurate.

To calculate the propeller's speed at any point along its length is easy. Take the prop tip in Figure 3; in one revolution, it moves from A to B; AB is the hypotenuse of a right-angle triangle. Recalling high school geometry: "the square of the hypotenuse of a right triangle is equal to the sum of the square of the other two sides." In formula form and Figure 3:

$$AB = \sqrt{(AC^2 + BC^2)}$$

A 12-inch-diameter prop, advancing 5 inches per revolution, would have a hypotenuse of:

$$\sqrt{(12 \times 3.1416)^2 + 5^2}$$

or 38.02 inches.

Tip speed for this prop turning at 10,000rpm would be:

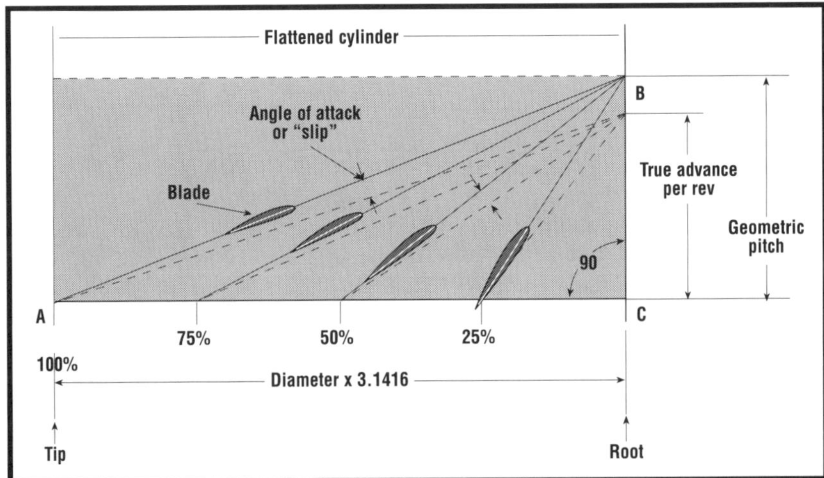

Figure 3.
"Constant pitch" propeller.

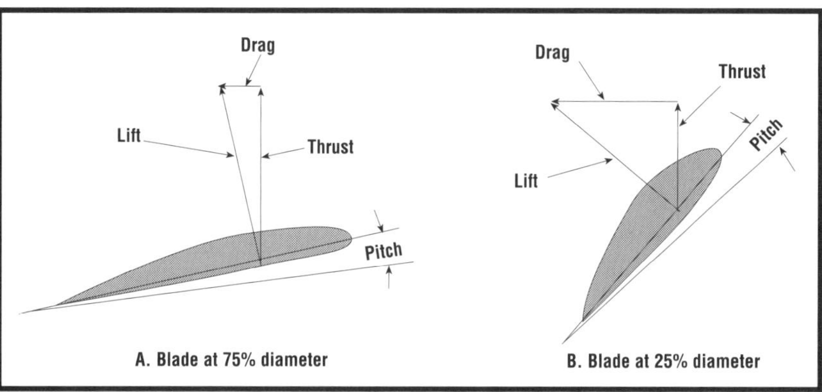

Figure 4.
Lift, drag and thrust vectors at 75% and 25% diameters.

$$\frac{38.02 \text{ in.} \times 10{,}000\text{rpm} \times 60 \text{ min./hr.}}{12 \text{ in./ft.} \times 5{,}280 \text{ ft./mi.}}$$

or 360.12mph.

At 50 percent of the blade length, the speed would be 50 percent of 360.12mph or 180.06mph. Those blades are lethal; take care!

Figure 4 shows blade cross-sections at 75 percent (A) and 25 percent (B) of the blade length from the hub. Both are operating at the same AoA. Note that at 25 percent, because of the blade angle, the lift is more inclined, the drag vector is increased and the thrust vector is reduced in comparison with the 75-percent point. This inner portion is less efficient, and from 25 percent to the prop center only worsens. A spinner of roughly 25 percent of the prop's diameter would cover this portion and would smooth out the airflow moving backward. For a 10-inch-diameter prop, a 2½-inch-diameter spinner does just that.

In Figure 4B, the higher blade angle, reduced thrust and increased drag reflect the effect of higher pitches for the prop as a whole. The increased drag reduces engine rpm; lower diameters are indicated. The reverse is also true; lower pitches with larger diameters.

THE AIRPLANE

The design of the model has a major bearing on the selection of its propeller diameter and pitch. The factors are:

■ **The weight and wing loading.** The heavier the model, for a given area, the higher its wing loading in ounces per square foot of wing area and the faster it must fly in level flight (or at higher AoA with higher drag).

Most models, in level flight, fly at C_L of 0.2 to 0.3. If you know the model's weight and calculate its wing area in square feet, its wing loading is easy to arrive at. Figure 5 provides a quick way to estimate the model's flight speed. Say the model's wing loading is 20 ounces per square foot; reading upward from 20 to C_L 0.2 and 0.3, level flight speeds are, on the left, 40 to 48mph. These speeds are minimums; something more is required for climbing and other maneuvers. Adding 25 percent gives speeds of 50 to 60mph and a mean speed of 55mph.

Now refer to Figure 15 (page 89): the rpm/pitch/speed nomograph. Place a straightedge at 55mph in the central, level-flight-speed column, and read off the static rpm and corresponding pitches that will provide 55mph. For example: a 7-inch pitch at 7,000rpm or an 8.5-inch pitch at 6,000rpm both provide 55mph.

The nomograph in Figure 15 is based on a 10-percent increase over the nominal pitch advance per rev and on a gain of 10 percent in engine revolutions as the prop "unloads" from a static position at high AoAs to the level flight speed at much lower AoAs. This graph will enable you to arrive at a reasonably close estimate of your model's top speed, based on the engine's static max rpm and its prop's nominal pitch. These results will never be 100 percent accurate, as the model's weight and drag will have an unavoidable impact, but they are close enough for all practical purposes.

■ **The model's aerodynamic drag.** A "clean" model such as the Swift will offer much less air resistance than one with an exposed engine, large flat windshield, large round or rectangular (in cross-section) wheels, unfaired landing-gear legs, dowels and rubber bands for wing-to-fuselage attachment, and other "built-in headwinds."

Parasite drag increases in proportion to the square of the speed. Doubling the speed results in a fourfold drag increase. High drag means increased "slip" (the prop will operate at higher AoAs) and rpm and flying speed will suffer adversely. Lower pitches and larger diameters are appropriate. While Figure 15 does not reflect the impact of high drag, it will put you "in the ballpark" as far as rpm and pitch are concerned.

■ **The weight-to-power ratio, or power loading.** A large engine powering a small, light model will obviously outperform a heavier, larger model powered by a smaller engine.

With the large variety of both models and engines available, some

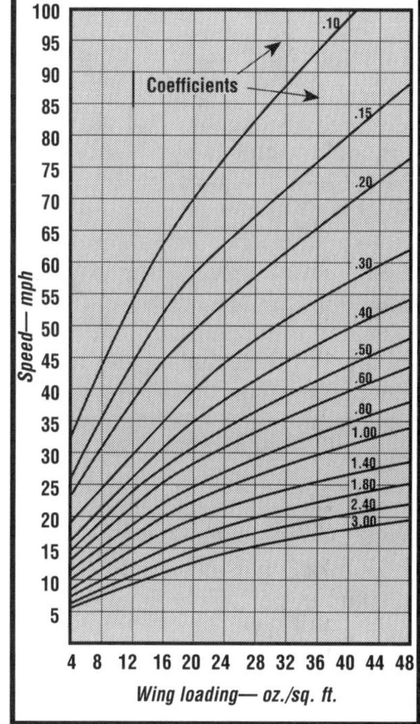

Figure 5.
Nomograph for quick determination of wing loading, lift and speed.

simple way of establishing the "weight-to-power ratio" is needed to permit ready comparisons. One way is to calculate what the weight in ounces would be if both engine and model were scaled up (or down) in proportion to 1 cubic inch of engine displacement (cid). For example, the Swift is powered by an O.S. Max .46 SF engine, and weighs, fueled, 92 ounces. Its weight-to-power ratio is 92/0.46, or 200 ounces per cid.

Another example is of a model weighing 300 ounces, powered by a 1.2ci engine. Its power loading is 300/1.2, or 250 ounces per cid. This comparison has obvious limitations. It assumes that power output of various sizes and makes of engines is proportional to their displacements—this assumption isn't too far off the mark. It's invalid for comparing 2-stroke with 4-stroke engines. Each class must be separately evaluated, e.g., 2-strokes should be compared with 2-strokes and 4 strokes with 4-strokes. Experience indicates that 2-stroke models with a 200-ounce per cid power loading that are well "propped" will have excellent performance. Higher power loadings, up to 300 ounces per cid, will result in diminished, but still acceptable, performance.

■ **The type of performance desired.** In designing a model, selecting a kit to build, or choosing a model to scratch-build from magazine plans, the modeler has performance objectives in mind that probably reflect his or her flying skills. The design goal may range from a slow, stable, easy-to-fly airplane (for a beginner) to a fast, high-powered, aerobatic model (for the expert). For the beginner, low wing loadings and a higher weight-to-power ratio of 275 to 300 ounces per cid would be in order.

At the other end of the scale, consider the Swift. Designed as a sport model with a wing loading of 22 ounces per square foot of wing area, a power loading of 200 ounces per cid and with the least drag that could be reasonably expected—short of retracts—it is fast, maneuverable and fun! It has flown with two propellers. The first, a 10x9, has a static rpm of 12,000. The second, a 10x10 (a "square" prop) turns 11,000rpm static.

From Figure 15, level flight speeds are estimated to be 125 and 130mph—very close! This model's vertical performance is that of a "homesick angel"; it performs vertical 8s with ease and grace.

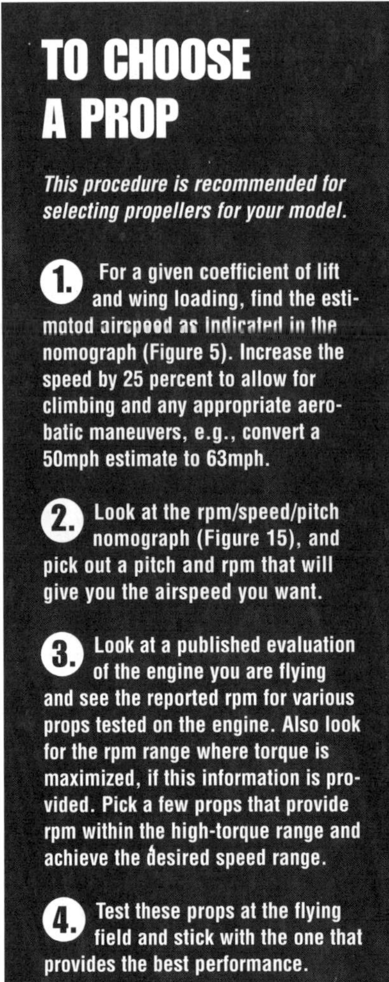

TO CHOOSE A PROP

This procedure is recommended for selecting propellers for your model.

1. For a given coefficient of lift and wing loading, find the estimated airspeed as indicated in the nomograph (Figure 5). Increase the speed by 25 percent to allow for climbing and any appropriate aerobatic maneuvers, e.g., convert a 50mph estimate to 63mph.

2. Look at the rpm/speed/pitch nomograph (Figure 15), and pick out a pitch and rpm that will give you the airspeed you want.

3. Look at a published evaluation of the engine you are flying and see the reported rpm for various props tested on the engine. Also look for the rpm range where torque is maximized, if this information is provided. Pick a few props that provide rpm within the high-torque range and achieve the desired speed range.

4. Test these props at the flying field and stick with the one that provides the best performance.

ENGINES

Today's model aircraft engines are fine examples of modern engine technology and precision machining. Most are "over square"—the bore diameter is larger than the stroke. This author prefers 2-stroke engines because they're simpler, more rugged, lighter, more powerful and less costly than the 4-stroke versions of the same displacement.

Engine-evaluation articles, such as those by David Gierke and Mike Billinton in *Model Airplane News,* and Clarence Lee in *R/C Modeler,* provide performance data on currently available engines and insight into their design and construction. They provide tabulations of static rpm of an engine while it is powering various diameters and pitches of propellers. Table 1 shows Billinton's recording of rpm for the Fox Eagle 74 *(Model Airplane News,* October '91) and Table 2 shows that of Lee for this engine *(R/C Modeler,* March '91). In addition, Billinton provides performance curves of the 74 in Figure 7. Note that with silencer and standard .330 carb, the brake horse-power (b.hp) peaks at 15,000rpm, and the maximum torque is in the 7,000 to 11,000rpm range.

Data of this type—and the engine manufacturers' recommendations—provide very useful guides in selecting the diameter to match the pitch and rpm determined from Figures 5 and 15.

MATCH THE PROP

As previously noted, for a 20-ounces-per-square-foot wing loading, a 55mph speed is indicated, and a 6-inch pitch prop turning 8,000rpm is one possible selection. Look at Table 1 (Figure 6) for the Fox Eagle 74. A 15-inch diameter by 8-inch pitch prop would turn at around 8,000rpm. Figure 7 indicates that these rpm aren't too far off the peak of the torque curve for this engine. Another choice could be a 12x10 prop also turning in the 9,000rpm range. Like low gears on a car, the lower pitch of 6 inches would provide quicker acceleration and better climb, but lower top speed.

TOOLS

There are two items of equipment every serious modeler should possess. First is a photocell tachometer, either digital or analog, to measure the static rpm of your engine. It is useful to compare the performance of props of various diameters and pitches with the published data as described above. These tachometers may be used safely from behind the prop, and they aren't expensive. The second tool is a propeller balancer, the type with two sets of overlapping, free-turning disks. Balance every prop—you'll be surprised how many require balancing—to avoid vibration. On reinforced plastic props, a coat of silver

TABLE 1

Prop diameter, pitch and make	RPM
18x8 Top Flite	5,190
15x8 Graupner	7,700
15x8 APC	8,030
16x5 Zinger	8,078
14x8 APC	9,180
13x6 MK	11,040
12x6 APC	12,814
11x5 Top Flite	13,960

Mike Billinton's evaluation of the Fox Eagle 74 with various names, diameters and pitches of propellers.

TABLE 2

Prop diameter and pitch	RPM
11x8	12,200
11x10	10,900
12x6	12,100
12x8	11,000
12x10	9,000
13x6	12,450
14x6	10,150

Clarence Lee's evaluation of the Fox Eagle 74 with various diameters and pitches of Zinger props.

Figure 6.

paint (after a gentle surface roughing with fine sandpaper for better paint adherence) will aid the photocell to "see" the prop. Any imbalance is easily corrected by adding paint to the lighter blade.

All this will narrow the choice to two or three props. However, there is just no substitute for actual flight tests in your final selection to obtain the performance sought and the optimum output of prop and engine.

PROPELLER MATERIALS

Props are available in wood, nylon and reinforced plastics. This author favors the reinforced plastic props because of their ruggedness and efficiency, even though they weigh roughly twice the weight of their wooden equivalents. Avoid unreinforced nylon props; they lack enough rigidity for use during high power.

PROPELLER EFFECTS

■ **Slipstream.** The slipstream (see Figure 1) moves as a helix rotating around the airplane in the same direction as the propeller's rotation, but at higher than flight speed. It strikes body, wing and tail surfaces at angles and increases the drag of any obstacle in its path. Its most unfavorable impact is on the vertical tail surface—it causes yawing that calls for rudder-trim correction.

The increase in the velocity of the oncoming relative wind (i.e., ahead of the prop) reduces the prop's effective pitch, as does one blade's downwash on the next. Such downwash further reduces the prop's efficiency. The situation is made worse with three or more blades. For model airplanes, such multi-blade props aren't recommended, except for scale models of aircraft so equipped.

In full-scale aircraft, multi-blade props are used to absorb the high power of modern piston and turboprop engines. They also reduce the propeller's diameter so as to avoid compressibility effects from tip speeds close to the speed of sound. The loss of efficiency in this reduction must be accepted.

■ **Asymmetric blade effect.** When the plane of the propeller is inclined to the direction of flight as in Figure 8, the advancing blade operates at a higher AoA than the retreating blade. Thrust on the advancing side is higher than on the retreating side. This causes a pitching or yawing couple.

■ **Pitching moment.** When the thrust line is tilted as in Figure 9, a vector is introduced that causes a pitching moment. It may combine with the asymmetric blade effect.

■ **Torque.** The resistance to rotation caused by the prop's drag tries to rotate the whole airplane in the opposite direction. This is particularly true in a steep climbing attitude at low forward speed and maximum rpm where the prop is operating at high AoAs, such as just after liftoff. A touch of opposite aileron input may be needed to off set the torque.

■ **Gyroscopic precession.** Like a gyroscope, a rotating propeller resists any effort to change the direction of its axis. The heavier the propeller and the higher the rpm, the greater this resistance. If a force is applied to tilt the plane of the prop's rotation, it is *"precessed" 90 degrees onward, in the direction of the prop's rotation.*

This effect shows up markedly on tail-dragger takeoffs if the tail is lifted too soon and too high. Precession causes a yaw to the left (for props rotating clockwise, viewed from behind) that could result in a ground loop unless corrected by rudder action.

The author's flying-boat design, Seagull III, was initially flown with a Graupner llx8 prop that was mounted in a pusher configuration with the propeller's plane of rotation directly over the CG (the thrust line was 6 inches above that CG). Coming out of a left-hand turn, the model would enter an uncommanded, gentle right-hand turn, nosing down slightly. It was easily corrected, but annoying. Replacing the Graupner (an excellent prop) with a Zinger wooden equivalent of half the Graupner's weight eliminated this peculiarity.

NOISE

Many clubs are experiencing problems because of noise that originates from two sources: the engine itself and the propeller. Engine mufflers and tuned pipes now available go a long way to reduce engine noise to acceptable levels.

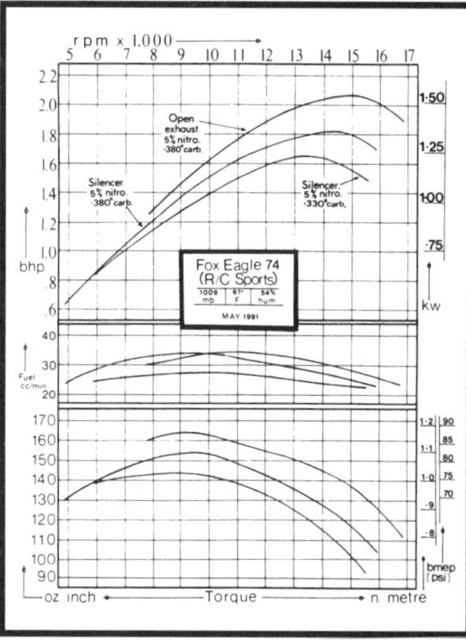

Figure 7.
Performance curves for the Fox Eagle 74.

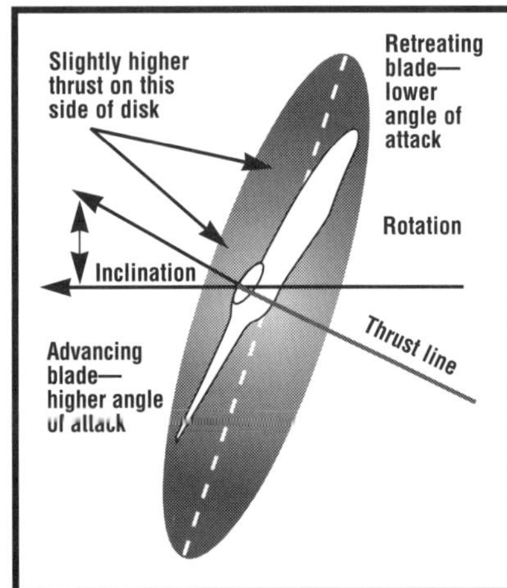

Figure 8.
Asymmetric blade effect.

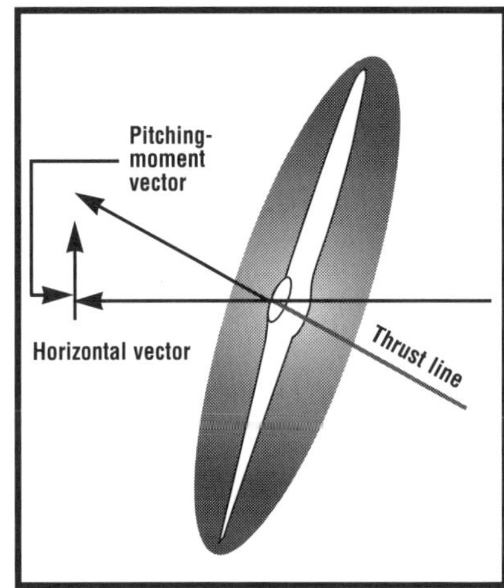

Figure 9.
Propeller pitching moment.

Regarding prop noise, there's a trend to long-stroke engines that develop their highest torque at lower rpm so that, for example, they can swing props with increased pitches. Higher pitches and lower diameters reduce tip speeds and prop noise. Propellers with pitches equal to their diameter or greater (over square), such as 11x11s, 11x12s, 11x13s and 11x14s, are now widely available.

LEVEL FLIGHT SPEEDS

For both full-scale and model airplanes, good design practice requires that the angle of incidence at which the wing is set (on the drawing board) result in the lowest fuselage and horizontal tail drag at the aircraft's selected cruising speed.

At lower speeds, the aircraft must nose-up, through elevator trim, to achieve the AoA that provides adequate lift. At higher speeds, the reverse takes place; down-elevator trim reduces the AoA.

To determine the wing's angle of incidence, you need the wing's airfoil and its lift/drag curves; the aircraft's gross weight in ounces; the wing's area in square inches; and last, but not least, the selected level-flight speed in mph.

It is assumed that the lowest drag will occur when the model flies with its fuselage centerline horizontal. The wing's angle of incidence, relative to that centerline, will then be the same as the calculated AoA.

Figures 10A and 10B show the effect of too much incidence or too little. In both cases, fuselage and horizontal tail drag is higher.

The problem is to estimate the model's level-flight cruising speed. Some chaps like to fly around the "pea patch" at maximum rpm and top speed; others, such as yours truly, are more conservative and enjoy flying at something less than top speed—say, 75 percent of the model's highest speed. Either way, evaluation of the aircraft's top speed is required.

Some years ago, a nomograph was developed for quickly determining a model's speed based on its engine's maximum static rpm and the nominal pitch of the propeller being rotated at those rpm. The nomograph was based on two assumptions:

- In top-speed flight, there would be a gain of 10 percent in rpm, since the prop is operating at a lower angle of attack, with less drag, than it would if the model was stationary.

- A loss of 15 percent in advance per revolution of the prop compared with the prop's nominal pitch advance. This was incorrectly based on the oft-repeated statement that a prop/engine combination developed only 85 percent of the engine's output in terms of thrust.

DAVID GIERKE'S INITIATIVES

David Gierke's "Real Performance Measurement" (RPM) reports in *Model Airplane News* on engine and propeller performance are, in this writer's opinion, outstanding—a real breakthrough and a major contribution to model airplane design.

For each engine under study, he provides not only horsepower and torque curves and details of its construction and handling, but also static and level-flight rpm and the model's actual airspeed at those rpm. He uses a variety of prop makes, diameters and pitches that are suitable for the engine being evaluated.

- Knowing static and flight rpm allows you to evaluate the gain in revolutions in flight.

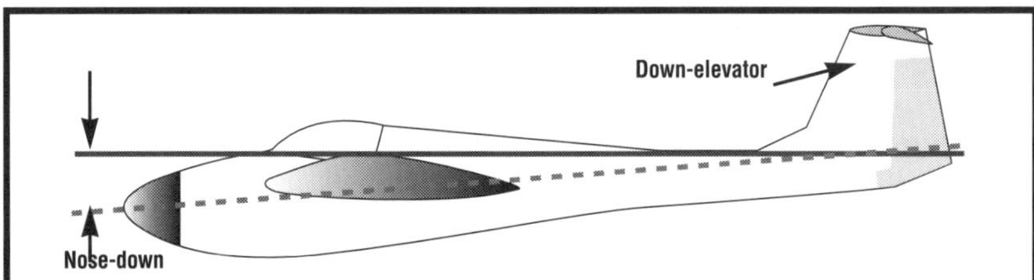

Figure 10A.
Too great an angle of incidence.

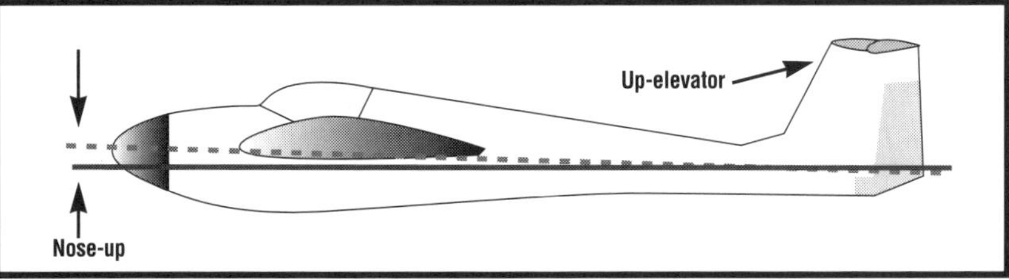

Figure 10B.
Too little an angle of incidence.

Propeller airfoil sections

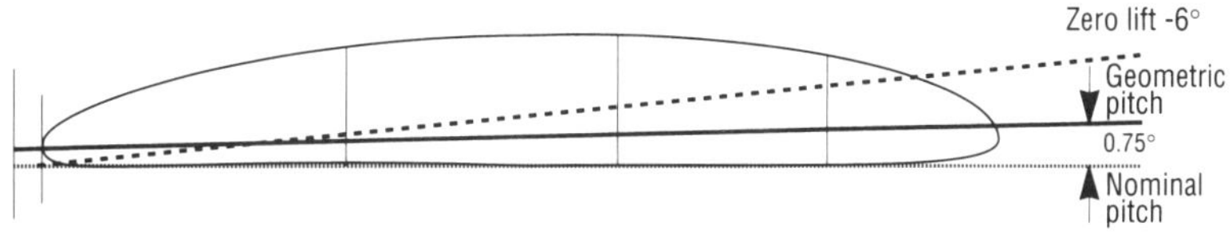

Zero lift -6°
Geometric pitch
0.75°
Nominal pitch

Figure 11.
Graupner prop section.

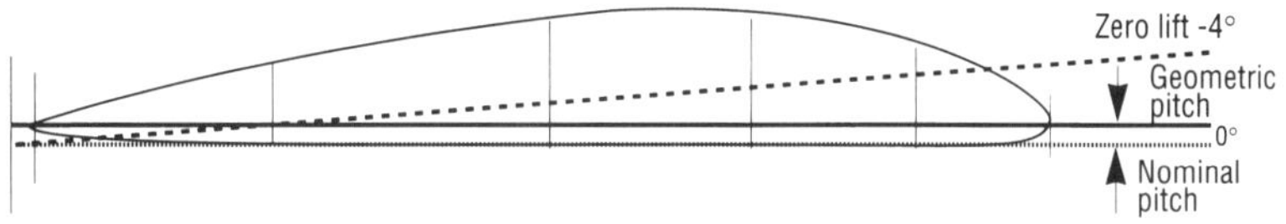

Zero lift -4°
Geometric pitch
0°
Nominal pitch

Figure 12.
APC prop section.

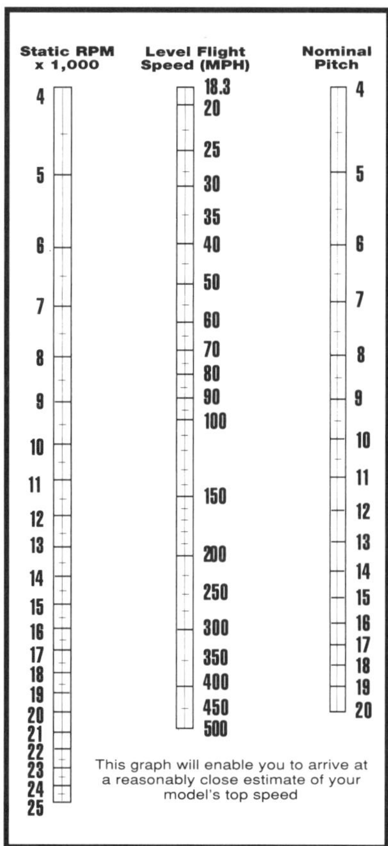

Figure 15.
This nomograph will enable you to arrive at a reasonably close estimate of your model's top speed. Align a straightedge from rpm (left) to prop nominal pitch (right). The speed in mph is read off the center scale.

■ Knowing in-flight speeds and rpm allows you to calculate the actual advance per revolution and compare it with the prop's "nominal" pitch advance.

This calculation is:

$$\text{Advance per rev} = \frac{\text{Speed} \times 5{,}280\ (\text{ft./mi.}) \times 12\ (\text{in./ft.})}{\text{rpm} \times 60\ (\text{min./hr.})}$$

Analysis of David's figures brought two facts to light:

■ The assumption of a 10-percent gain in rpm from static to level flight was not too far off.

■ The big surprise was that the advance per revolution exceeded the prop's nominal pitch by anywhere from 7 to 18 percent.

Figure 12 is a prop blade section. For the actual advance per rev to exceed the nominal pitch advance, the blade's actual AoA must be somewhere between the "nominal pitch" and "zero-lift" angles. The nominal pitch is measured, with a pitch gauge, on the blade's rear surface, at a point 75 percent of the blade's length, measured from the prop's center. The blade's airfoil, the leading-edge radius and its position relative to the nominal pitch all have a bearing (see Figures 11, 12, 13 and 14). ▲

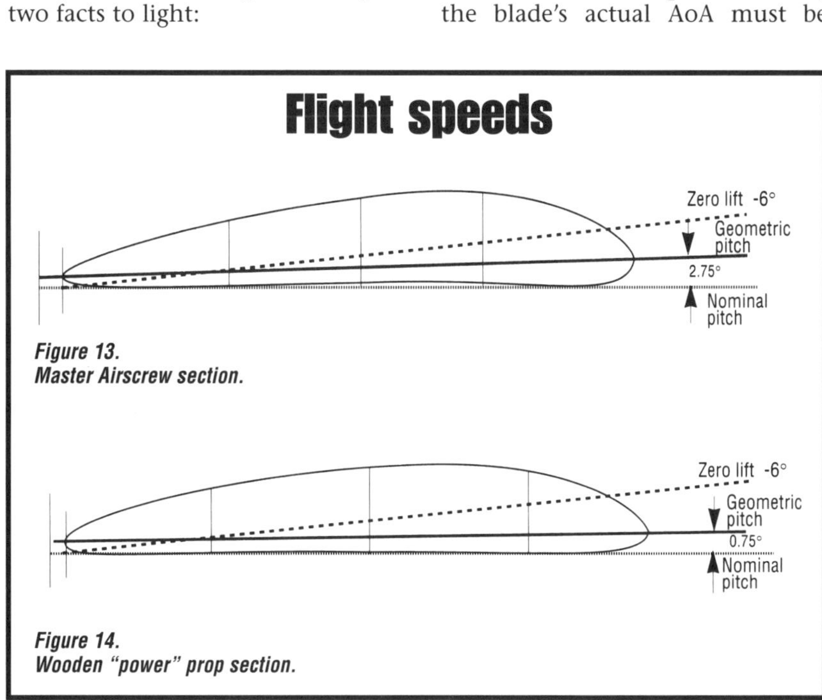

Figure 13.
Master Airscrew section.

Figure 14.
Wooden "power" prop section.

Chapter 19

Design for Aerobatics

In the design of an aerobatic model airplane, the first consideration must be for the heavy loads—both aerodynamic and structural—imposed by centrifugal force in high-speed, sharp, turning maneuvers. These loads are in addition to the model's own weight.

A pattern ship flying at 100mph in a 120-foot-diameter (60-foot radius) turn will sustain loads of more than 12 times its gross weight. If the combination of wing area and the airfoil's C_L max is incapable of supporting this load, a high-speed stall will result. A panicked pull-up from a steep dive, at low altitude, that results in such a stall could be very damaging. Similarly, the model's structure must not fail under such heavy loads (see Chapter 13, "Stressed Skin Design").

Model 1—the Swift.

It's true that at the higher AoAs needed to support these loads, the model's drag will increase enormously; this slows the model and reduces the load. The highest load, therefore, occurs at the start of the maneuver—before drag slows the model appreciably. The problem lies in selecting the wing area and airfoil section that will support these heavy loads. To better understand this, five model aircraft with wing areas of from 400 to 800 square inches were analyzed.

The basis for this analysis is model 3, which reflects the specifications of the author's Swift. This model has a wing area of 600 square inches and grosses 92 ounces with a full tank (a glow-powered airplane with an empty tank cannot fly!).

All five have the same 0.46ci engine, R/C equipment and landing gear. Analysis of the Swift's weight discloses that the power and control units, plus landing gear accounted for 48.5 ounces. It was estimated that for each 100 square inches of wing area added to or subtracted from the 600 square inches, there would be a weight change of 5 ounces; a 700-square-inch-area model would gross 97 ounces, and a 500-square-inch version would weigh 87 ounces.

The Swift's power loading of 200 ounces per cubic inch of engine displacement permitted sustained vertical climbs and vertical 8's with little discernible speed change.

All five wings used for this comparison *have AR 6* and taper ratios of 0.6, i.e., tip chord = 0.6 x root chord, and were unswept (see "Wing Area Analysis" chart).

AIRFOIL SELECTION

Symmetrical sections perform equally well inverted and upright, have zero pitching moments and are ideal for aerobatic models. The airfoil used in this study was NACA 64_1-012—an early laminar-flow airfoil. NACA Technical Note 1945 provides data on this airfoil and NACA 0012 at Rns down to 700,000 (0.7×10^6). A 10-inch-chord wing flying at 100mph at sea level is operating at an Rn of 780,000.

The disadvantage of symmetrical airfoils is their low maximum lift capability compared with cambered airfoils. This has two effects:

- At high-G loads, additional wing area is needed.
- Landing speeds will be higher, unless slotted flaps are used.

At Rn 700,000, NACA's 64_1-012 airfoil has a C_L max of 0.9 and a minimum C_D of 0.007.

NACA 0012 has C_L max of 1.05 and minimum C_D of 0.0065 at Rn

Model 2—the Wasp tandem wing.

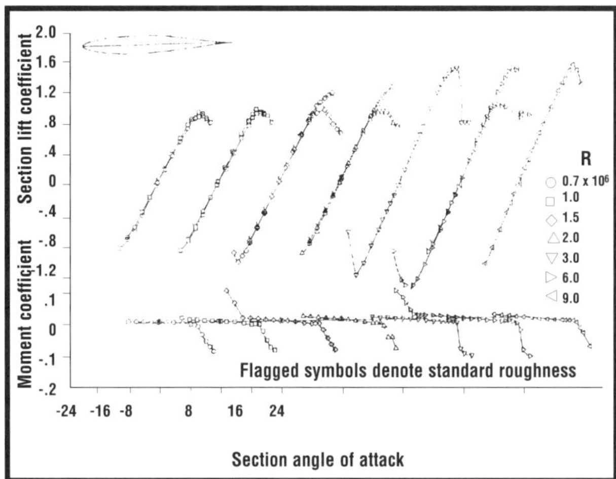

Figure 1.
Section lift and pitching-moment characteristics of the plain NACA 64_1-012 airfoil section, 24-inch chord.

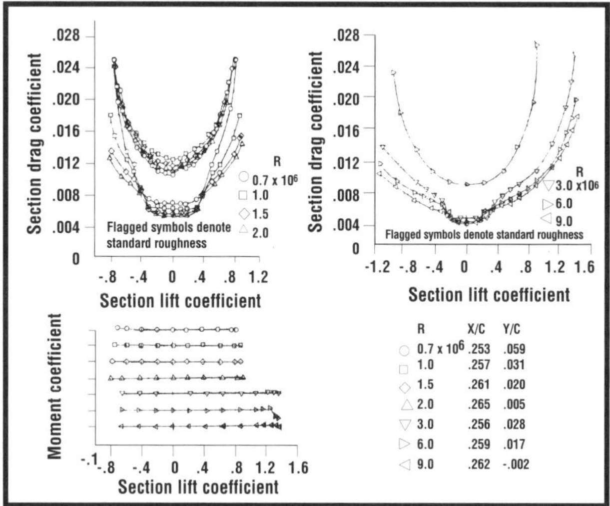

Figure 2.
Section drag characteristics and section pitching-moment characteristics about the aerodynamic center of the plain NACA 64_1-012 airfoil section.

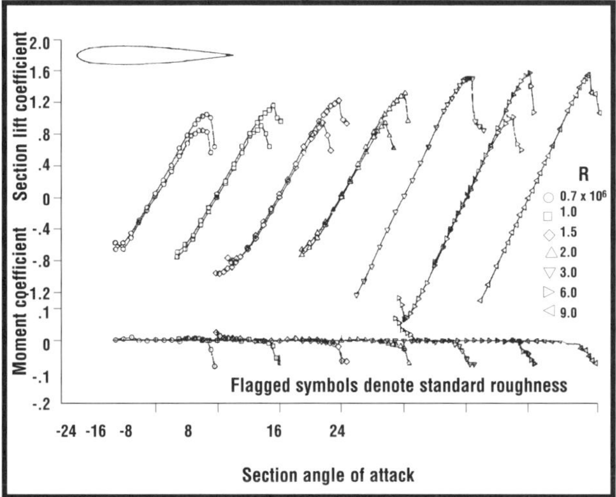

Figure 3.
Section lift and pitching-moment characteristics of the plain NACA 0012 airfoil section, 24-inch chord.

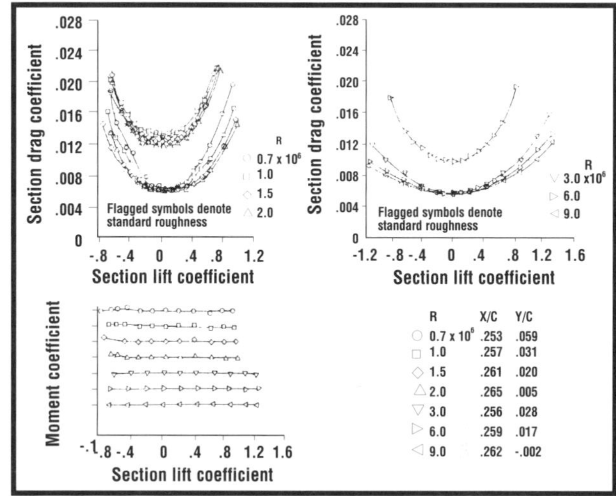

Figure 4.
Section drag characteristics and section pitching-moment characteristics about the aerodynamic center of the plain NACA 0012 airfoil section.

700,000 and would have been a better choice considering the Rns of these models. However, 64_1-012 was used in the calculations (see Figures 1, 2, 3 and 4).

Model 3—the Canada Goose canard.

DRAG

Other important considerations are wing drag, profile drag and particularly induced drag. A model with high wing drag in both level flight and under high G-force will not perform as well as one with lower drag under both. The chart shows some startling comparisons of level-flight drag to high-G-force drag.

This study considers only total wing drag; it does not include the drag contributions of fuselage, tail surfaces and landing gear. Although the tail feathers would vary in proportion to each model's wing area, the fuselages would all have the same cross-sectional area and would change only slightly in length; the difference in their contributions to each model's total drag would be minimal.

COMMENTS

■ **Model 1**—400-square-inch area. The C_L of 0.874 is dangerously close to 64_1-012's C_L max of 0.9. Since this model's level-flight drag is the lowest, it could exceed the 100mph speed, despite its high-G wing drag of 77 ounces, and it could stall at high speed. Its small size would adversely affect its visibility, and its landing speed is high.

■ **Model 2**—500-square-inch area. Much the same as for model 1, with

Wing Area Analysis

Model no.	Wing area (sq. in.)	Gross weight (oz.)	Wing load at 12.12 G's at 100mph (in oz.)	Wing drag at 12.12 G's at 100mph (in oz.)	Wing drag in level flight at 100mph (in oz.)	Wing loading (oz./sq. ft.)	Power loading (oz./cid)	Lift coefficient at 12.12 G's at 100mph	Landing speed (stall speed mph + 20%)
1	400	82	994	77	6.6	29.5	178	0.874	35
2	500	87	1,054	69	8	25	189	0.742	33
3	600	92	1,115	67	9.7	22	200	0.654	29
4	700	97	1,175	67	11.2	20	210	0.590	27
5	800	102	1,236	67	16	18.4	222	0.544	26

the exception that the lower C_L at high G's of 0.742 compared with the C_L max of 0.9 provides an improved safety margin against high-speed stalls. Landing speed is high.

■ **Model 3**—600-square-inch area, which is the optimum in this author's opinion. At 0.654, its high-G lift coefficient provides a good safety margin. Its level-flight wing drag of 9.7 ounces is good, and its high-G wing drag is reasonable. Landing speed of 29mph is acceptable. Its power loading of 200 ounces per cubic inch displacement proved satisfactory on the Swift, and it is large enough to be readily visible.

■ **Models 4 and 5**—700 and 800-square-inch areas, respectively. Both have the same high-G wing drag; but level-flight wing drag increases with the added wing area. Combined with the models' greater weights, this would adversely affect maneuverability. The greater wing area results in lower landing speeds and better visibility.

FORMULAS

In developing this comparison, formulas published in previous articles were used and are repeated below with examples for any fellow designer to follow.

■ Centrifugal force

$$G\text{'s} = \frac{1 + (1.466 \times \text{speed—mph})^2}{\text{Turn radius (feet)} \times 32.2}$$

At 100mph and turn radius of 60 feet,

$$\frac{1 + (1.466 \times 100)^2}{60 \times 32.2} = 12.12 \text{ G's}$$

■ Lift coefficient needed

$$C_L = \frac{\text{Gross weight (oz.)} \times 3519 \times G^*}{\text{Speed}^2 \times \text{Wing area (sq. in.)} \times K}$$

At sea level, K is 1.00; at 5,000 feet, 0.8616; and at 100,000 feet, 0.7384.
* If greater than 1G,

$$C_L = \frac{92 \times 3{,}519 \times 12.12}{100^2 \times 600 \times 1} = 0.654$$

Model 4—the Swan canard.

Model 5—the Wild Goose three-surface airplane.

■ Wing-drag coefficient

The profile C_D of airfoil 64_1-012 at a C_L of 0.654 is 0.0155 (see Figure 2). The total of both profile and induced drags is:

$$\text{Profile } C_D + \frac{0.318 \times \text{lift } C_L^2 \times (1 + \delta^*)}{\text{Aspect ratio}}$$

*δ (delta) is the wing planform correction factor. For a wing of taper ratio 0.6, it is 0.5.

$$0.0155 + \frac{(0.318 \times 0.654^2 \times 1.05)}{6} = 0.\,393$$

■ Wing drag (ounces)

$$\text{Drag (oz.)} = \frac{\text{Total wing } C_D \times \text{speed}^2 \times \text{wing area}}{3{,}519}$$

At 12 G's,

$$\frac{0.0393 \times 100^2 \times 600}{3519} = 67 \text{ oz.}$$

Plug in the numbers, and the formulas may be solved using simple arithmetic. Happy designing! ▲

Chapter 20

High-Lift Devices and Drag Reduction

High-lift devices (HLDs) on a model specifically designed to take advantage of the substantial lift and drag increase they provide, coupled with good drag reduction techniques, will result in smaller lighter, more nimble airplanes, with a greater range of speeds, from stall to top speed. Their appearance will be sleek—very similar to today's full-scale planes—yet they will be sturdy and capable of sustaining high-G loads of centrifugal force in their maneuvers.

The homebuilt movement, in cooperation with the Experimental Aircraft Association (EAA), has developed many superb full-scale, single-engine airplanes of composite construction. They have excellent performance on relatively low horsepower. These are the "Lancairs," "Glassairs," "Swift Lightning" and "Pulsars," to name a few. Their outstanding performance is due to good design and careful drag reduction. All have flaps to permit acceptable landing speeds. In contrast, most current models are reminiscent of the high-drag aircraft of the '30s.

The Crow in level flight.

Very few modelers take advantage of HLDs and drag reduction. Flaps are limited largely to scale models of aircraft so equipped. Hopefully, this article will persuade modelers to incorporate flaps and drag reduction in new and innovative designs; the benefits justify the effort.

STALL AND LANDING SPEED

Landing speeds have not been much discussed in the model airplane press, but are a major consideration in full-scale design. Landing speeds are a function of the model's stalling speed, which in turn, depends on weight, wing area and the airfoil's maximum lift capacity. Weight and wing area are combined in the form of "wing loading" in ounces per square foot of wing area.

SPECIFICATIONS	MODEL A	MODEL B
Wing area (sq. in.)	750	500
Fueled weight (oz.)	96	88
Wing planform	Constant chord	Constant chord
Aspect ratio	6	6
Span (in.)	67	54.75
Chord (in.)	11.2	9.13
Wing loading (oz./sq. ft.)	18.4	25.3
Wing airfoil	E 197	E197
Tail airfoil	Flat	E168
Airfoil C_L max	1.17	1.8 (flaps at 40°)
Power (cid)	0.46	0.46
Power loadings (oz./cid)	208.7	191.3
Propeller	11x6	10x9
Rpm	11,000	11,000
Est. max speed (mph)	75	100
Est. stall speed (mph)	19.5	18
Servos	4	5

At a wing loading of 16 ounces per square foot and wing max C_L of 1.00, the stall speed is 20mph. At a wing loading of 40 ounces per square foot, stall speed increases to 33mph. If the wing max C_L could be increased with the HLDs to 2.40, the stall speed would still be 20mph at 40 ounces per square foot. (See Figure 5 of Chapter 18, "Propeller Selection and Estimating Flight Speeds.")

The Crow at rest. Note the wing's high-lift devices (HLDs).

U.S. Federal Air Regulations (FARs) specify a stall speed of not more than 60 knots (or 69mph) for aircraft weighing less than 12,500 pounds of gross takeoff weight. Sixty-nine miles per hour is as fast as some models can fly at top speed! Most light, single-engine, full-scale aircraft stall, flaps extended 40 degrees, power-off and at gross weight at about 50mph. This is still too high for model aircraft. A "scale" speed is needed!

In "scale realism" *(Model Airplane News,* September 1993 issue), Kent Walters' suggestion that scale speeds be calculated using "the square root of the scale factor" is explained. This is a very sensible suggestion. Most

.40- to .50-powered models will be about ⅙ or ⅐ of the size of their big brothers. The square roots of these scale values are 0.408 and 0.378, respectively. Multiply 50mph by these numbers: 50 x 0.408 = 20mph and 50 x 0.378 = 18.9mph. A model's stall speed of 20mph seems reasonable. FAR no. 23 stipulates that approach speeds should be 1.3 times the stall speed, or 26mph. Twenty-five to 30mph are sensible speeds—fast enough for good control response, but slow enough for good pilot response.

In the absence of an airspeed indicator, it is not possible to judge a model's exact speed. If the glide is too flat and slow, most models will alert their pilots by gently stalling and nosing down (a signal to apply a bit of nose-down elevator trim).

A model with slotted flaps flying on a windy day lands into the wind *flaps up* for more airspeed with better penetration and control response. The higher wing loadings are less affected by gusts, and the touchdown speed is reduced by the wind's velocity. An unflapped model, with a lower wing loading, is easily disturbed by gusts, making landings more difficult.

MAXIMUM LIFT COEFFICIENT

To determine the C_L max for an unflapped wing, a simple and reasonably accurate method is to use the C_L max of the wing's airfoil. For E197, this is 1.17. For a wing with partial-span slotted flaps of 30 percent of the wing's chord in width, the flapped portion will produce an additional C_L of 1.05 at 40 degrees deflection (see Figure 10 of Chapter 3, "Understanding Aerodynamic Formulas"). Using E197 again, the flapped portion provides 1.17 + 1.05, or a C_L max of 2.22. The unflapped area has a C_L max of 1.17. To obtain the average C_L max, proceed as follows:

Flaps down, the Crow is descending.

Unflapped area (sq. in.) x 1.17 = x
Flapped area (sq. in.) x 2.22 = y
Total area = x + y

To find the average C_L max, divide (x + y) by the total area. That portion of the wing in or on the fuselage is considered as unflapped wing area.

Obviously, a tapered wing of equal area and aspect ratio, compared with a constant-chord wing and the same length of slotted flap, would have a higher C_L max, since a greater portion is "flapped" (see Figure 1). To determine the stall speed, flaps down, refer to Figure 3 of Chapter 1, "Airfoil Selection"; knowing the model's loading and C_L max, the stall speed is read off the vertical left-hand scale for sea-level conditions; otherwise, use this formula (WA = wing area; DF = density factor):

Stall speed mph =

$$\sqrt{\frac{\text{weight (oz.)} \times 3519}{C_L \text{ max} \times \text{WA (sq. in.)} \times \text{DF}}}$$

The density factor at sea level is 1.00; at 5,000 feet of altitude, it's 0.8616; and at 10,000 feet, it's 0.7384. This is one variation of the lift formula; involved are four factors: weight, wing area, speed and lift coefficient. Knowing three, the fourth is easily calculated as follows:

Lift (oz.) =

$$\frac{C_L \times \text{speed}^2 \text{ (mph)} \times \text{WA (sq. in.)} \times \text{DF}}{3{,}519}$$

Wing area (sq. in.) =

$$\frac{\text{Lift (oz.)} \times 3{,}519}{C_L \times \text{speed}^2 \text{ (mph)} \times \text{DF}}$$

Lift coefficient =

$$\frac{\text{Lift (oz.)} \times 3{,}519}{\text{Speed}^2 \text{ (mph)} \times \text{WA (sq. in.)} \times \text{DF}}$$

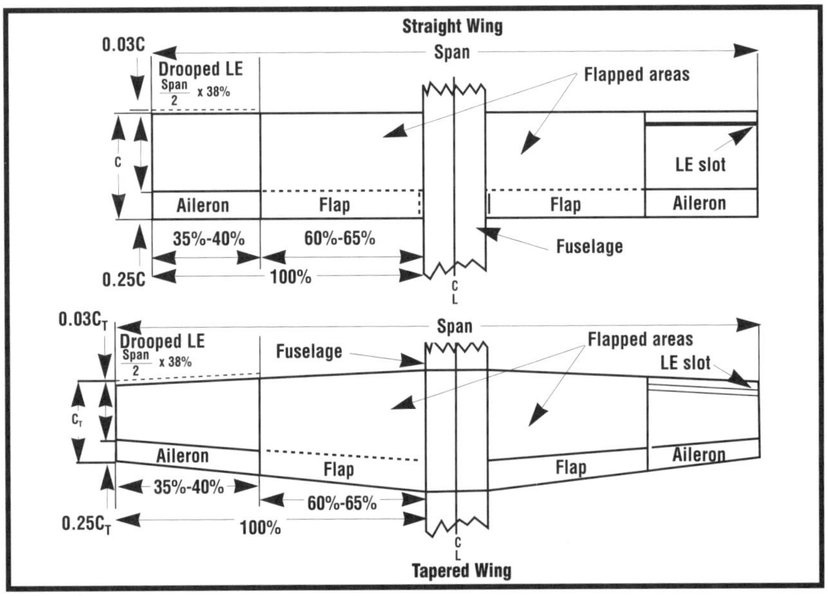

DESIGN COMPARISONS

To illustrate the advantages of HLDs and drag reduction, the specifications of two models (A and B) are outlined—both designed for stall speeds close to 20mph. Both are powered by .46ci engines and have the same control unit, but model B has an extra (fifth) servo for flap actuation.

Model A is typical of many models seen at any flying field: exposed engine; small spinner (or none); bare music-wire landing gear leg; big fat wheels, flat windshield; square cross-section fuselage; dowels; and rubber-band wing hold-downs; flat

Figure 1.
Desirable flap proportions for straight-wing and tapered-wing designs.

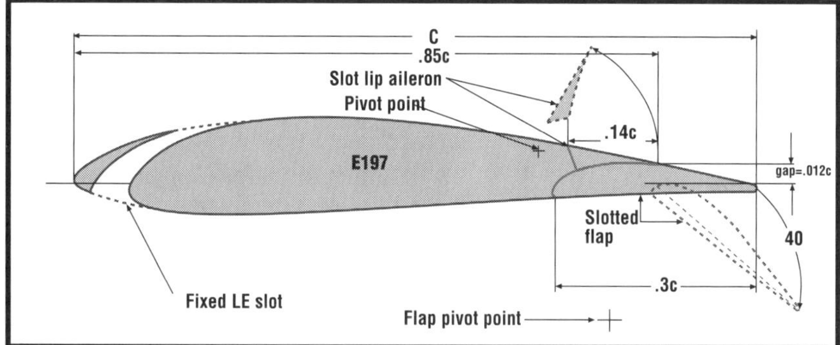

Figure 2.
The Crow's wing airfoil section.

balsa tail surfaces; exposed control horns; lots of "built-in headwinds" (beneficial for steepening the model's glide and making landings easy). It has no flaps. The wing is D-spar construction, plastic-film-covered; the fuselage is lite-ply; and the tail surfaces are ¼-inch balsa sheet.

Model B has a ducted cowl enclosing the engine; a large spinner; landing-gear leg fairings; small streamlined wheels; concealed wing hold-downs; balsa-sheeted, stressed-skin structure with a film overlay; streamlined windshield; and minimum exposure of control horns. It has slotted flaps, 30 percent of the wing chord in width and 60 percent of the semi-span in length.

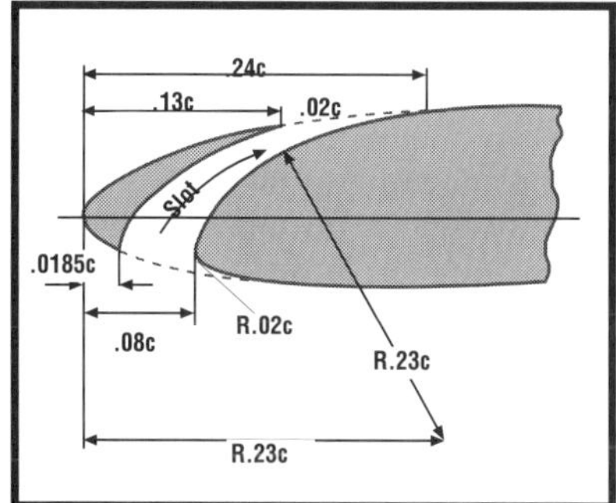

Figure 3.
Geometry of the fixed leading-edge slot.

Because of its sleek, low-drag design, similar to the Swift's, it is capable of high speeds. Mass balancing of ailerons, elevator and rudder is incorporated to avoid flutter that could be very damaging.

WEIGHT ANALYSIS

Look at the chart on page 93. The power and control units and landing gear of model A weigh 45 ounces, leaving 51 ounces for the structure of fuselage, wing and tail surfaces. Model B's wing area is two-thirds that of model A; it is reasonable to estimate that model B's *structural* weight would be two-thirds of model A's, or a weight reduction of 17 ounces.

Model B's weight would, however, be increased by the ducted cowl, large spinner, landing-gear leg fairings, full balsa stressed skins, flaps plus their servos and linkage, mass balancing of control surfaces and a 700mAh battery replacing the usual onboard unit of 500mAh. This is estimated to add 9 ounces, leaving 8 ounces, reducing model B's weight to 88 ounces. The Crow at 500 square inches of wing area, grossed 87.5 ounces, confirming model B's estimated weight.

As for model A, the Osprey had a wing area of 768 square inches and weighed 113 ounces. It had slotted flaps, six servos, a ducted cowl and heavy landing gear weighing 14.5 ounces The fuselage was heavily reinforced for use with twin floats. The fuselage, wing and tail surfaces were not fully balsa-sheet-covered. By comparison, model A's fueled weight of 96 ounces for 750 square inches of wing area is conservative.

■ **Drag comparison.** At 70mph, model B's wing would have 4 ounces less profile and induced drag than model A's wing; but that's not all! The engine cowl, spinner, shorter rounded fuselage, smaller tail surfaces, landing-gear leg fairings and small streamlined wheels, overall smoother surfaces and absence of dowels and rubber bands holding the wing are conservatively estimated to reduce drag by a further 8 ounces (at 70mph) for a total drag reduction of 12 ounces, permitting a higher top speed for model B. This is confirmed by experience with other previous designs.

■ **Takeoffs.** Assuming rotation at liftoff to 8 degrees AoA, unflapped model A would become airborne at 24mph. Model B, flaps extended to 20 degrees and similarly rotated to 8 degrees, would be airborne at 20mph with a shorter takeoff and steeper climb, flaps still extended. With its lower power-to-weight ratio (power loading) of 191.3 oz./cid, model B's lower drag would permit sustained vertical climb.

FLYING FLAPPED MODELS

Windy-day landings, flaps up, have been discussed. On a quiet day, wind-wise, the model may be slowed, flaps fully deployed, and nosed down as steeply as 45 degrees to the horizontal. The flap drag will limit the model's terminal velocity. There is no possibility of a stall and, at a reasonable height above the ground, the model is flared for a short-field landing. Landing flaps-up on such a day will be tricky; the glide is fast and flat, and overshooting the landing area is a real possibility. Maneuvers under power, flaps extended, can be almost incredibly tight, and the flaps themselves are sturdy enough to permit this treatment.

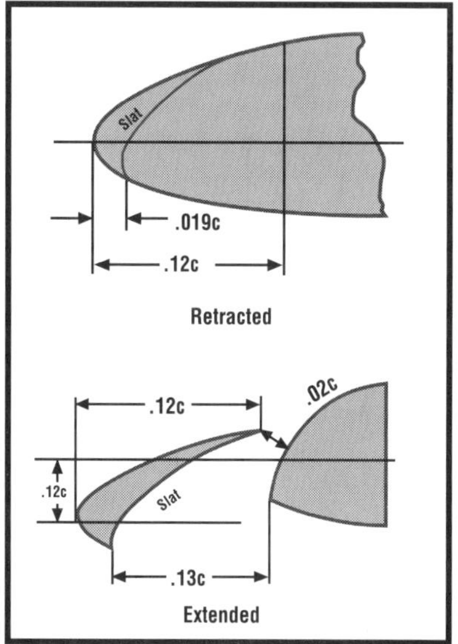

Figure 4.
Geometry of the retractable LE slat.

One advantage of the "30 percent of wing chord flaps with extended lip" is that there is very little pitch change when lowering the flaps. The Swift continued on its merry way on lowering full flaps, but it flew appreciably more slowly.

■ **Centrifugal force.** One concern with higher wing loadings, such as for model B, is that in a tight turn or sharp pull-up, centrifugal force plus the model's weight could exceed the wing's maximum lifting capacity. This could result in a dangerous, high-speed stall, particularly when pulling out of a steep dive at a low altitude. Assuming a turning radius of 60 feet (120-foot diameter), the following tabulates the G-forces involved compared with model B's maximum lift capacity, also in G, at various speeds.

Speed (mph)	Wt. + cent.* lift (G)	Wing max. lift (G)
60	5.00	6.80
70	6.45	9.25
80	8.11	12.00
90	10.00	15.30
100	12.12	18.90

****centrifugal***

For model B, lift exceeds load at all speeds. Note the loads the model's structure must sustain at higher speeds. In a tight turn at 90mph, the load is 880 ounces, or a surprising 55 pounds.

■ **Wing trailing-edge HLDs.** Figure 1 of Chapter 14, "Design for Flaps" and Figure 12 of Chapter 5, "Wing Design," describe and show the additional lift provided by five types of flap: plain, split, slotted, slotted with extended lips and Fowler.

The most practical type, giving the optimum additional lift with lowest added drag, is the 30 percent of chord slotted flap with extended lip. These are easily operated by one standard servo; they're rugged and very effective. Because of their low drag at 20 degrees extension, they may be used for takeoff advantage. Figure 2 illustrates the flap design for the Crow's wing. The only disadvantage is the longer streamlined arms from flap to pivot point needed to provide the backward movement from 0.7 percent of chord to 0.85 or 0.9 percent of chord.

Though the Fowler flap provides greater lift, its backward and downward motion demands complex pivoting arms or other mechanisms and powerful servos.

■ **Wing LE high-lift devices: LE slots.** Figure 3 illustrates fixed LE slots; Figure 4, retractable LE slats. Figure 5 shows the benefit of fixed LE slots: an increase in C_L max of 0.4 and a delay in stall to a 9-degree higher AoA, with only a small drag increase.

The retractable versions are self-opening at higher AoAs, but they demand smoothly operating, non-jamming mechanisms and should be linked so that the slats of both wing panels extend simultaneously for obvious reasons. They may also be servo operated.

To this author, the added complexity of the retractable slat is not justified by its benefits. The Crow has full-span, fixed LE slots, as shown in Figure 2.

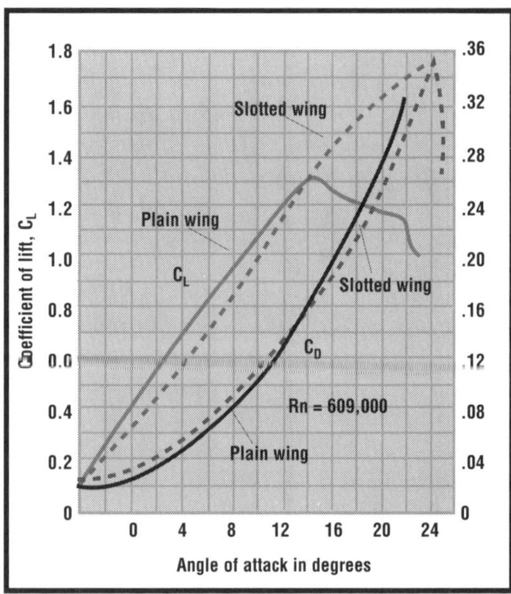

Figure 5.
The benefits of the fixed LE slot.

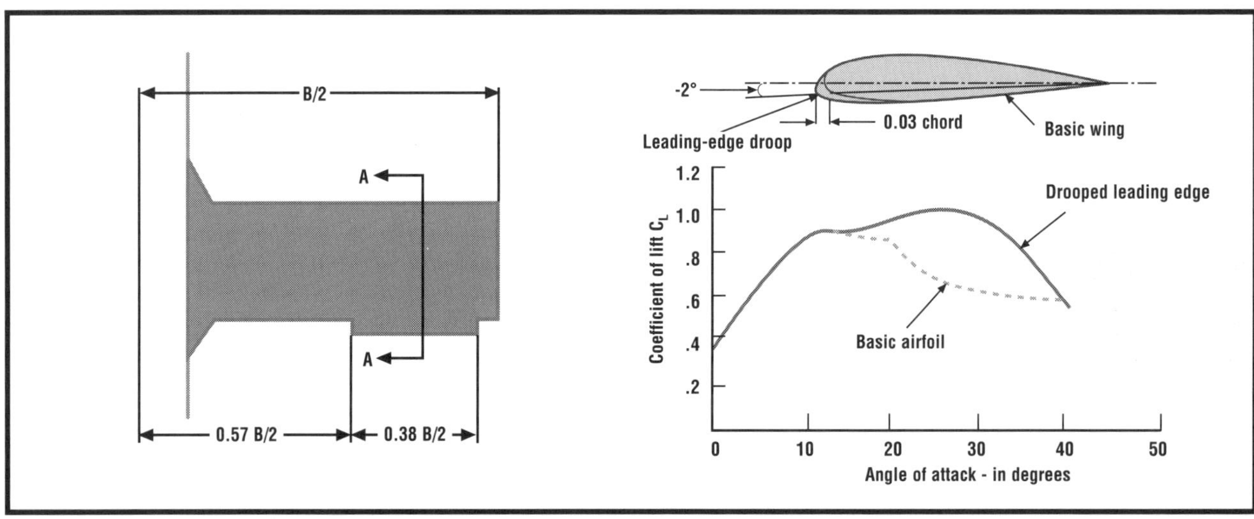

Figure 6.
Wing LE modification for improved stall/spin resistance.

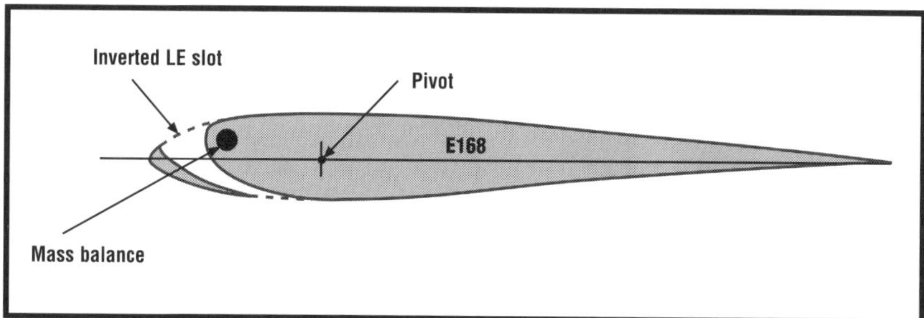

Figure 7.
The Crow's stabilator section.

■ **NASA LE droop**. As shown in Figure 6, these delay the stall by about 8 degrees; they provide extra lift at higher angles of attack; and they have low drag. Used as shown for 38 percent of the semi-span, ahead of the ailerons, they greatly improve aileron control effectiveness at high AoAs. The "droop" was used on the Swift to advantage.

■ **Horizontal-tail LE slots.** To obtain the high AoAs, before the stall, of the wings with LE slots and slotted flaps, a powerful downforce on the horizontal tail is needed to raise the model's nose. The Crane needed inverted LE slots on its horizontal stabilator to achieve this attitude. Similarly, the Crow STOL model's horizontal stabilator is equipped with inverted LE slots as shown in Figure 7.

■ **Slot-lip ailerons.** Illustrated in Figures 2 and 8, these replace normal ailerons when full-span flaps are used. On both the Crane and the Crow, these have proven to be very effective, and they work inverted. At any one time, only one works—that on the inside of the turn; the opposite one lies flat. The raised aileron reduces lift and has into-the-turn yaw. Both are lightly spring loaded to hold them down when they aren't being actuated. With flaps extended, they are even more effective. Raised, the slot effect over the flap is destroyed, reducing flap lift and adding into-the-turn drag. They provide crisp roll control at lower speeds of flap-extended flight—when most needed! The dimensions of these slot lip ailerons on the Crow were: width—15 percent chord; length—60 percent of semi-span.

■ **Landing-gear design.** Landing-gear design for models with HLDs is thoroughly discussed in Chapter 16, "Landing Gear Design." The "tail angle" (also called the "tip-back angle") must be large enough to permit the model to land at very close to its stall angle of attack and its slowest speed.

■ **Control unit.** Flap operation requires an extra servo, which may be operated by the retract switch on a 5-channel (or more) radio, but this provides only full-up or full-down flap positions—no in between! An auxiliary channel is desirable, controlled either by a three-position snap switch that provides full-up, 20 degrees down and 40 degrees down-flap positions; or a proportional slide switch that permits a choice of any flap position from full-up to full-down.

A TRIBUTE

Dick Murray and Ken Starkey—two friends and fellow club members—have test-flown each of this author's new designs. Both are pilots of consummate skills; and both offered valuable, constructive comments on the flight characteristics of each model. For lending me their skills and for their friendship, I am deeply grateful. Do try HLDs and drag reduction. Models of this type are highly versatile, and flying them is pure fun—well worth the extra effort their design and construction entails. Above all, they are sleek and beautiful. ▲

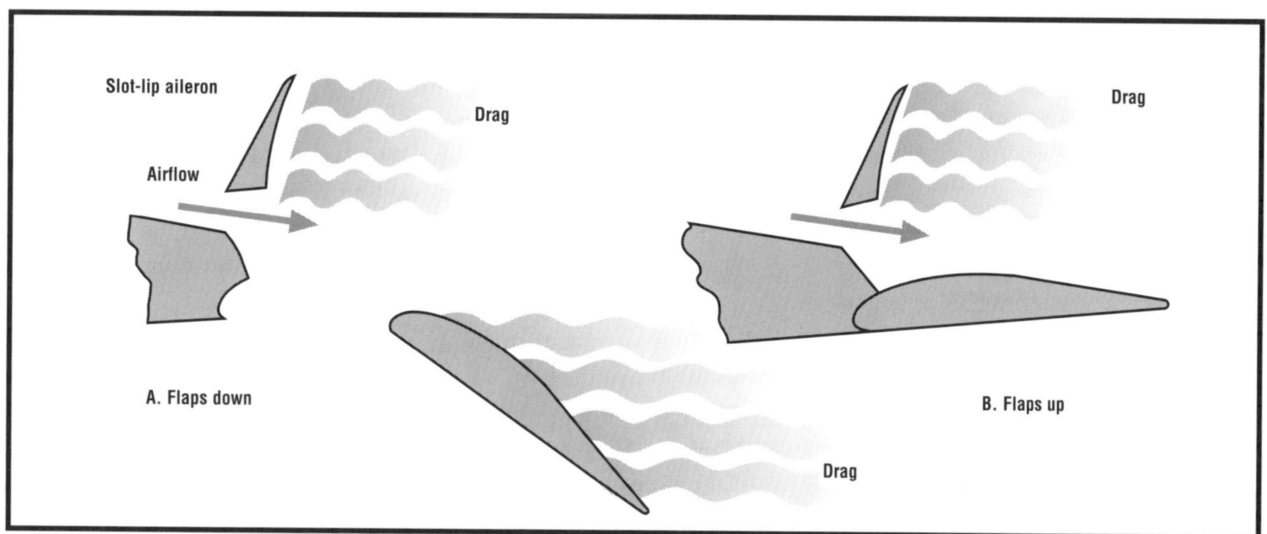

Figure 8.
Slot-lip aileron action.

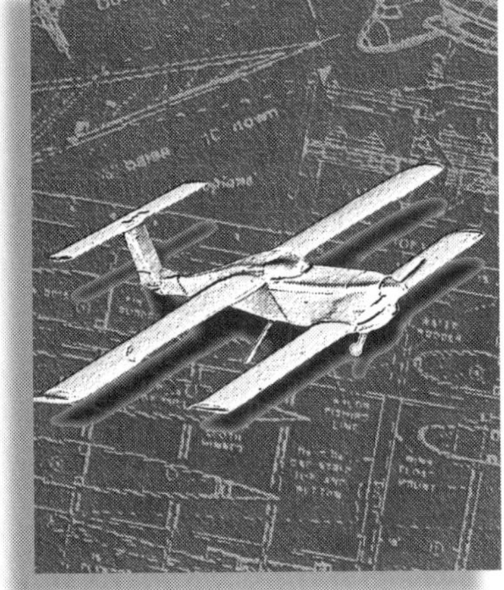

Chapter 21

Centrifugal Force and Maneuverability

In aerobatics, centrifugal force (CF) imposes both aerodynamic and structural loads on an airplane that may be many times the model's weight. It deserves serious consideration. CF acts at the plane's center of gravity (CG). The center of lift may be ahead of, on, or behind the CG in maneuvers.

■ If the center of lift is ahead of the CG, lift is upward; CF and weight pull downward at the CG. A force couple is created that causes the model to nose *up*, and this assists in the turn or climb.

■ If the center of lift is behind the CG, the force couple will cause the model to nose *down* and resist the maneuver.

■ If the center of lift and CG are vertically aligned, weight and CF are neutralized by lift and do not affect maneuverability.

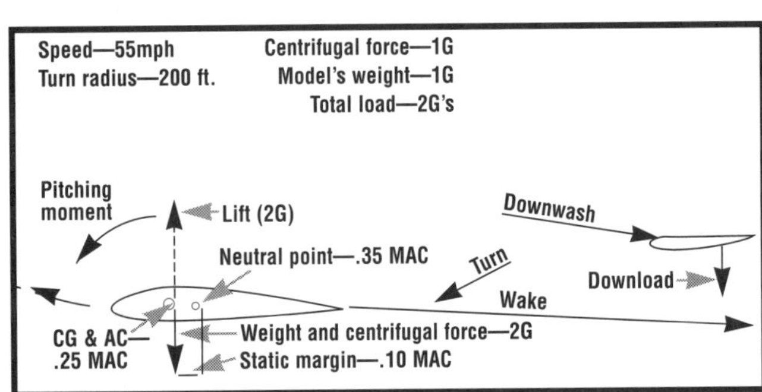

Figure 1.
Loads in a vertical turn (loop).

This chapter describes the evaluation of CF and analyzes various center of lift/CG positions for conventional (tail-last), tandem-wing, canard and three-surface configurations.

CENTRIFUGAL FORCE EVALUATION

It's easy to evaluate the maneuvering loads brought about by CF. Two important maneuvers will be considered: turns in a vertical plane and turns in a horizontal plane. Most aerobatics involve a combination of these.

■ **Turns in a vertical plane**—a series of loops. The CF will be evaluated at the bottom of the loop where weight and CF act downward.

■ **Turns in a horizontal plane**—a steady, level, coordinated turn in which weight acts downward but CF acts horizontally.

VERTICAL MANEUVERS

Assume that a plane flying at 55mph is at the bottom of a continuing 200-foot-radius (400-foot diameter) loop (see Figure 1). The combined weight and CF total 2G's, or twice the model's weight, and this force acts at the model's CG. The increase in the load the wing must support is modest. Had the loop been flown at 90mph,with a 100-foot radius, the CF would have increased to 5.4G's, plus the model's 1G weight, for a total load of 6.4G's.

Referring to Figure 1, the resulting force changes are:

■ **Lift.** The wing's AoA and C_L must increase to provide the additional lift needed.

■ **Drag.** Both profile drag and induced drag increase.

■ **Downwash.** The increased lift coefficient causes an increase in the downward deflection of the downwash striking either the horizontal tail or the aft wings of the tandem, canard, or three-surface configurations.

■ **Pitching moment** (PM). For cambered airfoils, the wing's PM may increase with increase in its angle of attack (AoA). The charts for the airfoils involved must be consulted.

■ **Thrust moment.** If the thrust line is above the CG, a nose-down moment results. If the thrust line passes through the CG, the result is neutral. If it is below the CG, a nose-up moment occurs.

■ **Drag moment.** If the center of lift is above the CG, the increased drag will cause a nose-up effect. If center of lift and CG coincide, the result is neutral. If the center of lift is below the CG, a nose-down action results.

■ **Maximum lift coefficient.** If the combined weight and CF in small-radius, high-speed turns exceeds the wing's maximum lift capacity, a high-speed stall will occur.

■ **Structure.** The model's structure must withstand the substantially increased load without failing.

HORIZONTAL TURNS

See Figure 2. With a plane flying at 55mph in a steady, level, coordinated, 200-foot-radius turn, CF acts horizontally; to provide lift to oppose it, the model must be

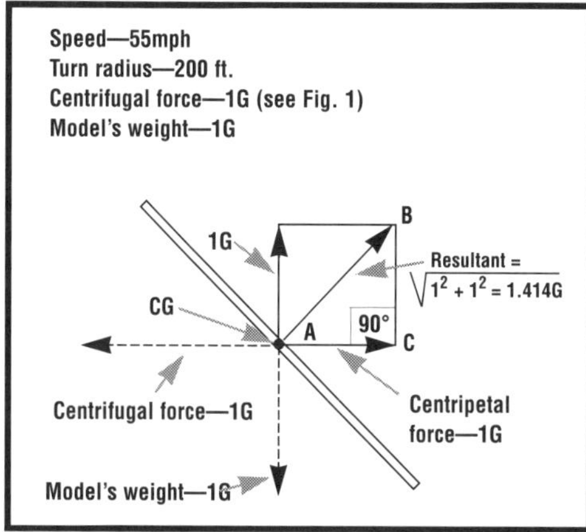

Figure 2.
Loads in a horizontal turn.

banked as shown. But the wing's lift must also overcome the model's weight. As in Figure 1, line CF represents 1G, and it must be opposed by a centripetal force of 1G. This results in a force diagram that is solved by vector analysis. In Figure 2, line AC is the centripetal force of 1G and line BC is the model's weight of 1G.

ABC is a right-angle triangle in which our old friend, "the square of the hypotenuse is equal to the sum of the squares of the other two sides" applies. As Figure 2 shows, the result is 1.414G's, and the angle of bank is at 90 degrees to line AB.

Obviously, in terms of turn radii and speeds, the horizontal turn is less demanding than the vertical turn. These comments on lift, drag, etc., for vertical turns, however, do apply to horizontal turns.

CG LOCATION

Figures 3 through 9 illustrate seven possible stable CG locations.

Figures 3, 4 and 5 are for conventional airplanes where only the wing's lift supports the model; the horizontal tail controls the wing's AoA and compensates for moments caused by thrust, drag, pitch and CG location.

Figures 6, 7, 8 and 9 display configurations in which two surfaces actively provide lift, share the model's weight and provide additional lift to overcome the various moments listed above.

Elevators for planes shown in Figures 3, 4 and 5 are on the horizontal tail's trailing edge. For the tandem wings shown in Figure 7, elevators may be on the trailing edges of either the fore or the aft wing.

Canard elevators are usually on the foreplane's trailing edge (Figure 8).

For the three-surface designs shown in Figure 9, the elevators are on the horizontal tail's trailing edge.

In all cases, the CG *must* be ahead of the neutral point (NP) for longitudinal stability.

Note the rearward shift of the CG from Figures 3 to 9 as the model's configurations change.

The following analyzes each configuration and its response to CF and other forces, both in level flight and under a 2G load.

■ Forward CG. The CG is at 15 percent of the wing's MAC, ahead of the wing's aerodynamic center of lift, which is at 25 percent MAC. The generous static margin of 20 percent MAC ensures that the model will be easy to fly and very stable longitudinally. In maneuvers, however, a force couple is created; CF and weight acting at the CG pull downward; wing lift at the aerodynamic center pulls upward; both cause the airplane to move away from the loop or turn, resisting the maneuver.

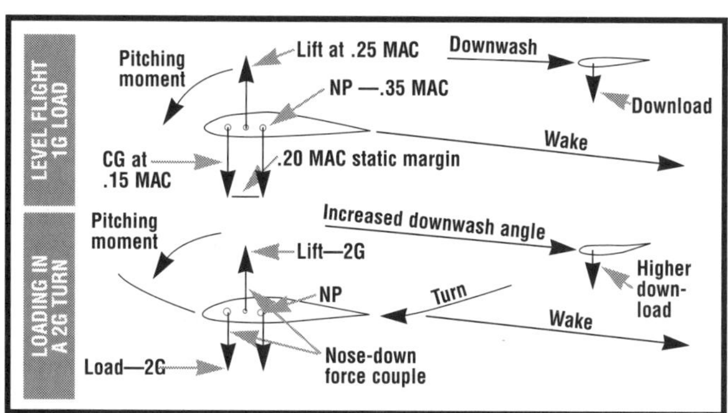

Figure 3.
Forward CG loading in 2G turns.

A substantial increase in tail download is required to overcome this. Elevators whose area is 40 percent of the total horizontal tail area will have adequate authority, but at high CF values, they simply can't provide adequate download, and the tail stalls. This limits the model's high-speed, low-radius turning capability and its maneuverability.

The increase in the downward deflection of the downwash striking the horizontal tail does assist, but this brings the tail closer to its stalling angle.

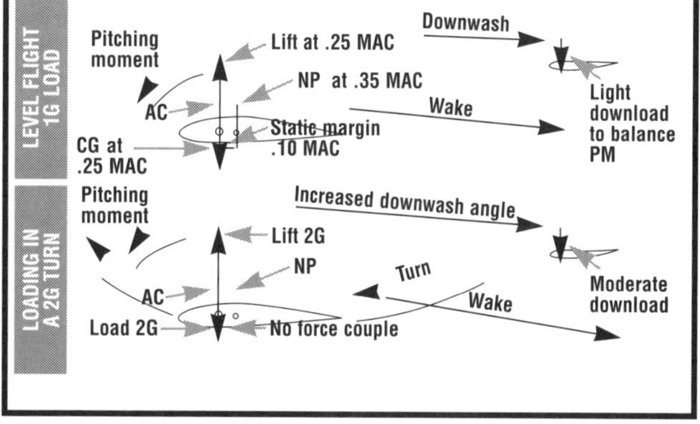

Figure 4.
Loading with CG at .25 MAC in a 2G turn.

■ CG on the aerodynamic center (Figure 4). The wing's lift, at its aerodynamic center, is vertically in line with the CG. In turns, CF neither adds to nor reduces the horizontal tail's load.

If the wing's airfoil is cambered, the tail must compensate for the nose-down pitching moment. If it is symmetrical, there is no pitching moment; this increases the horizontal tail's effectiveness. The increase in the downwash angle that results from the wing's increased lift coefficient aids the maneuver.

Elevators of 30 percent of the horizontal-tail area are suggested. The Swift typifies this arrangement.

■ CG aft of the aerodynamic center (Figure 5). In this configuration, the CG is slightly behind the wing's aerodynamic center at the 25 percent MAC location by 2 to 5 percent MAC. A modest increase in the horizontal tail's area of 3 to 5 percent of the wing's area will move the neutral point aft and maintain a healthy static margin of 10 percent MAC.

Under CF loads, the force couple is upward at the aerodynamic center and downward at the CG behind the aerodynamic center, and that helps the elevator action (as does the increase in downwash deflection). An elevator area of 25 percent of the horizontal-tail area is adequate.

LIFTING TAILS

See Figure 6. This type could almost be classified as a tandem-wing model; both wing and horizontal tail share in lifting the model's weight and in compensating for the various moments. It's an old free-flight setup, typified by the late Carl Goldberg's classic Comet design and advocated by H. deBolt.

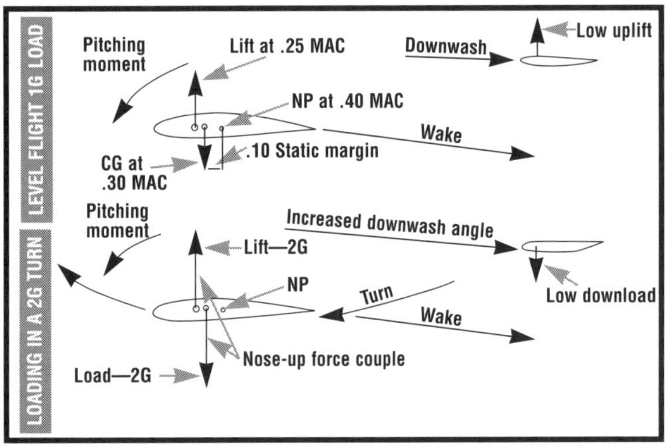

The lifting tail has a flat-bottom airfoil and is 35 to 40 percent MAC of the wing in area. This moves the NP aft to 45 percent MAC, permitting a CG at 35 percent MAC, well behind the wing's aerodynamic center at 25 percent MAC, but provides a healthy static margin of 10 percent MAC.

Up-elevator reduces the tail's upward lift. CF acting at the CG is behind the center of lift, and the resulting strong force couple actively assists up-elevator action, as does the increased angle of downwash. An elevator area of 20 percent of the horizontal tail is adequate.

The configuration is unsuitable for a model equipped with flaps on the wing. Fully extended, the flaps would:

- Substantially increase the wing's lift and lift coefficient.
- Sharply increase the down-ward angle of the downwash striking the horizontal tail, reducing its lift or reversing it to downlift.
- Move the combined center of lift of the wing and tail forward.
- Increase the moment arm between this combined center of lift and the CG, augmenting the nose-up force.

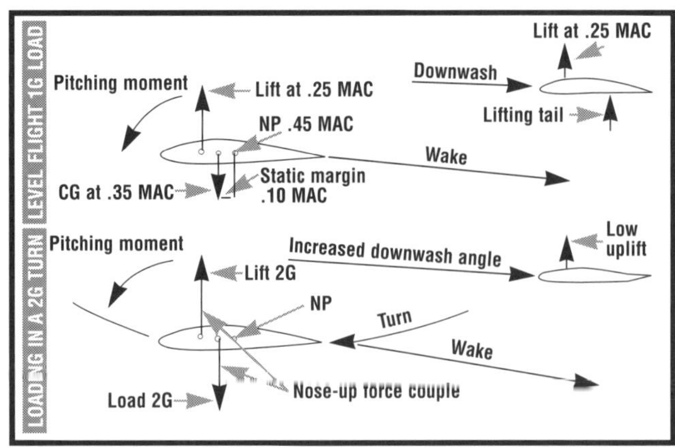

Figure 6.
Lifting tail load in a 2G turn.

Figure 5.
CG aft of .25 MAC loading in a 2G turn.

The combination of increased wing lift, reduced or reversed tail lift and the increased force couple between center of lift and CG would render the airplane dangerously unstable in pitch when the flaps were extended.

TANDEM WINGS

See Figure 7. This configuration is shown in the Wasp. Both wings share the lift to support the model, plus additional foreplane lift to compensate for the nose-down pitching moments of both wings' cambered airfoils. The combined center of lift of the two wings is thus ahead of the CG. Application of down-elevator on the foreplane does two things: it increases the foreplane's lift, and the downward angle of the downwash reduces the aft wing's lift. Both act to move the combined center of lift farther forward.

CF acting at the CG aft of this combined center of lift greatly aids the maneuver. In retrospect, the moment arm from CG forward to the foreplane's 25 percent MAC is short. A better option would have been to place smaller elevators on the aft wing's trailing edge, between the vertical surfaces, with ailerons on the foreplane. Flaps, if used, would be required for both wings.

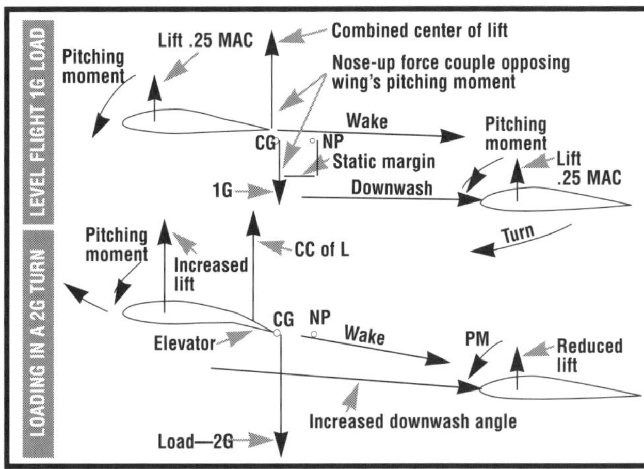

Figure 7.
Tandem-wing loading in a 2G turn.

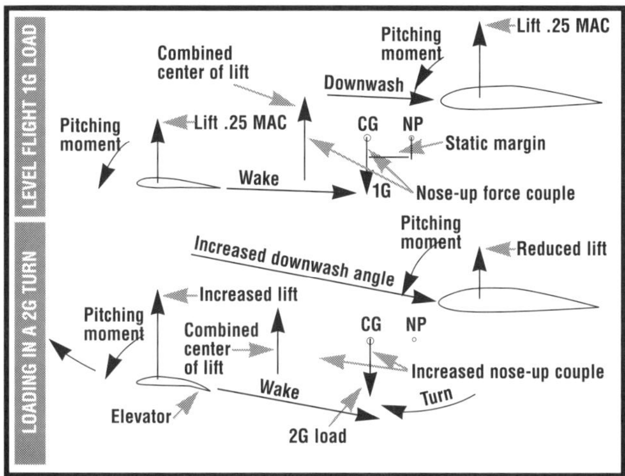

Figure 8.
Canard loading in a 2G turn.

CANARDS

See Figure 8. Like in the tandem-wing version, the foreplane must lift its share of the model's weight, plus provide additional lift to offset the cambered airfoils' pitching moments; this puts the combined center of lift ahead of the CG. Since the distance from CG to foreplane AC is greater than for the tandem type, the canard foreplane's pitching-moment load is less than for the tandem foreplane.

Depressing the foreplane's elevators increases its lift and increases the downwash deflection; this reduces the rear plane's lift in the portion "shadowed" by the front wing. Both move the combined center of lift forward. Under CF, a greater nose-up force couple results, and this helps with the maneuver.

The Canada Goose and the Swan had slotted flaps on both fore and aft wings.

THREE-SURFACE DESIGNS

See Figure 9. The Wild Goose shown in the photos illustrates this design. The horizontal tail controls pitch, and both wings have slotted slaps for slower landings. The tail's area moves the neutral point aft, and that permits the CG to move aft as well.

The closer spacing (longitudinally) of the wings results in a short moment arm from CG to foreplane AC. This results in a higher load on the foreplane to overcome the pitching moments of the two wings. The combined center of lift is thus ahead of the CG.

Up-elevator reduces the foreplane's load but does *not* reduce its lift. The combined center of lift moves forward; CF acting at the CG produces a nose-up force couple.

The combined elevator download and the reduced foreplane load are very effective in pitch. The

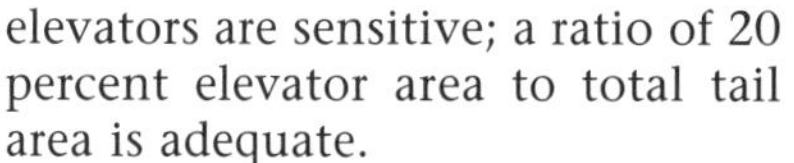
elevators are sensitive; a ratio of 20 percent elevator area to total tail area is adequate.

INVERTED FLIGHT AND MANEUVERABILITY

Of the seven configurations discussed so far, only Figures 1, 2 and 3 will easily fly inverted. The rest rely on two wings for support. Inverted, these types would not satisfy the two critical requirements for longitudinal stability:

- The foreplane must stall first.
- The aft plane must achieve zero lift first. For conventional tail-last types, optimum maneuverability is obtained by having a symmetrical airfoil and ensuring that thrust, drag and lift forces run through the CG. This arrangement neutralizes the disturbing moments and allows the tail full effectiveness, particularly if it is T-mounted.

Except for its airfoil, which is semisymmetrical, the Swift's design complies with these stipulations. ▲

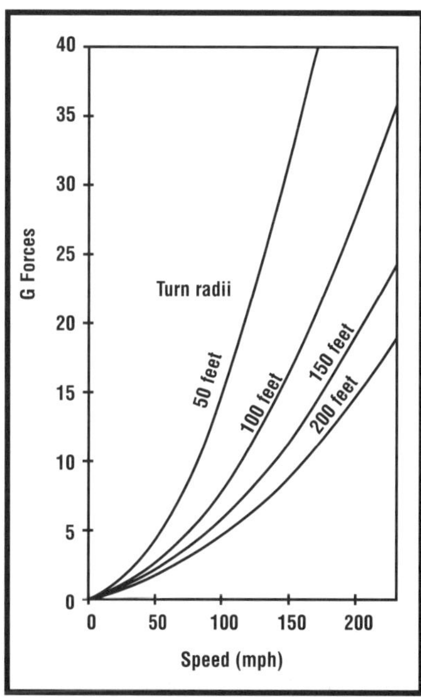

Figure 10.
G forces in pulling out of a vertical dive at various speeds and turn radii, including model's' 1G weight. Example: at 100mph in a100-foot turn radius, G forces are 7.7 times the model's weight.

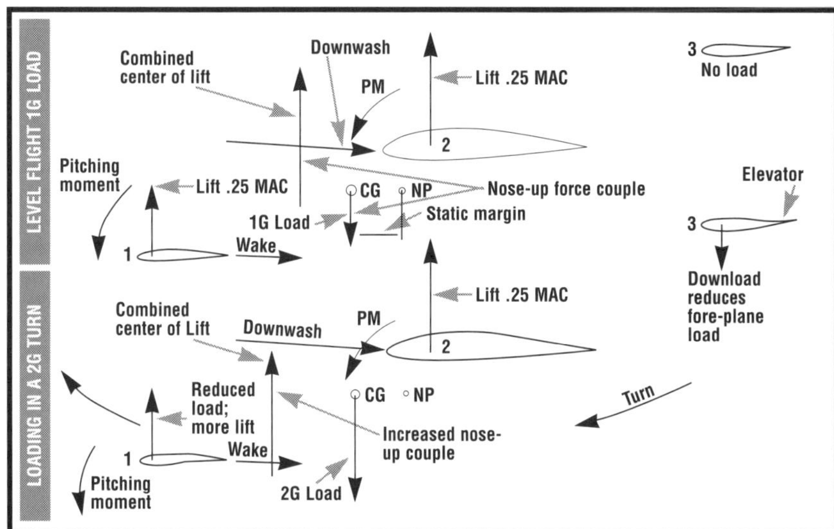

Figure 9.
Three-surface loading in a 2G turn.

Chapter 22

Canards, Tandem Wings and Three-Surface Designs

History repeats itself. The first successful powered flights were made by canards; subsequent designs incorporated both a canard foreplane and a tailplane behind the wing, i.e. three surfaces.

Eventually, the wing and rear tail versions predominated, and they're now the conventional configurations. Recently, however, largely owing to Burt Rutan's efforts, the canard, the tandem-wing and the three-surface versions have reappeared (Figure 1). Today, Burt's latest designs are more conventional, but still unique, and in this chapter, I'll discuss the design of these three configurations.

The Swan canard pusher.

ADVANTAGES

■ **Increased safety.** For well-designed, full-scale canard, tandem-wing and three-surface aircraft, the major advantage of their design is that it frees them from the too-often-fatal, stall-spin-at-low-altitude crash. Though the foreplane may stall, the main wing does not.

■ **Shared load; reduced main-wing area.** In a conventional aircraft, the wing does all the work; the horizontal tail is lightly loaded (downward in most cases) and simply controls the wing's AoA. On these three types of front-wing aircraft, their forward surfaces work hard and share the load with the main wing, which may, as a result, have a reduced area.

■ **Main wing spar may be out of the way** at the rear of the cabin; the conventional version's spar goes through the cabin and interferes with passenger seating (particularly true of low- and mid-wing types).

■ **Smaller, lighter, more compact airplane**—achieved by dividing the required wing area between two lifting surfaces.

DISADVANTAGES

■ **Heavily loaded foreplane.** For stability, the foreplane must be much more heavily loaded (in terms of ounces or pounds per square foot of wing area). The foreplane's loading controls the aircraft's stall speed, which is considerably higher than the main wing's stall speed. Canard and tandem-wing types take off and land faster and need a longer runway than conventional aircraft. The three-surface design is better in this respect because its foreplane loading may be reduced, but three surfaces mean more interference drag.

■ **Limited aerobatic capabilities.** The high foreplane loading, combined with the inability to stall the aft wing, limits the aerobatic capabilities of these three classes. (See Chapter 4, "Wing Loading Design.")

AIRFOIL SELECTION

For all three types of forward-wing aircraft, airfoil selection is very critical. There are three broad categories of airfoil: heavily cambered (such as E214); moderately cambered (such as E197); and no-camber, symmetrical type (such as E168). (See Figure 7 in Chapter 1, "Airfoil Selection.")

Figure 2 compares lift with AoA curves for these three airfoils. Note that, though the heavily cambered E214 stalls at a lower AoA, it starts lifting at a higher *negative* angle than the other two. The symmetrical E168 starts to lift only at a positive angle, and its max C_L is the lowest of all three. (See the appendix for the section characteristics of these airfoils.)

Since all three configurations have both forward and main wings sharing the lift, two requirements are of *critical* importance for successful, stable flight:

■ The front wing *must* stall before the main wing stalls. If the main wing stalls first, the scenario depicted in Figure 3 will result; at low altitude, a crash is inevitable.

■ The main wing *must* arrive at its angle of zero lift before the foreplane achieves zero lift. If the foreplane ceases to lift while the main wing still lifts, the behavior shown in Figure 4 results.

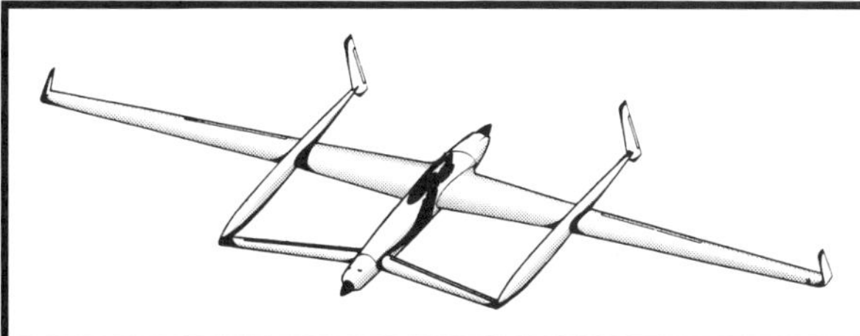

Figure 1.
Rutan's around-the-world Voyager.

With these considerations in mind, look again at Figure 2. Obviously, airfoil E214 would be an excellent choice for the front wing. Its early stall and high *negative* angle of zero lift satisfy both requirements, and its stall is gentle.

For the main wing, airfoil E197 would again be excellent. Its higher AoA at the gentle stall and its lower *negative* angle of zero lift comply with both manda-tory requirements. E168 would not be suitable for either front- or main-wing airfoils, but it would be a good section for the horizontal tail-plane of a three-surface design.

An airfoil's stall pattern at C_L max and at the wing's flight Rn is another important consideration. Obvi-ously, for a canard or tandem-wing foreplane to have sudden-lift-loss or sharply stalling airfoils invites trouble. In the landing flare, if the foreplane were to stall suddenly, landing would be very hard and would probably damage the nose-wheel landing gear.

For the three-surface airplane with a horizontal tail and elevators, a sharp foreplane stall is desirable to prevent up-eleva-tor action from stalling both the front and main wings. Elevator action would pre-vent a sudden nose drop. See Eppler E211—a foreplane airfoil with a sharp stall at low Rn—in the appendix. Note the reduction in the negative AoA of zero lift as Rn is reduced.

Using slotted flaps on the foreplanes of canard and tandem-wing models for pitch control has three effects (see Figure 5):

- The stall angle is reduced.
- The *negative* angle of zero lift is increased.
- C_L max is increased substantially.

REYNOLDS NUMBERS, ASPECT RATIO AND PLANFORM

High aspect ratios reduce the stalling angle (desirable for fore-planes) but result in lower Rns, particularly at landing speeds.

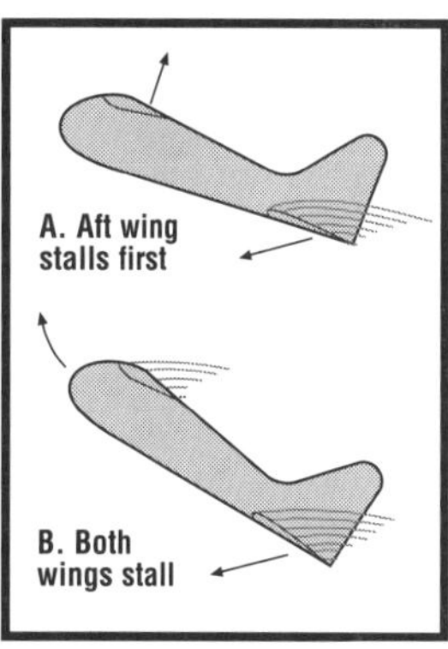

Figure 3.
Nose-up pitch as aft wing stalls first.

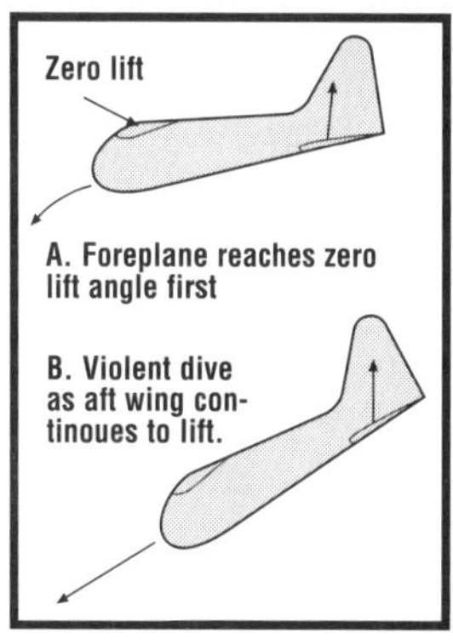

Figure 4.
Steep dive as foreplane hits zero-lift angle first.

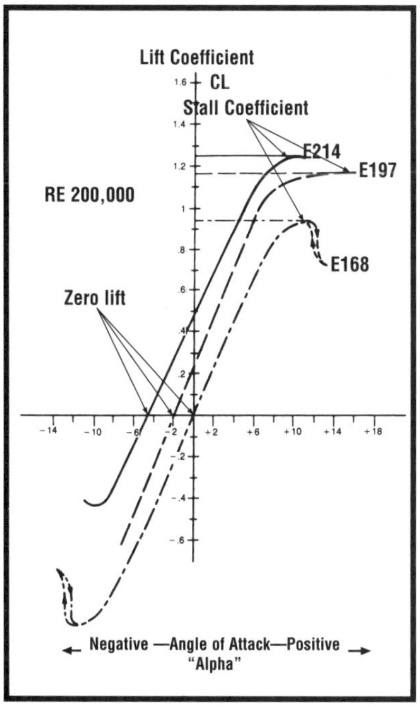

Chords of less than 5 inches are to be avoided. (For more on these subjects, refer to Chapter 1.)

Low aspect ratios increase the stalling angle (desirable for the main wings) of all three types. Shorter main wingspans improve roll response.

A mild forward sweep on the foreplane promotes root-stalling first (see Chapter 5, "Wing Design"). The result is a gentle, progressive stall as the angle of attack increases. Such forward sweep should not exceed 5 degrees on the ¼ MAC line. On a three-surface design, forward sweep would also benefit the horizontal tailplane.

DOWNWASH AND TIP VORTICES

Downwash is thoroughly discussed in Chapter 7, "Horizontal Tail Incidence", and charts for esti-mating downwash angles are provided. Each of the three, for-ward-wing aircraft is affected by downwash.

Figure 2.
Lift curves of three airfoil types.

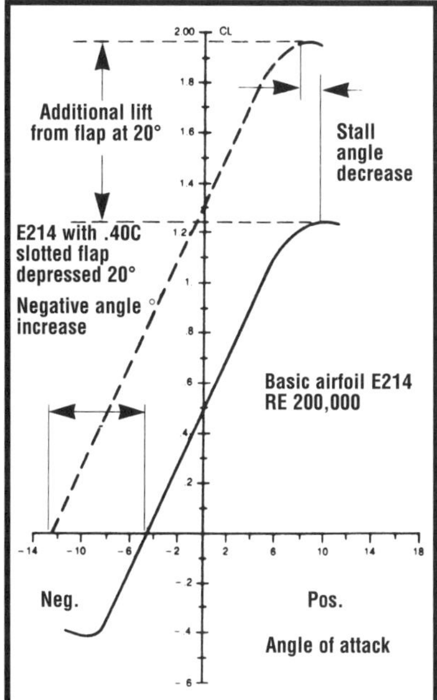

Figure 5.
Impact of a 40% chord slotted flap deployed to 20 degrees on airfoil section 214.

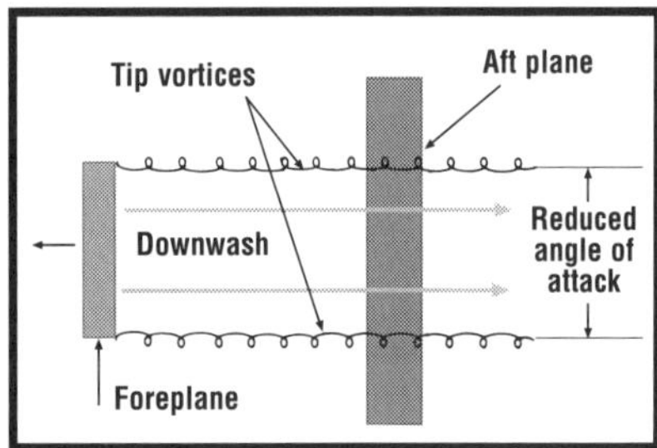

Figure 6.
Downwash impact on a canard.

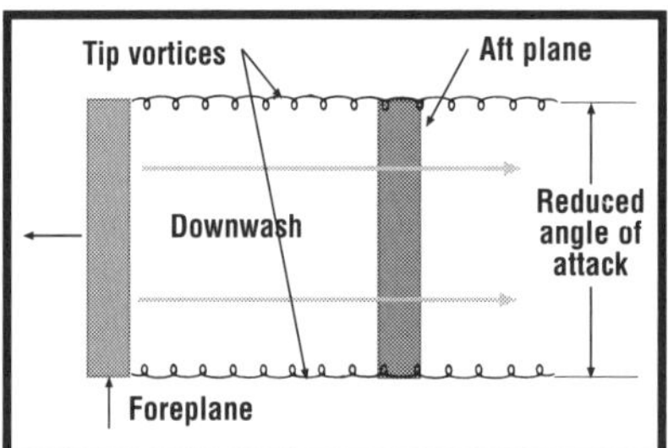

Figure 7.
Downwash impact on a tandem wing.

■ **Canards:** foreplane downwash impacts on a portion of the aft wing (equal in span to that of the foreplane), reducing the angle of attack and lift in the downwashed area (Figure 6).

■ **Tandem-wing aircraft:** the whole span of the aft wing is similarly affected (Figure 7).

■ **Three-surface models:** the main plane is affected as in the canard (Figure 6); and the horizontal tail is affected by the downwash from that portion of the main wing that's "shadowed" by the foreplane downwash. The reduced AoA of the "shadowed" portion of the main wing may be compensated for as follows:
—For tandem wings of equal span: for level flight at the designed cruising speed, the aft wing's AoA should be increased by the downwash angle generated by the foreplane.
—For canards and three-surface airplanes: shadowed portions of the main wing should have an increase in AoA that's equal to the foreplane's level-flight downwash angle. The part of the wing that's out of downwash is left at the AoA calculated to produce adequate lift. This calls for a "jog" in the wing and was used on the Swan.

A variation of this is to use the NASA droop for that part of the wing that's out of downwash, so that the inboard ends of the droop are just behind the foreplane tips.

A simpler method, where the foreplane span is roughly half that of the main wing, is to increase the whole main wing's AoA by half the foreplane level-flight downwash angle. The main wing outboard portions will have higher lift coefficients, closer to the stall. The Canada Goose used this method.

A third method is wing washout with increased root AoA and reduced tip AoA. An accurate built-in twist is needed, but it results in an increase in wingtip stall margin and is stabilizing on a sweptback main wing.

In all cases, the net lift should equal the calculated lift needed.

To avoid the impact of foreplane-tip vortices on the main wing, a vertical gap between foreplane and main plane of half the aft wing's MAC is suggested—either the foreplane low and the main plane high, or the reverse may be used. The foreplane-tip vortices will then pass under or over the main wing. Longitudinal separation or "stagger," between ¼ MAC points of each wing, of two to three times the aft wing's MAC, is appropriate.

For the three-surface design, it is suggested that the horizontal tail be "T"- mounted on the fin where it will be more effective, and the stagger be 1 to 2 times the aft wing's MAC.

LOGICAL DESIGN STEPS

■ **Power and control unit selection.** The power and control units together weigh 50 percent or more of most models' total weight. The first step in design is to choose these units and obtain their weights.

■ **Overall weight estimation.** Obtaining a rough preliminary weight estimate while the model is still in the conceptual stage is essential but not easy. The data on weight estimating in Chapter 13, "Stressed Skin Design and Weight Estimating," will help. When the model's size and proportions have been established, a more accurate weight appraisal is advisable. Chapter 5, "Wing Design," also provides insight into obtaining this estimate.

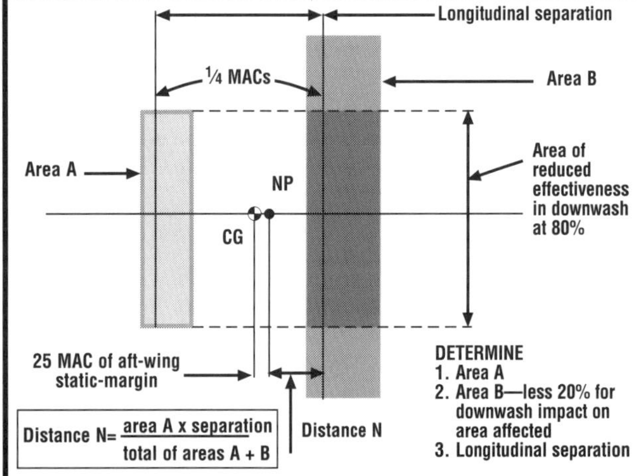

Figure 8.
Locating a canard's NP and CG.

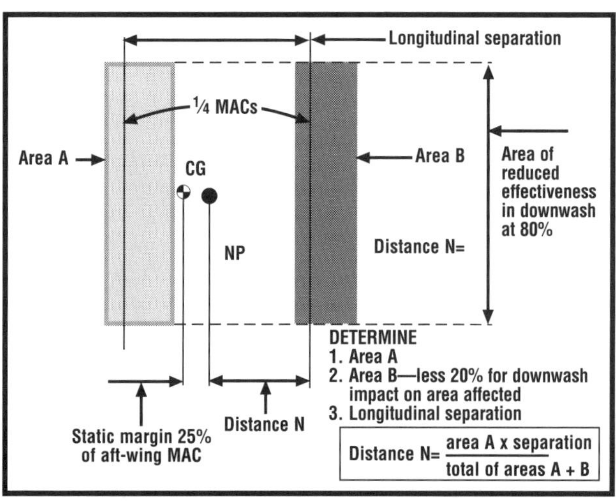

Figure 9.
Locating tandem-wing NP and CG.

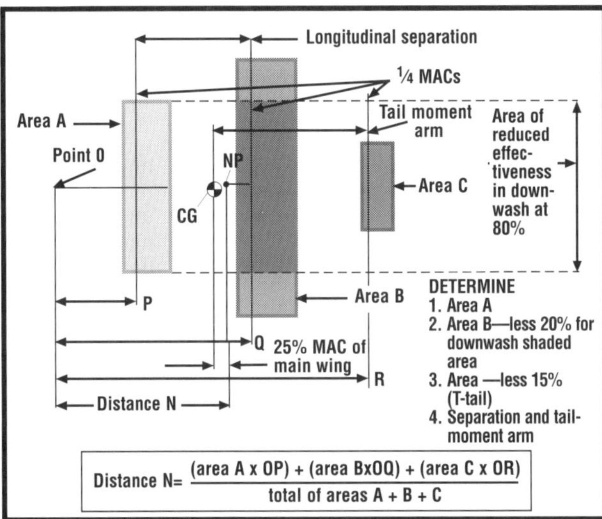

Figure 10.
Locating three-surface design NP and CG.

■ **Wing loading selection.** The type of performance desired governs the choice of wing loadings. Chapter 5 suggests wing loadings in ounces per square foot of wing area.

If the design is to incorporate flaps, then higher wing loadings are in order. When deployed, their additional lift and drag will provide reasonable landing speeds. With weight and wing loading established, the wing's total surface area is easily calculated:

Wing area (sq. in.) =

$$\frac{\text{Weight (oz.)} \times 144}{\text{Wing loading (oz./sq. ft.)}}$$

■ **Level-flight speed estimate.** This is essential in determining the angles of attack of the fore and aft wings.

■ **The neutral point and CG location.** The NP concept is discussed in the Chapter 6, "CG Location." For the three types of forward-wing models, both CG and NP will fall somewhere between the two lifting surfaces. Precisely calculating their locations is very complex and beyond the scope of this article. In full scale, the calculations are confirmed by wind-tunnel tests or actual flight tests with the CG at various locations.

A simplified method is proposed; it considers areas and their separation and effectiveness. Figure 8 covers NP and CG locations for canards, Figure 9 for tandem-wing designs and Figure 10 for three-surface models. The normal static margin for stability is 10 percent of the main wing's mean aerodynamic chord (MAC). Use of a 25-percent static margin as suggested leaves a 15 percent margin of error. Test-flying the model with cautious rearward CG movement will confirm your calculations.

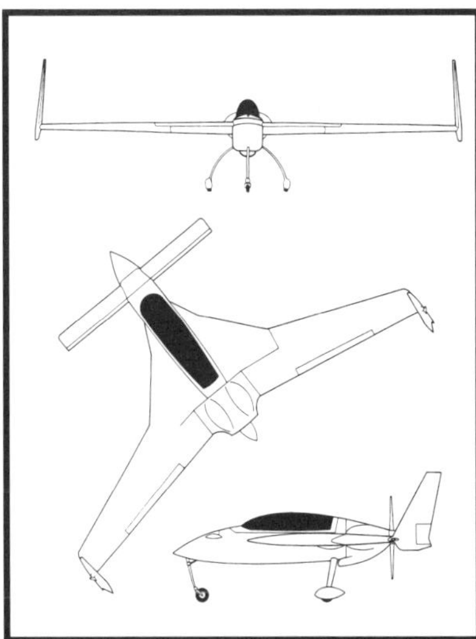

Figure 11.
Three-view drawing of the Rutan Long-EZ.

■ **Sizing of fore and aft wings.** The total wing area, having been established, must be divided between the two lifting surfaces.

CANARDS

From the discussion of NP and CG locations, it is apparent that the smaller the foreplane, the farther back NP and CG will be and vice versa. The area relationship between the two lifting surfaces determines NP and CG.

The heaviest component is the power unit. Its location dictates the area relationship of fore and aft wings. A pusher-engine design would require an aft CG, a small canard and a large wing. A front-engine design would reverse this situation.

If flaps are used, they must provide balanced lift when extended. Too much additional lift from either fore or aft wings would result in very serious pitch problems—either a dive or a stall. Obviously, both sets of flaps must be extended simultaneously for balance.

With a small canard of 15 percent of the aft wing in area, flaps on the aft wing would be much more powerful than those on the foreplane. Another disadvantage of a small canard and rearward CG is the reduction in moment arm to the MAC of the vertical tail surface(s); it necessitates very large vertical areas. Burt Rutan solved this problem by using aft-wing sweepback and placing the vertical surfaces at the wingtips (Figure 11). This substantially increases the moment arm. The Canada Goose design, with a modest 5 degrees of aft-wing sweepback, had the same philosophy applied to it.

Sweepback reduces lift. As model airplane designer John Roncz put it, "You get around 14 percent more lift per degree of angle of attack at zero sweep than at 30 degrees of sweep."

The Swan had a straight aft wing,

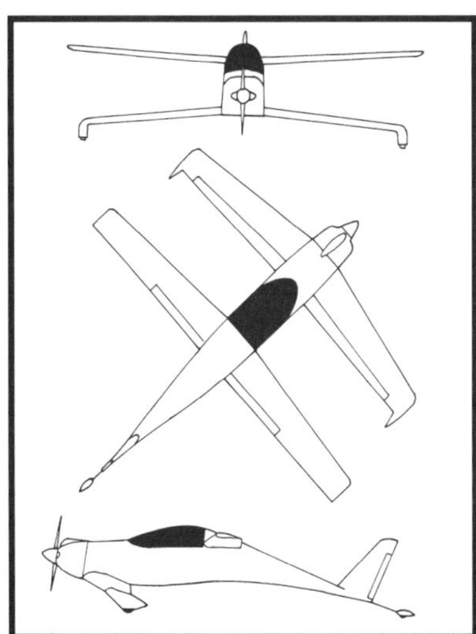

Figure 12.
Three-view drawing of the Rutan Quickie.

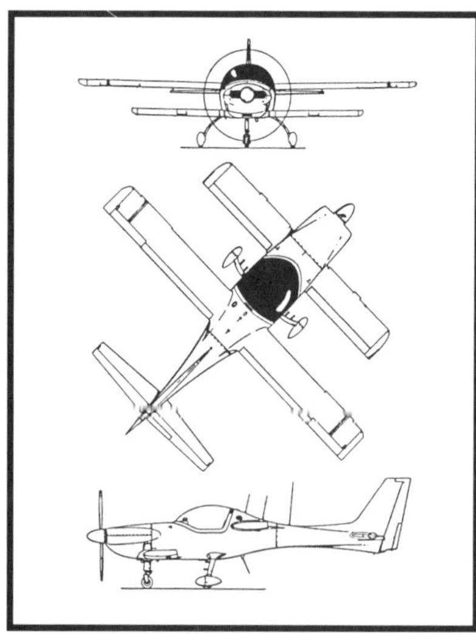

Figure 13.
Roncz's Eagle three-surface trainer.

but its vertical surfaces projected behind the wing. Twelve ounces of ballast were needed to correctly position its CG—as had been anticipated after doing the "Balancing Act" (see Chapter 6) for this model. The minimum canard area is 15 percent of that of the aft wing. For a front-engine aircraft, such as the ill-fated "Pugmobile," a foreplane area of close to 60 percent was used.

The Canada Goose had 31 percent foreplane; the Swan had 37 percent. Using a foreplane of 30 percent as an example, total wing area would be 130 percent.

For a total wing area of 600 square inches, foreplane area would be:

$$\frac{30 \times 600}{130}$$

or 138.5 square inches; and aft wing area would be:

$$\frac{100 \times 600}{130}$$

or 461.5 square inches in area.

The designer needs to take the area relationship into consideration.

TANDEM WINGS

This type has wings with close to equal area. The NP and CG are well forward. A pusher engine *behind the aft wing* would present an impossible CG problem.

Rutan's Quickie (Figure 12) illustrates a front-engine tandem-wing version, with its vertical tail mounted on an extension of the fuselage.

The Wasp is another tandem-wing version. The pusher engine is just behind the front wing. The aft wing and vertical surfaces were supported on booms. This model was very stable, but it had no flaps owing to its low wing loading.

THREE-SURFACE AIRPLANES

The comments on wing sizing for a canard apply to the fore and main planes of the three-surface type. The presence of a horizontal tail causes both NP and CG to move rearward (compared with a canard). The tail's elevators provide pitch control. Slotted flaps on both fore and aft planes permit higher wing loadings with reasonable landing speeds.

Figure 13 shows John Roncz's "Eagle"—a successful trainer that proved safe and easy to fly. Its forward wing area is 67 percent of the main wing area, and both wings are equipped with slotted flaps.

Rutan's "Catbird" (Figure 14) is another three-surface design. Note the slight forward sweep of both canard and horizontal tail. The Piaggio P180 "Avanti" is a twin-pusher-engine, three-surface, slotted-flap airplane (Figure 15). The author's "Wild Goose" was built according to the design approach outlined in this chapter and flies very well. All four illustrate the added flexibility offered by this three-surface configuration.

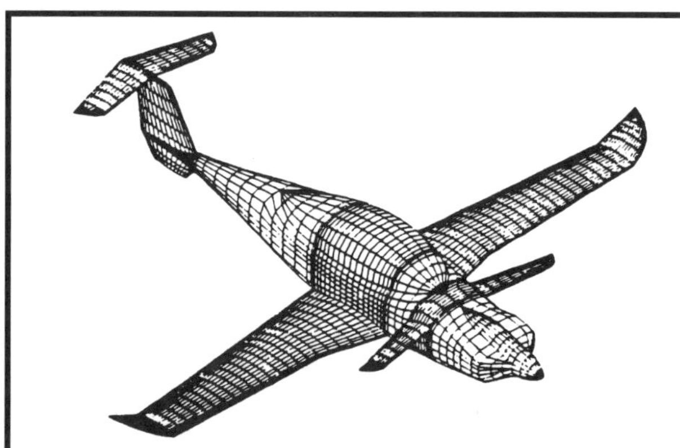

Figure 14.
Rutan model 81 Catbird (VSAERO model); note three surfaces.

■ **Aspect ratio and planform selection.** In addition to determining the areas of the wings, you must also select their aspect ratios and planforms as previously discussed.

■ **Longitudinal and vertical separation.** Longitudinal separation (stagger) measured from the 25-percent-MAC points ranges from 1 to 3.25 times the aft wing's MAC.

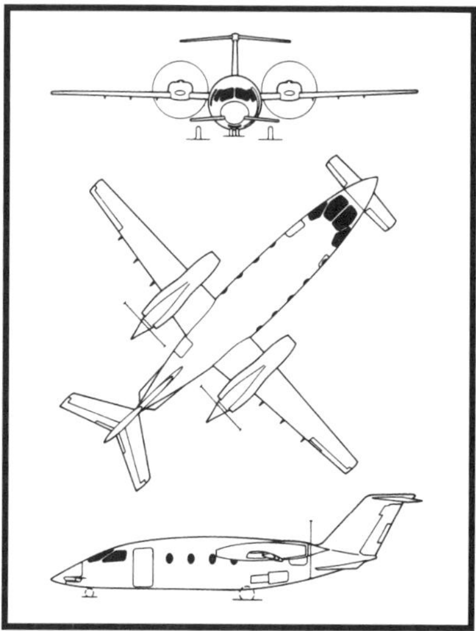

Figure 15.
Piaggio P 180 Avanti three-surface twin.

Vertical separation (gap) should be ½ the aft wing's MAC as discussed.

Tail surfaces of a three-surface design should have a tail-moment arm as outlined in Chapter 7. A T-tail design is favored.

■ **Airfoil selection.** As previously explained, this is critical for stable flight. Additional information and formulas can be found in Chapter 1. The horizontal tail airfoil of a three-surface design should be of symmetrical section

LEVEL FLIGHT

In level flight, at the selected cruising speed, the fore and aft wings must support the model's weight. The calculation of the weight distribution, leading to loadings for both wings, is shown in Figure 16. The foreplane must, however, support

The Wild Goose, a successful three-surface design.

an additional load beyond that resulting from weight alone. This results from:

- The fore and aft wing's pitching moments always being nose-down or negative.
- Propeller thrust loading.
- Drag moments of both fore and aft wings.

Explanation and evaluation follows:

Pitching moments are explained in Chapter 1, and Formula 10 of Chapter 1 permits the calculation of these moments in inch-ounces. Symmetrical airfoils have no pitching moment.

If the propeller thrust is above an imaginary horizontal line drawn through the CG, a nose-down (or negative) moment results. Below that horizontal line, thrust produces a nose-up moment that reduces the foreplane load. If the CG is on the thrust line, there is no thrust loading. The thrust, in ounces, required to propel the model at the design's level flight speed is difficult to evaluate; an estimate would be 40 percent of the model's gross weight. For a weight of 100 ounces, thrust would be 40 ounces.

Figure 17 provides formulas for calculating the wing pitch and thrust-related foreplane loads in ounces. Fore- and aft-plane drag moments consist of the total of profile and induced drags, in ounces, multiplied by the distance, in inches, the wing's ¼ MAC is above or below the CG. If it's above the CG, the moment is nose-up, or positive, and below it, it is nose-down, or negative (see Formulas 5 and 9 of Chapter 1).

Figure 18 provides simple formulas for establishing the effect of drag moments on the foreplane load in ounces. The total foreplane load is composed of its share of the model's weight plus the net sum of the moment source loads, pitching moments, thrust moments and drag moments (in ounces). Both thrust and drag loads may be positive or negative; take care to identify each so that the net value will be correct.

LIFT COEFFICIENTS

Having determined the wings' areas in square inches and their loadings in ounces, the level-flight design speed estimated (see Formula 7 in Chapter 1) permits calculation of the lift coefficients required for each wing's airfoil. Applying "Special Procedures" A and B will determine the angles of attack to provide those lift coefficients.

Decide which of the procedures will be used to compensate for the reduction in AoA caused by the downwash affecting the aft wing behind the foreplane.

The foregoing provides conditions for level flight at the design speed; any variations from that speed will require the same trim adjustments as for a conventional model.

■ Stability test. Two points of critical importance for longitudinal stability are:
—The foreplane must stall first.
—The aft plane must hit zero-lift first.

Now that the angles of attack of both wings have been calculated, it is time for this test:

Using "Special Procedure" C in Chapter 1, determine the stalling angle for each wing and the zero-lift angles from the airfoils' curves at the landing speed Rns.

Compare the spread from AoA to the stalling angle, but *before* estimating the downwash compensation. Raising the foreplane's lift by lowering its flaps will bring it to its stall attitude; the increased lift produced by both the foreplane and its flap will increase the angle of downwash, increasing the aft wing's stall margin, but only for that portion of the aft wing in the foreplane's downwash; that part out of downwash isn't affected. If your foreplane's calculated angle of attack is 3 degrees and it stalls at 12 degrees, there's a spread of 9 degrees. With an aft wing at 1 degrees, stalling at 14 degrees, the spread is 13 degrees so that the foreplane stalls first.

Similarly compare the spread from zero-lift angles of attack to your calculated angles for both wings. That of the foreplane should be substantially higher than that of the aft

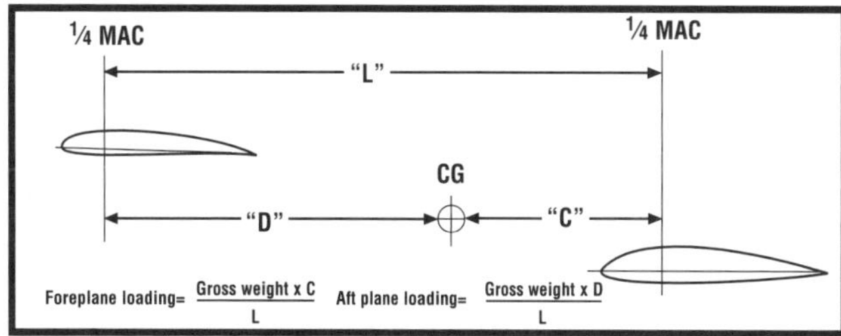

Figure 16.
Calculation of wing loadings due to weight only.

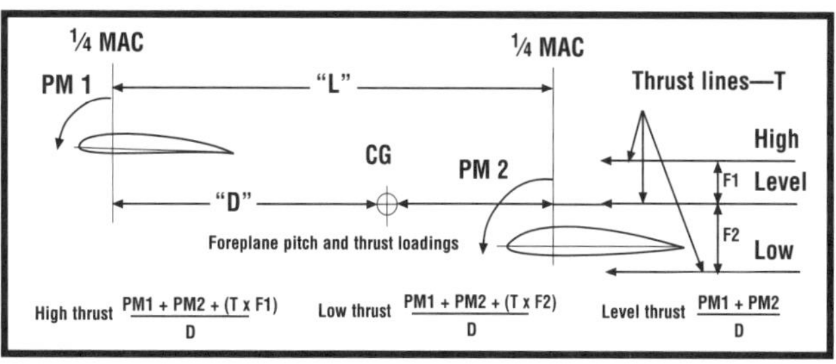

Figure 17.
Additional foreplane loading from wing pitching moments and thrust.

plane. As the foreplane moves toward zero lift, its downwash angle is reduced, increasing the aft wing's lift in the downwashed area and increasing the spread from zero lift to actual AoA.

Eppler E214 has a zero-lift angle of minus 4.75 degrees; if set at 3 degrees, as above, the spread is plus 3 degrees to minus 4.75 degrees, or 7.75 degrees. Eppler E197 has a zero-lift angle of minus 2 degrees. Set at plus 1 degrees, the spread is plus 1 degree to minus 2 degrees or 3 degrees, leaving a healthy margin of 4.75 degrees.

THREE-SURFACE AIRPLANE

This type presents more options than either canard or tandem wing configurations as regards the lift distribution between all three surfaces.

1. The canard and main wing provide all the lift needed. The horizontal tail provides no lift at the selected speed, but its elevators control pitch and trim.
2. Have the canard provide most of its share of the needed lift with the horizontal tail providing a compensating download.
3. Have all three surfaces share the lift. This author's choice would be "1" above—canard and main wing doing all the lifting. Calculation of wing loads would be that for canards and tandem wings described previously.

■ **Unique behavior of the three-surface configuration.** Flight tests of the Wild Goose disclosed unique behavior that relates directly to the three options outlined above. Option 1 had been selected for this model. During its design, the airplane's wing loadings were calculated to be 46 ounces. per square foot for the foreplane and 22 ounces. per square foot for the aft plane in level flight at 60mph.

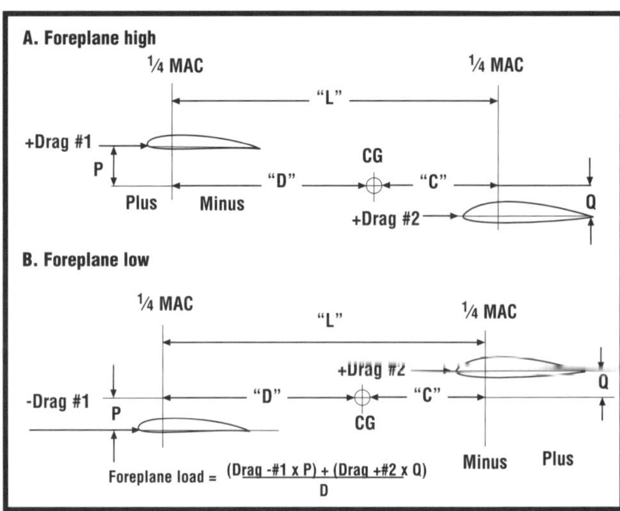

Figure 18.
Foreplane loading from fore and aft wing-drag moments.

The foreplane's loading consisted of 18 ounces. per square foot for its share of the model's weight, plus 28 ounces per square foot due to the nose-down load from the airfoils' pitching and the airplane's thrust and drag moments. This high foreplane loading was of concern; but slotted flaps on both fore and aft wings were calculated to bring takeoff and landing speeds to reasonable levels.

During test flights, two unusual characteristics became very evident:

■ Elevator pitch control was *very* sensitive.

■ Landing speed, *flaps-up,* was more in keeping with the aft wing's lower loading and comparatively slow—an estimated 25mph.

The explanation of this surprising behavior was reasoned as follows: a conventional, tail-last, airplane with its CG well ahead of its wing's center of lift requires a tail-down load (up-elevator) for level flight. The CG of the three-surface design is well ahead of the aft wing's center of lift, and in level flight, the

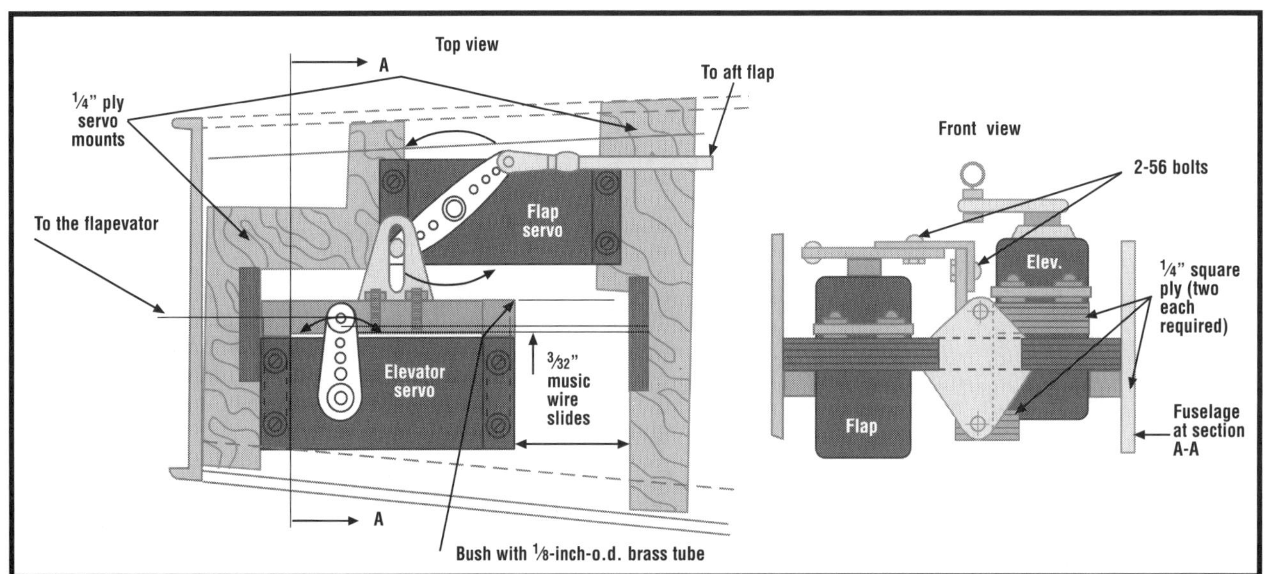

Figure 19.
Elevator-flap servo installation.

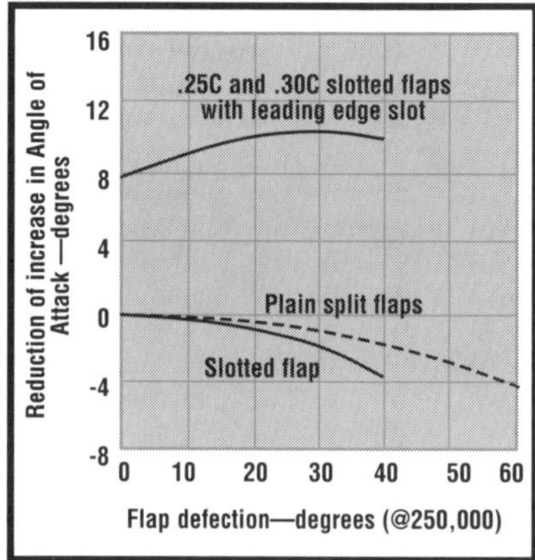

Figure 20.
The effect of flaps and leading-edge slots on the angle of maximum lift.

foreplane's lift provides the balancing upward lift. Up-elevator downloads the tail and unloads the foreplane, reducing its wing loading substantially. The foreplane's *surplus* lift is then adding to the up-elevator action, causing the elevator sensitivity.

This results in a very beneficial reduction in landing and takeoff speeds, both flaps-up and flaps-down. This unique behavior has an impact on the three options listed above.

Option 1 is considered above; option 2 would reduce the foreplane's wing loading, its angle of attack, its lift coefficient and its downwash angle. The aft wing's loading would increase, requiring an increase in its angle of attack. This would bring both wings' airfoils closer to dangerously unstable conditions, but it could reduce elevator sensitivity.

Option 3—having the horizontal tail lift upward—would add to the foreplane's loading and would result in even greater elevator sensitivity.

In this author's opinion, option 1 is best. Elevator sensitivity may be overcome by use of the elevator's *low* dual rate, or by reducing the elevator's area to 20 or 25 percent of the horizontal tail's area instead of the Wild Goose's 40 percent.

■ Longitudinal control methods. The dominant pitch control for canards is a slotted flap on the canard. Another method is a flap on the foreplane and simultaneous up or down action of ailerons on the aft wing. The major method for tandem wings is a plain flap of full or partial span on the foreplane. The horizontal tailplane's elevators are the sole pitch control for three-surface designs.

If option 1 is chosen and fore and main planes provide the necessary lift, the horizontal tailplane's AoA should be zero degrees to the downwash from the main wing. That downwash angle is based on the level-flight lift coefficient generated by the main wing, which is, itself, in the foreplane's downwash! Chapter 7 provides charts for estimating downwash.

■ Directional control. Chapter 9, "Vertical Tail Design and Spiral Stability," provides the basis for obtaining good directional control. For tandem-wing and three-surface models, the moment arm from CG to MAC of the vertical tail surfaces is large enough to permit reasonably sized surfaces.

Canards, particularly those with small foreplanes and pusher engines, do not have adequate moment arms. Recourse is:
—Larger vertical surfaces
—Booms or fuselage extensions supporting smaller surfaces.
—Aft wing sweepback and wingtip vertical surfaces.

FLAPS

Flaps were previously mentioned, and their limitations were briefly outlined. Since both fore and main wings share the provision of lift, the additional lift provided on flap extension *must not upset* the lift distribution between the wings. Too much lift from either wing would result in dangerous nose-up or nose-down pitch. Both sets of flaps must be lowered simultaneously for the same reason.

Both of this author's canard designs—the Swan and the Canada Goose—had slotted flaps on both wings. The foreplane flaps also provided pitch control as "flapevators." On both models, one servo actuated the foreplane slotted flap for pitch control, but it was mounted on a slide that permitted it to move backward under control of a second fixed servo (Figure 19), lowering both the fore and aft plane flaps simultaneously—foreplane flaps to 20 degrees deflection and aft-plane flaps to such deflection as balanced the increased foreplane lift.

Slotted flaps provide their maximum additional lift at 40 degrees deflection so that the foreplane flap, still under control of the first servo, may move up to neutral or down to the full 40-degree deflection from its 20-degree position for pitch control. Deflecting the foreplane flap results in a substantial increase in downwash on the aft wing, reducing its lift and that of the aft flaps in the area "shadowed" by the foreplane's downwash.

Any attempt to calculate the aft flap deflection angle to balance the front flap's 20-degree deflection would have been very complex. Instead, cautious flight tests were performed, progressively increasing aft flap deflection on each flight, until balance was achieved. Bear in mind that the foreplane flap could be raised or lowered to correct any minor imbalance, and if the imbalance was major, retracting both sets of flaps would restore the model to normal, flaps-up, flight. This worked; the Swan's aft wing slotted flaps, of partial wingspan, were extended to 35 degrees in balancing the foreplane's full-span slotted flaps deployed to 20 degrees.

In flight, lowering the flaps caused the model to "levitate"—at much slower speed, but with no up or down pitch—and the foreplane flap continued its function as

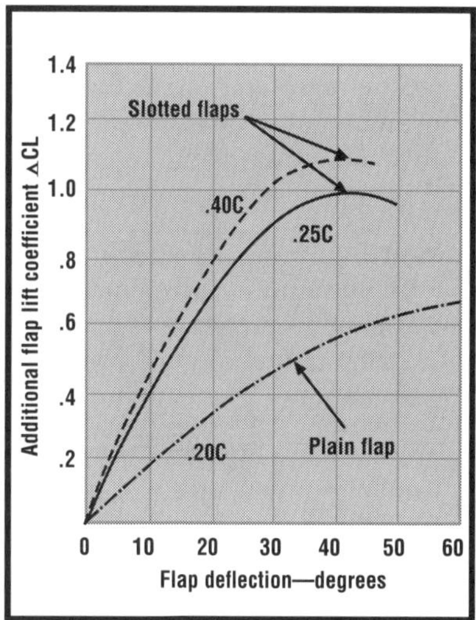

Figure 21.
Additional flap C_L example: .40 slotted flap depressed 20 degrees provides ΔC_L of 0.80 to lift of basic airfoil section.

elevator under control of the first servo. Almost full foreflap deflection was needed, in ground effect, to raise the nose for a gentle landing.

Flap deflection reduces the stalling angles of both fore and aft wings and greatly increases the foreplane's angle of zero lift (Figure 20). For three-surface designs, the same comments regarding balanced flap lift and simultaneous extension of both sets of flaps apply. However, the foreplane flap serves only as a flap; pitch control is effected by the tailplane's elevators so that the foreflap may be deflected 40 degrees.

Slotted flaps on a tandem-wing design would present the same problems as canard flaps. Slotted flaps with chords of up to 40 percent of the wing's chord may be used on foreplanes, as shown in Figures 20 and 21. Use of such wide-chord flaps on the aft plane is not recommended. Chapter 14, "Design for Flaps," provides insight into flap design, construction and actuation.

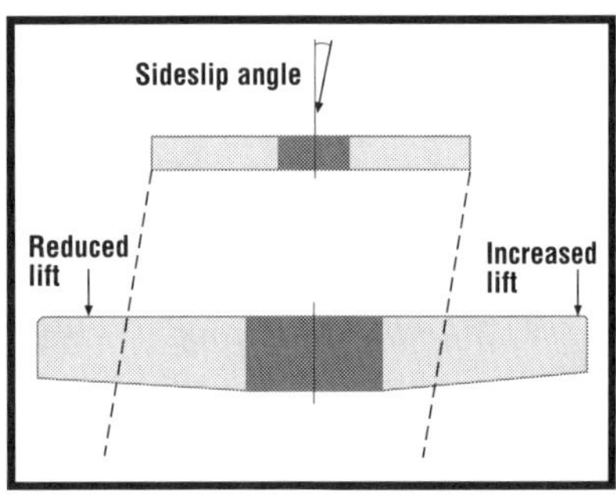

Figure 22.
The aymmetric canard downwash due to sideslip.

■ **Dihedral.** Foreplane downwash impacting asymmetrically on the aft wing in a side slip creates a powerful dihedral effect when the plane yaws (Figure 22). John Roncz's three-surface "Eagle" has no dihedral; its wings are "flat." Flight tests confirmed that dihedral was not required. The same would apply to canards and, to a lesser extent, to tandem-wing design

■ **Landing-gear design.** Chapter 16, "Landing-Gear Design" covers this subject. The stalling characteristics of the foreplane govern landing-gear design, for all three versions.

■ **Structural design.** The discussion of stressed-skin design in Chapter 13 applies to all three types of front-wing-first airplanes. Use of this type of structure would simplify weight estimating and provide optimum weight-to-strength ratios.

GLIDER EXPERIMENT

At first glance, the "Plover" appears to be a tailless glider; in fact it's a canard. The forward-swept inner panels are the aft plane, and the unswept outer panels are the canard. The inner and outer panel aerodynamic centers are shown in Chapter 26, "Construction Designs," as are the area's airfoil sections' neutral point and CG locations.

First test glides, with a vertical surface of normal size, were a disaster and the treacherous behavior of swept-forward wings was forcibly revealed.

When yawed, the retreating panels' centers of drag and lift move outboard. The advancing panel's centers move inboard. The drag imbalance greatly exaggerates the yaw, and the lift imbalance causes a violent roll in the opposite direction. After a couple of damaging crashes and some pondering, the vertical surface was enlarged by 300 percent of its original area. The model then flew well.

The forward panels were readily damaged on landing. After a summer of repeated flying and repairing, it was put to one side. The basic concept has merit; it avoids the impact of foreplane downwash on the aft plane. A powered version would be an interesting design challenge. ▲

The Plover glider canard.

Chapter 23

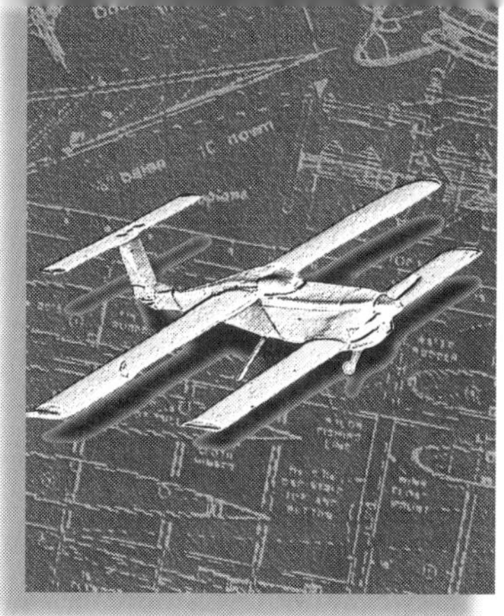

Tailless Airplane Design

The flying wing has intrigued designers since the early days of flight. Its structural simplicity, graceful flight and low weight and drag potential have major appeal. Despite this, no full-scale, tailless airplane or flying wing has ever been produced in quantities that could rival those of conventional aircraft. This chapter explores the pros and cons of tailless design.

CENTER OF GRAVITY LOCATION

For longitudinal stability, the CG of any type of airplane must be ahead of its neutral point (NP). On a conventional (with tail) airplane, the horizontal tail's area and its distance from the wing (both horizontally and vertically) determine the NP location. It is possible to have the CG ahead of the wing's aerodynamic center (which lies at 25 percent of the wing's MAC) or behind it and still maintain an adequate static (stability) margin between the CG and the NP behind it (see Chapter 7, "Horizontal Tail Design").

On a tailless aircraft, the wing's aerodynamic center (AC) and the NP coincide. For longitudinal stability, the CG must be ahead of the AC/NP location. This results in a nose-down imbalance. For equilibrium, the wing must provide a balancing force as shown in Figures 1A, 1B and 1C.

For a conventional airplane, this balance is achieved by the horizontal tail, which is at some distance behind the CG to provide a long moment arm, so that a relatively small tail area does the job.

For a tailless aircraft, the wing itself must provide this balancing force. On a straight wing (Figure 1A), the moment arm is short, so a larger balancing force is required to produce the moment needed. To increase the length of the moment arm, designers have resorted to using wide chords, forward and backward sweep and delta wings (an extreme example of sweepback).

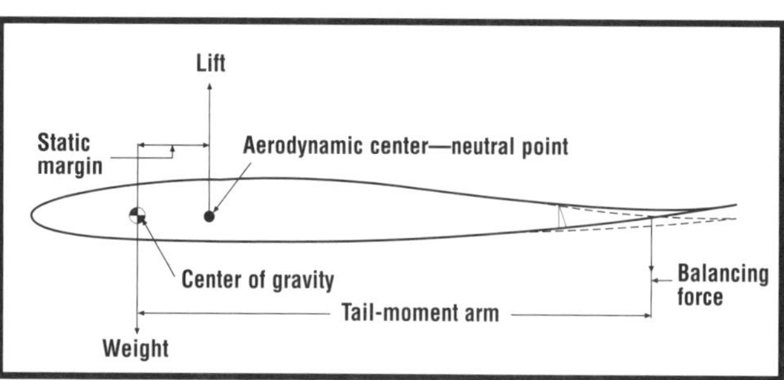

Figure 1A.
Plain tailless force diagram; Eppler 184 airfoil.

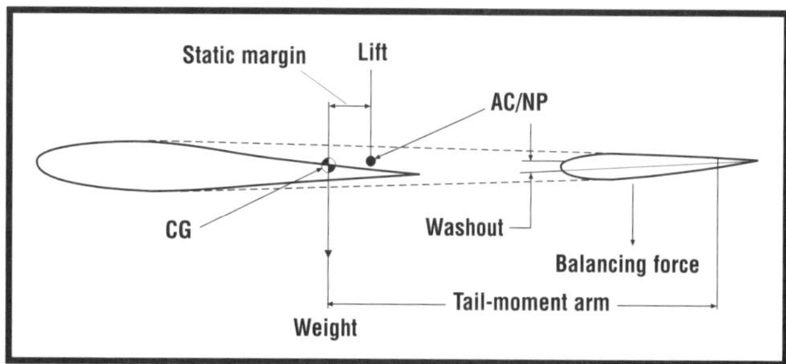

Figure 1B.
Sweptback tailless force diagram; Eppler 168 airfoil.

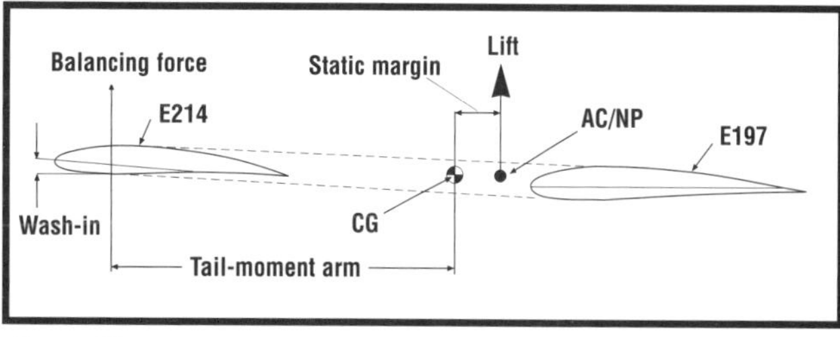

Figure 1C.
Swept-forward tailless force diagram.

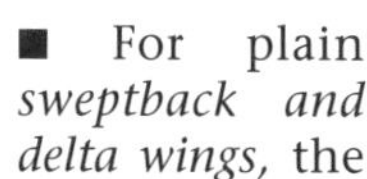

■ For plain *sweptback and delta wings,* the balancing force acts downward, *reducing* the wing's lift and requiring additional wing area to compensate (Figures 1A and 1B).

■ For a *forward-swept wing,* the balancing force acts upward, *increasing* the wing's lift. This allows less wing area and higher wing loadings (Figure 1C).

Owing to the high balancing forces needed, a tailless airplane is especially sensitive to CG location.

AIRFOIL CHARACTERISTICS

With their limited tail-moment arms, tailless airplanes—with the exception of forward-swept versions—can't tolerate airfoils that produce high nose-down pitching moments; such airfoils include those that have heavily cambered mean lines.

See the lift, drag and pitching moments for cambered airfoils E197 and E214 in the appendix. Such airfoils, when used on a tailless airplane, call for a substantially greater balancing force. Some early, full-scale, tailless designs that employed cambered airfoils had sweepback and inverted, washed-out airfoil sections toward the wingtips. This provided the balancing force, but certainly did not improve the wing's lift.

To reduce or eliminate the airfoil's nose-down pitching moment, symmetrical airfoils or airfoils with reflexed mean lines were used. In the appendix, E184 and E230 are two reflexed airfoils; E184 has a low nose-down pitching moment, and E230 has a nose-up moment. An E184 airfoil placed inboard with an E230 airfoil placed outboard on a swept-back wing could provide sufficient balancing force. E168 is a symmetrical airfoil that has no pitching moment, except at the stall during which the airfoil becomes nose-down and is stabilizing.

Reflexed and symmetrical airfoils have substantially reduced max lift coeffients; E214 has a C_L max of 1.25, whereas E230 has a C_L max of only 0.78. Since both stall and landing speeds are directly related to the airfoil's C_L max, these reduced values result in substantially higher landing speeds or they necessitate an increase in wing area (lower wing loadings) to achieve those lower speeds.

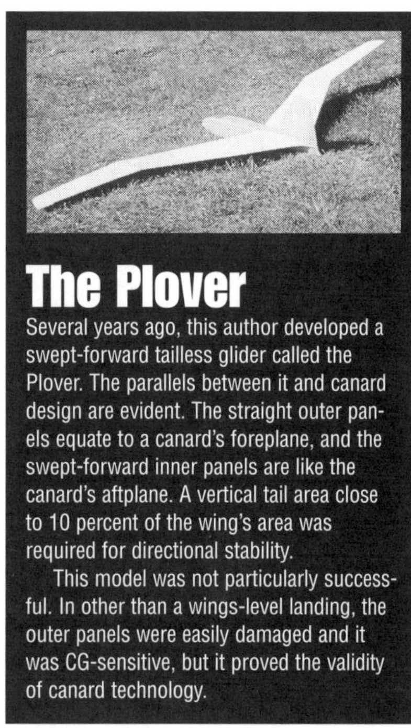

The Plover

Several years ago, this author developed a swept-forward tailless glider called the Plover. The parallels between it and canard design are evident. The straight outer panels equate to a canard's foreplane, and the swept-forward inner panels are like the canard's aftplane. A vertical tail area close to 10 percent of the wing's area was required for directional stability.

This model was not particularly successful. In other than a wings-level landing, the outer panels were easily damaged and it was CG-sensitive, but it proved the validity of canard technology.

HIGH-LIFT DEVICES

The lift that a wing generates is equal to the square of its flying speed. Assuming a constant AoA, doubling the speed increases lift fourfold.

At high speed, it's obvious that less wing area is required (see Chapter 5, "Wing Design"). At high speeds, less wing area means reduced drag—both profile and induced—but substantially higher stall and landing speeds. The Gee Bee racers of the '30s reflected this philosophy, and they landed "hot."

To provide slower landing speeds with reduced wing area, the modern approach is to use high-lift (HL) devices (such as split, slotted, or Fowler flaps) on the wing's trailing edge (combined, in some cases, with leading-edge slots and flaps). Use of these devices results in very large increases in the wing's C_L max.

Under the conditions described above, the wing's area is determined by its HL-device-assisted C_L max and the landing speed desired. Unfortunately, when deployed, these high-lift devices produce heavy nose-down pitching moments that are beyond the capability of tailless aircraft (with the exception of forward-swept types). To overcome this, small split flaps, which produce more drag than lift, are sometimes used.

On conventional "tailed" airplanes, the increased nose-down pitching moment is compensated for by the heavy downwash angle increase provided by the deployed HL devices striking the tail, and by stabilizer/elevator action. Obviously, on a tailless airplane, the wing's downwash provides no such compensating force.

For tailless airplanes (except swept-forward configurations) all three factors—CG location, reduced airfoil C_L max and limited use of HL devices—require an increase in wing area compared with conventional aircraft, and this reduces the tailless craft's efficiency.

This author's Swift has 600 square inches of wing area and weighs 92 ounces (gross) for a wing loading of 22 ounces per square foot. Its airfoil is the E197, and it is equipped with slotted flaps whose chord is 30 percent of wing chord, and which occupy 60 percent of the wing's trailing edge. The C_L max (flaps extended 40 degrees) is 1.80; stall speed is 17mph.

For an aircraft with a wing C_L max of 0.90 to achieve the Swift's stall speed would require a wing loading of 11 ounces per square foot. Because of the lower loading, a substantial increase in wing area and weight would result. It is not improbable that this increase would equal the weight savings that would result from using a shorter fuselage and absence of a horizontal tail. Using the Swift's gross weight of 92 ounces, to achieve the 17mph stall, the wing area for a tailless model would be 1,200 square inches—a 100-percent increase. Top-speed performance would be adversely affected.

SWEPT-FORWARD TAILLESS AIRCRAFT

Of the tailless configurations, only the swept-forward (SF) has an upward lifting balancing force, which adds to the wing's overall lift, rather than the downward, lift-reducing balancing force of the other configurations.

Very few SF tailless aircraft—either full-scale or model—have been designed and built, owing to two major factors:

- The SF wing has a strong tendency to twist under load, increasing its AoA. Unless the wing is torsionally very strong, this tendency leads to flutter and disastrous failure. A stiff, heavy structure is needed. Modern, composite, stressed-skin design has largely overcome this problem.

- An SF wing is directionally unstable and requires large vertical surfaces for directional stability.

Since lift is all upward, the nose-down pitching moment of cambered airfoils is easily overcome with an SF wing. Such airfoils, with their higher C_L max, may be used.

High-lift devices, such as slotted flaps, may be incorporated at the inboard trailing edges. Elevators are depressed at the wingtips to increase lift forward of the CG and offset both the added lift and the nose-down pitch of the extended HL devices that are behind the CG. In this condition, both elevators and flaps add to the wing's total lift.

An SF wing characteristically stalls at the wing root first. Because

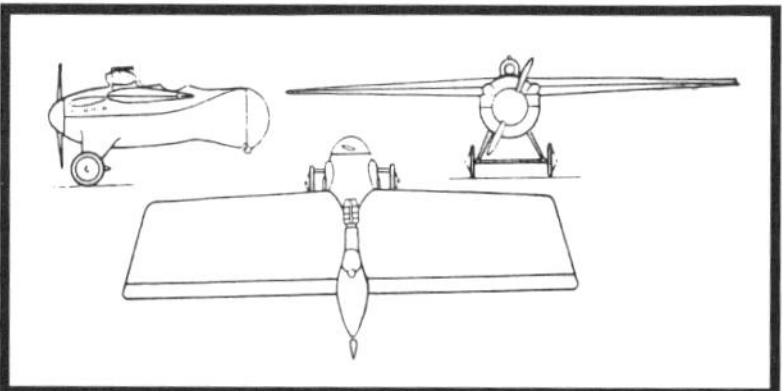

Figure 2.
The 1922 Arnoux "Simplex" racing monoplane designed by Carmier.

this area is aft of the CG, such a stall causes the airplane to nose-up. To permit the SF wing to stall ahead of the CG *first* (causing nose-down), an increase in the wing's angle of attack toward the tip (wash-in) is desirable. This adds to the wing's twisting tendency and reinforces the need for torsional strength.

It does not require much imagination to see a parallel between this SF wing and a canard configuration:

- In both, lift is upward.
- The canard foreplane and the SF wing's outboard areas must both stall first.
- The aft wing of a canard and the inboard portions of a SF wing must arrive at their angles of zero lift before that of the foreplane or outboard panel.

Canard design technology is thus applicable to SF tailless design, with one major difference: the inner portions of the SF wing are not affected by downwash from the outer portions. In canard design, downwash from the foreplane significantly affects the aftplane and is a design consideration.

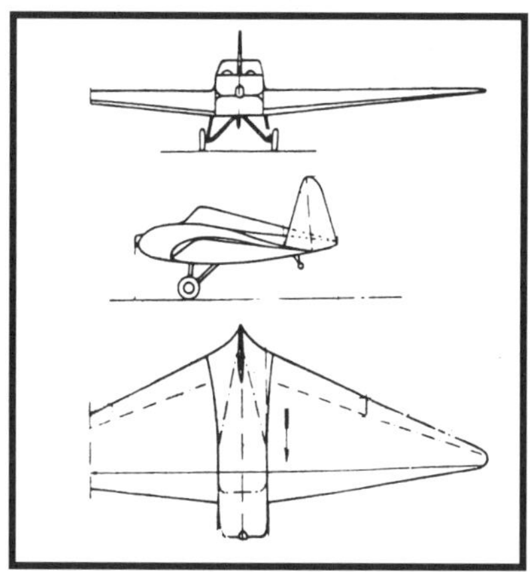

Figure 3.
The 1935 Fauvel A.V. 10 tailless light airplane.

PLAIN TAILLESS AIRCRAFT

Figure 2 is a three-view drawing of the Arnoux "Simplex"—a 1922 racing monoplane, which was powered by a 320hp Hispano-Suiza engine. Its top speed was 236mph and its landing speed a brisk 84mph. It crashed during a test flight before the Coupe Deutsch.

Flight controls were elevons and rudder, and the airfoil was a symmetrical Goettingen 411. The very short tail-moment arm from the CG to the elevons must have made longitudinal control and CG location very sensitive; stops restricted the downward movement of the elevons. Roll and yaw control was satisfactory, and the structure was good. To obtain the correct CG, a tractor engine and propeller were the only choices. The major disadvantage, longitudinally, of the plain wing is the short tail-moment arm.

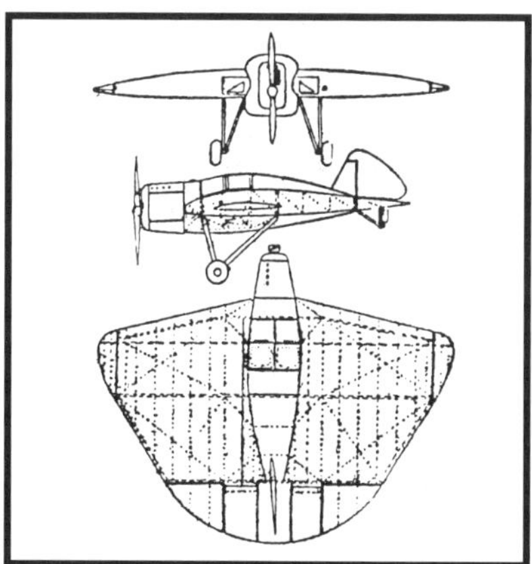

Figure 4.
Hoffman disk-type airpane.

Obviously, lower aspect ratios with the resulting longer chords would be an improvement. Coupling low AR with heavy taper results in even longer central moment arms.

Figure 3 illustrates the concept—the Fauvel A.V. 10 of 1935. Powered by a 75hp Pobjoy engine, it had a sharply tapered wing with an AR of 5.4. Its airfoil was heavily reflexed, without washout, and uniform across the span. Inboard trailing-edge elevators provided pitch control; outboard ailerons provided roll control; and a rudder controlled yaw.

The AV 10 performed well and was granted a French certificate of airworthiness, but no further developments occurred. Structurally, the wide, thick wing was light. A tractor engine and prop were the only choices.

The low-AR, wide-chord configuration was developed into the Hoffman disk-type airplane shown in Figure 4. The airfoil was a stable, reflexed M-section; the ailerons were the wingtip, floating variety; the elevators were inset at the semicircular trailing edge, and a large vertical surface was provided. An 85hp tractor engine and prop were used. It flew well, but no further developments took place.

Low-AR wings do not stall until they reach high angles of attack; and the danger of spins is remote. Slow, safe, landings at high angles of attack are possible. The Hoffman's long main landing gear reflects this capability.

In R/C model terms, the tailless plain wing concept is alive and well in Bill Evans' "Scimitar" series.

SWEPTBACK AIRCRAFT

Sweepback (SB) favors higher aspect ratios. For a given angle of SB (measured on the ¼ chord line) higher ARs result in longer tail moment arms for better longitudinal control. Higher SB angles have the same effect but result in lower lift.

High ARs demand greater strength and higher weight. Also, sweepback induces twist under flight loads, and that tends to reduce the wingtip's angle of attack. Good, torsional stiffness is required to remedy this.

During the '30s, the German Horten brothers developed a series of flying wings as shown in Figures

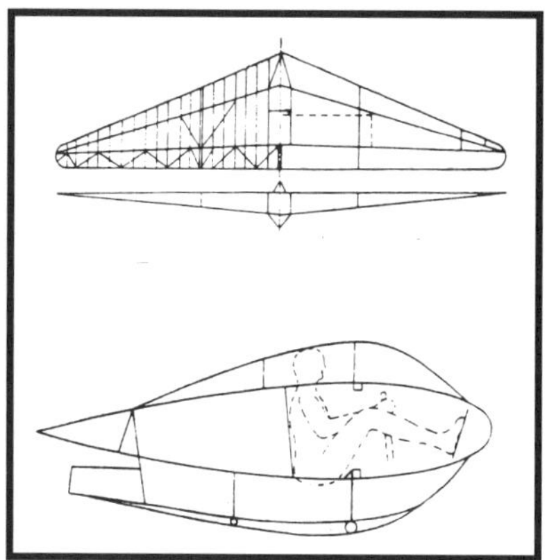

Figure 5.
The Horten brothers' first "flying wing" sailplane of 1933.

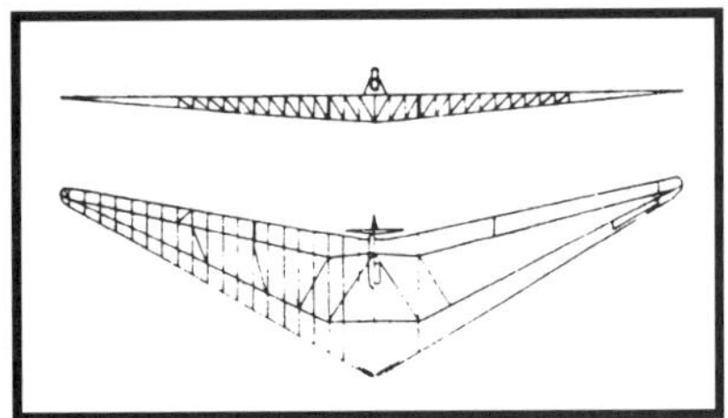

Figure 6.
A 60hp pusher prop on a Horten glider.

5 and 6.

The Horten flying wings had:

- Thick, sharply tapered planforms of symmetrical airfoil sections.
- Washout toward the wingtips.
- Elevators inboard and ailerons outboard on the trailing edges.
- Yaw control was provided by air brakes placed outboard on both the top and bottom surfaces, flush with those surfaces when not being used. No vertical surfaces were used.
- Dihedral on the lower wing surface.
- A cabin arrangement that, in later models, required that the pilot lie in a prone position, completely enclosed in the wing.

One version had an enclosed 60hp engine driving a pusher prop on an extension shaft (Figure 6). For R/C models, an electric motor enclosed in the wing, with an extension shaft, driving a pusher prop at the wing's trailing edge would be practical.

Figure 7 illustrates the Buxton glider of 1938. This interesting design had a thin, high-AR wing, symmetrical airfoils washed out to the wingtips, and vertical fins and rudders at the wingtips. Outboard elevons provided pitch and roll control. The pilot was housed in a pod below the wing. Small split flaps were used at the wing roots.

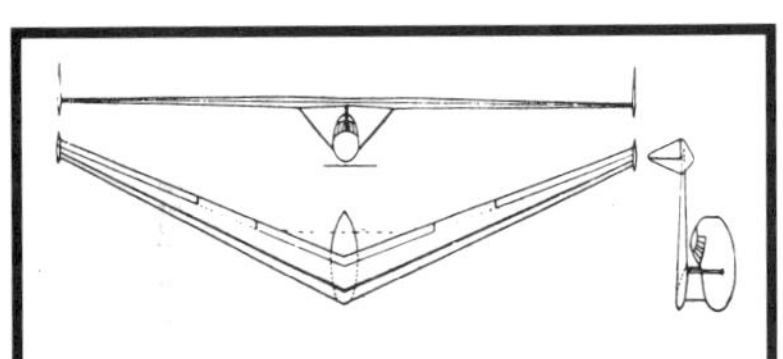

Figure 7.
The Buxton glider of 1938.

A more recent flying-wing design, the Davis Wing, is shown in Figure 8. It incorporates the design features of the ill-fated Northrop flying-wing bombers of the '40s. It also bears a close resemblance to the Horten designs.

The engine is a 65hp, water-cooled Rotax 532, in a well-streamlined pusher installation.

This wing had an AR of 6.67, a surprisingly large wing area of 240 square feet and a gross weight of 975 pounds for a wing loading of 4.06 pounds per square foot (low for a powered full-scale light airplane). A Cessna 172 weighs 2,300 pounds, has 174 square feet of wing area and wing loading of 13.2 pounds per square foot.

The Davis's top speed was a brisk 150mph—excellent, on 65hp; stall speed was a modest 42mph, thanks to its low wing loading. Its empty weight was 565 pounds, so it carried 73 percent of its weight as useful load.

The wing is sharply tapered and swept back 28 degrees on the ¼ chord line. Controls consist of split-drag rudders outboard and elevons inboard. Wisely, the narrow tips are equipped with fixed leading-edge slots to delay wingtip stalling. Obviously, the pusher engine and prop are best. No dihedral is needed on sweptback wings.

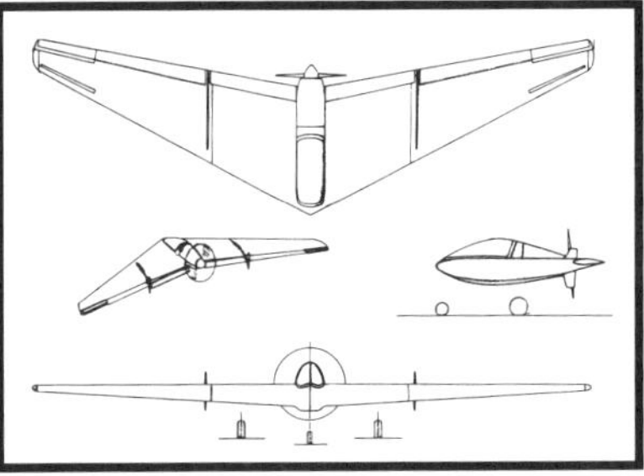

Figure 8.
The Davis Wing.

Richard Engel's "Winglet" *(Model Airplane News,* March 1994), powered by a pusher .40 and with a wing area of 900 square inches, is a good example of a flying-wing design.

COMBINED PLAIN AND SWEPTBACK AIRCRAFT

Figures 9 and 10 show the 1921 Wenk-Peschkes "Weltensegler" sailplane. This design illustrates the combined plain and sweptback wing planform, with a rectangular, dihedralled center section and anhedralled, sweptback, outer panels. The outer panels are set at lower angles of attack to provide the download to balance the forward CG. Controls were on the trailing edge of the outer panels.

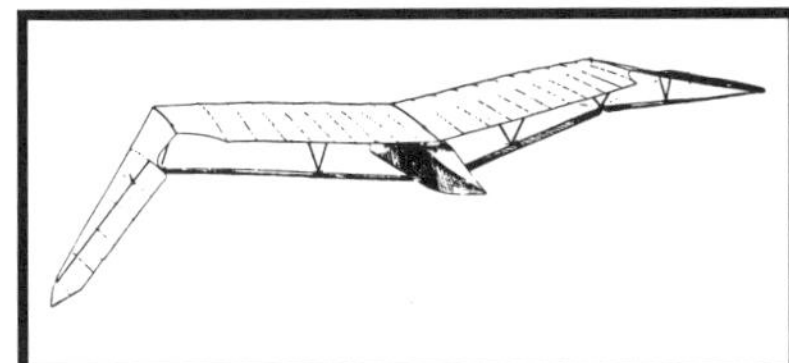

Figure 9.
The Wenk-Peshkes "Weltensegler" sailplane at the 1921 Rhön Competition.

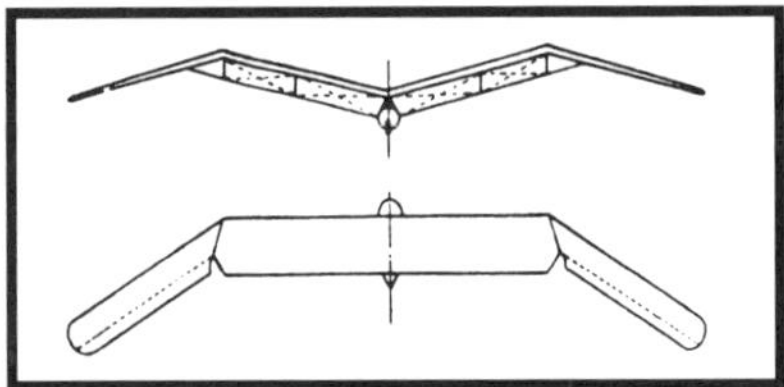

Figure 10.
Wenk-Peschkes "Weltensegler" sailplane (1921 type).

These outer panels, like an inverted V-tail, provided both horizontal and vertical surfaces. The elevons acted, in concert, as elevators; but differentially as ailerons. The downswept controls also acted as rudders into the elevon-induced turn, thus overcoming any adverse yaw.

As Figures 9 and 10 illustrate, the wing was externally braced, it had an AR of 11, and it weighed a low 93 pounds for a span of 53 feet and an area of 195 square feet. It flew successfully, but later broke up in flight, causing the pilot's death.

Figure 11 portrays a British pro-

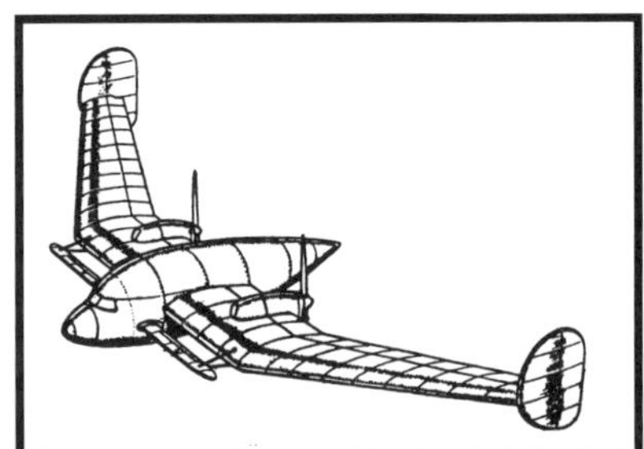

Figure 11.
Tailless airplane of F. Hadley Page and G.V. Lachmann.

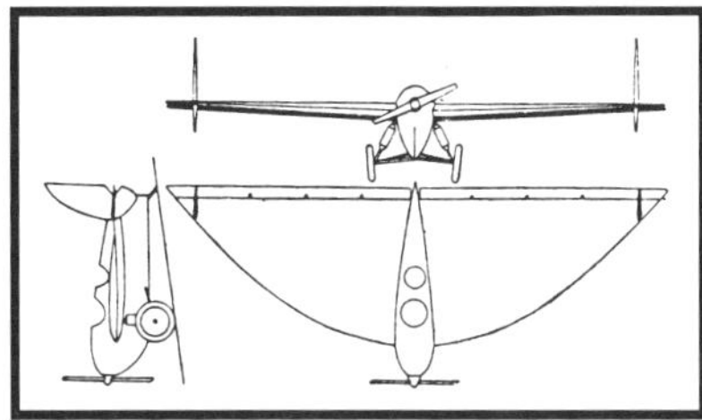

Figure 12.
The Tscheranowsky-Gruhon "Parabola."

ject: the Handley Page-Lachmann twin-pusher-engine tailless. This craft had the combined plain and swept planform, but with large vertical surfaces at the wingtips. This compensated for the fuselage and countered an "engine-out" situation.

The tab on the floating airfoil in front of the main plane is coupled with the landing flaps to counteract the nose heaviness caused by the deflected landing flaps. The advent of WW II probably stopped further development of this interesting design.

DELTA WINGS

The delta planform has the advantage of flying to very high angles of attack before stalling. High-lift devices are neither practical nor needed on this type of wing.

Over the years, many delta-wing designs have evolved. Figures 12 and 13 illustrate two such planes. Figure 12 is of the Tscheranowsky-Gruhon "Parabola," which was built by the Z.A.H.I. in 1931. Its wing section had a thickness of 7.7 percent. Figure 13 shows a design that might raise problems with lateral stability–the 1930 Abrial A-Viii light airplane. It was powered by a 95hp engine; it had a 22.4-foot span and 173 square feet of wing area; and it weighed 1,320 pounds. Note the reflexed airfoil.

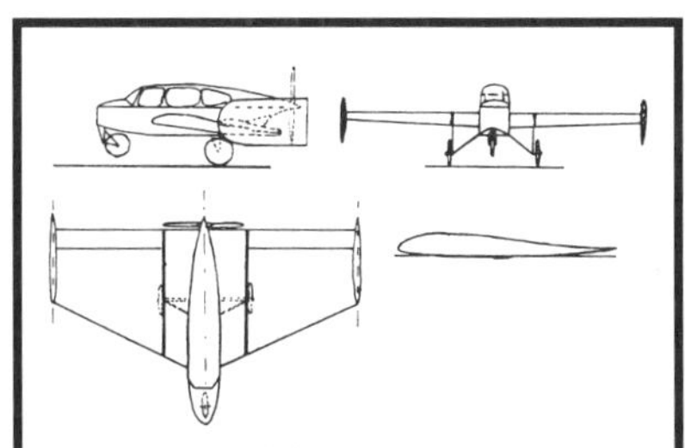

Figure 13.
The 1930 Abrial A-Viii light delta-wing airplane.

Figure 14 illustrates the original configuration of a Delta RPV (remotely piloted vehicle), which underwent wind-tunnel and flight tests at the Langley Research Center in Virginia.

Figure 15 shows the modifications resulting from wind-tunnel tests, confirmed by subsequent flight tests. Note the NASA leading-edge droop (*Model Airplane News,* June 1990—NASA Safewing) and RAO slots on the outboard wing panels to improve stall resistance. An R/C model based on the modified design would be an interesting project. The low AR, wide chord, and thick airfoil result in a light, strong structure. Obviously, a

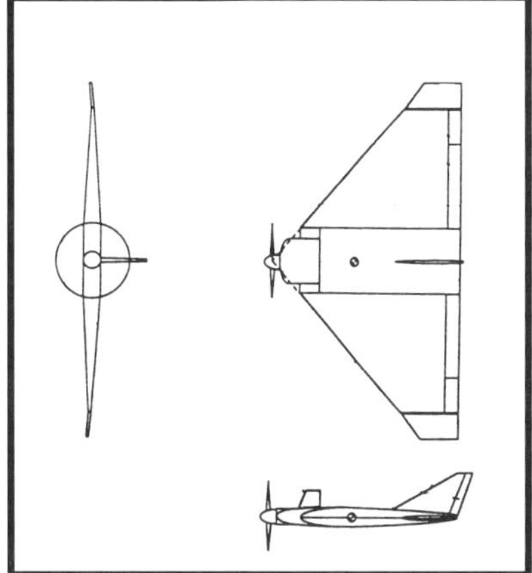

Figure 14.
Delta RPV; three-view sketch of base-line configuration.

tractor power unit is required; a pusher installation would present serious problems in correctly positioning the CG.

SWEPT-FORWARD WINGS

Few swept-forward tailless airplanes have been developed. Figure 16 shows one such design—the Landwerlin-Berreur racing monoplane of 1922. This "Buzzard"-type aircraft featured separate elevators and ailerons and a low-aspect-ratio tail fin. It was powered by a 700hp engine.

Figure 17 (from an *Aeromodeler* annual) shows a swept-forward, tailless, free-flight model. Note the heavily cambered airfoil sections and the large vertical surface.

AILERONS AND ELEVONS

Adverse yaw is an important consideration when dealing with high-aspect-ratio (AR) wings of plain, swept-back or swept-forward configurations—particularly for ailerons or elevons located near or at the wingtips. On this author's designs, the modified frise aileron (see Figure 1A in Chapter 10, "Roll Control Design") with heavy differential has been proven to provide roll control without adverse yaw. However, if they're used as elevons for elevator control, they should have equal up and down action. A two-servo arrangement, where the elevator servo moves the aileron servo back and forth, will provide the elevons with equal up and down action as elevators, and with differential action as ailerons.

On plain or delta wings of low AR, the need for anti-yaw differential is greatly reduced. On swept-forward wings (without high-lift devices), modified frise ailerons located at the wingtips and with anti-yaw differential are suggested. Elevators are then located at the inboard trailing edges where their moment arm from the CG is the greatest.

For swept-forward wings with

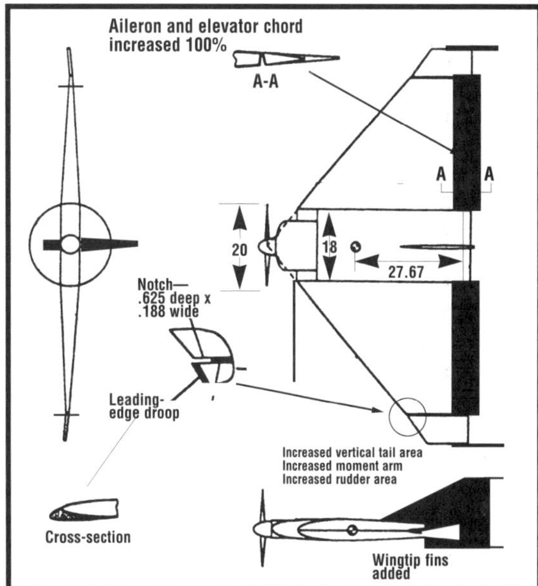

Figure 15.
Delta RPV configuration modifications.

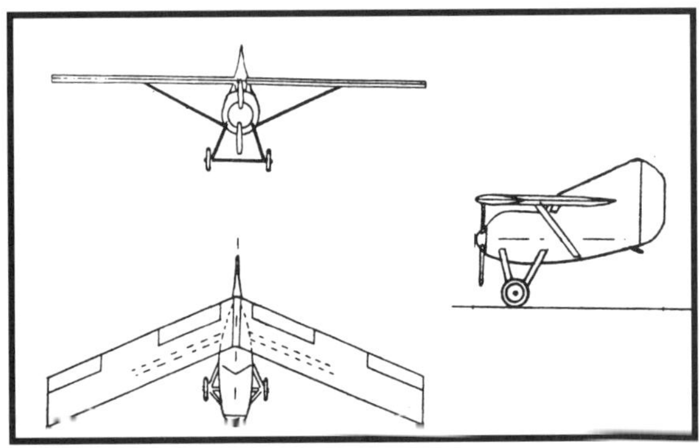

Figure 16.
1922 Landwerlin-Berreur.

inboard, high-lift devices, slotted elevators/elevons (similar to the slotted flap shown in Chapter 14, "Design for Flaps") are suggested. These provide additional lift to balance that of the high-lift devices.

It's suggested that elevators that are separate from ailerons be used where possible. The top-hinged variety (see Figure 1C in Chapter 10) with equal up/down action is suggested.

VERTICAL SURFACES

For plain, delta and swept-forward tailless planforms, a single vertical surface on the centerline is optimum. Placing the rudder-hinge line at or behind the wing trailing edge provides a healthy moment arm. Positioning ¼ to ⅓ of the vertical tail area below the wing will improve its effectiveness at wing-high angles of attack where the above-wing portion may be blanketed by the wing's turbulence. The anhe-draled and swept-back outer panels of the combined plain and sweptback tailless configuration present side areas that act as vertical surfaces. (The vertical tail area is described in Chap-ter 9, "Vertical Tail Design and Spiral Stability.")

Note that the sideways-projected areas are proportional to the angle at which these outer panels are anhe-draled; and their plan-view area is inversely proportional to this angle.

On sweptback tailless wings, the location that provides the greatest vertical tail-moment arm is at the wingtips (control surfaces with greater moment arms need less area for equal effectiveness). If symmetrical airfoil sections are used in the dual-wingtip vertical surfaces, "toeing-in" their chord lines by 2 or 3 degrees is suggested.

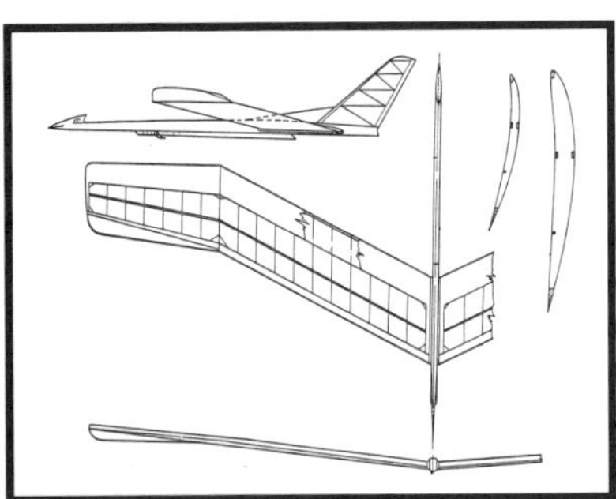

Figure 17.
M-tailless (with negative sweepback) by K. Ginalski of Poland.

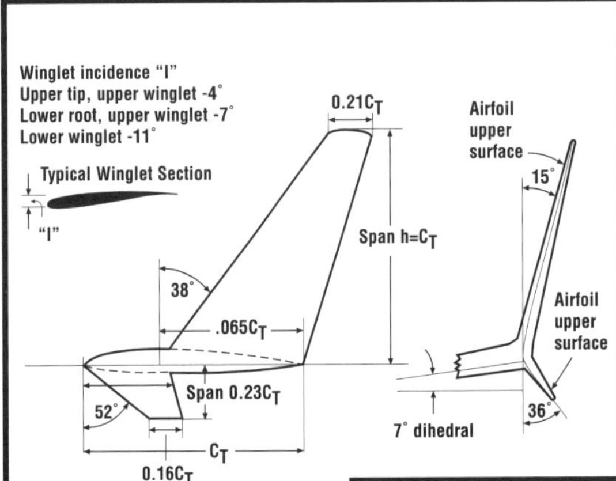

Figure 18.
Whitcomb Winglet

Two forms of winglets—the Whitcomb and the Grantz—may be used as wingtip vertical surfaces (see Figures 18 and 19). The dimensions of both are related to the wingtip chord and will provide vertical areas that may or may not be adequate. Determine the areas needed and, maintaining the same proportions, size the winglets to the desired area. Rudder area should be 30 percent of the area of any of the vertical surfaces discussed. On swept-forward wings, because of the directional instability of this planform, large central vertical surfaces are mandatory.

This author's Plover glider (see Chapter 26, "Construction Designs") had a vertical tail-moment arm of twice the wing's MAC and an area 10 percent of the wing's. A large vertical surface could result in spiral instability

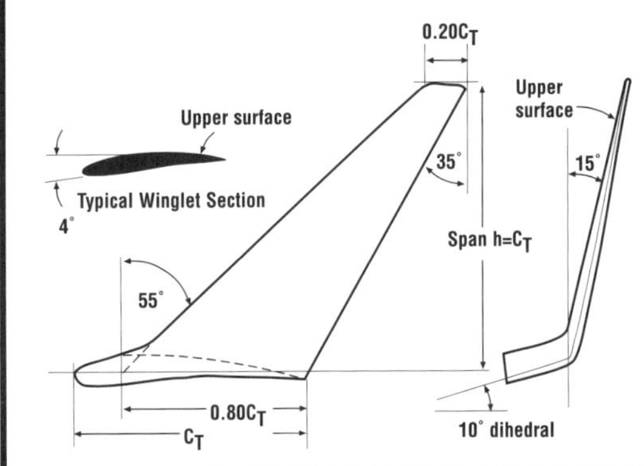

Figure 19.
Grantz Winglet.

SPLIT-DRAG RUDDERS AND SPOILERS

Northrop and Davis flying wings employed split-drag rudders at the wingtips as in Figure 20. Opened on one wing panel, the added drag acted like rudders. Engel's "Winglet" also has split-drag rudders.

Spoilers may be used for both glide control and directional control, but they may also replace ailerons for roll control when used on the wing's upper

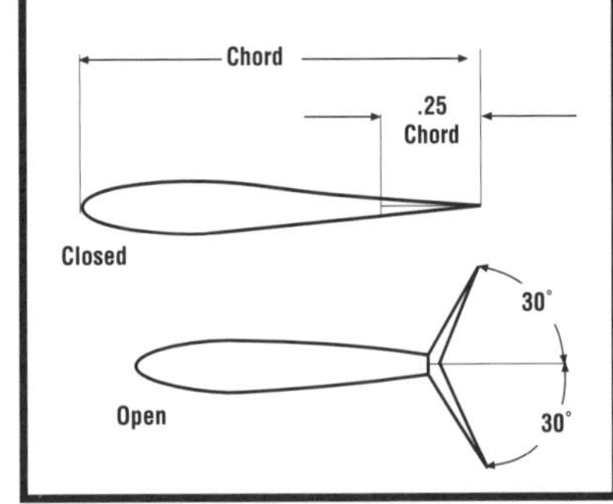

Figure 20.
Split-drag rudder design.

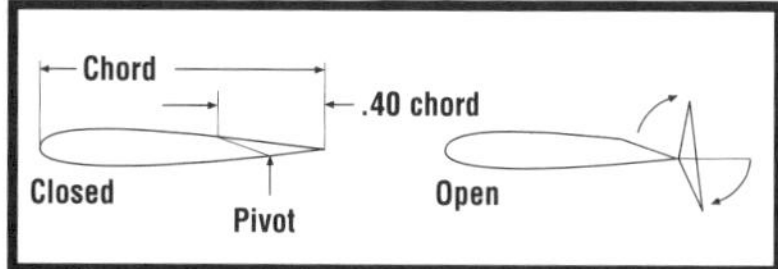

Figure 21.
Spoil-flap design.

surface only.

Placing the spoiler's LE beyond 70 percent of the wing chord avoids the lag between control action and response, which is characteristic of spoilers located farther forward on the wing chord.

Spoilers create desirable into-the-turn yaw, because only the spoiler on the inside of the turn is raised; its mate remains flush with the wing.

The Hortens used spoilers on both upper and lower wingtip surfaces for directional control. When not in use, both split-drag rudders and spoilers lie flush with the wing surface and cause no drag.

SPOIL FLAPS

Spoil flaps are shown in Figure 21. They were used on this author's "Dove"—a powered glider. The spoil flaps were used for glide control and proved to be successful. Their combined areas were 7 percent of the Dove's wing area. Extended, they didn't change the Dove's in-flight attitude, but they did cause a greater sink rate. They were used for slow, steep descents from height and for short, no-float landings. Used separately, they could act as drag rudders.

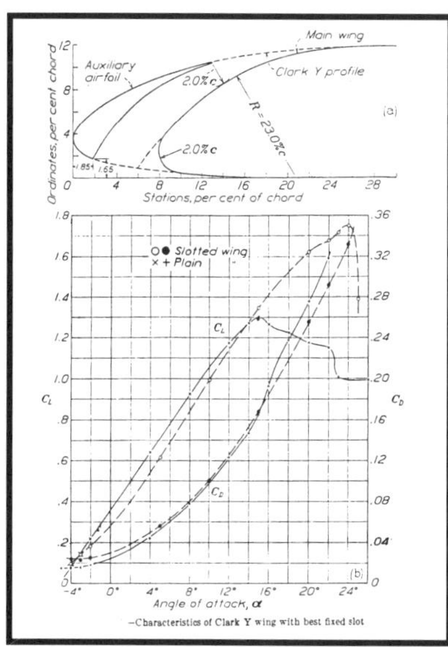

Figure 22.
Fixed leading-edge slot at Rn 600,000.

LEADING-EDGE FIXED SLOTS

Despite washout, swept-back, highly tapered wings are prone to tip-stalling at high angles of attack. This results in loss of longitudinal control. Fixed LE slots, as shown in Figure 22, delay the stall about 9 degrees and increase the max C_L substantially, but have very low drag. Both Northrop and Davis used them at the wingtips, extending for 25 percent of the wing's semi-span.

The basic dimensions for the slot shown in Figure 22 may be applied to any airfoil section.

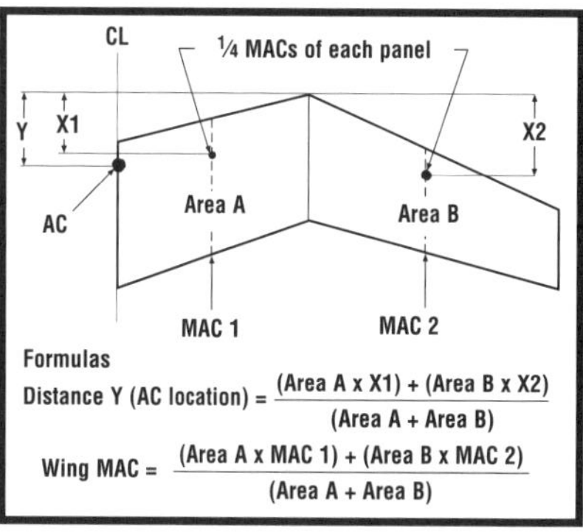

Figure 23.
AC and MAC of multi-tapered wings.

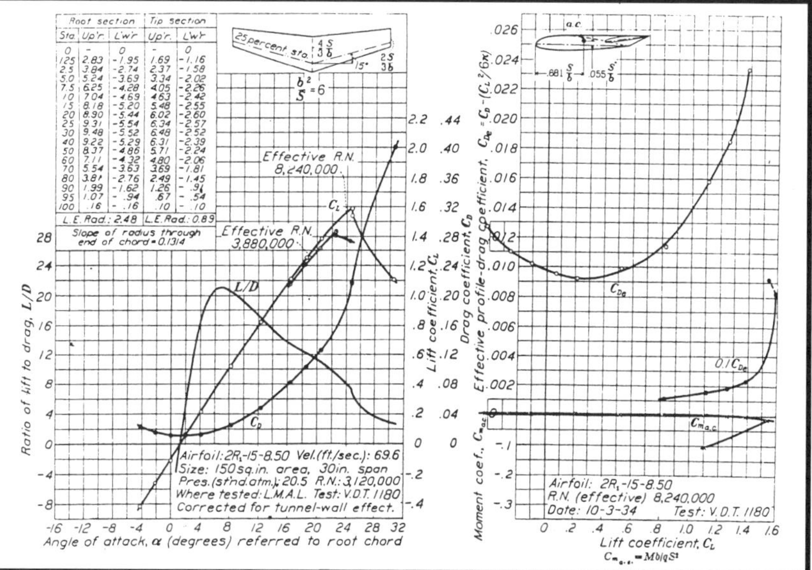

Figure 23.
Tapered NACA $2R_1$—15—8.50 airfoil.

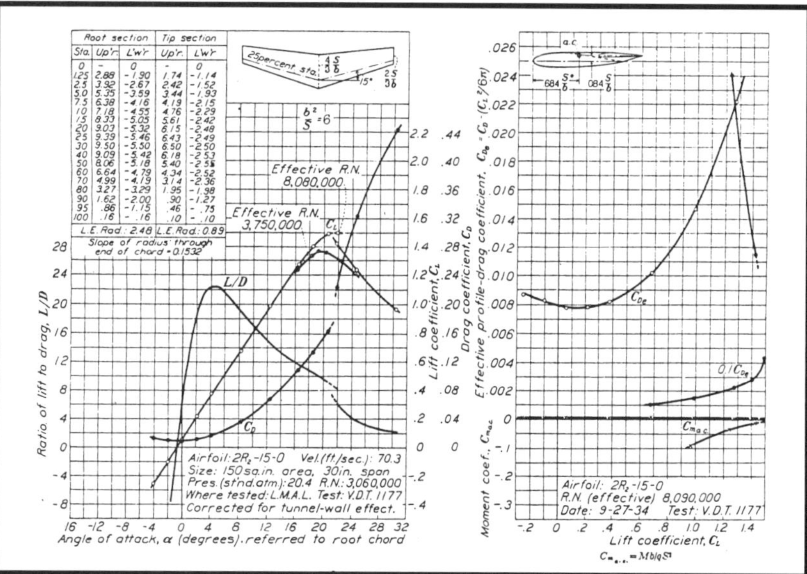

Figure 24.
Tapered NACA $2R_1$—15—0 airfoil.

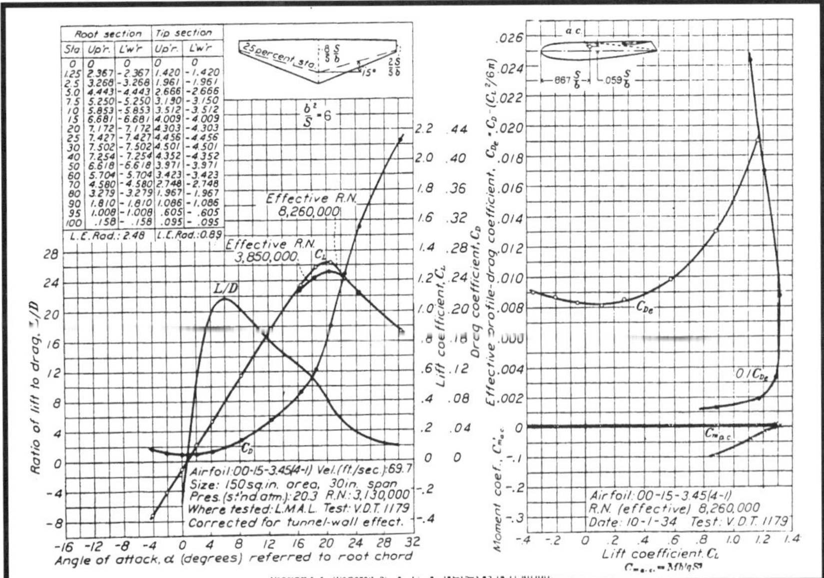

Figure 26. Tapered NACA 00—15—3.45 (4 to 1) airfoil

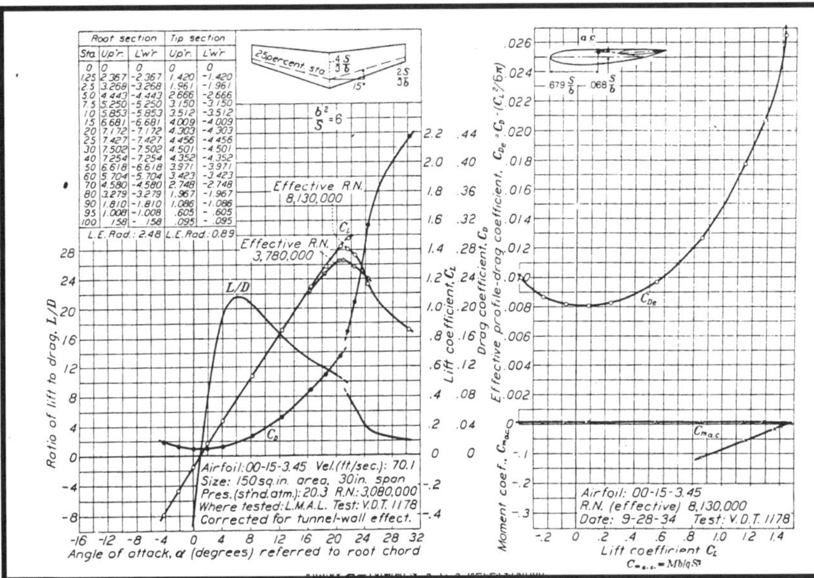

Figure 27. Tapered NACA 00—15—3.45 airfoil

WASHOUT AND SWEEPBACK

Figures 24, 25, 26 and 27 reflect wind-tunnel tests performed by NACA on four different wings. All were stable at the stall (pitching moment becomes negative). The wing shown in Figure 24 has a reflexed airfoil and 8.5 degrees of washout. The wing in Figure 25 also has a reflexed airfoil but no washout. The wings shown in Figures 26 and 27 have 3.45 degrees of washout.

In Figures 24, 25 and 27, the taper ratios are 2 to 1 from root to tip. In Figure 26, the wing's 4-to-1 taper invited early tip-stall, along with reduced C_L max. These figures provide root and tip airfoil ordinates and aerodynamic center location. "S" is wing area and "b" is span. Although tested at high Rns, these wings are a useful guide for swept-back designs.

DIHEDRAL

Sweptback and delta wings need no dihedral. The plain and swept-forward types should have the dihedral angles that are suggested in Chapter 9. Combined plain and sweptback wings need a healthy amount of dihedral in the plain section to compensate for the anhedraled tips.

STATIC MARGIN

As previously discussed, the AC and NP of tailless airplanes coincide. For stability, the CG must be ahead of the AC/NP. This produces a "force couple"—lift upward and CG downward—that must be balanced by a rear download.

The larger the static margin (the distance between the CG and AC/NP), the greater the aft download necessary. Centrifugal force created during maneuvers requires an increase in all three: lift, weight at the CG and balancing force.

Large static margins, however, are more stable longitudinally; small margins promote maneuverability, but reduce stability. A safety margin (SM) of 5 to 10 percent of the wing's MAC is suggested.

The swept-forward wing obtains equilibrium by increased lift created toward its tips. This permits the use of cambered, high-C_L-max airfoils, healthy stability margins and high-lift devices.

WEIGHT DISTRIBUTION

This is important, longitudinally, for tailless airplanes, because of their limited longitudinal control when compared with "tailed" airplanes (Chapter 11, "Weight Distribution in Design"). Massing the fixed weights of power and control units as close to the CG as possible is recommended for tailless designs. Positioning the fuel tank on the model's CG will avoid a possibly destabilizing shift of the CG as fuel is consumed and the tank becomes lighter.

LOCATING THE AC AND MAC

In Chapter 1, "Airfoil Selection," graphic methods for locating the AC and MAC of straight, tapered and sweptback wings are explained.

For multi-tapered wings—such as the one shown in Figure 23—obtain the ¼ MACs of each panel (A and B) using the methods shown in the aforementioned article. Calculate the area of each panel (in square inches) and, using the simple formulas that accompany Figure 23, obtain the wing's AC and its MAC. ▲

Chapter 24

Hull and Float Design

Few events give greater satisfaction than the successful first flight of a model airplane that one has conceived, designed and built. Ensuring the success of that first flight and of subsequent flights is what this series is all about.

Flying off water adds two new elements: hydrostatics (buoyancy) and hydrodynamics (planing lift).

Flying boat or floatplane flying is, if anything, more fun than flying off land. There are few trees over water to reach up and grab your model, and water is more forgiving than terra firma.

■ **Float and hull basics.** Figure 1 shows views of a float, or hull, with three cross-sections. Note the following key points:

—The "step" separates the forebody from the afterbody.

—The "keel flat" is the reference line for the "trim angle" shown in Figure 2.

—The "sternpost angle" governs the hull's (or float's) trim angle at the "hump."

—The "beam" is a critical dimension.

—The "step depth" is also a critical dimension.

—The "angle of deadrise" bears on the hull's planing performance.

—The "deck" is only a reference line. The top contour is the designer's choice.

■ **Float and hull factors.** For successful water flying, the following conditions must be met:

—There must be adequate buoyancy with substantial reserve while afloat.

—Planing surfaces should have a wetted area that's large enough to permit the model to accelerate to flying speed quickly.

—The hull's (or float's) trim angle at the hump should not cause the wing's airfoil to exceed its stalling angle of attack.

—Spray should be well-controlled; in particular, it should be prevented from hitting the propeller.

—There should be no porpoising on takeoff, and no skipping on landing.

—The model should weathercock to face into the wind when at rest, or when taxiing on water at low speeds.

PLANING ACTION AND THE STEP

Figure 2 illustrates the step's function. Planing at speed, the forebody creates a trough in which the afterbody planes. With adequate step depth, the hull or float rides on two areas, and porpoising, or skipping, is minimized.

HULL DEVELOPMENT

The hull or floats described here were developed by NACA scientists and tested in 2,000-foot-long towing basins. Recorded were:

■ Water resistance, with a range of loads.

■ Trim angles, "free to trim" under hydrodynamic forces in the displacement range, i.e., up to the hump and at various controlled trim angles at planing speeds in excess of hump speed.

■ Scale-wing lift forces were included in the tests.

■ Spray, porpoising and skipping tests were conducted during simulated takeoffs and landings.

■ Optimum CG locations, relative to the step.

Two hull or float designs were selected for this chapter. The

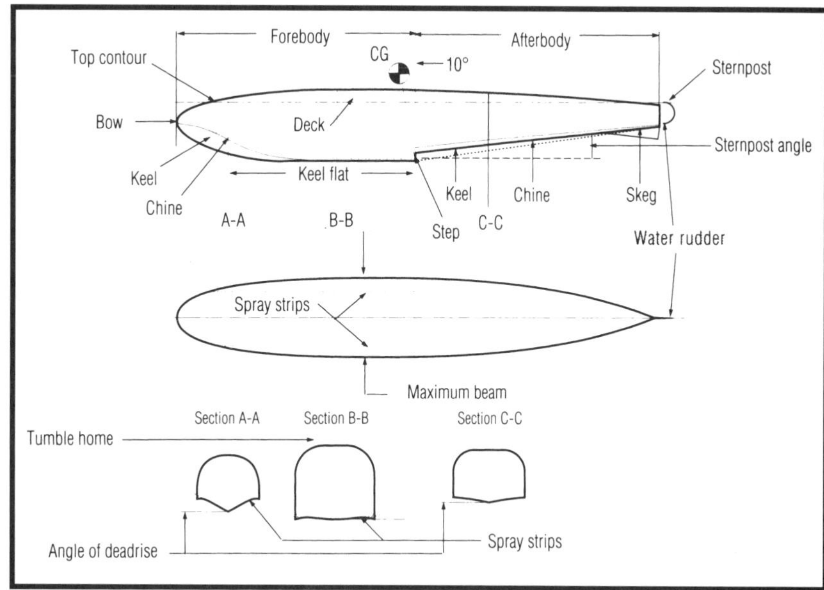

***Figure 1.* Hull or float basics.**

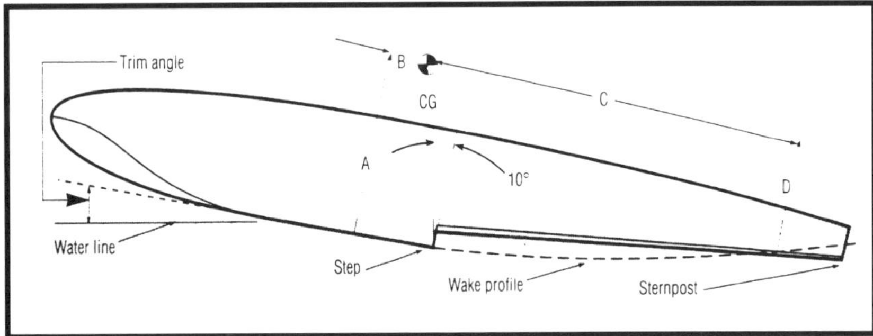

Figure 2.
Forces on a hull in two-step planing.

dimensions of both are comparable to those of R/C model water planes.

The first design has a short afterbody that's suitable for floatplanes. The second, with a long afterbody, is suitable for flying boats. Both designs were tested with sternpost angles of 6 , 8 and 10 degrees.

THE "HUMP"

Figures 3 and 4 provide resistance and trim angles for the short and long afterbody hull/floats. Both figures merit close scrutiny.

Note the high points in the resistance curves—known, for obvious reasons, as the "hump." Not surprisingly, the maximum trim angles coincide with the hump. Beyond hump speed, trim and resistance fall off as the hull accelerates to plane "on the step."

Up to the hump, trim is controlled by both hydrostatic and hydrodynamic forces with little effective elevator action. Beyond the hump, trim is progressively elevator-controlled as speed increases to liftoff velocity. Notable is the influence that sternpost angles have on trim angles *at the hump* for both afterbody lengths. By judicious selection of the sternpost angle, one can control hump trim angles within a fairly wide range.

There are two causes of hump resistance:

- The hull is transitioning from being a floating object supported by hydrostatic buoyancy to being a planing object supported by hydrodynamic forces that act mainly on the forebody bottom, but with buoyancy still having some effect.

- The hull/float must rise from full displacement depth, floating, to its planing depth aided by wing lift as it accelerates.

If the wing's AoA is above its stalling angle at hump trim, the wing will stall, and its contribution to raising the aircraft will be largely lost. Stalled, the wing will lose roll damping and aileron control, and the wing floats may dig in and cause water looping.

A model wing's stall angle—at low Rn, in ground effect, and with slotted flaps extended—may be as low as 10 degrees. A short afterbody hull/float with a sternpost angle of 10 degrees has hump trim of 12.5 degrees—well above the wing's stalling angle.

A properly designed forebody bottom and spray strips will run very cleanly. Spray hitting the wings, tail, or propeller can slow takeoff, not to mention damage the prop. At prop-tip speeds of close to 300mph, water is pretty "solid."

BEAM AND CG LOCATION

The hull/float maximum width, or beam, is critical for good water performance. *Too much beam* adds weight and air drag and makes the model hydrodynamically ready to lift off *before* the wing provides adequate lift. Skipping and wing stall may result.

With *too little beam,* the model sits low in the water and has higher hump resistance and heavier spray. Takeoff runs are longer. Too much beam is better than too little.

A study of NACA reports on hull design indicated that a hull, planing at the wing's stall speed, should generate enough hydrodynamic lift to support the model's gross weight. Further, at this speed, the "wetted" length of the forebody bottom would roughly equal the beam. The wetted area would then be the beam multiplied by the beam (beam^2).

The stall speed of a model depends on two factors: the wing's C_L max and its wing loading in ounces per square foot of wing area.

Model airfoils have a broad average C_L max of 1.00, so wing loading is the major factor governing a model's stall speed. It was concluded that a planing area (beam^2) relationship to wing loading could be used for float/hull-beam determination.

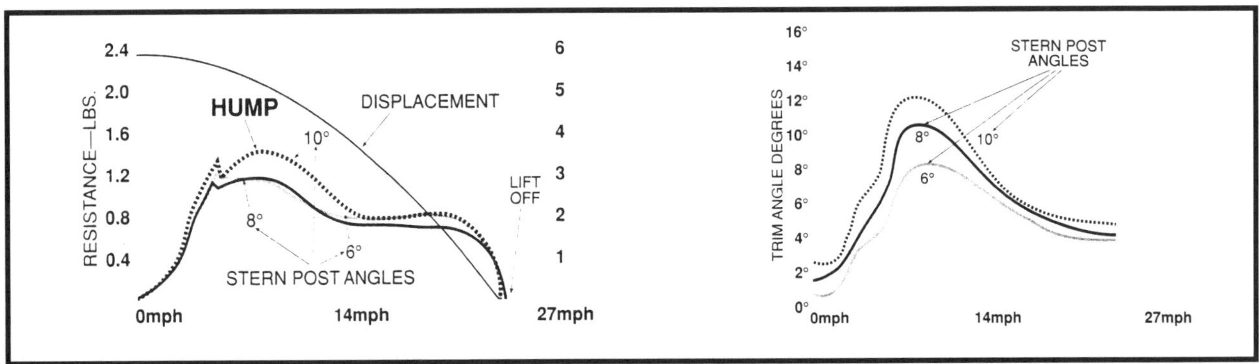

Figure 3.
Resistance and trim angles; short afterbody and sternpost angles of 6, 8 and 10 degrees; beam^2 loading at 2.5 oz. per square inch.

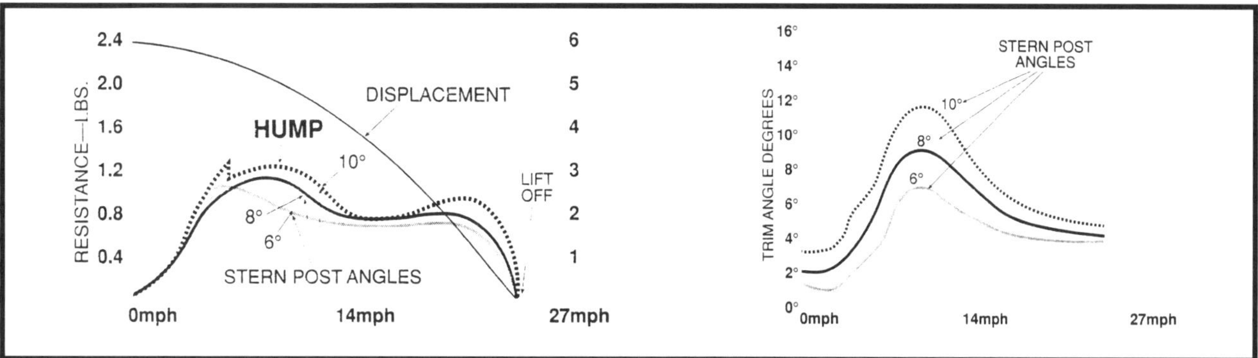

Figure 4.
Resistance and trim angles; long afterbody and sternpost angles of 6, 8 and 10 degrees; beam² loading at 2.5 oz. per sq. in.

An empirical solution to the beam problem was developed by an analysis of the wing loadings versus beam² loading of some 25 model flying boats and floatplanes, as shown in Figure 5.

The curve in Figure 5 averages the various points and may be used to determine your model's beam as follows:

- Estimate your design's gross weight (Figure 6 will help).
- Divide gross weight in ounces by the model's wing area in square feet to provide its wing loading in ounces per square foot.
- Refer to Figure 5, and select the beam² loading that corresponds to the wing loading. For example, a wing loading of 20 ounces per square foot (horizontal) calls for a beam² loading of 2.6 ounces per square inch of beam (vertical).
- Divide gross weight by the beam² loading. The result is the forebody's wetted area in square inches. A gross weight of 93.6 ounces, divided by a beam² loading of 2.6 ounces per square inch gives a wetted area of 36 square inches.
- The beam is the square root of the wetted area. For 36 square inches, the beam would be the square root of 36, or 6 inches.
- For a twin-float plane, divide the beam in half for each float, i.e., 6 divided by 2, or 3 inches per beam for each float. Step depth should be based on the total beam (6 inches, in this example) and would be 8.5 percent of 6 inches, or 0.5 inch for each float.

Figures 1 and 2 show the best CG location: along a line at 10 degrees to the vertical, ahead of the step/forebody bottom corner.

The wing's optimum location is with its center of lift (¼ of MAC) vertically in line with the CG.

PORPOISING AND SKIPPING

Porpoising is the up-and-down oscillation of the bow that occurs beyond hump speed. Skipping occurs on landing when the plane touches down several times. Landing too fast contributes to skipping, but adequate step depth (8 to 9 percent of the beam) avoids both of these undesirable characteristics.

PLANING TAIL HULLS

During the 1940s, in search of improved performance, NACA continued its towing-basin tests, but on a new hull form.

This hull featured a deep pointed step and a CG positioned at or behind the step. The aim was to have the afterbody contribute more to the hull's hydrodynamic lift—hence, the name: "planing tail hull."

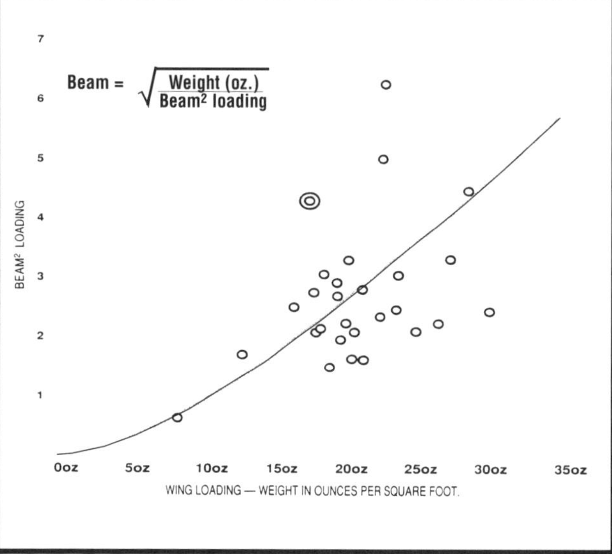

Figure 5.
Beam chart.

This author designed, built and flew a model with this hull—the Flamingo (see Chapter 26, "Construction Designs"). Powered by a Torpedo 0.15cid engine and controlled by a Babcock receiver and escapements, it flew well; the hull was efficient.

Some years later, it was modernized with an O.S. Max 0.35cid engine and a 4-channel radio that provided rudder, elevator aileron and engine control.

One very undesirable trait surfaced: the Flamingo always weathercocked pointing downwind—not good for takeoffs! This was because of its narrow afterbody, rearward CG and deep step, all of which combined to make the model's stern sink low in the water.

Above-water side areas were well forward; *below-water* side areas were well aft. Wind striking the side caused the model to weathervane—but pointing downwind. Water- and air-rudder control tried hard to correct this condition, but the downwind wingtip float's water drag rendered these controls ineffective.

NACA tested further variations of this hull and arrived at a configuration with no afterbody, just a very deep pointed step. Two booms extending back from twin engine nacelles replaced the afterbody and carried horizontal and twin vertical surfaces at their aft ends. This concept is reflected in the author's Sea Loon (Figure 7). It flew well.

But the booms, which also provided lateral stability on the water, did not sink into the forebody's wake as in Figure 2, but rode on or just under the undisturbed water on either side of the forebody, as in Figure 7.

Figures 3 and 4 do not apply to this configuration. Hump trim for the Sea Loon was established by carefully selecting the vertical-step depth to provide a 9-degree sternpost angle. The objective was to avoid wing stall at hump trim. Once past the hump, the twin booms were clear of the water.

FOREBODY

Figure 8 provides typical forebody cross-sections of full-scale water aircraft. Type A "flat" is the most effective hydrodynamically, but it planes with heavy spray. V-bottoms (type B) absorb landing shock, but reduce effectiveness and have heavy spray. Types C, D and E are designed to reduce "pounding" on takeoff and landing. Type F "cathedral" is popular for motorboats; spray is well-controlled without external spray strips, which are fragile and cause high air drag.

Type G "suggested" combines the efficiency of the flat bottom with the spray control of the flared and cathedral types. Above all, its construction is both simple and rugged (as shown in Figure 9) and applies to both hulls and floats.

Afterbodies do not require spray strips; otherwise, construction is the same as that shown in Figure 9 and based on the principles in Chapter 13, "Stressed Skin Design."

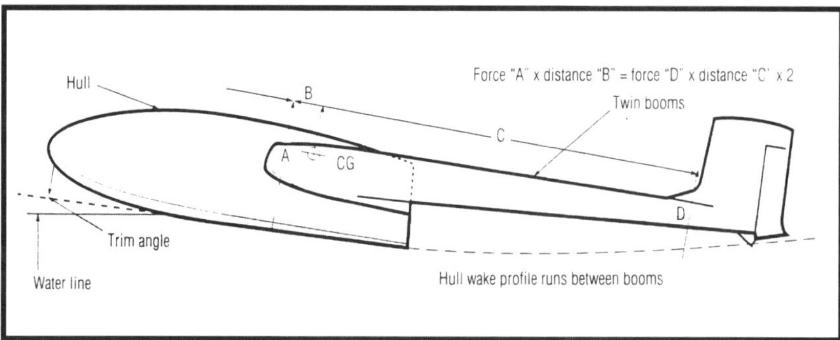

Figure 7.
Sea Loon II—planing action of hull and twin boom afterbodies.

BOW CONTOURS

Bow contours for full-scale aircraft depend on the aircraft's function. Flying boats for heavy sea duty would have boat-like bows; for more moderate duty, bows may have a more streamlined shape. The type illustrated in Figure 10 has proven itself for model hulls and floats, and it's not difficult to make.

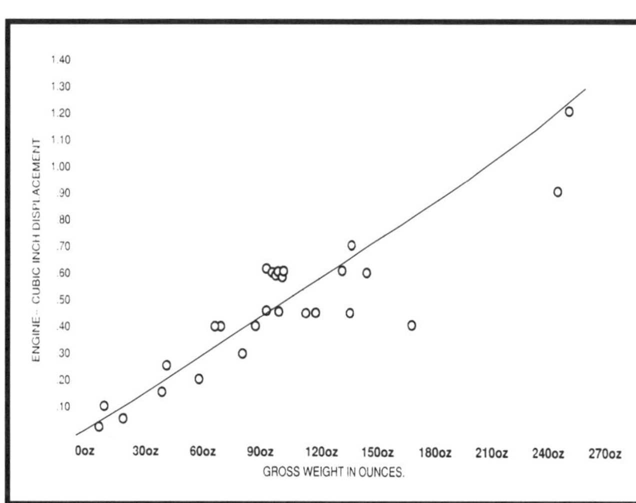

Figure 6.
Engine displacement vs. gross weight.

BUOYANCY

A cubic inch of water weighs 0.58 ounce. A model weighing 100 ounces would require a displacement of 100 divided by 0.58, or 173 cubic inches, *plus* 100 percent reserve buoyancy, for a total of 346 cubic inches.

The NACA models on which Figure 10 was based were designed with 100 percent reserves for a 94-ounce model (at the hull's lowest load). Adequate buoyancy is not a problem.

For twin floats, a maximum depth that's equal to the maximum beam and a length that's 60 to 70 percent of the airplane's length provide adequate buoyancy and reserves.

FLOAT OR HULL PROPORTIONS

Figure 10 provides proportions of both short- and long-afterbody hulls or floats. The short version, if used for a flying boat, would require an extension to provide an adequate tail-moment arm (TMA) for longitudinal stability. The long version provides such a TMA.

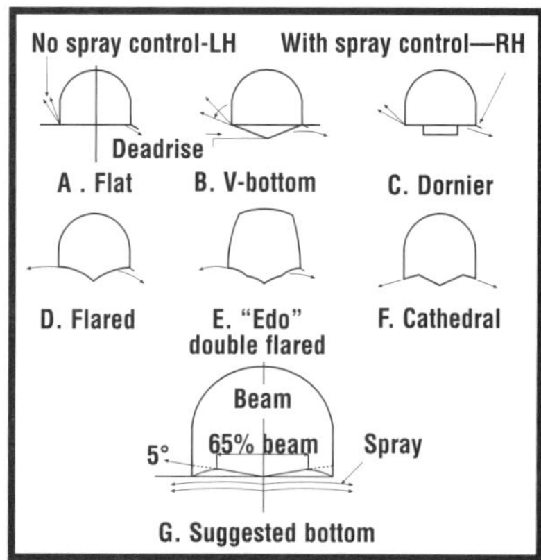

Figure 8.
Hull and float forebody bottoms and spray control.

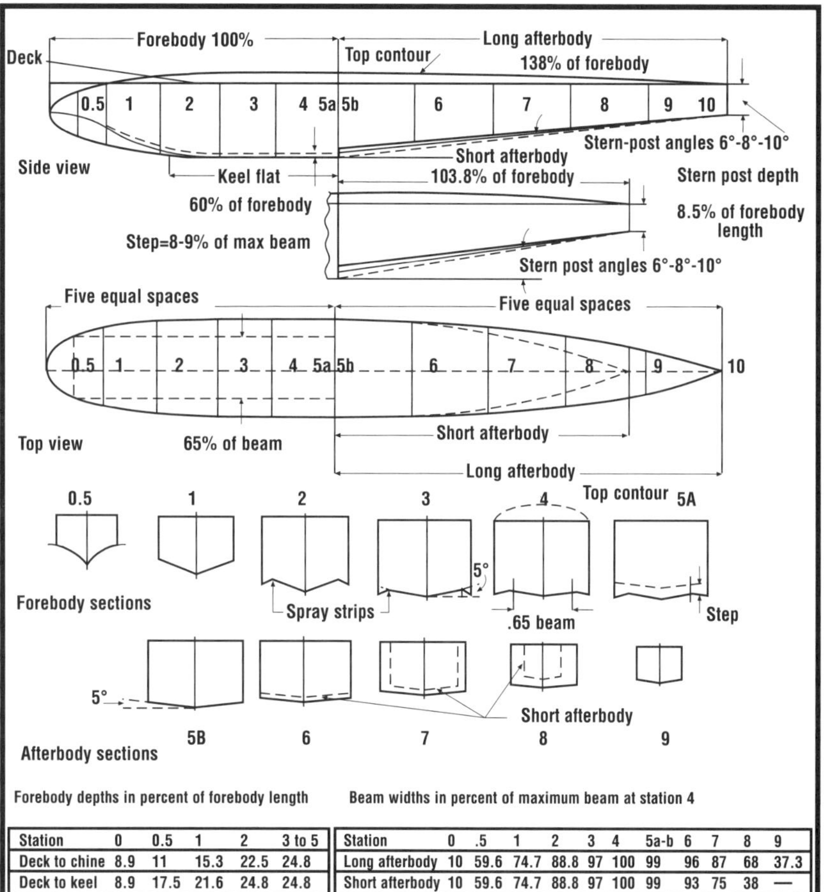

Station	0	0.5	1	2	3 to 5
Deck to chine	8.9	11	15.3	22.5	24.8
Deck to keel	8.9	17.5	21.6	24.8	24.8

Station	0	.5	1	2	3	4	5a-b	6	7	8	9
Long afterbody	10	59.6	74.7	88.8	97	100	99	96	87	68	37.3
Short afterbody	10	59.6	74.7	88.8	97	100	99	93	75	38	—

Figure 10.
Hull or float proportions.

Knowing the hull's (or float's) total length and having arrived at the beam, the dimensions of either version are easily calculated. Note that hull or float depths are based on the forebody length, and widths are in percentages of the beam.

For twin-float planes, the calculated beam is divided by 2 to provide each float's beam. Overall float length is 60 to 70 percent of the plane's length. The step depth is based on the total beam and is applied to each float.

WING ANGLE OF INCIDENCE

Chapter 18, "Propeller Selection and Estimating Level Flight Speeds," provides the basis for calculating the angle of incidence necessary to provide adequate lift at the model's estimated level cruise speed. For the Seagull III, this was 0.5 degree.

WING'S STALLING ANGLE AND HUMP TRIM

Chapter 16, "Landing Gear Design," details the calculations necessary to arrive at the wing's stalling angle (at landing-speed Rns, in ground effect and with flaps extended).

The Seagull III's net stalling angle during the takeoff run is 15 degrees. Since the wing is set at 0.5 degree in level flight, the stall would occur 14.5 degrees later.

The Seagull III's hull is the long-afterbody type with a sternpost angle of 10 degrees. Hump trim for this hull is 12 degrees; but because the forebody keel flat is set at *plus* 2 degrees for level flight, this model's *hump* trim angle is reduced to 10 degrees. With a wing stall at 14.5 degrees and hump trim of 10 degrees, there is a good safety margin—and wing stall at hump trim is avoided.

Beyond the hump, the elevators take control of the model's trim, and at liftoff speed, moderate up-elevator causes the model to become airborne.

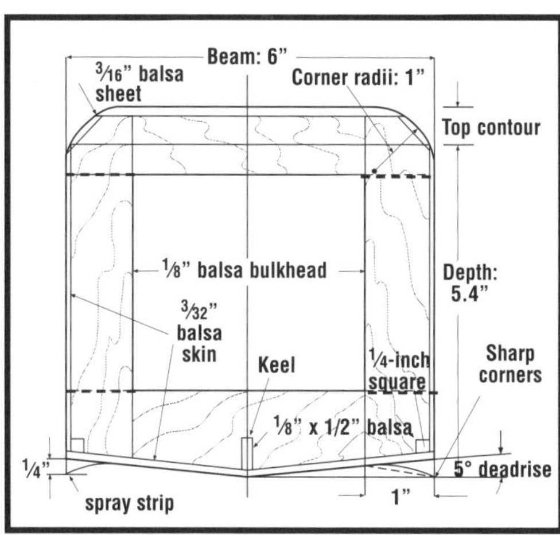

Figure 9.
Typical hull or float construction.

FLYING BOAT LATERAL STABILITY AFLOAT

Flying boats and single-float seaplanes need wing floats to prevent them from tipping over. These must provide sufficient buoyancy to cover a situation in which the model is slowly taxiing crosswind with the hull (or single float) on the crest of a wave and the downwind float in a nearby trough. The upwind wing panel is elevated at a considerable angle to the wind, tending to submerge the downwind float or even capsize the model.

These wing floats may be located anywhere from the wing's tip to its root. Mounted close to the root, the floats must be larger to provide the greater buoyancy needed; farther out, they may be smaller and lighter and have less drag.

The planing surfaces of these wing floats must be of adequate area and set at a great enough angle to the hull's keel flat to cause the float to recover quickly while planing when disturbing forces cause the model to heel, lowering one wingtip float to the water surface.

WINGTIP FLOAT DESIGN

Refer to Figure 11. When the model heels to submerge one float, the CG is displaced a distance "X." This distance, in inches, multiplied by the model's weight in ounces, gives the unbalancing moment in inch-ounces. The corrective force is the buoyancy of the submerged float in ounces, multiplied by the distance

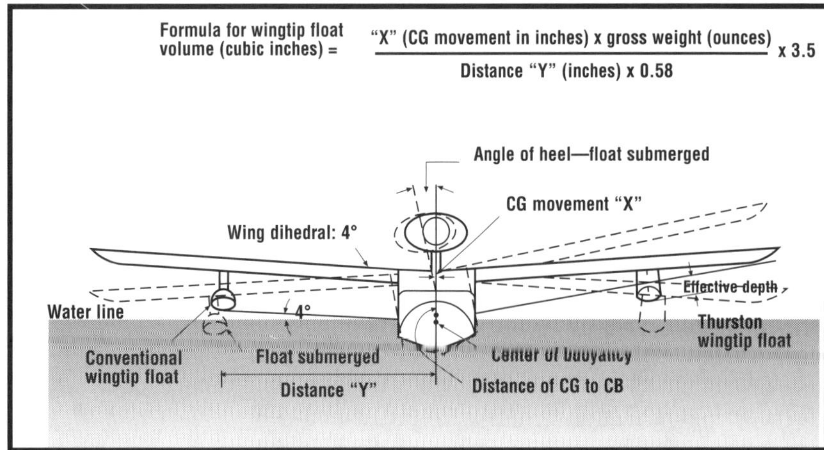

Figure 11.
Wingtip-float-volume calculation.

Seagull III in a flaps-down landing. Note the well-controlled spray from the forebody bottom and the plane's "at the hump" attitude.

between the float and hull centerlines. The corrective buoyancy in ounces has to be converted to cubic inches and increased for the reserve buoyancy. The formula in Figure 11 for float volume does all this and includes a 250-percent reserve.

To design a float that has low drag *and* the required volume is not difficult. Lay out a block that will provide the volume in cubic inches that provides the calculated buoyancy (Figure 12). The width is the float beam based on the hull beam^2 loading; its length will be roughly four times that of the beam. Both depth and beam are calculated using the formulas in Figure 12. Draw the 3-views of your float in and around this block as shown. The float bottoms should be flat with sharp chine corners.

The float bottom should be set at 3 degrees to the hull's keel flat, as shown. Viewed from the front, the float bottom should parallel the water surface at contact for maximum recovery action when planing.

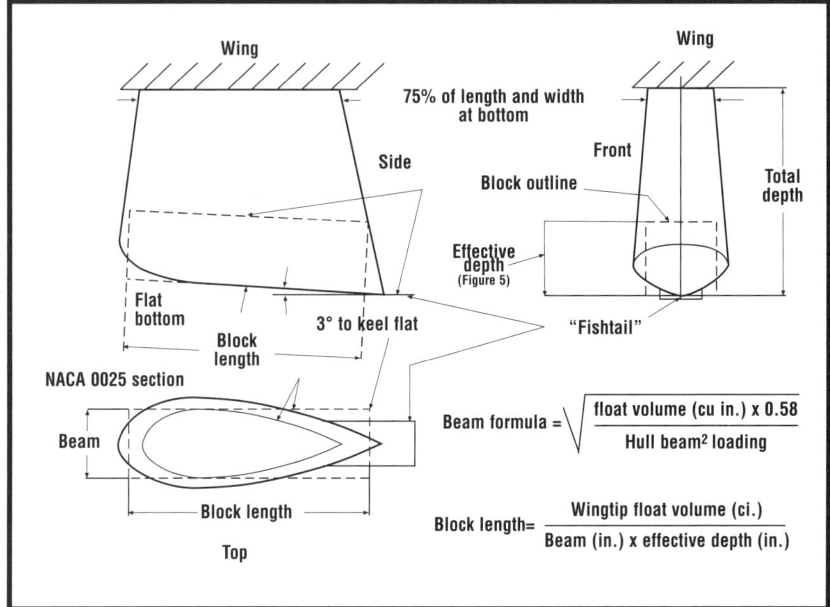

Figure 13.
Development of "Thurston" float from basic block.

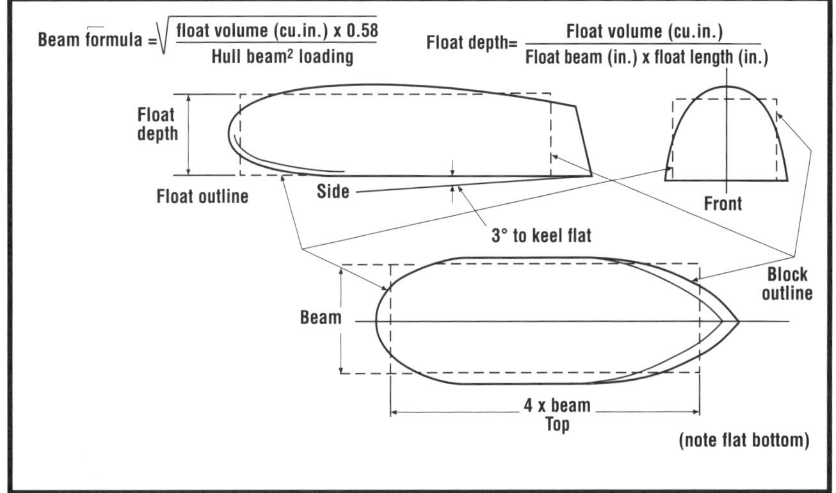

Figure 12.
Method of developing float lines from basic block of wingtip float volume.

THE THURSTON FLOAT

The Seagull III incorporates the Thurston float at its wingtips. These are light and rugged, easily made using sheet balsa and have low drag. Figure 13 provides their design basis.

WATER RUDDERS

Water planes should have water rudders for directional control because the air rudder is ineffective when the plane taxies at low speed. The Seagull III has a water rudder at the base of the air rudder. The Osprey and Seahawk have water rudders operated by separate servos twinned to the receiver's rudder channel. All have good water control. ▲

Chapter 25

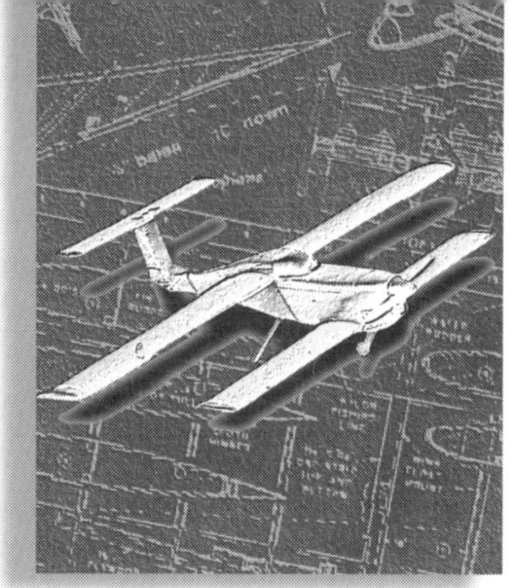

Basic Proportions for R/C Model Aircraft

Many modelers design their models to reflect their own individuality. For many reasons, they do not choose to follow the detailed and sometimes complex suggestions presented by authors such as me.

The basic proportions presented here are for a range of models to help modelers exercise their urge to originate unique, yet successful, models. They are easy to follow and require a minimum of calculation; and they're divided into six categories represented by:

■ **Figure 1.** Basic proportions for eight models with engine sizes of from .10 to .60.

■ **Figure 2.** Basic twin-float proportions.

■ **Figure 3.** Basic flying boat proportions.

■ **Figure 4.** Basic glider proportions.

■ **Figure 5.** Proportions for aerobatic models powered by .40 to .50 engines.

■ **Figure 6.** Airfoil layout procedure and ordinates for six airfoils. See appendix for performance curves.

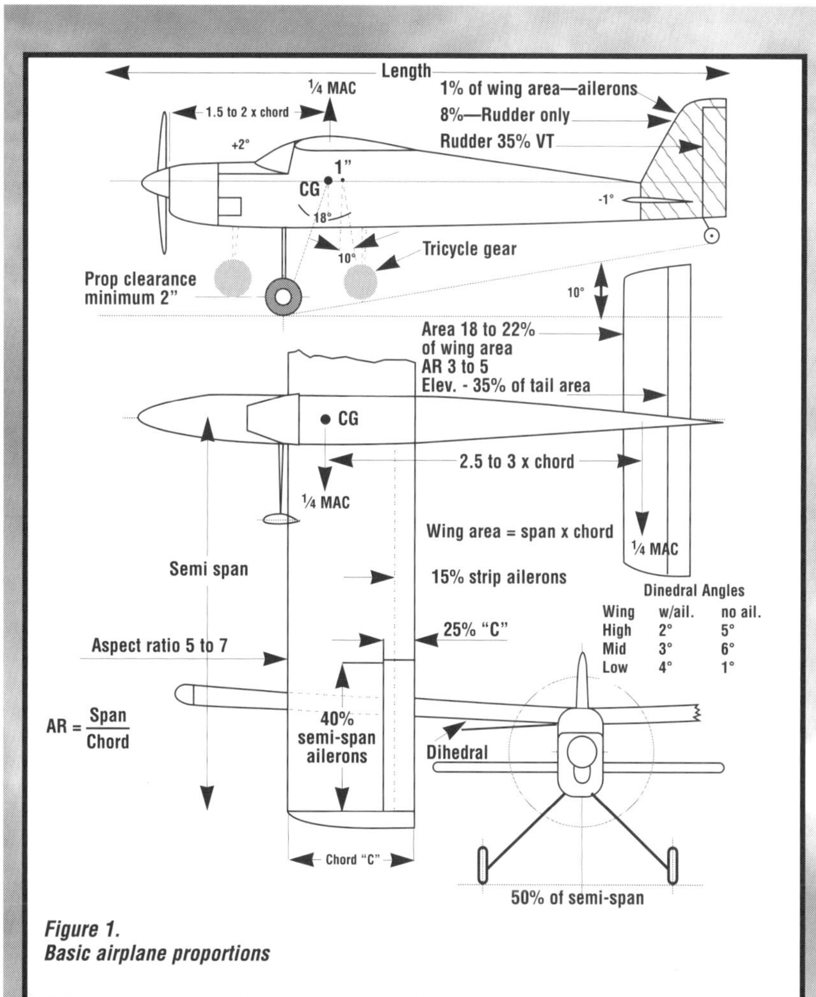

Figure 1.
Basic airplane proportions

Engine disp. (cid)	Wing area (sq. in.)	Wing loading (oz./sq. ft.)	Estimated gross wt. (oz.)	Power loading (oz./cid)	Prop (d x p) (in.)	Wheel diameter (in.)	Speed at C_L 2.0 (mph)
0.10	300	14	29	290	7x4	1.75	42
0.15	325	15	34	226	8x4	1.75	44
0.25	450	17	53	212	9x4	2	46
0.35	550	19	73	208	9x6	2	48
0.40	600	19	79	198	10x6	2.25	48
0.45-6	700	20	97	215	11x6	2.5	49
0.50	750	20	104	208	11x6	2.5	49
0.60-1	800	20	111	185	12x6	3.0	49

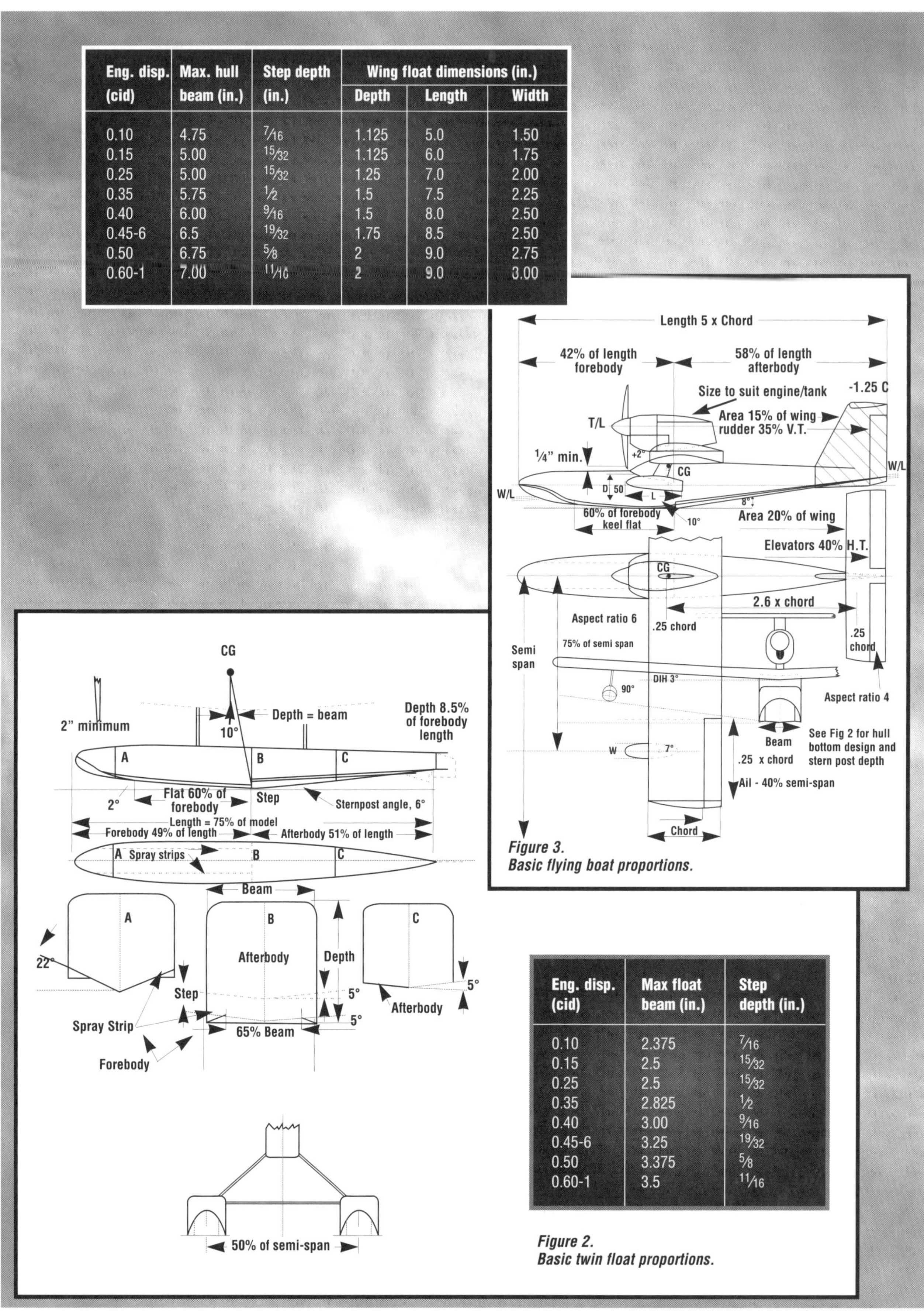

Eng. disp. (cid)	Max. hull beam (in.)	Step depth (in.)	Wing float dimensions (in.)		
			Depth	Length	Width
0.10	4.75	7/16	1.125	5.0	1.50
0.15	5.00	15/32	1.125	6.0	1.75
0.25	5.00	15/32	1.25	7.0	2.00
0.35	5.75	1/2	1.5	7.5	2.25
0.40	6.00	9/16	1.5	8.0	2.50
0.45-6	6.5	19/32	1.75	8.5	2.50
0.50	6.75	5/8	2	9.0	2.75
0.60-1	7.00	11/16	2	9.0	3.00

Figure 3.
Basic flying boat proportions.

Eng. disp. (cid)	Max float beam (in.)	Step depth (in.)
0.10	2.375	7/16
0.15	2.5	15/32
0.25	2.5	15/32
0.35	2.825	1/2
0.40	3.00	9/16
0.45-6	3.25	19/32
0.50	3.375	5/8
0.60-1	3.5	11/16

Figure 2.
Basic twin float proportions.

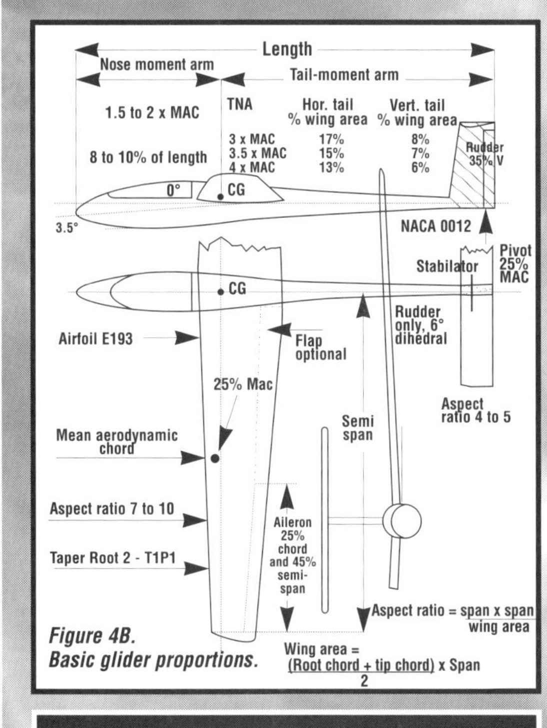

Figure 4B.
Basic glider proportions.

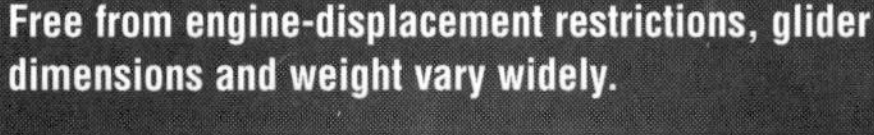
Free from engine-displacement restrictions, glider dimensions and weight vary widely.

Wing area	500 to 1,000 sq. in.
Span	60 to 100 in.
Aspect ratio	7 to 15
Wing loadings	6.5 to 12 oz. per sq. ft.
Weight	25 to 75 oz.
Controls	Rudder and elevator only to aileron, rudder, elevator, flaps (or spoilers)
Wing airfoils	Clark Y, E193, E197—your choice
Tail airfoils	NACA 0012, E168
Control weights	Rudder and elevator only—6.25 oz. (receiver, 2 small servos, 250mAh battery)
	Aileron, rudder, elevator, flaps (spoilers)—12 oz. (4 standard servos, 500mAh battery)

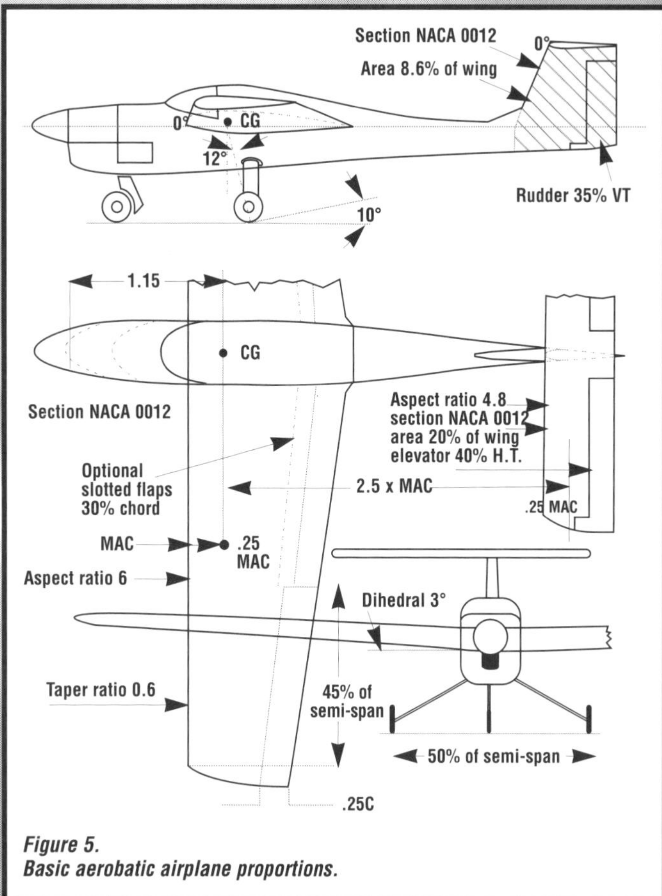

Figure 5.
Basic aerobatic airplane proportions.

All five models are powered by .46 engines and have APC 10x9 props

Wing area	Wing chords (in.)		Wingspan	Weight	Wing loading
(sq. in.)	Root	Tip	(in.)	(oz.)	(oz./sq. ft.)
400	10.2	6.12	49	82	29.5
500	11.4	6.85	54.75	87	25
600	12.5	7.5	60	92	22
700	13.5	8.1	64.80	97	20
800	14.4	8.7	69.25	102	18.4

AIRFOIL LAYOUT PROCEDURE

Every serious modeler should know how to develop an airfoil from its published ordinates.

These describe each airfoil by three measurements:

- Chord length and stations along the chord.

- Depth (ordinates) above and below the chord line at each station.

- Leading-edge radius and location of its center.

All measurements are *percentage of the chord length.* An exception is the Clark Y, whose depth is measured from its flat bottom, *not* its chord line. With the bottom level, the Clark Y is at an angle of attack of 2 degrees, measured on its chord line.

This author measures the stations in 1⁄10-inch intervals, along the chord line, from the leading edge. Some interpolation is necessary.

Depths above and below the chord line are measured in 1⁄50-inch intervals; some interpolation is needed. The necessary calculations are simple.

Stations

Chord length x station percentage. Example: chord 7 in. x station 50 is 3.5 inches from the leading edge.

Ordinates (depths)

$\frac{\text{Chord length (in.)}}{2}$ x percent depth

Example: a 7-inch chord with 7.88% depth at station 50 is 7 ÷ 2 x 7.88 = 27.58 fiftieths above the chord line at station 50.

Most calculators have a "Constant" feature. Using it, the chord length is entered once; the station or ordinate percentages only are needed to complete the calculation.

Note that ordinates below the chord line are negative, e.g., -2.5.

Nose radius

Quoted as a percentage of the chord's length, NACA airfoils, such as NACA 2412, locate the *center* of the nose radius by "slope of radius through the end of chord 2/20." Simply measure 2 inches from the chord leading edge; erect a vertical line 0.2 inch high, above the chord line. The diagonal, from the chord line to the top of the vertical line, locates the center of the nose radius. On a 10-inch wing chord, this radius would be 0.158 inch. Laying out one airfoil section takes 15 to 20 minutes. For an untapered wing, this is no problem. However, for a high-aspect-ratio tapered wing with many different ribs, this procedure is both long and tedious.

Given chord lengths, airfoil setion designations, skin thickness/spar location and sizes various companies can provide very accurate computer-generated airfoil sections at a reasonable cost.

Figure 6A illustrates a layout of a 7-inch chord E193 section with vertical line at each chord station. In Figure 6B, the ordinate lengths, above and below the chord line have been measured. Using French curves, the points are joined smoothly to outline the airfoil. ▲

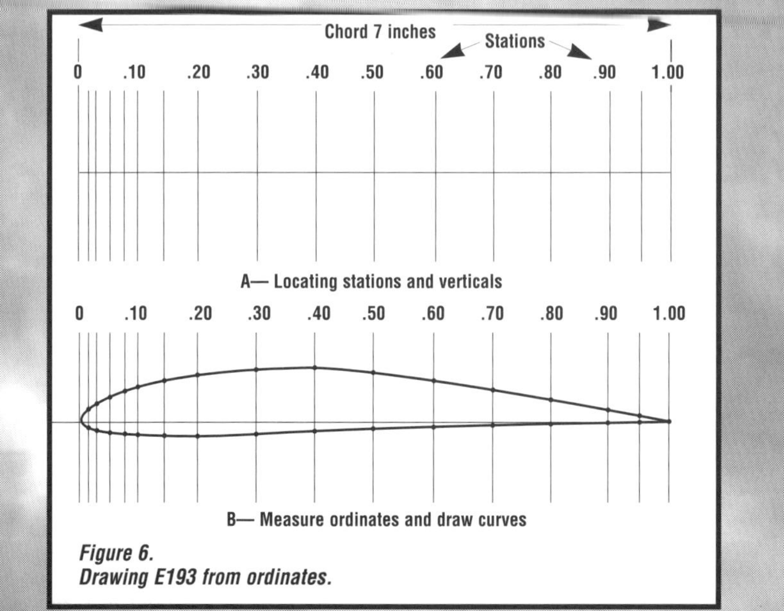

Figure 6.
Drawing E193 from ordinates.

STATION % OF CH	FLAT BOTTOM				SEMISYMMETRICAL				SYMMETRICAL			
	CLARK Y		E193		NACA 2412		E197		NACA 0012		E168	
	U	L	U	L	U	L	U	L	U	L	U	L
0	3.50	3.50	0	0	0	0	0	0	0	0	0	0
1.25	5.45	1.93	1.78	-1.14	2.15	-1.65	2.00	-1.46	1.894	-1.894	1.95	-1.95
2.50	6.50	1.47	2.44	-1.30	2.99	-2.27	2.64	-1.82	2.615	-2.615	2.60	-2.60
5.0	7.90	0.93	3.76	-1.78	4.13	-3.01	4.12	-2.60	3.555	-3.555	3.68	-3.68
7.5	8.85	0.63	4.74	-2.00	4.96	-3.46	5.16	-3.14	4.2	-4.200	4.34	-4.34
10	9.60	0.42	5.52	-2.16	5.63	-3.75	6.08	-3.46	4.683	-4.680	4.84	-4.84
15	10.68	0.15	6.68	-2.24	6.61	-4.10	7.36	-3.96	5.345	-5.340	5.60	-5.60
20	11.36	0.03	7.54	-2.40	7.26	-4.23	8.24	-4.26	5.738	-5.738	6.06	-6.06
25	–	–	–	–	7.67	-4.22	–	–	5.941	-5.941	–	–
30	11.70	0	8.5	-1.78	7.88	-4.12	9.340	-4.20	6.002	-6.002	6.18	-6.18
40	11.40	0	8.48	-1.40	7.80	-3.80	9.38	-3.88	5.803	-5.803	5.80	-5.80
50	10.52	0	7.76	-1.04	7.24	-3.34	8.76	-3.00	5.294	-5.294	4.88	-4.88
60	9.15	0	6.66	-0.60	6.36	-2.76	7.40	-2.38	4.563	-4.563	3.76	-3.76
70	7.35	0	5.2	-0.36	5.18	-2.14	5.48	-1.64	3.664	-3.664	2.86	-2.86
80	5.22	0	3.58	-0.08	3.75	-1.50	3.70	-0.96	2.623	-2.623	1.80	-1.80
90	2.80	0	2.0	-0.01	2.08	-.82	2.16	-0.38	1.448	-1.448	0.84	-0.84
95	1.49	0	0.84	-0.00	1.14	-.48	1.00	-0.20	0.807	-.8070	0.40	-0.40
100	0.12	0	0	-0.00	0.13	-0.13	0	0	0.126	-0.126	0	0
LE radius	1.50		0.67		1.58 Slope 2/20		0.84 0		1.58		1.24	

Key: CH = chord; U = upper; L = lower.

Chapter 26

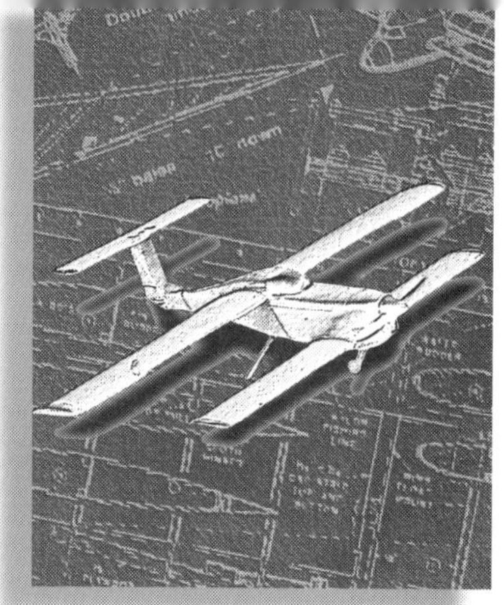

Construction Designs

Here are a few of the innovative R/C airplane models that the author has designed. The various sport planes, canards, three-surface and amphibious designs and gliders included illustrate a variety of the design elements and approaches described in this book.

SEAHAWK

Type	*amphibious sport*
Gross weight	*110 oz. (land); 121 oz. (water)*
Wing area	*655 sq. in.*
Wing loading	*24.3 oz./sq. ft. (land); 26.6 oz./sq. ft. (water)*
Beam^2 loading	*3.33 oz.*
Engine	*46*
Prop	*11x8*
Power loading	*239.9 oz./cid(land); 263 oz./cid (water)*

(Model Airplane News, Oct. '92)

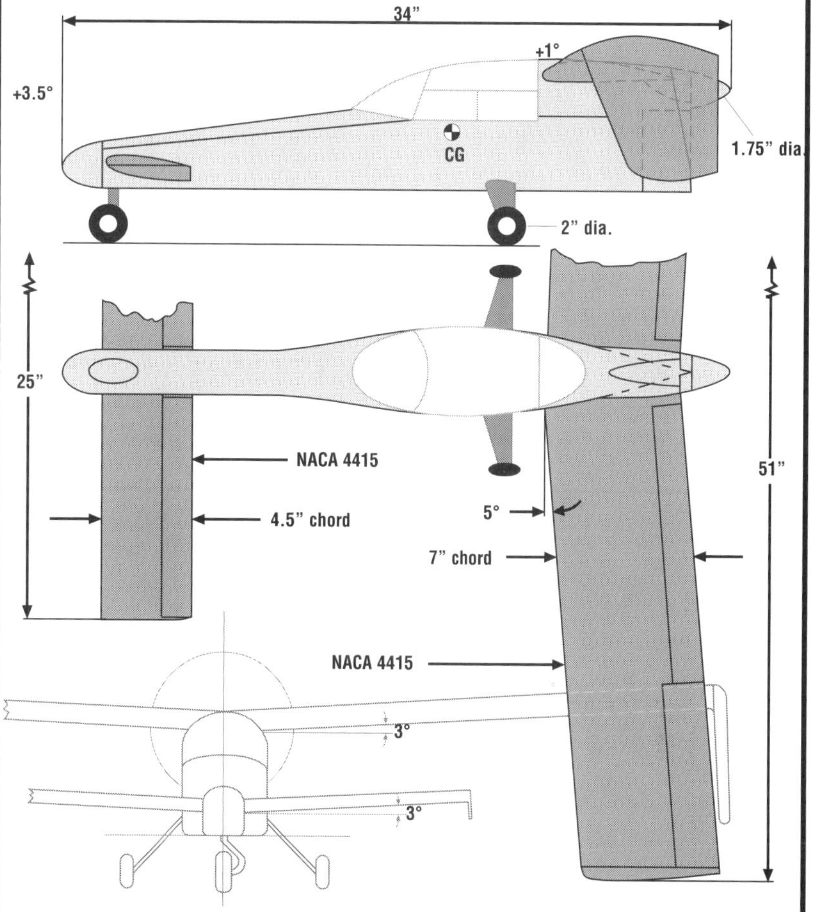

34"
+1°
+3.5°
CG
1.75" dia.
2" dia.
25"
51"
NACA 4415
4.5" chord
5°
7" chord
NACA 4415
3°
3°

CANADA GOOSE

Type	*canard*
Gross weight	*75 oz.*
Wing area	*444 sq. in.*
Wing loading	*24.3 oz. sq. ft.*
Engine	*30 to .35*
Prop	*10x5 or 10x6 pusher*
Power loading	215 oz./cid

(Model Airplane News, Jan. '81)

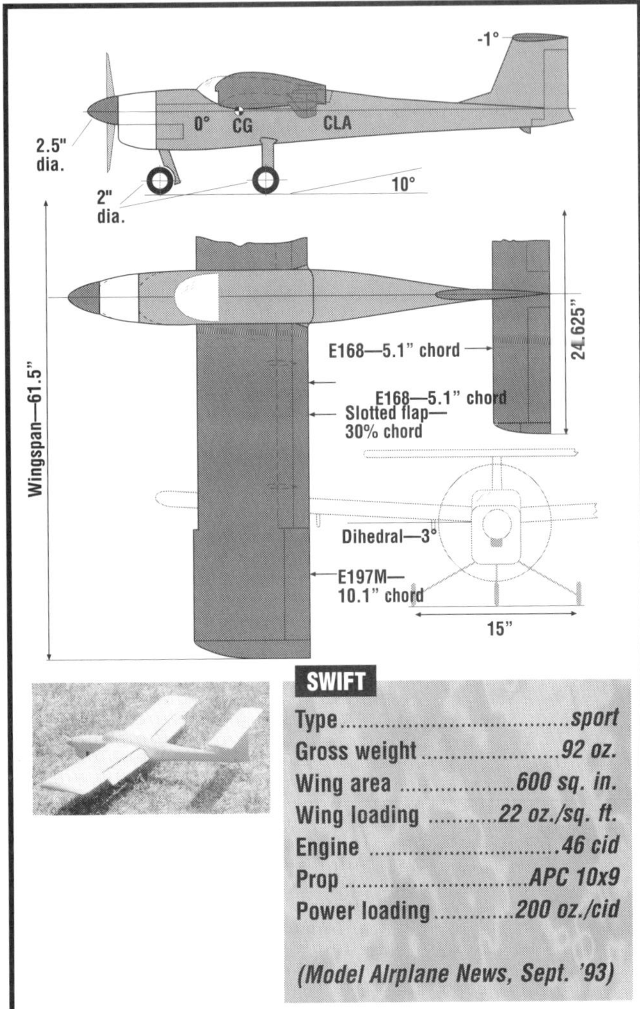

SWIFT

Type .... *sport*
Gross weight .... *92 oz.*
Wing area .... *600 sq. in.*
Wing loading .... *22 oz./sq. ft.*
Engine .... *46 cid*
Prop .... *APC 10x9*
Power loading .... *200 oz./cid*

(Model Airplane News, Sept. '93)

DOVE

Type .... *powered glider*
Gross weight *55.375*
Wing area .... *602 sq. in.*
Wing loading .... *13.16 oz./sq. ft.*
Engine *15*
Prop .... *APC 8x4*
Power loading .... *367 oz./cid*

(Model Airplane News, Nov. 1994)

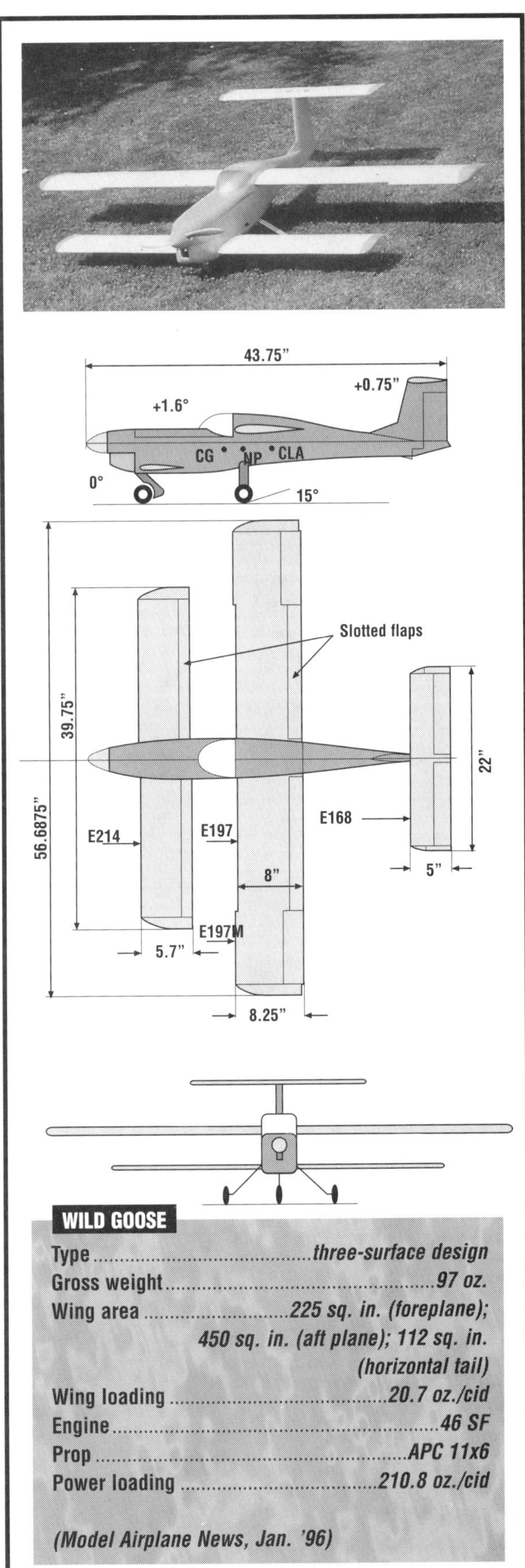

WILD GOOSE

Type .... *three-surface design*
Gross weight .... *97 oz.*
Wing area .... *225 sq. in. (foreplane); 450 sq. in. (aft plane); 112 sq. in. (horizontal tail)*
Wing loading .... *20.7 oz./cid*
Engine .... *46 SF*
Prop .... *APC 11x6*
Power loading .... *210.8 oz./cid*

(Model Airplane News, Jan. '96)

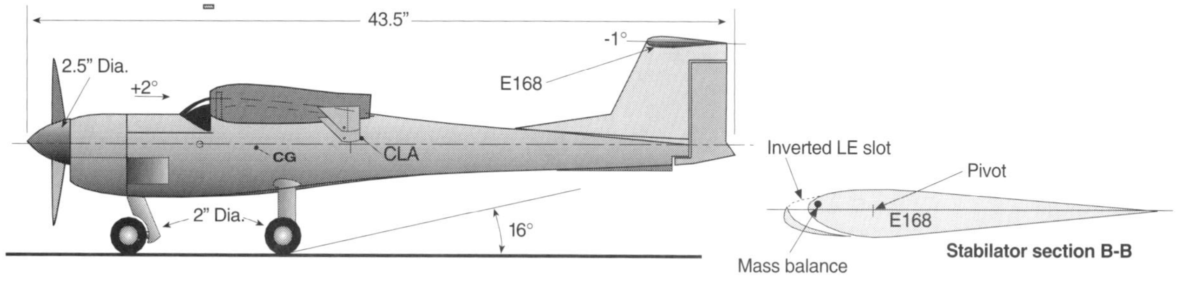

43.5"
-1°
2.5" Dia.
+2°
E168
CG
CLA
Inverted LE slot
Pivot
2" Dia.
16°
E168
Mass balance
Stabilator section B-B

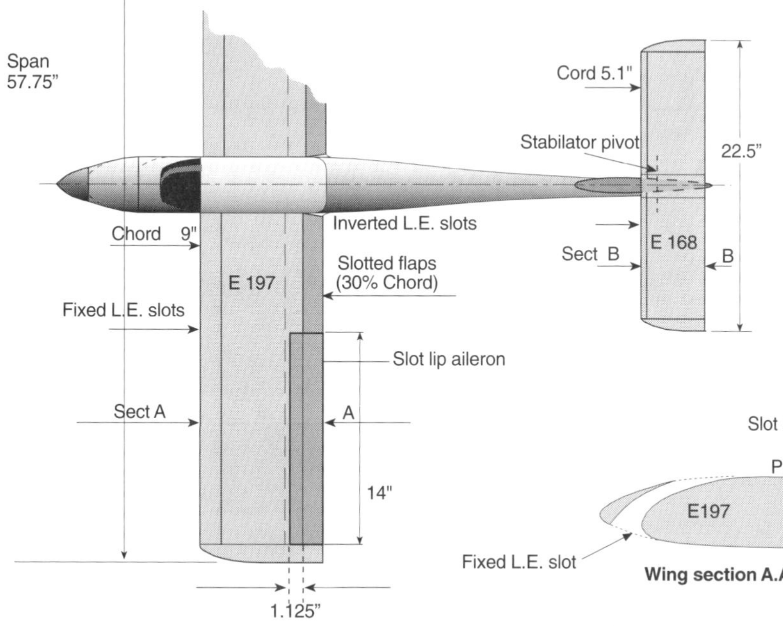

Span
57.75"
Cord 5.1"
Stabilator pivot
22.5"
Chord 9"
Inverted L.E. slots
Sect B
E 168
B
E 197
Slotted flaps
(30% Chord)
Fixed L.E. slots
Slot lip aileron
Sect A
A
14"
1.125"

Slot lip aileron
Pivot
Slot lip
E197
Fixed L.E. slot
Wing section A.A
Slotted flap
40°
Flap pivot
Dihedral 3°

CROW

Type .... ***STOL***
Gross weight .... ***88 oz.***
Wing area .... ***500 sq. in.***
Wing loading .... ***25.4 oz./sq. ft.***
Engine ***46***
Prop .... ***APC 11x6 or 11x7***
Power loading .... ***191.3 oz./cid***

(Model Airplane News, Aug. '96)

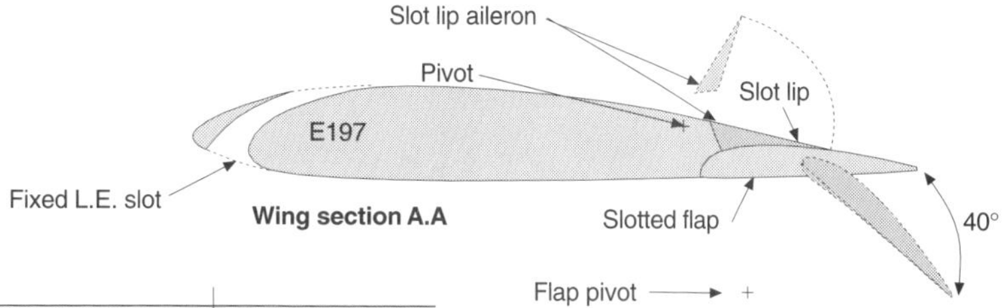

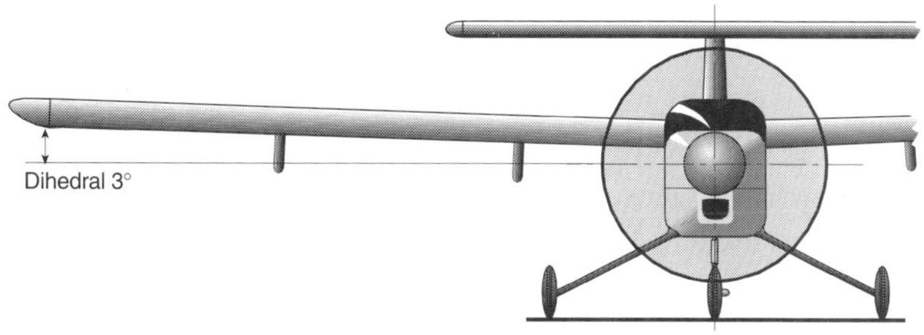

OSPREY

Type .... ***sport/float plane***
Gross weight .... ***113 oz.; 143 oz. (w/floats)***
Wing area .... ***768 sq. in.***
Wing loading .... ***20.92 oz./sq. ft.;***
26.5 oz. (w/floats)
Engine ***45***
Prop .... ***APC 12x6***
Power loading .... ***251 oz./cid;***
317 oz./cid (w/floats)
(Model Builder, June '91)

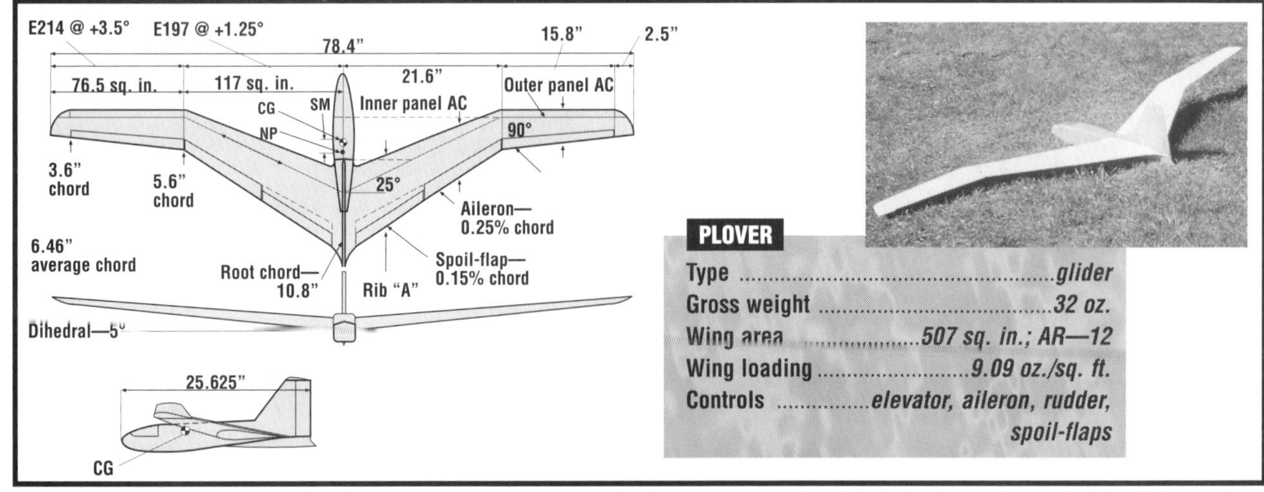

PLOVER

Type ....glider
Gross weight ....32 oz.
Wing area ....507 sq. in.; AR—12
Wing loading ....9.09 oz./sq. ft.
Controls ....elevator, aileron, rudder, spoil-flaps

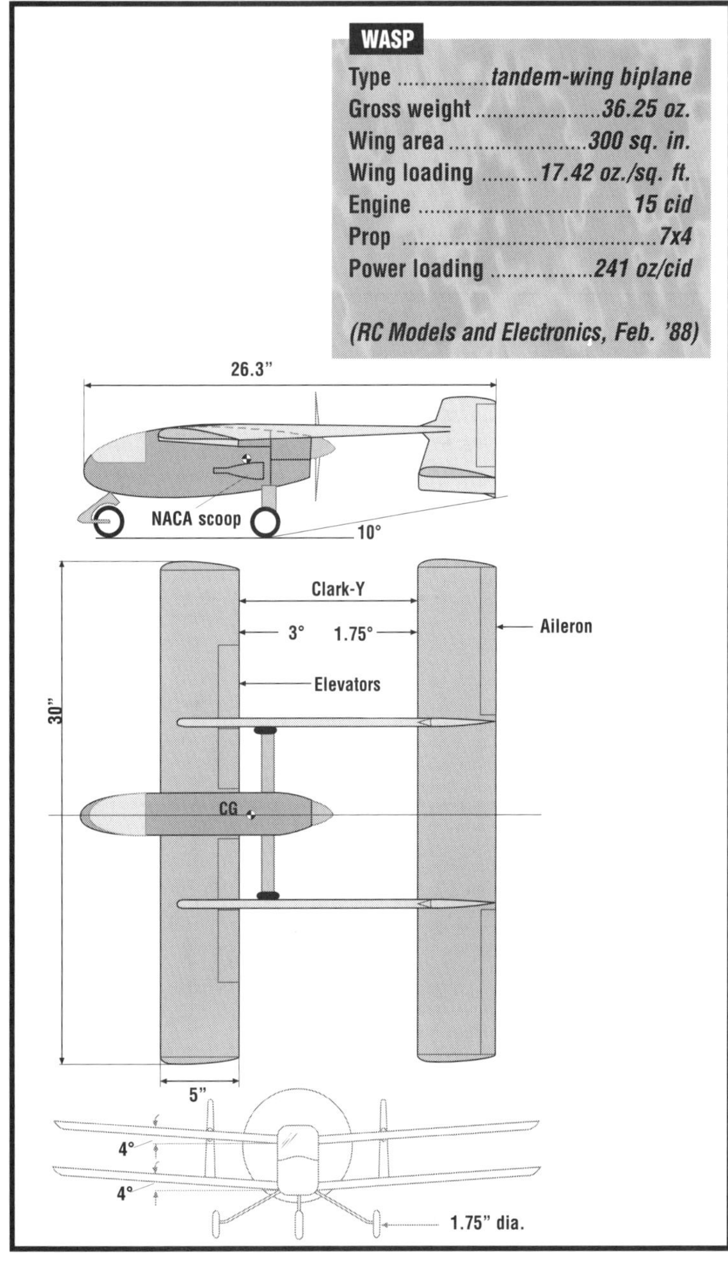

WASP

Type ....tandem-wing biplane
Gross weight ....36.25 oz.
Wing area ....300 sq. in.
Wing loading ....17.42 oz./sq. ft.
Engine ....15 cid
Prop 7x4
Power loading ....241 oz/cid

(RC Models and Electronics, Feb. '88)

SWAN

Type ....canard
Gross weight...........................115 oz.
Wing area ....669 sq. in.
Wing loading ....24.75 oz./sq. in.
Engine ....45 cid
Prop................................10x6 pusher
Power loading...................211 oz./cid

(Model Builder, Oct. '89)

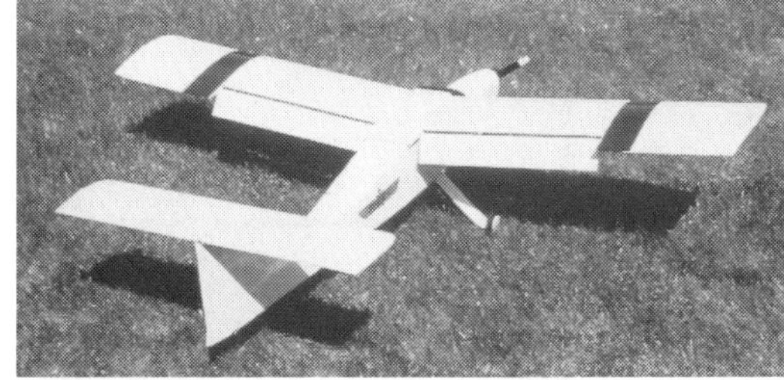

SNOWY OWL

Type ....sport
Gross weight ....98 oz.
Wing area ....643 sq. in.
Wing loading ....22 oz./sq. ft.
Engine...40
Prop 11x6
Power loading ....245 oz./cid

(RC Modeler, Jan. '89)

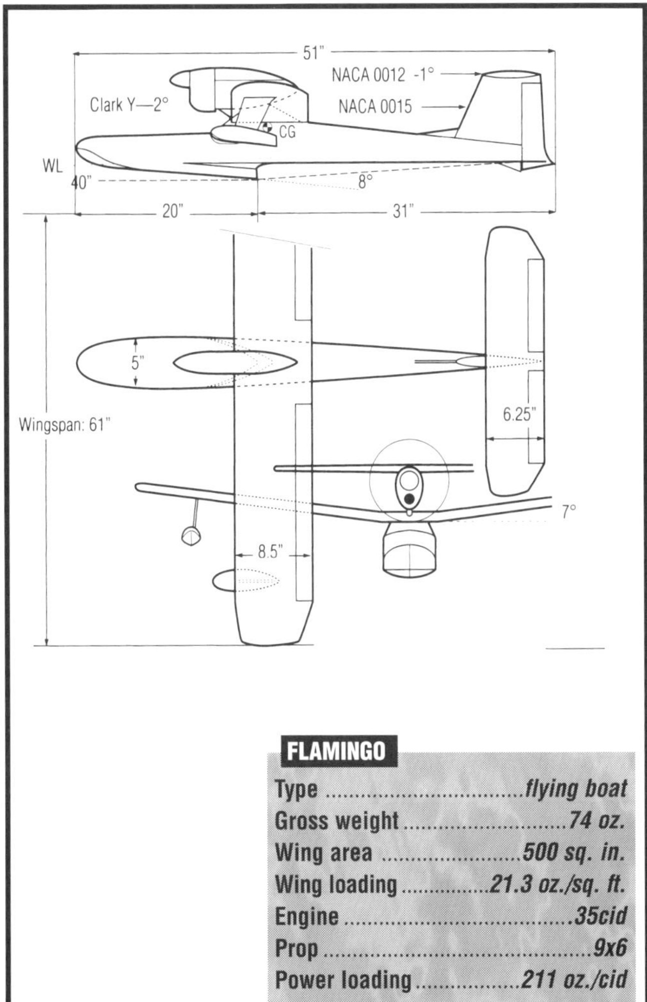

FLAMINGO

Type	*flying boat*
Gross weight	*74 oz.*
Wing area	*500 sq. in.*
Wing loading	*21.3 oz./sq. ft.*
Engine	*35cid*
Prop	*9x6*
Power loading	*211 oz./cid*

(Model Airplane News, Oct. '57)

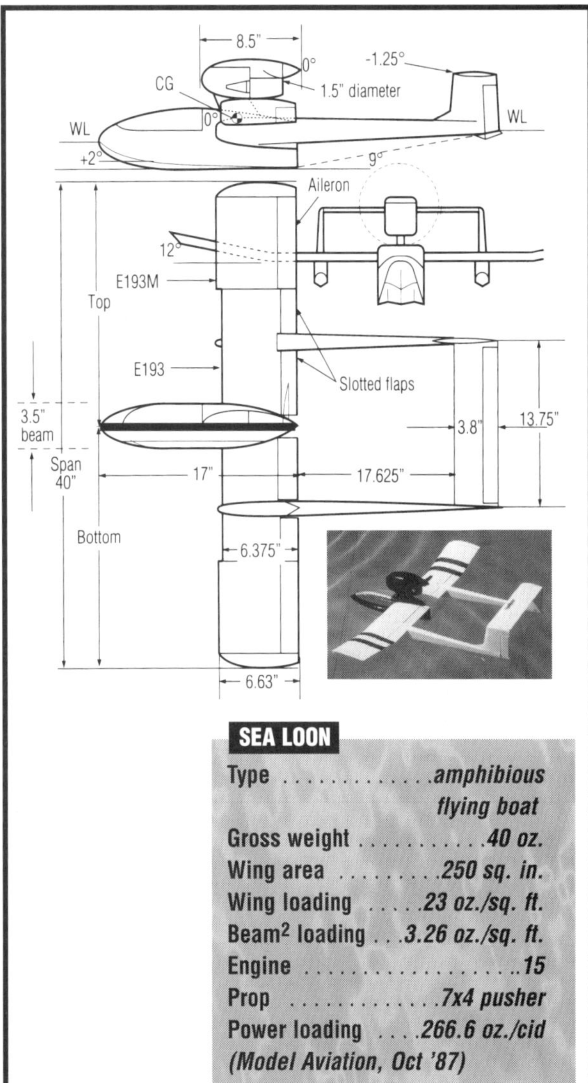

SEA LOON

Type	*amphibious flying boat*
Gross weight	*40 oz.*
Wing area	*250 sq. in.*
Wing loading	*23 oz./sq. ft.*
Beam² loading	*3.26 oz./sq. ft.*
Engine	*.15*
Prop	*7x4 pusher*
Power loading	*266.6 oz./cid*

(Model Aviation, Oct '87)

SPARROWHAWK

Type	*sport*
Gross weight	*38 oz.*
Wing area	*250 sq. in.*
Wing loading	*22 oz./sq. ft.*
Engine	*15cid*
Prop	*7x6*
Power loading	*253.3 oz./cid*

(Model Aviation, Jan. '87)

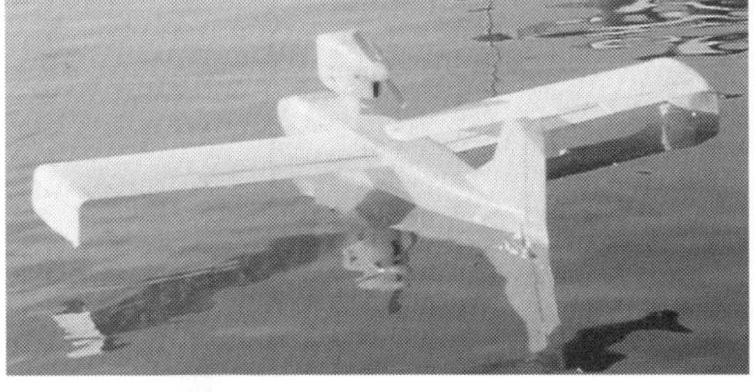

SEAGULL III

Type	*flying boat*
Gross weight	*112 oz.*
Wing area	*694 sq. in.*
Wing loading	*23.3 oz./sq. ft.*
Beam² loading	*3.11 oz./sq. in.*
Engine	*46 cid*
Prop	*11x8 pusher*
Power loading	*243 oz./cid*

(RC Modeler, Oct. '92)

▲

Appendix

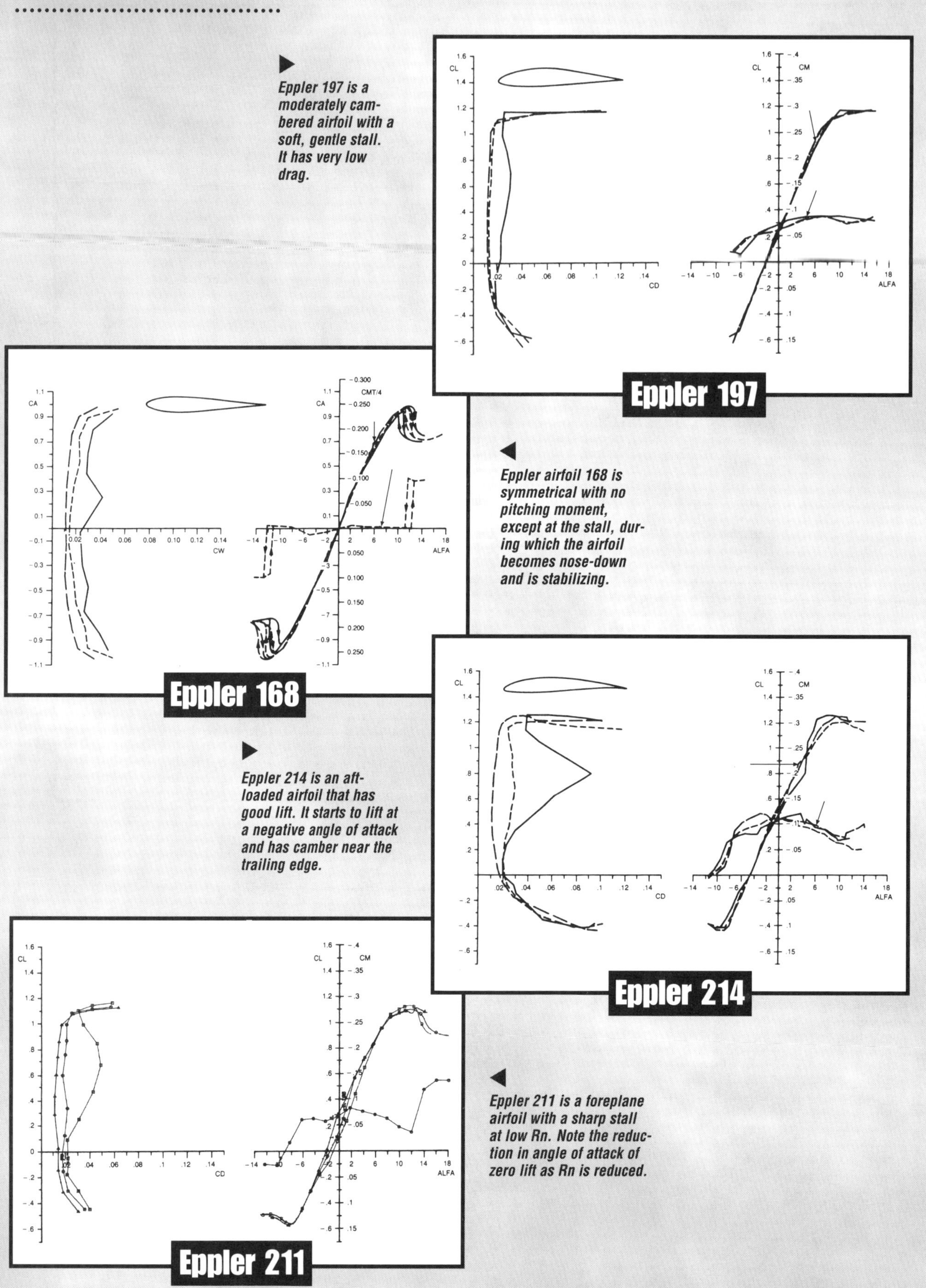

Eppler 197 is a moderately cambered airfoil with a soft, gentle stall. It has very low drag.

Eppler airfoil 168 is symmetrical with no pitching moment, except at the stall, during which the airfoil becomes nose-down and is stabilizing.

Eppler 214 is an aft-loaded airfoil that has good lift. It starts to lift at a negative angle of attack and has camber near the trailing edge.

Eppler 211 is a foreplane airfoil with a sharp stall at low Rn. Note the reduction in angle of attack of zero lift as Rn is reduced.

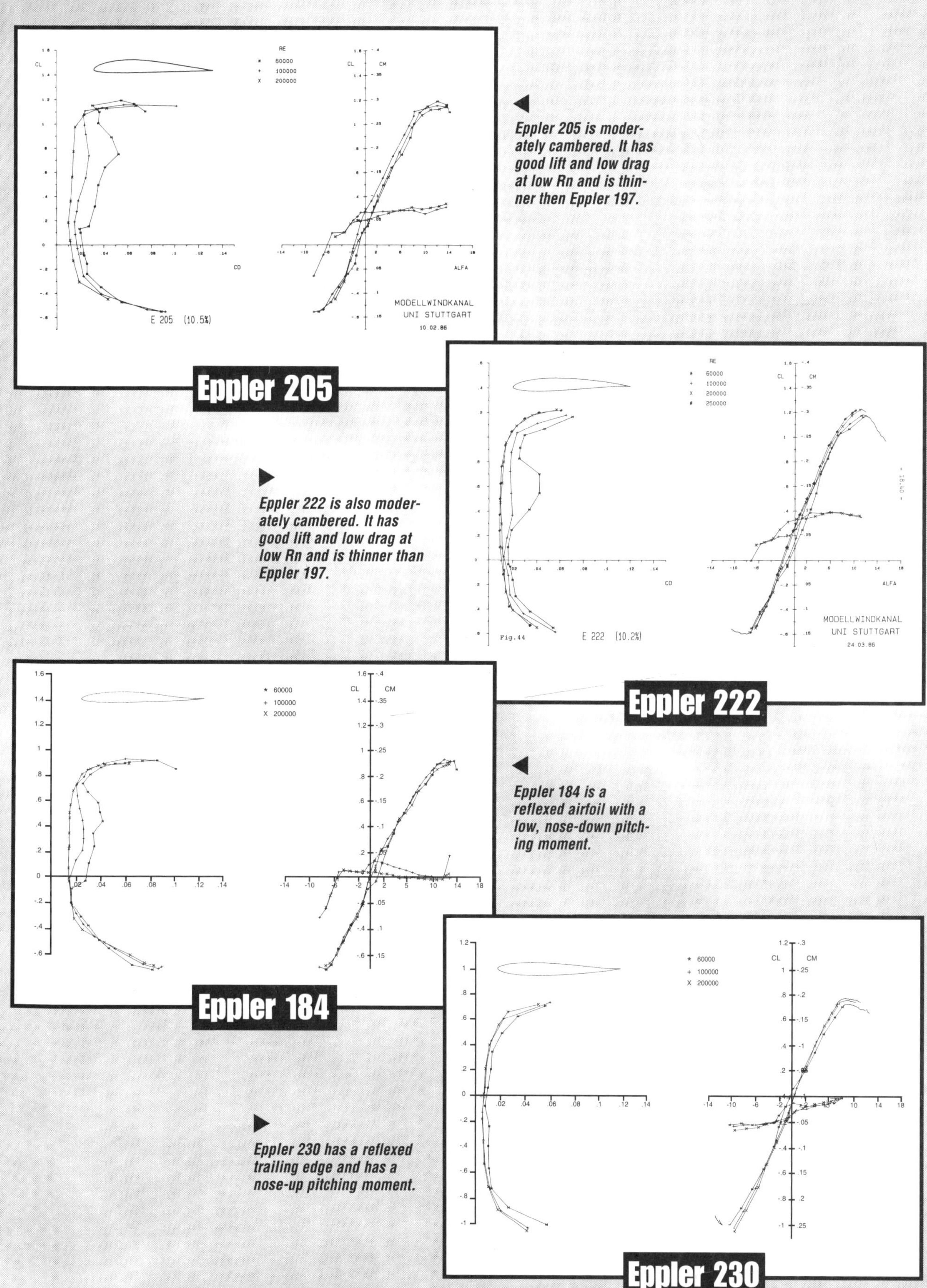

Eppler 205 is moderately cambered. It has good lift and low drag at low Rn and is thinner then Eppler 197.

Eppler 222 is also moderately cambered. It has good lift and low drag at low Rn and is thinner than Eppler 197.

Eppler 184 is a reflexed airfoil with a low, nose-down pitching moment.

Eppler 230 has a reflexed trailing edge and has a nose-up pitching moment.